CHILDREN WHO REMEMBER PREVIOUS LIVES

A QUESTION OF REINCARNATION

CHILDREN WHO REMEMBER PREVIOUS LIVES

A QUESTION OF REINCARNATION

Ian Stevenson

University Press of Virginia
Charlottesville

THE UNIVERSITY PRESS OF VIRGINIA
Copyright © 1987 by Ian Stevenson
First published 1987

Library of Congress Cataloging-in-Publication Data

Stevenson, Ian.
  Children who remember previous lives.

  Bibliography: p.
  Includes index.
    1. Reincarnation—Case studies. 2. Psychical research and
children—Case studies. I. Title.
BL515.S747   1987   133.9′01′3   87-8262
ISBN 0-8139-1140-0

Printed in the United States of America

For Margaret

Contents

Preface

This book aims at presenting for the general reader an account of my research on cases suggestive of reincarnation. It does not provide detailed evidence for reincarnation. Rather, it offers a summary of the way I have conducted my research, of the more important results obtained, and of my present conclusions.

In order to familiarize readers with the types of cases from which the evidence derives, I have included summaries of twelve typical cases. These, however, are unfleshed skeletons compared with the detailed case reports that I have published elsewhere, in which I have tried to marshal all the evidence bearing on the cases reported. (I have now published 65 detailed case reports and have more than 100 in various stages of preparation for future publication.) I should regard disapprovingly anyone who, solely from reading this book, moved from skepticism—or ignorance—concerning reincarnation to a settled conviction that it occurs. I shall be content if I have succeeded in making the idea of reincarnation plausible to persons who have not thought it was; and if some of them then think it worth their while to examine the evidence in my detailed case reports, I shall have accomplished more than I set out to do.

I have also drastically abbreviated my discussion of the interpretation of the evidence, although I have tried to give a balanced exposition of its strengths and weaknesses. I hope that the brevity of this part of the book will induce readers to study my longer deployment of arguments in other books.

In addition to providing an outline of my methods and principal results, this book will perhaps serve several other purposes. First, I hope that it will help to correct some common misconceptions about reincarnation. For many Westerners the idea of reincarnation seems remote and bizarre. They often associate it with, and only with, Hinduism and Buddhism and the Hindu and Buddhist ideas concerning retributive *karma*[1] and rebirth in nonhuman animal bodies. I shall take some pains to show that the cases I have studied rarely furnish evidence supporting these ideas. Moreover, many of the numerous peoples other than Hindus and Buddhists who believe in reincarnation do not link it with concepts of reward, punishment, or rebirth in nonhuman animal bodies. A belief that reincarnation must happen in a particular way can impede useful thought about the subject almost as much as can total rejection of the idea; some correspondents who write me with dogmatic assurance about how reincarnation occurs seem to have almost as much to unlearn as those who insist that reincarnation is impossible.

I have a second, subsidiary motive for writing this book: my hope that it will elicit reports of new cases that we can investigate. I am convinced that cases of the reincarnation type are underreported, particularly in the West. Correspondents sometimes tell me that a child of their family seemed to speak about a previous life when he[2] was about three years old; but by the time the correspondent writes, the child is often already ten or fifteen years of age, or even older. Some persons repentantly mention that when the child was younger they ignored him or even derided him for talking about a previous life. Later, the child forgot what he had seemed to remember earlier. If I and my successors can study cases among young children of the West while the cases are still active, as we have been doing in Asia and other parts of the world for many years, our research should make more rapid progress.

It may seem contradictory, just after inviting readers to send me information about new cases, to mention that I wish also in this book to discourage a deliberate searching for memories of previous lives— whether through the use of drugs, meditation, or hypnosis. Unfortunately, some hypnotists have stated that anyone can recover memories of previous lives by means of hypnosis, and great therapeutic benefits from this are claimed or hinted at. I shall try to quench misguided and sometimes shamefully exploited enthusiasm for hypnosis, especially when it is proposed as a sure means of eliciting memories of previous lives.

The cases that seem to me most deserving of our attention have nearly all occurred outside areas of Western culture, that is, among the peoples of Asia, West Africa, and the tribal groups of northwestern North America. There are reasons for this geographical disproportion, and although we have little understanding of them, I have offered some speculations about it. Here I wish to offer two related comments. First, not all cases come from the areas where most occur; some excellent ones have occurred in Europe and North America (among nontribal peoples). Second, cases suggestive of reincarnation show significant similarities in their main features to phenomena that have been carefully studied in the West for more than a century: apparitions, telepathic impressions, telepathic dreams, and lucid dreams. Here and there throughout this book I have drawn attention to these parallels. I hope these allusions will help to make the cases that I mainly discuss seem less remote and exotic, and therefore more credible, than they might otherwise appear to be.

NOTES, REFERENCES, AND DETAILED CASE REPORTS

This book is written for the person in the street. But which one? One who moves rapidly may read it without examining a single note or reference. Such a reader may resent paying one-sixth of the cost of a book for notes that do not interest him. However, I would also like to attract readers whose study of this book will not slake their thirst for knowledge, but increase it. I hope that these readers will find the extensive notes and references useful. They are all placed at the end of the book.

How to Find a Reference to a Source

If I have not included a note about an author whose name I mention in the text, the reader may turn to the list of references, where I have listed published sources alphabetically by authors' names.

Guide to Detailed Case Reports

If a reader wishes to read a detailed report of a case, he will find a reference to the report (if one has been published) in the list of cases given in the Appendix; the cases are listed there by the *first* or given names of the persons who say they have had a previous life (or, in rare instances, who are said by other persons to have had a previous life). I refer to these persons as the subjects of the cases.

ACKNOWLEDGMENTS

In my books containing detailed case reports, I have already thanked many persons who have ably and selflessly assisted my investigations. I will not repeat all their names here, but instead will confine my thanks to those persons who have helped me in the field work of recent years and in the preparation of this book.

For special assistance in my recent field work I should like to thank Rita Castrén (Finland), Daw Hnin Aye (Burma), Nicholas Ibekwe (Nigeria), Tissa Jayawardene (Sri Lanka), Madj Mu'akkasah (Lebanon), Satwant Pasricha (India), Godwin Samararatne (Sri Lanka), Nasib Sirorasa (Thailand), and U Win Maung (Burma). Can Polat (Turkey) has sent me information about cases in his country.

Several colleagues and friends have generously read and given me helpful comments to improve one or several chapters, and for this invaluable aid I wish to thank: Carlos Alvarado, John Beloff, Stuart Edelstein, Brian Goodwin, Nicholas McClean-Rice, George Owen, and James Wheatley. They have removed numerous faults, and at least some of those that remain may be due to my not having followed their advice on all points.

My former and present Research Assistants have also greatly improved the book with their suggestions. For this help I thank Carolee Werner, Susan Adams, and Emily Williams Cook, the last with special gratitude, because she read through the entire book twice.

Thanks are due also, and warmly given, to Elizabeth Byrd and Patricia Estes for typing—and much retyping—of high quality.

Elsevier Science Publishers (Biomedical Division) gave permission for a quotation from one of their journals. The National Technical Information Service of the United States Department of Commerce authorized citation of a passage from a monograph by L. L. Vasiliev.

I drafted much of the book during a sabbatical leave at Darwin College, Cambridge University, and I cordially thank the Master and Fellows of Darwin College for providing me with this opportunity.

My wife, Margaret, generously gave up much time that we could have spent pleasantly together so that I could finish this book, and I dedicate it affectionately to her.

Finally, I acknowledge gratefully the support of my research by the Bernstein Brothers Parapsychology and Health Foundation.

CHILDREN WHO REMEMBER PREVIOUS LIVES

CHAPTER ONE

Introduction

It may disappoint some readers to learn that this book is not about reincarnation directly; instead, it is about children who claim to remember previous lives. From studying the experiences of such children some understanding about reincarnation may eventually come. Before that can happen, however, we must become confident that reincarnation offers the best explanation for these children's apparent memories.

When I refer to these memories, I shall at times omit qualifying adjectives, such as "apparent" or "purported"; but I do this only to make reading easier and with no intention of begging the main question that the cases of these children present. From the perspective of the child subject of a case, however, the memories that he experiences of a former life seem just as real—just as much true memories—as memories he may have of events since he was born. The verified statements he makes about the other life derive from memories of *some* kind.[1] Those who observe him need to decide whether they are memories of a life that he lived in a former incarnation or ones that he acquired in some other way. If readers remember this point, they should not find the title of this book misleading.

I have another reason for saying little about reincarnation itself. Although I shall be drawing on the information of over two thousand cases,[2] this is a miniscule number compared with the billions of human beings who have lived. It would be rash to generalize from so few cases, even if we were sure they are all best interpreted as instances of reincarnation (which we cannot be); furthermore, although the cases show considerable uniformities, we cannot say that they are representative of the lives of ordinary people. Indeed, when I later describe the recurrent features of the cases, readers will quickly realize that the lives apparently remembered are *not* ordinary ones. This is only partly due to the haphazard methods I have had to use, faute de mieux, in collecting cases. The cases are also unrepresentative because remembering a previous life is an unusual experience that occurs to only a few persons for reasons that we are, at most, just beginning to understand.

Although I am not writing directly about reincarnation, the central issue of my research and of this book is whether or not reincarnation occurs, at least sometimes. This amounts to asking whether a human personality (or a component of it) may survive death, and later—perhaps after an interval passed in some nonphysical realm— become associated with another physical body. Reincarnation is not the only conceivable way in which a human personality might survive death. It is not the form of survival that most Christians and Moslems expect. Nor is it the only form of survival that scientific investigators of this possibility have envisaged.[3]

Most scientists today do not believe that any survival of human personality after death does or can occur.[4] Nearly all scientists who do believe in a life after death derive their conviction in the matter from faith in a particular religious teaching. Most of them would deny that the question of human survival after death could be studied scientifically. Nevertheless, a little over one hundred years ago a handful of scientists and scholars in England began to discuss the possibility of obtaining evidence of survival after death through the collection and analysis of data with methods customary in other branches of science. They and their successors have obtained a variety of such data. The cases discussed in this book represent only one block of information that anyone studying the subject of survival after death should try to appraise.[5]

In the two paragraphs above I referred to human personality. The *Oxford English Dictionary* defines the word *personality* as: "The quality, character, or fact of being a person as distinct from a thing. . . . Personal existence, actual existence as a person; the fact of there being or having been such a person; personal identity. . . . That quality or assemblage of qualities which makes a person what he is, as distinct from other persons." The first part of the definition indicates the crux of this matter. Are human beings things, or are they more than that? If they have "something more" than a thing has, can that "something more," whatever it is, survive death? The persistence of a person's stream of consciousness after death can be known directly only to that person. Other persons who outlive him can obtain only indirect evidence of his survival. What criteria should they adopt for deciding that a particular person has survived death? What is meant, in the definition above, by "personal identity?" Philosophers have much debated what constitutes a person's identity.[6] Most seem to agree that, each life being unique, the memories of it will be unique; therefore, evidence of the persistence of memories will provide the best—and perhaps the only—indication that a particular person has survived the death of his body.

Thus, the search for evidence that someone has survived death has usually involved studying indicia of the continuation of that person's memories. The information examined must, however, extend beyond mere imaged memories of past events; we can have such memories on a video tape, yet we would not say that the tape and its electronic player were personalities. The concept of personality should also include feelings and purposes and at least some degree of consciousness. We could allow for a temporary lapse of consciousness after death, just as we do when we sleep and awake to another day; but I do not think we should regard anyone as having survived death if he did not resume what we call consciousness, even though the kind of consciousness that he had after death might differ greatly from that familiar to us when alive.

The evidence of survival after death deriving from children who remember previous lives differs in one important respect from some of the other types of evidence of survival, such as that obtained from some apparitions of the dead. An apparition may suggest that a person who is dead has somehow survived death and become able to communicate evidence of his identity to living persons, whereas a child who claims to remember a previous life is a living person who claims to have had an earlier life in which he died. In some respects it is easier to work forward from a dead person to a presumed still-living one than it is to work backward from a living person to the dead one whose life the child claims to have lived. I shall next try to explain why I think this.

So far as the evidence goes, dead persons—at least up to the stage where any evidence of their discarnate existence can be obtained[7]—may undergo comparatively little change of personality solely as a result of dying. In contrast, the association of a discarnate personality with a new physical body would entail major adaptations as it becomes housed in a new and smaller physical frame with still-rudimentary sensory organs. Moreover, this new body might be born in a different family, to which the personality would need to adapt, and this would inevitably lead to further modifications. By the time a child could communicate memories of a previous life, the different ingredients of his personality would have blended, more or less, and become difficult for an investigator to distinguish from each other. This makes the evidence for the survival of a deceased person that we derive from such children less easy to evaluate—at least as to the deceased person's identity—than that provided by, for example, an apparition of a deceased person as he was at the time of his death. There are several rival interpretations to consider in appraising an apparition, but at least the figure seen is often—although not always—that of a whole person and a recognizable one.[8] It is not the same with children who remember previous lives. From the information they furnish, which often comes in fragments only, an investigator must decide whether the pieces he can put together credibly evoke a particular deceased person and no one else. I shall return later to the important topic of the criteria for identifying a particular person.

The evidence for reincarnation that we have suggests that living human beings (and perhaps nonhuman animals also) have minds, or souls if you like, that animate them when they are living and that survive after they die. Most biologists will stigmatize this suggestion as vitalism[9] and declare it to have been discredited decades ago. However, new evidence—and even examination of older, neglected evidence—may restore the credit of vitalism. I do not think scientists in other disciplines need lose anything except some of their assumptions—such as that a person is nothing but a physical body—if they examine open-mindedly the evidence we have of life after death. Reincarnation, at least as I conceive it, does not nullify what we know about evolution and genetics. It suggests, however, that there may be two streams of evolution—the biological one and a personal one—and that during terrestrial lives these streams may interact. How they might do this we can barely envisage at present, although in a later chapter I put forward some tentative speculations about processes that may occur.

The idea of reincarnation offers a contribution to the understanding of the uniqueness of individual persons. Geneticists use the word *phenotype* to indicate the living person produced by the interaction of a person's genes and his environment (the only elements involved that most geneticists now acknowledge). Most biologists recognize the uniqueness of each phenotype—even those of one-egg (identical) twins. They believe that genetics and the influences of environment will ultimately explain this uniqueness. Almost infinite possibilities exist for variations in genetic composition: these include the random distribution of chromosomes into gametes (the male and female cells that unite when conception occurs), the recombination of genes among chromosomes, and occasional mutations of genes. Environments also vary widely. Even twins have somewhat different environments, and someone once remarked that not even conjoined (Siamese) twins have precisely the same environment, because one of them has to go through a door first. [10]

Ideas that seem to have general validity, however, may prove insufficient when tested against all relevant observations. Some persons have unique attributes that we cannot now explain satisfactorily as due solely to a combination of genetic variation and environmental influences. Reincarnation deserves consideration as a third factor in play.

If we are, through the shuffling of our genes, the products of "chance and necessity," to use Jacques Monod's phrase, we can expect no solution to the problem of the inequalities in the conditions of different persons at birth. And we can draw little comfort from the analogy of being dealt a hand at cards with the opportunity to play it well or badly; a person born blind cannot even see the cards in his hand. The belief in reincarnation provides no quick reparation for congenital blindness. The research that this book reviews may, however, ultimately offer a better understanding of why a particular person is born blind than any other explanation now available. The important question to be answered is not that of why *any* person is born blind; it is that of why a *particular* person is born blind when others are not. Just to ask this question assumes that there is a person associated with a body during life; and that we can distinguish the person (or personality) from the body.

Furthermore, if reincarnation occurs, the congenitally blind person can rationally hope ultimately to enjoy vision—in another life. Critics of the evidence of reincarnation have sometimes pointed to its element of hopefulness with the dismissing suggestion that such evidence as we have derives only from man's wishful thinking. This objection wrongly assumes that what we desire must be false. We might be more easily persuaded to believe what we wish to believe than the contrary; nevertheless, what we wish to believe may be true. Our inquiry into the truth or falseness of an idea should proceed without regard to whether it fortifies or undermines our wishes.

Apart from this, the cases that I have studied include some for which informants have given testimony opposing their own beliefs and wishes. This occurs sometimes when a case develops in a family whose members do not believe in reincarnation; or who would rather not accept the claims of their child to remember a particular previous life. This also is a topic to which I shall return later.

In the remainder of this chapter I shall define some terms that I shall use, or usages that I have adopted, with which many readers will be unfamiliar. Along the way I shall digress to present some cases illustrating the occurrence of telepathy in everyday life; the reader who has some knowledge of such cases will be better able to judge the cases of children who claim to remember previous lives. I shall then briefly outline the later chapters of the book.

TERMS USED IN PSYCHICAL RESEARCH

The cases I describe in this book fall within the branch of science called psychical research and sometimes parapsychology. These are not satisfactory terms for the study of phenomena that we cannot account for by our present understanding of the known sensory powers and muscular activity of humans (and perhaps other animals). The word *parapsychology*, which was first used (in Germany) in the late nineteenth century, is especially unsatisfactory. It emphasizes the relationships of this branch of science to psychology, whereas most of the scientists working in the field now realize that its links with physics and biology are just as important as those with psychology. Also, the word implies (or has come to suggest) phenomena that do not show the same lawfulness that psychologists like to think the phenomena they study show. Scientists working in this field believe that they also study lawful phenomena, but ones that may follow laws other than those of modern physics and physiology. The recurrence of similar features in many cases occurring far apart from each other provides some support for this belief.

The word *parapsychology* has another disadvantage. It tends to isolate the phenomena under investigation—and also the scientists who study them—from other endeavors in science. It has not always been this way. Modern science is a recent and parochial activity. It arose in the West around A.D. 1600. Up to that time, in Europe (and still today throughout most of the world not counted as the West), the phenomena now considered paranormal were accepted without question. I do not mean that they were not considered unusual or that individual reports of such phenomena were never doubted. I mean only that they were not treated with the *general* skepticism toward them that later developed among scientists in the West and, following them, many other educated Westerners. For example, Descartes referred casually to the communication of thoughts between two persons separated by a long distance; and Bacon, another founder of modern science, proposed experiments in what he called "binding of thoughts" and also ones with the throwing of dice to study the influence of "imagination" on the outcome.[11] Even up to the end of the nineteenth century, scientists interested in what we now call psychical research associated on equal terms with psychologists and attended the same professional conventions (then usually called congresses). How they and their successors came to be illegitimated and sent into exile may form a chapter in the histories of science that will be written in the next century. Here I wish only to add that most scientists working in this field look forward with hope and expectation to the ultimate reunion of their branch of science with the rest of it. When that happens, words that are now current may be superseded.

In the meantime, however, we must make the best use we can of the words our predecessors adopted for phenomena that are still little understood, but that undeniably occur. I shall therefore define a few terms that the reader will meet in this book.[12] We speak of an experience or an event as *paranormal* when we cannot account for it by any known sensory or muscular process. We usually now refer to paranormal sensory experiences as *extrasensory perceptions*, but I myself prefer to speak of them as *paranormal cognitions* or—better yet—as instances of *paranormal awareness*. Paranormal sensory experiences contrast with *normal means of communication*, by which we mean all the ways in which information reaches our minds through the recognized senses, particularly from reading, other visual perception, and hearing.

Extrasensory perception may occur through *telepathy* or *clairvoyance*. The word *telepathy* refers to communication between two minds and has come to replace the older terms *thought-reading* and *thought-transference.* The word *clairvoyance* refers to extrasensory perception (usually of an object) without the mediation of another person's mind. [13] Telepathy and clairvoyance are processes of obtaining knowledge about contemporary events. Extrasensory perception also subsumes two other modalities: that of *precognition* (sometimes called *paranormal foreknowledge*), which refers to noninferential knowledge of the future, and that of *retrocognition*, which refers to paranormal knowledge of the past.

We refer to a person who has an experience of extrasensory perception—whether spontaneously or during the course of an experiment—as the *percipient* or the *subject*. And we call the person about whom the percipient obtains information the *agent* or, sometimes, the *target person*. The word *agent* is not satisfactory; it suggests that the person concerned is an active, willing participant in the experience, and although he sometimes is, he may also be passive and unaware of any communication that occurs.

A few persons claim to obtain communications that appear to have originated in the minds of deceased persons who are conceived of as still living in a discarnate state. The persons who do this are called *mediums* or *sensitives,* and the discarnate persons who purport to give information through them are called *communicators.* I shall occasionally refer to such *mediumistic communications.*

In some places I shall use the words *psychic* and *psychical* as approximately synonymous with *paranormal* and *parapsychological.* I shall use these terms especially in considering the possible influence of presumed discarnate persons on living persons or living embryos.

Investigators have studied paranormal phenomena in two ways. They have tried to observe the phenomena as they occur spontaneously or obtain reports from other persons who have observed them; and they have tried to elicit them under experimental conditions. By means of experiments scientists can control circumstances and vary them so that when they interpret their results they can often confidently exclude explanations other than that of some paranormal process. These opportunities are nearly always lacking in the study of spontaneous cases. Occasionally, investigators can themselves observe some phenomenon as it occurs; but most of the time they must construct as accurate a picture as possible of events that happened before they reached the scene. This is an unsatisfactory situation. However, scientists working in this field cannot forego the study of spontaneous cases without impoverishing the subject by depriving it of its most important phenomena. Most spontaneous paranormal experiences are concerned with critical events in people's lives, such as death, and these events almost never occur in a laboratory. The cases about which I am writing in this book illustrate this point; but so do most other spontaneous cases. It would be helpful to study reincarnation with the rigor that an experimental situation permits, but wrong to abandon the study because we cannot do this. I believe it is better to learn what is probable about important matters than to be certain about trivial ones.

Here I should say that as a reader of this book you will have to decide—if you have not already done so—whether you believe that thoughts can be communicated between persons (and other knowledge acquired) without the known sensory organs. You should do this because telepathy (perhaps combined with clairvoyance) is an important alternative interpretation for the cases with which this book is concerned. To look ahead a little, there are about half a dozen possible interpretations of the cases, each of which may, for a few cases, prove the best explanation. For the majority of the stronger cases, however, we need consider only three interpretations: serious flaws in the testimony, telepathy and clairvoyance on the part of the subject, and reincarnation. Readers who do not believe in paranormal cognition (telepathy and clairvoyance) may find themselves with an uncomfortably limited choice.

If you have not yet made up your mind concerning the existence of such capacities as telepathy and clairvoyance, and if your temperament resembles mine, you will wish to decide after examining the evidence and not on the basis of what your relatives, neighbors, and professors tell you to think. Ample materials are available for your assistance. A satisfactory stock of reliable books on the subject can fill bookshelves on three sides of a medium-size room. Books that are *not* reliable could fill shelves on all the walls of all the rooms of a ducal mansion—Blenheim Palace, for example—but a few sound introductory texts and outlines can prevent anyone from wasting time with these. [14]

A DIGRESSION TO ILLUSTRATE
TELEPATHY AND APPARITIONS

For me the most important evidence of telepathy derives from unusual experiences that occur from time to time in everyday life, and

I shall present a few examples of these so that readers may test their own attitudes toward reports of such events.

The first experience that I shall cite occurred to a man who was a Confederate army soldier captured at the battle of Shiloh in 1862. While a prisoner of war at Camp Douglas, on the outskirts of Chicago, he had a vision, which he later described as follows:

> *On the next day (April 16th) . . . I proceeded to my nest and reclined alongside of my friend Wilkes, in a posture that gave me a command of one-half of the building. I made some remarks to him upon the card-playing groups opposite, when, suddenly, I felt a gentle stroke on the back of my neck, and, in an instant, I was unconscious. The next moment I had a vivid view of the village of Tremeirchion [in Wales], and the grassy slopes of the hills of Hiraddog, and I seemed to be hovering over the rook woods of Brynbella. I glided to the bedchamber of my Aunt Mary. My aunt was in bed, and seemed sick unto death. I took a position by the side of the bed, and saw myself, with head bent down, listening to her parting words, which sounded regretful, as though conscience smote her for not having been so kind as she might have been, or had wished to be. I heard the boy say, "I believe you, aunt. It is neither your fault, nor mine. You were good and kind to me, and I knew you wished to be kinder; but things were so ordered that you had to be what you were. I also dearly wished to love you, but I was afraid to speak of it, lest you would check me, or say something that would offend me. I feel our parting was in this spirit. There is no need of regrets. You have done your duty to me, and you had children of your own, who required all your care. What has happened to me since, was decreed should happen. Farewell."*
>
> *I put forth my hand and felt the clasp of the long, thin hands of the sore-sick woman, I heard a murmur of farewell, and immediately I woke.*
>
> *It appeared to me that I had but closed my eyes. I was still in the same reclining attitude, the groups opposite were still engaged in their card games, Wilkes was in the same position. Nothing had changed.*
>
> *I asked, "What has happened?"*
>
> *"What could happen?" said he. "What makes you ask? It is but a moment ago you were speaking to me."*
>
> *"Oh, I thought I had been asleep a long time."*

On the next day, the 17th April, 1862, my Aunt Mary died at
Fynnon Beuno [her home in Wales]!

I should explain that the aunt of whose death the soldier became
aware had taken him in as a child, when he had been orphaned and
homeless. She had done this from a sense of duty, even though already
overburdened by the responsibilities of her own family. That she had
not, nevertheless, been able to give the boy much love appears to have
been a subject of regret on both sides and a theme of the soldier's
experience in saying farewell to her as she died.

In the next case the percipient was a young Scotsman who was
traveling in Sweden in 1799. Setting out from Gothenburg for Nor-
way, he and his party traveled all day and into the night before finally
arriving at about 1:00 A.M. on December 19 at an inn, where they
decided to stop for the rest of the night. In his journal he wrote:

Dec. 19 . . . . Tired with the cold of yesterday, I was glad to take
advantage of a hot bath before I turned in. And here a most re-
markable thing happened to me—so remarkable that I must tell the
story from the beginning. After I left the High School, I went with
G———, my most intimate friend, to attend the classes in the
University [of Edinburgh]. There was no divinity class, but we
frequently in our walks discussed and speculated upon many grave
subjects—among others, on the immortality of the soul, and on a
future state. This question, and the possibility, I will not say of ghosts
walking, but of the dead appearing to the living, were subjects of much
speculation; and we actually committed the folly of drawing up an
agreement, written with our blood, *to the effect, that whichever of*
us died the first should appear to the other, and thus solve any doubts
we had entertained of the "life after death." After we had finished our
class at the college, G——— went to India, having got an appoint-
ment there in the civil service. He seldom wrote to me, and after the
lapse of a few years I had almost forgotten him; moreover, his family
having little connection with Edinburgh, I seldom saw or heard
anything of them, or of him through them, so that all the old school-
boy intimacy had died out, and I had nearly forgotten his existence. I
had taken, as I have said, a warm bath; and while lying in it and
enjoying the comfort of the heat, after the late freezing I had under-
gone, I turned my head round, looking towards the chair on which I

had deposited my clothes, as I was about to get up out of the bath. On the chair sat G———, looking calmly at me. How I got out of the bath I know not, but on recovering my senses I found myself sprawling on the floor. The apparition, or whatever it was, that had taken the likeness of G———, had disappeared. The vision produced such a shock that I had no inclination to talk about it, or to speak about it even to Stuart [a traveling companion]; but the impression it made upon me was too vivid to be easily forgotten; and so strongly was I affected by it, that I have here written down the whole history, with the date, 19th December, and all the particulars, as they are now fresh before me. No doubt I had fallen asleep; and that the appearance presented so distinctly to my eyes was a dream, I can not for a moment doubt; yet for years I had had no communication with G———, nor had there been anything to recall him to my recollection; nothing had taken place during our Swedish travels either connected with G——— or with India, or with any thing relating to him, or to any member of his family. I recollected quickly enough our old discussion, and the bargain we had made. I could not discharge from my mind the impression that G——— must have died, and that his appearance to me was to be received by me as proof of a future state; yet all the while I felt convinced that the whole was a dream; and so painfully vivid and so unfading was the impression, that I could not bring myself to talk of it, or to make the slightest allusion to it. I finished dressing; and as we had agreed to make an early start, I was ready by six o'clock, the hour of our early breakfast.

Many years later, the percipient, in publishing an account of his experience, added the following information:

Soon after my return to Edinburgh, there arrived a letter from India announcing G———'s death! and stating that he had died on the 19th of December!! Singular coincidence! yet when one reflects on the vast number of dreams which night after night pass through our brains, the number of coincidences between the vision and the event are perhaps fewer and less remarkable than a fair calculation of chances would warrant us to expect.

I give the next case in the words of a man (a Russian) who, as a child, was apparently seen as an apparition by his mother:

I was then twelve years old and had just passed into my second year of high school; I went to the cottage not far from Pskov. My mother who had a severe liver ailment had gone with her husband (my father) for treatment to Karlsbad (now Karlovy Vary), leaving me, my sister and brother in the charge of her younger sisters. We, the children, were given a greater than usual freedom of action and used it. Once, in the evening, we decided to recreate one of the adventures of the children of Captain Grant, who had saved themselves from a flood by climbing a tree. We chose a big willow leaning over the water on the bank of the river. I was to play Paganel and became so engrossed in this part that, just like him, I fell off the tree into the water and, unable to swim, began drowning. Only grabbing a branch, I managed to reach the steep bank, with great difficulty. In silent horror, my brother and sister were witnessing this event from the tree. We were particularly worried by the inevitability of the punishment. We could not conceal from our aunts this adventure: I was completely wet and my brand new high school cap with its white peak—the object of pride and love—had been carried away by the current. At home, our young aunts, sympathizing, decided not to report to Karlsbad of the event (they also were uneasy about it). They made us promise that we would not repeat it. You can imagine the amazement and confusion—both ours and our aunts'— when the moment she arrived, our mother described this incident in all details, pointed out the willow, mentioned the cap which had been carried to the dam, etc. She had dreamed of all this in Karlsbad and, waking up in tears, and disarray, asked her husband immediately to cable home asking whether everything was all right with the children. Father admitted that he had not sent a cable but, in order to calm the sick woman, dozed for half an hour in the reception room of the hotel and returned saying that he had cabled.

For the next case, I again quote the words of a person directly concerned in it. Here is his account of how his sister became aware, while a long distance away, of an accident he had:

As a 19 year old [German] student, I had a serious accident during a military exercise near Würzburg and barely escaped certain death. Riding on the narrow edge of a steep ravine through which a road led, I fell with my rearing and tumbling horse down into the path of a mounted battery and came to lie almost beneath the wheel of one of the

guns. The latter, pulled by six horses, came to a stop just in time and I
escaped, having suffered no more than fright. This accident happened
in the morning hours of a beautiful spring day. In the evening of the
same day, I received a telegram from my father who enquired about my
well being. It was the first and only time in my life that I received such
a query. My oldest sister, to whom I had always been particularly
close, had occasioned this telegraphic enquiry, because she had suddenly
told my parents that she knew with certainty that I had suffered an
accident. My family lived in Coburg at the time. This is a case of
spontaneous telepathy in which at a time of mortal danger, and as I
contemplated certain death, I transmitted my thoughts, while my
sister, who was particularly close to me, acted as the receiver.

Armchair critics sometimes say of reports such as those I have
cited that they all derive from woolly-minded persons who have no
credibility. No one can reasonably say this of the persons concerned in
these cases. I did not mention their names earlier, because I did not
wish any reader to accept the authenticity of the cases from the mere
dropping of names. However, I will now tell you that the reporters of
these experiences were, in order: H. M. Stanley, the African explorer
and "discoverer" of Dr. Livingstone; Lord Brougham, a notable British orator and statesman, who was Lord Chancellor in the Whig government of 1830; L. L. Vasiliev, who became professor of physiology
in the University of Leningrad; and Hans Berger, the discoverer of the
electroencephalogram.[15]

Berger's experience affected him so much that he dropped any
intention he had had of becoming an astronomer and decided instead
to devote his life to the study of the relationship between the mind and
the physical world, with consequences for which we should all feel
grateful. The experiences of the other persons concerned deeply affected them also, in different ways. Vasiliev cited his experience in one
of his books on parapsychology (to which he made notable contributions), and his childhood experience with telepathy seems to have
been a factor in his later undertaking research in parapsychology.
However, I mainly wish to emphasize that the persons who had these
experiences deserve to be listened to thoughtfully when they recount
them, because they have earned our respect through their competence
in unrelated activities.[16]

Skeptics have also suggested that apparitions of the dead coincide by chance with the deaths of the persons perceived. The early psychical researchers paid much attention to this objection, and they refuted it with a careful appraisal of the likelihood that an apparition of a person might be seen at the moment of his death by chance.[17]

Even if it were not wrong, the argument of chance coincidence could only be brought against instances in which a person was identified in a dream or apparition at the moment of his death *without specific details* of the death. When such details occur—as they do in many instances—and are outside the percipient's normal powers of inference, we are considering a unique perception, at a long distance, of a unique event. To illustrate this point I shall present another case. The percipient was Agnes Paquet, whose brother, Edmund Dunn, drowned in the harbor of Chicago in 1889. She made the following statement:

I arose about the usual hour on the morning of the accident, probably about six o'clock. I had slept well throughout the night, had no dreams or sudden awakenings. I awoke feeling gloomy and depressed, which feeling I could not shake off. After breakfast my husband went to his work, and, at the proper time, the children were gotten ready and sent to school, leaving me alone in the house. Soon after this I decided to steep and drink some tea, hoping it would relieve me of the gloomy feelings aforementioned. I went into the pantry, took down the tea canister, and as I turned around my brother Edmund—or his exact image—stood before me and only a few feet away. The apparition stood with back toward me, or, rather, partially so, and was in the act of falling forward—away from me—seemingly impelled by two ropes or a loop of rope drawing against his legs. The vision lasted but a moment, disappearing over a low railing or bulwark, but was very distinct. I dropped the tea, clasped my hands to my face, and exclaimed, "My God! Ed. is drowned."

At about half-past ten a.m. my husband received a telegram from Chicago, announcing the drowning of my brother. When he arrived home he said to me, "Ed. is sick in hospital at Chicago; I have just received a telegram," to which I replied, "Ed. is drowned; I saw him go overboard." I then gave him a minute description of what I had seen. I stated that my brother, as I saw him, was bareheaded, had on a heavy, blue sailor's shirt, no coat, and that he went over the rail or bulwark. I noticed that his pants' legs were rolled up enough to show

*the white lining inside. I also described the appearance of the boat at
the point where my brother went overboard.*

*I am not nervous, and neither before nor since have I had any
experience in the least degree similar to that above related.*

My brother was not subject to fainting or vertigo.

Agnes Paquet's husband, Peter, provided the following corroboration of his wife's experience and his brother-in-law's death:

*At about 10.30 o'clock a.m., October 24th, 1889, I received
a telegram from Chicago, announcing the drowning of my brother-
in-law, Edmund Dunn, at 3 o'clock that morning. I went directly
home, and, wishing to break the force of the sad news I had to convey
to my wife, I said to her: "Ed. is sick in hospital at Chicago; I have
just received a telegram." to which she replied: "Ed. is drowned; I saw
him go overboard." She then described to me the appearance and dress of
her brother as described in her statement; also the appearance of the
boat, &c.*

*I started at once for Chicago, and when I arrived there I found
the appearance of that part of the vessel described by my wife to be
exactly as she had described it, though she had never seen the vessel;
and the crew verified my wife's description of her brother's dress, &c.,
except that they thought that he had his hat on at the time of the
accident. They said that Mr. Dunn had purchased a pair of pants a
few days before the accident occurred, and as they were a trifle long
before, wrinkling at the knees, he had worn them rolled up, showing
the white lining as seen by my wife.*

*The captain of the tug, who was at the wheel at the time of the
accident, seemed reticent. He thought my brother-in-law was taken
with a fainting fit or vertigo and fell over backward; but a sailor
(Frank Yemont) told a friend of mine that he (Yemont) stood on the bow
of the vessel that was being towed and saw the accident. He stated that
my brother-in-law was caught by the tow-line and thrown overboard,
as described by my wife. I think that the captain, in his statement,
wished to avoid responsibility, as he had no right to order a fireman—
my brother-in-law's occupation—to handle the tow-line.*

*My brother-in-law was never, to my knowledge, subject to faint-
ing or vertigo.*[18]

To state the obvious, one can die only once in a lifetime. Therefore, the precise details of how one dies are always unique. Some

deaths resemble others, and we can sometimes predict, in a general way, how a particular person will die. Other deaths, however, have unusual features, and I place that of Edmund Dunn in this category. His kind of death—from drowning when his foot got caught in a tow-line—cannot have happened to more than a few people at any time, and it can only have happened once to him. [19] We cannot reasonably argue that his sister just happened by chance to have a vision with details corresponding to those of her brother's death at about the time he did die in the manner she described. It makes more sense to conclude that she somehow became aware (at a long distance) of the details of his death. If we cannot state exactly how she did this, we should not for that reason deny that she did. "Rarities and reports that seem incredible are not to be suppressed or denied to the memory of men." [20]

Confronted with cases like Agnes Paquet's, some critics have suggested that we cannot trust the accounts of such experiences because they were usually written down after the percipient obtained knowledge of the corresponding events and often only many years later, when faulty memories could have blurred details and permitted a forgetting of discrepancies. This is an objection that we must take seriously in the appraisal of these cases (and of the children's cases with which this book is mainly concerned). We do not know when H. M. Stanley first wrote down his account of his experience, but it could only have been many years after he had it; and it was not published, so far as I know, until 1909, after Stanley's death. There are, nevertheless, a substantial number of cases in which a percipient (or someone else) made a written record of a seemingly paranormal dream or vision before normally obtaining information about the corresponding events. Lord Brougham's case gives us a good example of this type, because he recorded in his diary the vision of his friend that he had in Sweden before he learned of the friend's death in India.

I shall describe another case of this type, one that I investigated myself. In it the percipient, Mrs. Georgina Feakes, had a vision of her cousin, Owen Howison, who had been killed in action during World War II. Mrs. Feakes already knew about Owen Howison's death at the time of her vision, and indeed, his mother, Beatrice Howison (Mrs. Feakes's aunt), had asked her whether she had had any visions of Owen. (Mrs. Feakes had some reputation in her family for having such experiences.) These circumstances prepared Mrs. Feakes to have a vision of her cousin, but not for the one she had. In this vision, she saw him take a blue flower out of his shirt and then replace it; he repeated this unusual action and then vanished. This action of bringing a flower out of a shirt and then hiding it again made no sense to Mrs. Feakes, but she described what she had seen to her aunt. The latter replied that Mrs. Feakes' vision closely matched an incident in her son's life. He and his family had lived in Cape Town, and once when he had been climbing on nearby Table Mountain he had illegally plucked a protected blue flower, which he had brought to his mother. He had carried it home inside his shirt. It then happened that just as he was showing the flower to his mother, two unexpected visitors arrived separately and knocked on the door. Each time this happened, Owen Howison quickly put the flower back in his shirt. Mrs. Feakes had no normal knowledge of this incident. It may or may not be interpreted as evidence of Owen Howison's survival of death; Mrs. Feakes might have obtained her information about the episode by telepathy from Mrs. Howison. (Other details of the case not germane to my present point make me think this unlikely.) However, I have cited the case here not to press its interpretation as evidence of Owen Howison's survival after death, but because I obtained copies of letters that Mrs. Feakes wrote to Mrs. Howison concerning her vision and the related events. These showed that Mrs. Feakes had written to Mrs. Howison about her experience before Mrs. Howison had told Mrs. Feakes to what events it corresponded. The letters did not contain all the details of Mrs. Feakes's experience as she later described it to me, but corroborated enough of them to warrant my including the case in the group for which we can say that faults of memory did not lead the informants to believe that a perception matched an apparently corresponding event more than it did.[21]

No case, including Mrs. Feakes's, is perfect. One may argue that Mrs. Howison somehow told Mrs. Feakes about the incident of Owen's putting the blue flower in his shirt and that subsequently she and Mrs. Feakes forgot that she had done this. One can also suppose that Mrs. Howison had docilely conformed her memory of the event so that it seemed to correspond more than it really did with Mrs. Feakes's vision. Individual spontaneous cases always remain assailable by persons of skeptical inclinations, and this is why some psychical researchers invest their efforts in experiments, which they believe to be less vulnerable to criticism.

How common are experiences like the six cases I have just cited?

We do not know, but we do know that in Great Britain and the United States several surveys have shown that between 10 and 17 percent of respondents (from the general population) *believe* that they have had at least one experience of perceiving an apparition (not always visually).[22] Many more persons report having had other types of paranormal experiences, such as impressions of unusual events, occurring at a distance, of which they had no normal awareness. We know that when we investigate such experiences, many of them do not stand up to scrutiny; their authenticity weakens when inquiries reveal flaws of observation or memory regarding either the percipient's experience, the related events, or both.[23] In another large block of cases, persons who believe they have had a paranormal communication cannot provide sufficient detail about it for an adequate appraisal. And in still other cases, a strong desire, or some other normal factor, may best account for a conviction of having had a paranormal communication. For example, hope and expectation may well explain the majority of the experiences in which a widow or widower believes that she or he has felt the presence of a deceased spouse, seen the spouse, or seemed to have some other type of communication from the spouse.[24] Some of these experiences may have elements of paranormal communication, but it is rare to find satisfactory evidence of this.[25]

The foregoing difficulties lead students of psychical research to emphasize the distinction between *authenticity* and *paranormality*. By authenticity we mean the accuracy of reports of a case that we receive from the persons experiencing it (or from those who have investigated it) measured against the imagined "case as it really happened." In practice, we almost never know exactly what happened; but we can sometimes detect or infer inaccuracies, omissions, and embellishments in the reports, and these may lead us to rank a case low in authenticity. However, we can rank a case high in authenticity and still say that it provides no evidence of paranormal communication. An obvious example of this occurs when two people sitting in the same room together seem spontaneously to think of the same person or topic at the same time. Their description of the experience may be highly accurate, but their sensory contact with each other makes it impossible to show that they were communicating without their senses; they may have been, but we cannot demonstrate this or ask anyone else to believe that they were.

Many authentic cases are therefore valueless with regard to evidence of a paranormal process. However, even if we were to make a generous allowance for cases having a normal explanation and deduct 95 percent of those initially reported to investigators, an impressive number of genuine paranormal experiences would remain. Moreover, paranormal experiences of different types show remarkable uniformities from case to case. As far back as the eighteenth century, enough was known of these uniformities that Immanuel Kant, who had a keen interest in psychical phenomena, wrote of them:

> *The same ignorance makes me unwilling to deny utterly the truth in divers ghost stories, because I have the curious reservation that, although I doubt each one taken by itself, when they are considered as a group I have some belief in them. (Kant, 1976/1766, p. 52; my translation)*

What uniformities do we find in them "considered as a group?" We find in case after case two main themes: love and death. The persons who are concerned in the experiences nearly always love each other. (They are often members of the same family, but the links can be marital as well as biological, so we are not concerned with a genetic factor here.) And the communication exchanged between them has usually to do with death or with some life-threatening illness or injury.[26] (The six cases I have cited are typical in both these features.) The cases of the children who remember previous lives likewise show many similarities to each other; and I will explain later that the themes of love and death figure prominently in them also.

I hope that the foregoing digression about telepathic experiences in everyday life will suffice to prepare the reader to consider later whether telepathy provides an adequate explanation for the cases of the children who claim to remember previous lives. I shall now resume my notes on terminology and explain some terms that I have adopted in reporting and discussing these cases.

TERMS USED IN DESCRIBING CASES OF THE REINCARNATION TYPE

I use the phrase *previous personality* to designate some aspects of the deceased person of whom the child having memories of a previous life is presumed to be the reincarnation. The word *personality* in this phrase may seem inappropriate to some readers. The deceased person in question was more than a personality; he also had a physical body that died. Many would say that was the end of him, but the cases I have investigated suggest that something of the person may have persisted after his death and later become associated with a new physical body. For the interval between death and presumed rebirth we can no longer describe whatever parts of him survived as a "person," because his physical body is dead; but we can, I think, describe these elements as a "personality" or a "discarnate personality." I have, therefore, used the word *personality* to designate *both* a deceased person of whom the child is said to be the reincarnation *and* those aspects of that person that may have survived death and contributed to the new person (and personality) of the child.

I am not opposed to using the word *soul* in reference to the hypothetical elements of a person that may survive death and reincarnate. However, as this word carries for many readers connotations of particular religious views, I generally avoid it and prefer to use the word *personality* in referring to these potentially surviving elements. The word *mind* also occurs in my vocabulary, particularly when I refer to whatever a person experiences directly that is private to him.

Two other terms need defining: *solved cases* and *unsolved cases*. I refer to cases in which my associates and I are satisfied that the child's statements refer to one deceased person, and only one, as *solved;* and cases for which we cannot find any such person as *unsolved*.

The subjects of these cases usually have two types of memories of the previous lives they seem to remember. First, they have *imaged memories*. These are memories of events, often represented to the subjects—it seems—like the visual representations of ordinary memories that we all have of earlier events in this life. I also include under imaged memories the information the subject may have about names of persons and places, sometimes even dates and ages, that is not ordinarily inwardly represented to him in imaged form, although it may be. These memories differ from the second type, which I designate *behavioral memories*.

The concept of what I call *behavioral memory* is so important to the cases and their interpretation that I shall explain in some detail what I mean by this term. Psychologists have studied the frequent occurrence of behavior, such as a habit or a seemingly irrational reaction to a situation, although the person showing it has no memory of how he developed the behavior. Posthypnotic suggestions provide a particularly useful method for investigating this separation of behavior from memories of its origins. A posthypnotic suggestion is one given by a hypnotist to a subject, in which the hypnotist tells the subject to perform a certain action after he comes out of hypnosis; but when the hypnotist gives this suggestion, he often gives a second one at the same time, and this is that the subject will forget that the hypnotist has given him the first suggestion. For example, the hypnotist may tell the subject that after the subject comes out of hypnosis he (the hypnotist) will drop his handkerchief on the floor, and that as soon as the hypnotist does this the subject is to open his umbrella. The hypnotist further tells the subject that he will not remember that he has been told to open the umbrella on this signal. Then he brings the subject out of hypnosis. After a suitable interval the hypnotist casually drops his handkerchief on the floor. The subject may startle a little and seem puzzled, but he proceeds to get his umbrella and open it in the room. The hypnotist asks him why he is doing this, and the subject tries to explain his behavior. He says that the ceiling of the house seems a little leaky, a storm might come up, and he would need the open umbrella if water leaked into the room; or he may say that he wanted to make quite sure that his umbrella was working properly. He has completely forgotten that his behavior of opening the umbrella in the room really derives from the hypnotist's earlier instruction. Thus, the subject performs an action without consciously knowing why he is doing it. [27]

Our ordinary behavior does not derive from posthypnotic suggestions, and I only mentioned them here to emphasize that we can develop patterns of behavior, and even make them fully automatic, while forgetting the events from which they derive. We can walk, but few of us remember our first stumblings as we learned to do so. A skilled pianist may learn a piece of music so well that he can play it while carrying on a conversation with another person; yet he may forget most or even all the details of the practice by which he earlier learned the piece. We can also have unpleasant behavioral memories without imaged memories of their origin. For example, a strong fear or phobia often persists long after the frightening event that caused it has been forgotten. I think most psychologists and psychiatrists agree that we bring many behavioral memories from childhood into adulthood while forgetting how we acquired them. [28] I am only adding the suggestion that we may similarly bring behavioral memories from a previous life.

In order to complete the list of memories—additional to imaged and behavioral ones—that we may bring over from one life to another, I should mention *subliminal cognitive memories*. The phrase *behavioral memories* refers to habits and other types of more or less automatic behavior of a whole person; by *subliminal cognitive memories* I mean information a person has but cannot remember learning. In a later chapter I shall discuss, as examples of these, foreign languages that one has learned—early in life or perhaps in a previous life—without remembering how one learned them or even, in some instances, *that* one had once learned them.

For the remaining chapters of this book I have adopted the following plan. In the next chapter I show that a belief in reincarnation is widespread throughout the world, and I discuss how people may come to hold the belief. I also mention that the different peoples who believe in reincarnation often have widely varying beliefs about it: for example, about who can reincarnate and under what circumstances.

I follow the chapter about the belief in reincarnation with one (chapter 3) about the types of evidence that are used to justify a belief in it. In this chapter I explain why I reject as of little value nearly all types of alleged evidence of reincarnation, except that provided by young children who claim to remember previous lives. Next I present in chapter 4 summaries of twelve typical cases of children who have remembered previous lives. Then (in chapter 5) I survey some of the recurrent characteristics of cases of this type.

In chapters 6 and 7 I present an account of my methods of investigating and analyzing the cases.

In chapter 8 I return to the variations in the cases in different cultures and, with further examples of these variations, discuss possible reasons for them.

In the last three chapters—especially chapter 11—I become more speculative. In chapter 9 I discuss a variety of presently unsolved problems in psychology, psychiatry, and medicine, to the solution of which the idea of reincarnation may contribute. I have, I hope, increased the plausibility of these conjectures by referring (for each topic I discuss) to examples of actual cases in which reincarnation seems to have had some explanatory value. In chapter 10 I offer some answers to questions that are frequently raised in connection with these cases. And finally, in chapter 11, I give some of my conjectures about processes involved in reincarnation, if it occurs. Here I have ventured—contrary to my earlier assertion—to say something about reincarnation. But I have also tried to keep what I say, if not firmly grounded in the data of the cases that I have studied, at least within sight of the data.

CHAPTER TWO

The Belief in Reincarnation

Many persons believe they have lived before being born into what we may call the present life. To those who have this belief, it does not seem strange at all. They would agree with Voltaire, who wrote: "It is not more surprising to be born twice than once." [1] Yet persons unfamiliar with the idea of reincarnation often find it unreasonable and even absurd. They, however, may form a minority of all the inhabitants of the earth; believers in reincarnation possibly outnumber those who reject the idea or have never heard of it.

Many Westerners mistakenly think that only the inhabitants of Southeast Asia believe in reincarnation. This error probably arose because the Hindus and Buddhists of that region recorded the belief in their ancient religious scriptures and they emphasize it in their modern teachings. Their doctrines have diffused into the West in translations, through the efforts of their missionaries, and in not-always-reliable popular distillates.

The inhabitants of many other parts of the world, however, also believe in reincarnation. Large groups of Shiite Moslems of western Asia believe in it. So do the inhabitants of West Africa and East Africa who have not been completely converted to Islam and Christianity. A large minority of the inhabitants of Brazil believe in reincarnation; their belief appears to derive from ideas about it brought by Africans to Brazil, where they became emulsified with concepts of spiritualism imported from France in the nineteenth century.

Another substantial number of persons who believe in reincarnation live in northwestern North America. The native tribes of that region have preserved the belief in reincarnation (which forms a part of their traditional religion) despite some erosion of it through the efforts of Christian missionaries and educators, both of whom have, from different points of view, inculcated a belief in "one life" on earth.

Numerous other peoples also believe in reincarnation, but I shall mention only a few additional examples. Anthropologists (of this century) have reported the belief among the Trobriand Islanders, the tribes of central Australia, and the Ainu of northern Japan.[2]

The widespread occurrence of belief in reincarnation led Schopenhauer to remark: "Were an Asiatic to ask me for a definition of Europe, I should be forced to answer him: It is that part of the world completely dominated by the outrageous and incredible delusion that a man's birth is his beginning and that he is created out of nothing."[3]

The belief has spread in the West since Schopenhauer's time. By the late twentieth century, many Europeans had lapsed from the disbelief that he deplored. A survey conducted in 1968 by Gallup International showed that 18 percent of persons in eight countries of West Europe believed in reincarnation. A year later, a similar survey in North America showed that 20 percent of Americans and 26 percent of Canadians questioned said that they believed in reincarnation. In a later survey in the United States (reported in 1982), 23 percent of the respondents said they believed in reincarnation.[4]

It would be incorrect to say that all the peoples of industrially undeveloped countries not influenced by Christianity or orthodox Islam believe in reincarnation. A few have remained impervious to these teachings and have retained traditional religions that do *not* include this belief. These few exceptions, however, subtract little from the generalization that nearly everyone outside the range of orthodox Christianity, Judaism, Islam, and Science—the last being a secular religion for many persons—believes in reincarnation. I shall consider next how this may have happened.

Did the belief arise in one place and then diffuse to other parts of the world, rather as we suppose the ancestor of the Indo-European languages to have spread out from one fairly small region? If this happened, it would explain the occurrence of the belief in some far-separated areas of the world that communicated with each other in historical times or earlier. For example, traders and other travelers have linked South Asia and West Asia for at least two millennia and possibly much longer. We can trace the belief in reincarnation in India at least to the period of the later Vedas, which were written about 1,000 B.C.[5] The Indologist Norman Brown suggested that the authors of the accounts of walking on water recorded in the Bible may have borrowed and adapted them from earlier narrations or legends of Buddhism. If this happened, it follows that the Indians could also have exported their belief in reincarnation to western Asia and Europe. Apollonius, a Greek born in Tyana (now in southern Anatolia, Turkey), traveled in the first century A.D. to India and there engaged in a philosophical discussion with a sage, Iarchus. A modern Indian would find nothing surprising in the almost casual references to reincarnation that are recorded from their conversation.[6] The beliefs in reincarnation held by people living in different parts of Asia *may* have had a common origin.[7] As I shall explain later, the peoples of South Asia and those of West Asia (who believe in reincarnation) now have different concepts about some important details of reincarnation; but this does not preclude a common ancestry for the central idea.

If, however, we try to show that all the other peoples who believe in reincarnation also derived their ideas on the subject from central or southern Asia, we encounter serious difficulties. How shall we account, on this hypothesis, for the belief in reincarnation among the Eskimo and the other tribes of northwestern North America? Their ancestors migrated from Asia to America thousands of years ago, and it is generally believed that afterward there was no important contact (in protohistorical times) between Asia and America. It is barely possible that an Eskimo in northern Canada and a villager of the Ganges Valley acquired their beliefs in reincarnation from the same source.[8] It is even less likely that the belief in reincarnation spread from South Asia to West Africa or to central Australia.

If, however, the belief did not diffuse to other regions from one central place of origin, it must have arisen in different parts of the world independently and, no doubt, at different times. This leads us to ask how such an idea might arise in the first place.

The belief in survival of personality after death diminishes the grief of mourners and the fear of those who await their turn to die. Yet the idea of reincarnation is not necessary for such solace; it could be obtained from simply believing in a prolonged or eternal sojourn in some paradisal realm where we would live after death. We need to ask, therefore, what would generate the more specific belief that aspects of a person who had survived death could enter into a new physical body and start another terrestrial life.

A desire by grieving relatives for the return of loved ones from death may promote the conviction that they have reincarnated among them; but this explanation seems less than fully satisfactory when the presumed rebirth occurs in a family completely different from that of the deceased person, which we find to be almost the rule in India,

Thailand, Turkey, and Sri Lanka. Bereaved persons hearing of a child born in another family who claims to have belonged to theirs may derive some comfort from this information, if they accept the claim; but it is unlikely that the reassurance provided by such cases could alone support the extensive edifice of belief in reincarnation that, for example, the Hindus and Buddhists of South Asia have erected.

The easiest way to acquire any belief is to accept as true what one's parents tell one; and their task of inculcating a belief becomes easier when they can draw on the support of scriptural authority, as Hindus and Buddhists can. (Some Christians use the Bible with similar authority in arguments *against* reincarnation.) Most children in South Asia grow up believing in reincarnation as something entirely natural, and they may discover with surprise that peoples of other countries do not share their belief.

Religious tradition, however, does not require a written embodiment. No scripture imposes it on the Tlingit of Alaska, because they have none. The Alevis of south-central Turkey also seem to have no written authority for their belief in reincarnation.[9] The Igbo of Nigeria offer still another example of a people having a robust belief in reincarnation that has been transmitted wthout a written book of reference.[10]

However, understanding how a belief in reincarnation may pass from generation to generation—through scripture or oral tradition—does not explain how it arose in the first place. This may have happened in more than one way.

One may reach a conviction about reincarnation through philosophical argument. A number of philosophers, including such superior ones as Plato, Schopenhauer,[11] McTaggart, Broad, and Ducasse,[12] have taken the idea of reincarnation seriously and argued on its behalf.

In the *Meno* Plato described Socrates' demonstration of how a young boy was able to solve a geometrical problem when it was presented to him, seemingly for the first time. Socrates attributed the boy's success to his having a subliminal memory of the solution, which he had learned in a previous life, even though the boy had no imaged memories of such a life.

According to Plato, Socrates spoke dogmatically about the knowledge we bring from one incarnation to another: "The soul then being immortal, having often been born, having beheld the things which are here, the things which are in Hades, and all things, there is nothing of which she has not gained knowledge. No wonder, therefore, that she is able to recollect, with regard to virtue as well as to other things, what formerly she knew. . . . For inquiry and learning is reminiscence all." [13]

In a similar vein, McTaggart said that reincarnation might explain—and that nothing else could—such common observations as the strong attractions some people have for others on first or slight acquaintance, and the unusual aptitudes and interests they often show, contrary to the expectations of their families.

Other philosophers, as I mentioned in chapter 1, have concerned themselves with how we should define personal identity; in grappling with this problem they have tried to answer the question of what criteria we should have for saying that a particular person has survived death and been reincarnated.

I think it fair to say that philosophers have added only a little to the evidence for reincarnation or to the belief in it. Someone balancing between belief and disbelief might find himself tipped toward believing in reincarnation by philosophical arguments, such as those used by McTaggart and Ducasse [14]; but I do not think that these arguments alone would suffice to establish a belief that did not already have roots. Nevertheless, some philosophers have contributed to removing the rubbish of unwarranted assumptions that seem for many persons to make belief in reincarnation unreasonable.

Although we have no evidence on the matter, it seems to me likely that the belief in reincarnation has originated sometimes, and perhaps often, from the claim of someone to remember having lived before. News of such a person may travel from place to place, and an account of his memories may pass down several generations or more in time. Yet such diffusion must have some outer limits. Traders notoriously narrate extraordinary tales of distant places; but the entertainment of their listeners does not require them to present convincing evidence, and as the site for some unusual event becomes more remote, listeners become less inclined to believe that it happened. We cannot anyway account for the widespread belief in reincarnation among the Eskimo—from Greenland through northern Canada to Alaska—by supposing that hunters and sledders carried accounts of reincarnation cases from settlement to settlement across vast distances of tundra and ice. [15] Moreover, when two neighboring peoples believe in reincarnation, this does not necessarily mean that one has proselytized the other. The ancestors of the Athabaskan Indians (of north-western Canada and central Alaska) and of the Eskimo appear to have migrated from Asia to the North American continent at different times, and these peoples speak mutually unintelligible languages. Although they formerly quarreled over territory, they otherwise appear to have had little contact with each other, at least of a type that would include an exchange of ideas about the nature of man and his destiny after death; and yet both the Athabaskan and the Eskimo believe in reincarnation.

I conclude, therefore, that persons of cultures having no written scriptures who believe in reincarnation may have reached their belief through exposure to a person within their trading area who claimed to remember a previous life. [16] This person could have lived in the same or a nearby village; and he could have lived a few generations back, so that the tradition of his memories outlived the man himself. Perhaps many such persons have independently claimed to remember a previous life and thereby have established the belief in reincarnation in different parts of the world.

Although the belief in reincarnation among different peoples was probably initiated by claims to remember previous lives, once the belief becomes established it may persist for many years in the absence of supporting evidence. For example, although Hindus have believed in reincarnation for several thousand years, we find no trace of anything corresponding to a modern case of the reincarnation type in India until the beginning of the eighteenth century. And this case appears to have had no successors—certainly none known to me—until the early years of the twentieth century. [17]

We should, however, remember that many cases may have occurred in India before this century without our having any record of them. I am sure that the cases about which I have learned in *this* century represent only a small fraction of all that have occurred; and in former centuries our modern facilities for reporting and disseminating information about cases would be lacking. Moreover, the beliefs of Hinduism might have made memories of previous lives seem normal and in no need of being recorded, or even noticed.

The Cathars of southwestern France provide another example of a group having a strong belief in reincarnation, although we have received from them almost nothing in the way of cases. The Cathars were a heretical Christian sect during the twelfth and thirteenth centuries.[18] In the middle of the thirteenth century the forces of King Louis IX of France and northern French nobles effectively extirpated the sect. The records of the Cathars themselves seem largely to have been destroyed, and most of what we know about them derives from records of their persecutors, the monks of the Inquisition. Here again, however, the paucity of cases known to us does not mean that no others occurred.

It also seems probable that a belief in reincarnation may become established without the evidence that memories of a previous life may provide. Otherwise, I find it difficult to explain the frequent belief in reincarnation expressed at present by many persons in the West, especially young persons. They may have had some exposure to the popular books about Asian religions and theosophy, but these (for the most part) give assertions, not evidence; and the evidence from investigated cases has only recently become more widely available. Perhaps they reached a belief in reincarnation through some process of intuition or self-conducted philosophical argument. Anyone, perhaps particularly a thoughtful child, may find incredible the orthodox Christian doctrine according to which God makes a new soul for each new baby born. And if one rejects that assertion without dismissing the idea of a soul, one may easily suppose that each soul had some existence prior to its association with its (present) physical body and that it was, therefore, associated with an earlier physical body. "Whoever believes that man's birth is his beginning," wrote Schopenhauer, "must also believe that his death is the end."[19] The teaching that we have only a single life, as I mentioned in the last chapter, also offends many persons' sense of justice when they contemplate the different conditions at birth of different persons. From dissatisfaction with this teaching they might turn toward the idea of reincarnation.

If reincarnation occurs, intimations about it may derive from previous lives that are not remembered in detail.[20] About 2,000 years ago, the great Indian sage Patanjali explained the almost universal fear of death as due to fear of undergoing another postmortem review of one's life, such as, according to Hinduism and some other traditions, each soul experiences at death. The subliminal memory of this experience—unpleasant as it must be for many persons—would generate fear of another death, since this, in turn, would precipitate another (and possibly equally unpleasant) review of one's actions.[21, 22]

The belief in reincarnation, like other beliefs, can rise and fall in acceptance within particular nations and cultures. If we consider the belief over a long period of time, we can find one clear instance of its arising in a people and several of its disappearing among peoples who had held it for a long time.

The Tibetans provide an example of the development of a belief in reincarnation—or perhaps I should say a belief in a particular style of reincarnation—where none existed before. Buddhism reached and spread in Tibet between the seventh and tenth centuries A.D. The version of Buddhism imported into Tibet included the belief in reincarnation; but this, as derived from India, did not have the features that the Tibetans developed and that make their belief in reincarnation, and most of their cases of the reincarnation type, distinct from those of other peoples. I refer to the ideas that spiritually advanced monks (*lamas*) may acquire the ability to control their next lives, and that after rebirth they may give indications of their previous identities. (Such persons are called *tulkus* among Tibetans.) These concepts developed in Tibet during the eleventh to fifteenth centuries A.D. They gradually became codified, and to some extent hardened, into a system of succession for the abbotships of monasteries through reincarnation. Although the Tibetan concept of reincarnation did not begin with the Dalai Lamas, they and their associates of the Gelugpa, or "Yellow Hat," school of Tibetan Buddhists adopted it. They have since developed it to the point where the ritual procedures associated with the identification of each new Dalai Lama now provide a model for similar discoveries of other senior lamas. [23]

Among cases of peoples who had once believed in reincarnation but have ceased to do so, the Moslems of India provide one of the most impressive examples. We know that only a handful of the millions of Moslems living in India have descended from the Moslem raiders and invaders who eventually established the Mogul empire whose leaders dominated India for four centuries. The majority of Moslems in India today are descendants of Hindu ancestors who converted to Islam. [24] The Ismailis, a Shiite sect that originated in western Asia and spread into other parts of Asia and Africa, at one time believed in reincarnation, but the modern Ismailis (of western Asia) do not. [25] The Celts of Great Britain believed in reincarnation, [26] as did the Vikings of Scandinavia and Iceland [27]; the majority of their descendants (Christians for the most part) do not.

We also know that at least some Christians of southern Europe believed in reincarnation up to the sixth century. It did not then form part of official instruction, but leaders of the church appear to have tolerated it as an acceptable concept until the Council of Nice in A.D. 553.[28] We may debate whether the actions of this council as a whole, and those of a group of clerics outside the council but associated with it, constituted a binding official ban on the teaching of reincarnation. Yet certainly a decline in the acceptability of the idea set in among orthodox Christians at about this time and has persisted since.

I have also obtained evidence of a decline in the belief in reincarnation in my journeys to northwestern North America, where I have studied cases of the reincarnation type among the natives (Indians and Eskimo) of that area for many years. I once conducted a small, informal survey of Eskimo informants concerning their knowledge of the idea of reincarnation among their own people and their belief in it. I questioned 108 Eskimos in this survey. Of the 66 persons who were forty years or older, 47 (71 percent) had heard of the belief in reincarnation among the Eskimo; but of the 42 persons who were thirty-nine years or younger, only 13 (31 percent) had heard of this belief. I asked 47 of the informants who had heard of the belief whether they believed that reincarnation does in fact occur, and 29 (62 percent) said that they believed it does. This is a much higher percentage of believers than we find among persons of the conjoined forty-eight states, so the belief in reincarnation persists rather strongly among the Eskimo, even though many younger people have not heard of the belief among their own people.[29] I should mention, however, that some young persons among the tribes of northwestern North America have a lively interest in reincarnation, and some mothers who were still under the age of thirty proved to be among my best informants for cases in this region.

The processes that promote skepticism about reincarnation probably resemble in reverse those that stimulate a belief in it. After a Hindu had converted to Islam in India (say in the sixteenth century), the members of his family might have mused nostalgically about the idea of reincarnation for one or several generations, but then it would have begun to seem at first remote and eventually ridiculous. If during this later period any child among the converts started saying that he remembered a previous life, he might have been discouraged by derision or sterner measures, if these were needed. And if I am correct in believing that the cases and the belief strengthen each other in a cir-

cular way, the resulting loss of cases (by suppression) would have removed empirical support for the doctrine among the new Moslems,
who could then have belittled the idea of reincarnation as a foolish
superstition that the faithful in Islam had happily outgrown. As an
eraser of credibility, remoteness in time works as well as physical distance. The editor of the Norse poems about the hero Helgi provides
and example of this: "It was believed according to ancient lore . . .
that folk were reborn; but this is now said to be old women's lying
tales. Helgi and Sigrún are said to have been reborn; he was then
called Helgi Haddingjaskati and she Kara Hálfdanardóttir, as is related in *Káruljóth;* and she was a Valkyrie." [30]

When persons who know about cases suggestive of reincarnation
that they believe are authentic encounter aggressive skepticism, they
may remain silent but not completely abandon their previous convictions. Dissembling their real beliefs, they may appear to have changed
them when they have not. I have found evidence of this among the
Tlingit and the Eskimo, whose traditional religions now stand on the
defensive against Christianity and Western science.

Not long after I began my investigations among the Indians and
the Eskimo of northwestern North America (in the early 1960s), I
met a nurse who had worked among the Eskimo for many years. I
mentioned my research to her, and she told me that the belief in
reincarnation had already died out; I had come, she said, twenty years
too late. She was wrong. I found more than 170 cases of the reincarnation type among the Eskimo and Indians of northwestern North
America. The cases existed plentifully but were revealed only to in-
quirers judged sympathetic.

The nurse I met is not the only nonnative from whom these cases
have been hidden. I met or corresponded with six professionally
trained persons who had lived and worked among the Tlingit for periods varying between a few months and several years. Four of them
were anthropologists. Tlingit bands had given two of them tribal
names and thus shown that they accepted these outsiders into the
Tlingit group; I mention this to emphasize how close these Western
persons were to the natives of whose belief in reincarnation they remained (with one exception) completely ignorant. Of the six, only
one knew anything about the Tlingit belief in reincarnation; she had
also obtained some information about their cases, although she had
not investigated any. The remaining five knew nothing about either

the belief or the cases related to reincarnation among the Tlingit until I mentioned these to them. They could have learned about these topics, as I did, if they had asked about them; but why should their Tlingit friends have risked mockery by broaching the subject first?

In the foregoing discussions of the belief in reincarnation among different peoples, I have considered only what I call the primary (or central) belief in reincarnation: whether the personality (soul or mind) of a person may, after the person's death, become associated with a new physical body. Attached to this primary belief, however, we find a wide variety of subsidiary beliefs about who reincarnates, how it occurs, and how causes in one life may have effects in a later one. I think it important to study these secondary beliefs about reincarnation separately from the primary belief, and I shall now describe some of them.[31]

When Westerners who have mistakenly thought that only the people of Southeast Asia believe in reincarnation learn for the first time about the belief among other peoples, they are inclined to imagine that these other peoples must have concepts about reincarnation similar to those of the Hindus and Buddhists. This is wrong. The Southeast Asians believe that moral conduct in one life influences the circumstances of a later life; this is the essence of the doctrine of *karma*. Many persons, however, believe in reincarnation without believing in karma or in any concept like it. At least three other concepts of reincarnation have been or are held by persons who believe in reincarnation just as earnestly as the Hindus and Buddhists do.

The members of the Shiite Moslem sects of western Asia who believe in reincarnation do not think that what a person does in one life has any effect on what happens to him in another. Instead they believe that a soul passes through a succession of lives in different circumstances, in each of which lives he must strive his best for moral perfection. Whether he succeeds or fails in one life has no effect on his condition in a later one. Ultimately, however, at the Day of Judgment, the books of his actions are examined, the accounts of good and bad deeds summed up, and, according to the reckoning, God assigns each person to Heaven or Hell for eternity.[32]

The peoples of West Africa hold a belief in reincarnation that has almost no connection with their moral values. I do not mean to imply that West Africans have undeveloped moral concepts; on the contrary, they have an elaborate system of moral codes and of sanctions for their enforcement. Their concept of reincarnation, however, has few connections with these codes. They regard life as basically pleasant and desirable. (This attitude contrasts with the life-negating attitude of the Hindus and Buddhists.) Accordingly, West Africans consider the after-death state a limbo from which discarnate spirits are eager to return for a new terrestrial incarnation. They hope for an improvement in status or circumstances in another incarnation, but have no expectation that this will come from meritorious conduct. They attach more importance to wishes for improvement that a person may express before he dies.[33]

The Tlingit of southeastern Alaska hold similar beliefs. Like the West Africans, they do not believe that moral conduct in one life governs or even has the slightest effect on what happens in the next one; and they also believe that wishes expressed in one life may shape conditions in the next one. Thus, we often find an older Tlingit who senses that he may soon die choosing the parents he wishes for his next incarnation; and he may also speak about what he would like modified in himself in that next life. He may say, for example, that he hopes to be stronger, better educated, and no longer troubled with flat feet.[34]

A fourth concept about the ways in which one life is tied to another may be the most important; it is the only one for which we have some evidence, although not much of that. I refer to the idea that a person (before his death or in the discarnate state) chooses the family of his next incarnation and thereby indirectly selects also the conditions for starting it. When I say there is evidence for this concept I am thinking of a small number of cases among the Tlingit, a few among Tibetan lamas, and occasional ones among other peoples in which a person has indicated before his death in what family he would be reborn; the subject of such a case later provides evidence suggesting the success of the deceased person's intention.[35] All the cases with an announcing dream also suggest a choice on the part of the discarnate personality appearing in the dream. This is particularly true of the petitionary types of announcing dreams so common among the Burmese. The discarnate personality communicates—and sometimes the dreamer hears him say explicitly—that he has chosen a particular family, usually that of the dreamer, and wishes their agreement to his rebirth among them.

This idea that we can choose the circumstances of our next incarnation has a long history in Europe also. It occurred among some of the ancient Greeks, and Plato expounded it. In the *Republic,* he described souls who are about to be reborn as choosing the lives they will have after birth.[36] According to this belief, persons who have acquired wisdom in prior lives can choose better future lives than those who have squandered their previous lives and learned nothing from them. Plato did not, however, suggest that one's conduct in a prior life influences the next life, except to the extent that the wisdom needed for prudent selection of that life derives from previous efforts to attain such wisdom.

Numerous other differences occur among the ideas that different peoples have concerning reincarnation. I shall return to this topic in chapter 8; but I shall serve my readers best if I first describe the evidence bearing on the question of whether reincarnation occurs.

CHAPTER THREE

Types of Evidence for Reincarnation

Many persons have had apparent memories of previous lives in a wide variety of circumstances. All but one of these circumstances—the spontaneous experiences of very young children—seem to provide little of value as evidence of any paranormal process. Nevertheless, in each of them a small number of experiences have occurred that may derive from memories of previous lives. Consequently, I shall discuss them in this chapter while trying to explain my preference for the cases of young children that occur spontaneously instead of those of adults that are induced or deliberately sought.

PAST-LIFE READINGS

I believe the weakest evidence for reincarnation comes from persons who claim they can describe or "read" other persons' previous lives. Surely such claims provide as good an example as we can find of beliefs sustained in the absence of evidence. I suppose that those who pay for "past-life readings" have confidence in what they are told, but I can find no support for such faith in any results known to me. Without their almost invariable commercial exploitation, past-life readings would evoke more laughter than sadness. The "previous lives" depicted almost always occurred in the centers of history's cyclones. Such events as the Crusades, the French Revolution, the American Civil War, and, above all, Jesus Christ's crucifixion, figure repeatedly in the readings of other persons' previous lives. I sometimes think that if all those said to have watched the crucifixion of Jesus (in previous lives) had actually done so, the Roman soldiers at that event would have had no place to stand.

I find it surprising that most persons who have had one past-life reading seem to have had no more. If they tested one "reader" against others, they might quickly wish to have their money back.[1] I am almost afraid to say anything positive about past-life readings for fear of increasing gullibility in the matter. And yet I should mention two instances known to me in which different sensitives independently gave the same (or similar) information about the previous lives of a person when they had no opportunity of communicating with each other. And I know of two other instances in which a sensitive described details of another person's previous life that corresponded to spontaneous memories that person had already had. None of these instances, however, necessarily offers evidence of reincarnation. At best, they suggest telepathy between the sensitive and the person whose past life was read, although we should not deny the possibility that the sensitive really did discern information about the other person's previous life.

HYPNOTIC REGRESSION

Experiments with hypnotic regression to ostensible previous lives provide a level of evidence just perceptibly stronger—in a few instances—than that from past-life readings. Yet to judge by my mail and by the stacks of books generated by such experiments, many persons in the West have become firmly convinced that hypnosis can cut a breach through our amnesia and allow real memories of previous lives to pour out. If they would stop to learn something about hypnosis, they would soon feel less assurance.

I shall not rashly attempt a definition of hypnosis, especially since some experts now deny that hypnosis constitutes a special state of consciousness. Experiments have demonstrated that at least some of the phenomena of hypnosis can occur without the formal induction of hypnosis, but simply with a sufficient change in the subject's willingness to follow directions and respond to suggestions. If he becomes adequately motivated to behave differently, he may perform mental and physical feats that at one time were thought to require hypnosis. In short, although hypnosis may alter a subject's capacities, so may other types of psychological influence.

However, I think all students of hypnosis agree that during this state, whatever its nature may be, the hypnotized subject's attention becomes remarkably concentrated and his mind freed of extraneous stimuli and intruding irrelevant thoughts. In this condition, he can focus on particular scenes of the past with a vividness and clarity not often otherwise experienced. He may remember details of his childhood that remain ordinarily forgotten, such as the day of the week of his tenth birthday and the teachers and classmates in his grade school.[2]

So far so good. But in the process of achieving this greater power of concentration, the subject surrenders direction of his thoughts to the hypnotist and thus becomes less able, or at least unwilling, to resist following the latter's instructions. These instructions tell the subject that he should remember something, and when he cannot do so accurately, he often furnishes an incorrect statement in order to please the hypnotist. Most subjects doing this do not realize that they are mixing truth and falsehood in what they tell the hypnotist.[3]

A hypnotized subject is likely to conform just as much to the hypnotist's instructions when told to return to a previous life as he does when told to return to the age of five, and perhaps more so.[4] When the hypnotist says: "You will go back before your birth to another time and place," the subject tries to oblige. He will show equal pliancy even when the hypnotist phrases his instructions less explicitly by saying, for example: "You will remember the cause of these headaches somewhere in your past." In the peculiar condition of conformity that hypnosis induces, the subject is impelled—one could almost say compelled—to furnish a plausible past of some kind; and if he cannot present one from this life he may construct one from an apparent previous life, even when he has never before had any memories of such a life that he might use as ingredients. He may then reach for other materials in his mind, and he usually seizes on the tags of history that even the least educated person has picked up from reading, radio, and television. If he knows no history, and even if he does, he may engage in speaking fiction in order not to disappoint the hypnotist.

In addition, the subject often employs a third common feature of hypnosis: heightened powers of dramatization. He links the various latent items of information in his mind and animates them into a "previous personality." This previous personality may show appropriate emotions and consistency of character even when it is evoked at different times over many months.

With regard to the integration of ordinarily latent mental contents and their dramatic presentation in a more or less coherent form, hypnosis has much in common with dreams. This makes it somewhat surprising that some persons who attach no importance to their dreams uncritically accept as true whatever they experience during

hypnosis. Such folly probably derives from the glamour that hypnotists, and the dramatic inductions of hypnosis, have achieved. Stage
hypnotists and other promoters of sensational claims connected with
hypnosis have nourished the misconception that hypnosis is an infal-
lible means of recovering memories, when, in reality, this is far from
being true.

One can sometimes show the most absurd anachronisms in the
reports of hypnotically induced "previous personalities." In one published example the evoked "previous personality," who described himself as a courier for the king of France in the time of the Crusades,
claimed that he carried messages between the court at Versailles and
Bordeaux. In the time of the Crusades (eleventh to thirteenth centuries), however, Versailles had no important connection with the
government of France; it only achieved that status in the seventeenth
century.[5]

Another hypnotized and regressed subject recounted a life in
seventeenth century England as James, Earl of Leicester (pronounced
by him "Lechester"). He described how "Lord Cromwell" had evicted
him and his family from their castle. In fact, the Earl of Leicester of
this period was *Robert* Sidney (1595 -1677), not James; he was never
evicted from his country seat (at Penshurst) and Oliver Cromwell was
not known generally—if at all—as Lord Cromwell, although he was
Lord Protector.

Anachronisms and other mistakes of the kind I have just mentioned would embarrass the average high school student, but they
demonstrate another feature of hypnosis—the abeyance of ordinary
critical faculties. (Writers who publish such incorrect details without
comment have no such defense, since they presumably enjoy normal
judgment when writing their books; but it seems that things too silly
to be put in historical novels may still be fobbed off as "previous
lives.") The two examples I just gave also show, as do many other
hypnotically induced "previous lives," a tendency the subjects have to
assign themselves in these previous lives a role of historical importance, or to locate themselves in relation to well-known people and
places.

We may overlook a number of inaccuracies in such cases, and
perhaps we should. This indulgence, however, would not remove all
the obstacles to accepting hypnotically induced "previous lives" as
what they appear to be. The lives portrayed occurred in a past of

imperfect records that are devoted mainly to political leaders and perhaps a few other outstanding persons, such as great artists and inventors. Of almost any life before the middle of the nineteenth century, we can say the following: If detailed records of this life—needed for verification—exist, then the subject could, at least in principle, have had access to them; and if the person concerned lived an obscure life, we can probably verify little or nothing about it.[6]

In some instances of ostensible regression to previous lives, the hypnotist has afterward asked the hypnotized subject—in the same or a later session—to tell the source of the material embodied earlier in the evoked "previous life." Some subjects questioned in this way have then remembered and named a book or other source for some of the information included in the "previous life."[7]

Apart from the unjustified reputation of hypnosis as a means of eliciting accurate information, the dramatic powers of the mind that hypnosis releases provide for the subject (and sometimes the observers) a convincing appearance of realism. Two subjects whom I hypnotized myself illustrated well the power of fantasies to present themselves as memories.

The first subject regressed easily to three different "previous lives." The only one of these that contained any verifiable information was that of a priest of the late seventeenth century in France, who figured marginally in the religious controversies of that period. I happened to know that the subject had learned about this person through normal reading and conversation. In another "previous life," the subject saw herself as an English sailor in the sixteenth century. The ship ran onto rocks in a storm, and the sailor found himself in the water, drowning. The enactment of the drowning by the subject included expressions of fear and difficulty in breathing. On one occasion when the subject seemed to relive this drowning, her physical condition alarmed me so much that I quickly gave suggestions that she would imagine another, more tranquil scene; she immediately did this and became calmer. Although I am convinced that the subject who seemed to remember these three lives had engaged in fantasy, using information that she had normally obtained, she herself believed afterward that she had remembered and relived actual previous lives. The apparent realism of the experiences out-weighed other considerations for her.

Another subject I hypnotized recalled a "previous life" in nineteenth-century Amsterdam. She seemed at times to be making an effort to speak Dutch, so I asked a Dutch-speaking colleague to attend a session; he quickly learned that she could not speak the Dutch language at all. (She knew a few words of tourist German, and she had tried to work these into a semblance of Dutch.) Nor did she show knowledge of the main parts of Amsterdam with which a resident of that city would have been familiar. Of relevance here, however, is the intense impersonation of the Dutch woman that the subject showed during the hypnosis. I could easily regress her upwards and downwards within the life of the supposed previous personality. Placed at her wedding day, the "previous personality" showed the joyful exuberance of a bride. Advanced in years to the day of her husband's death, she burst into tears and expressed an intense grief that moved all observers. (I had with me at the time two colleagues, both experienced psychologists, and the subject's expression of appropriate emotions impressed them so much that I had difficulty in persuading them to adopt my view that she was only enacting fantasies.)

In fairness, however, I must add that this subject did show a little knowledge about nineteenth-century Holland that she may not have acquired normally. For example, she correctly named a ship, *Nederland*, as being in the harbor of Amsterdam in 1866. The previous life in this case may, therefore, have been mostly fiction, but contained a few ingredients of fact, some of them perhaps obtained paranormally.

Promoters of hypnosis as a means of recovering memories of previous lives frequently cite improvements in the patients following the hypnotic sessions. For example, if a patient loses a long-standing phobia of water after describing how he drowned in a "previous life," the patient and the hypnotist may both attribute the improvement to the recovery of the apparent memory of the drowning. However, this exemplifies a common fallacy of psychotherapists: the unwarranted belief that a patient's improvement vindicates the theory favored and the technique used. Improvements and recovery from the neuroses occur with a wide variety of therapists and techniques. The successful therapist should receive credit after others have failed, but the credit should go to the therapist (and the patient), not to the therapist's technique or theory. As I shall explain later, children who claim to remember previous lives (with verified details) often have phobias appropriate to the mode of death in the previous life they remember.

However, such a phobia may manifest before the child speaks about the previous life and explains the origin of the phobia; it may continue manifesting during the period when the child talks about the traumatic origin of the phobia; and sometimes it still continues long after the child has forgotten the imaged memories of the previous life. These phobias provide no grounds for believing that recovering a seemingly related memory of a previous life abolishes a phobia derived from one. Despite these reservations I do not mean to deny absolutely the beneficial effect that remembering the traumatic events initiating a phobia may sometimes have. (I continue this topic in chapter 5, especially in note 15.)

Although I am skeptical about the results of most experiments with hypnotic regression to ostensible previous lives, I do not reject all of them as worthless. In a few instances the subject has communicated obscure information about a particular place in an earlier period of history, which it seems most unlikely he could have learned normally, so far as I could discover. I consider the case described in Bernstein's *The Search for Bridey Murphy* in this small class.[8] Moreover, in two cases that I have investigated, hypnotized and regressed subjects proved able to speak foreign languages they had not learned normally. This ability is called *xenoglossy,* which means "foreign tongue." They spoke these languages responsively, that is, they engaged in a sensible conversational exchange with other persons speaking the same language.[9]

The foolish implausibilities that disfigure most hypnotically induced previous personalities should not influence us to overlook one legitimate question that these cases raise: Why does the subject of such an experiment, given all the times and places that he might choose for his previous life, select one time and place instead of others? Why, when requested to go back to *any* time and place, should he choose to narrate a life in, say, seventeenth-century Scotland instead of one in eighteenth-century France or nineteenth-century Germany? If he had had a real previous life in seventeenth-century Scotland, this could have influenced him to reconstruct a life of that place and time instead of another one. Then, once committed to the erection of such a previous life, he would draw on everything his now concentrated memory could mobilize from his depots of normally acquired information. During this process a few items of memories from the real previous life might become dislodged and attracted, like iron filings in a magnetic field, to the otherwise mainly fictional previous life. This could result in a kind of historical novel.[10] The subject I mentioned earlier who remembered a previous life in Amsterdam may have illustrated this process. We can often see it occurring in dreams. Some dreams contain obviously unrealistic elements that are combined with accurate memories and—much more rarely—information obtained through extrasensory perception.

One might suppose that subjects who have spontaneously a few apparent memories of a previous life might mobilize additional details under hypnosis. I expected this myself and have attempted to use hypnosis with some persons reporting spontaneous apparent memories of previous lives. Although the apparent memories these persons had had might have derived from a previous life, they lacked sufficient detail, especially of proper names, to permit any verifications. I hoped that during hypnosis the subjects might remember some (or more) proper names of people and places, so that we could verify the existence of the persons whose lives they seemed to remember.

I have conducted or initiated thirteen such experiments; in some I was the hypnotist myself, in others I arranged for another hypnotist to conduct the experiment. Not a single one of the experiments succeeded. Perhaps these efforts failed because the subjects were all (with one exception) older children or adults by the time we undertook the experiments.[11]

These experiments should be repeated and extended with more young subjects, say children about seven or eight years old. Children of this age enter hypnosis easily; and, if they have memories of real previous lives, these may lie closer to the surface of consciousness than they would later in life. In addition, one can usually obtain more definite knowledge concerning the exposure of young children to normal sources of information about the topics figuring in the previous lives. In contrast, adults have had longer and more abundant contacts with a variety of sources of information potentially available for use in fantasies about previous lives.

THE EXPERIENCE OF DÉJÀ VU

Some persons have had the experience of believing, on visiting a place for the first time, that they have seen it before. Psychologists call this experience déjà vu ("already seen"). As many as 76 percent of people surveyed report having had such an experience.[12]

Some children subjects of cases of the reincarnation type experience déjà vu when they first go to the villages where they say they lived in a previous life. All or much of the village seems familiar to such a child, although he may also remark on changes in doors, rooms, trees, and other features of the local buildings and grounds that have been altered since the life he remembers.[13] Perhaps other persons who have experience of déjà vu, but who do not have any imaged memories of a previous life, remember just the tip of such a life, so to speak, and cannot bring further memories into consciousness.

Most cases of déjà vu, however, probably require no such interpretation. Several other explanations account for many instances of this experience better than reincarnation does.[14] For example, some instances may be due to the kind of noninferential knowledge of the future that we call precognition. Precognition sometimes occurs during dreams. Suppose that a person dreams of a place that he has never seen before, but that he will later visit, although he does not know this at the time. He may then forget the dream, although residues of it may remain just below the threshold of consciousness. Experiments with memory have shown that "recognition is greater than recall." This means that although we may try unsuccessfully to recall a name, for example, we may recognize it if we see it in a list along with other names. In the present example, the dreamer, when he actually visits the place dreamed about, may find that it seems familiar and may even think that he has seen it before, although he cannot explain why he thinks this. A few instances of déjà vu seem to support this explanation. In these the person having an experience of déjà vu has later recalled a dream he had earlier about the place that seemed familiar.

Some déjà vu experiences may have an even simpler explanation. The scene that appears familiar may resemble one previously seen by the person having the experience without his recognizing the similarity. Something like this happens when we approach and even address by name a complete stranger whom we have mistaken for someone we know. In the latter situation the stranger quickly tells us we are wrong, if we do not realize the error ourselves before he does so. A stretch of scenery, however, or an event in progress cannot speak and correct our errors; and so when they appear familiar we may persist in thinking incorrectly that we have "been there before."

A neurological explanation has also been suggested for some déjà vu experiences. If the two hemispheres of the brain should function slightly out of phase with each other, information reaching conscious-ness through one hemisphere would be recorded by that hemisphere as new while the other side of the brain, a millisecond later, might regis-ter it as old. I know of no experimental evidence that this can happen; and even if it could, it would not explain those few instances of déjà vu in which the person having the experience showed knowledge of a place that he could not have obtained normally. [15]

DREAMS AND NIGHTMARES

Some persons have dreams in which they seem to see themselves in another place and wearing clothes of a different epoch. Many such dreams are recurrent and may have an unpleasant, nightmarish qual-ity. Some of the persons having such dreams say that they first started in childhood and have recurred often thereafter. Sometimes the dreams diminish in frequency as the person becomes older, and they may eventually cease altogether.

In the more valuable of such dreams—as I judge them—the dreamer seems to experience a reliving of the events in the dream. He may not find it easy to describe the difference between these unusual dreams and his ordinary ones. He will likely say, however, that his ordinary dreams seem disjointed, incongruous, and generally unre-alistic, even though he may not recognize these features until he awakens. In contrast, in the "previous life" dreams the scenes are completely realistic and coherent. The details of the surroundings are as vivid and as natural as waking perceptions are, and they lack the bizarreness that objects and surroundings so often have in ordinary dreams. If the dream is recurrent, each dream of the series is usually exactly like all the others, with the dreamer always awakening at the same point—often a crisis in the event enacted—of the dream. Fi-nally, dreams of this type become strongly fixed in the memory and do not fade away as do the majority of ordinary dreams. This fixation in memory may occur even in dreams of this kind that do not recur, so it does not necessarily depend upon repetition.

Many persons have described such dreams to me. The majority of them have no verifiable details, although a few correspond with other aspects of the dreamer's personality, such as unusual fears or interests in particular countries.

In one case an American girl, Alice Robertson (pseudonym), suffered for many years (beginning in early childhood) from recurrent nightmares, the vivid details of which never changed. In the night-mares she was an adult woman dressed in an ankle-length garment and walking tranquilly along a road with a young girl whom she knew to be her daughter. It was evening and the sun was approaching the horizon. Suddenly, she became aware of a deafening roar, and the earth seemed to give way beneath her. At this point she would awaken in terror, screaming. This would bring her solicitous mother running to her side. The child—as Alice then was—would try to explain to her mother that she had really lived the scene of the nightmare; but her mother, the wife of an Episcopalian bishop, would assure her that this could not be possible and that she had "only been dreaming." Even-tually Alice gave up trying to persuade her mother that in her night-mares she was remembering real events that she had once experienced. The nightmares, however, persisted, although in later life they grad-ually diminished in frequency.

After Alice grew up, she identified the ankle-length garment that she wore in the dream as a sari. This detail harmonized with a strong attraction she felt for India. When she was a young woman, she saw a moving picture about Darjeeling (in northeastern India), which produced in her a strong sense of déjà vu. She then for the first time read something about Darjeeling and learned that disastrous land-slides had occurred there on a number of occasions between 1890 and 1920. She thus became convinced that the previous life of her night-mares had occurred in Darjeeling. I could not verify this, because Alice could not give sufficient details of personal names and places to permit an attempt at this. She was one of the persons I mentioned earlier with whom an effort was made with hypnosis to elicit addi-tional memories; but during the hypnosis she merely relived the fa-miliar terrifying experience of the nightmare without adding any new details.

Another American girl, Mary Magruder (pseudonym), had equally distressing nightmares, which also began in her early child-hood. In hers she seemed to be a young girl who was being chased by an (American) Indian during a raid by Indians on a settlement of white pioneers. Like the dreams of Alice Robertson, those of Mary Magruder were vivid and the details similar at each recurrence. How-ever, the dream did not always run to its full length. In some of the dreams Indians were only chasing her; in others an Indian had actually caught her and was holding her by the hair. At this point she would awaken, screaming. Sometimes she would say: "Mother, they are taking my curls." Mary particularly noted that whereas her own hair was light and straight, that of the young girl she seemed to be in the dream was brown and curly.

Although Mary appeared to be reliving a previous life in the nightmares, she did not think much about the matter until a chance visit brought her to a place in western Virginia where her ancestors had lived during the eighteenth century. (She had grown up in the Midwest and had not known anything about this region or her ancestors there before her visit to the area in adulthood.) She then learned that a part of the ancestral property of her family was known as Burnt Cabin from its having been burned in an Indian raid. I visited the area in order to learn more about the place at first hand. A historical marker by the road 4 kilometers from the site of "Burnt Cabin" records that the last Indian raid in Virginia took place near there in 1764. The present owner of the Burnt Cabin tract, who was a distant cousin of Mary, confirmed to me the tradition that the site derived its name from an Indian raid, which he thought had occurred around 1745–50.

Mary could furnish no additional details about the possible previous life of her nightmares, and those that she did give remain unverified. So far as they go, however, they are historically plausible.[16]

The memories of most of the children whose cases I have studied occurred to them in their ordinary waking state. Some of them, however, have also had dreams or nightmares in which scenes of the remembered previous life appeared to them.[17] Distortions may occur in such dreams, as they often do in dreams having paranormally derived elements and, for that matter, in ordinary dreams also.

In one such case a Lebanese child, Arif Hamed (pseudonym), recalled a previous life that ended when a large building stone fell off a balcony and struck the person whose life he remembered. This man had been sitting under the balcony and died instantly when the stone hit him on the head. According to Arif's memories, some goats browsing in the area around the house provided the last images seen by the man before he died. Arif had recurrent dreams of goats climbing over piles of building stones and knocking some of them over. I have verified some of Arif's memories, although not that goats were actually in the area around the previous personality's house when he died. I think it likely nevertheless that this detail is accurate; goats are common domestic animals in rural Lebanon. If it is accurate, it then became incorporated and distorted in Arif's recurrent dream, which seems to derive from the manner in which the previous personality of this case died.

I do, therefore, think that some vivid and recurrent dreams may stem from actual memories of previous lives. I do not, however, know of any method, or any discriminating detail, that would justify our making a more positive statement about dreams of this type that have no verified details. The quality of vividness in a dream may provide an indication of paranormality, but no proof if it: a vivid dream is more likely to have a paranormal component than a nonvivid one, but most vivid dreams do not have have this component.[18] And we must examine even those containing verified details with regard to the possible origin in normal sources of the information included.

I would particularly warn persons having such recurrent dreams against interpreting them precipitately. Some such dreamers have rushed to encyclopedias and searched them for information about a person whose life matches the scene or event of their dream. One of my correspondents had a vivid dream in which she seemed elegantly dressed in the clothes worn in Europe during the first half of the nineteenth century. An aristocratic man, similarly well turned out, was paying court to her. I think it would have been wiser for her to remain content with examining only the details in the dream itself. Unfortunately, she did not do this and soon decided that she must have been in her previous life the notorious dancer Lola Montez, the femme fatale who cost King Ludwig I of Bavaria his throne. (Another of my correspondents also thinks, for different reasons, that *she* was Lola Montez. Perhaps I should introduce these two correspondents to each other.)

ILLNESSES AND DRUGS

Some persons have had the experience of seeming to relive a portion of a previous life when under the influence of drugs, such as lysergic acid diethylamide (LSD). We know from other experiences with this drug that it can revive in the most powerful manner the memories of events of this life; I am therefore prepared to believe that, if reincarnation occurs, LSD (and similar drugs) may facilitate the recovery of memories of previous lives. I do not, however, know of anyone who has recalled verified details of a previous life through their use.[19] Moreover, such memories as come into consciousness in this way may undergo distortions similar to those of dreams.

LSD may induce unpleasant side effects and complications,

sometimes serious ones. I think it a drug whose usefulness we have not yet adequately studied and exploited; but I also think it potentially harmful when taken under unsuitable conditions, by which I mainly mean in the absence of adequate medical supervision. Therefore, I am far from recommending that it be taken as a means of inducing possible memories of previous lives.

In a few persons, what seem to be memories of a previous life have come into consciousness during a serious illness—usually one with fever and delirium. For example, a woman (interviewed by one of my associates) who was stricken severely with the neurological disease known as Guillain-Barré syndrome experienced vivid imagery both of earlier events in her (present) life and of what seemed to her to be events in a previous one, perhaps in France during the nineteenth century. These latter images were not derived, so far as she could tell, from any events that she remembered having experienced since her birth, although they were mixed with memories of such events. In addition to being seriously ill, however, the patient was also under the influence of medication; so it would be difficult to identify the immediate physical cause of the unusual images she experienced.

Several of the children subjects of cases of the reincarnation type have had an increase in memories of a previous life during an illness (usually with a fever), and a few have made their first statements about the previous life during an illness.[20]

MEDITATION

Some persons have seemed to recover memories of previous lives during meditation. The *siddhis* (spiritual and paranormal powers) said to be acquired incidentally by spiritual aspirants in Hinduism and Buddhism include the ability to remember previous lives. In some instances known to me, apparent memories of previous lives have erupted suddenly and unexpectedly into consciousness during meditation; but I know of only one person who has obtained verifiable memories in this way. This is Pratomwan Inthanu (a Buddhist nun of Thailand), who recovered, while meditating, some subsequently verified memories of the lives of two infants who had lived in places far removed from where Pratomwan herself was born and lived.

Apparent memories of a previous life that occur spontaneously during meditation may have value for the meditator, even though they are unverified and contribute nothing to evidence. (Meditators are not usually seeking evidence.)

However, I think I should warn against attaching importance to apparent memories of previous lives evoked during meditation when the meditator has deliberately set out to recover such memories. This merely invites fantasies that appear deceptively as memories of a previous life. A person searching for memories of a previous life during meditation is in no better position than someone under the influence of a hypnotist; in both situations there is a task to do and the likelihood of fulfilling the task with a fantasy.

Even without such deliberate elicitation, fantasies may emerge during meditation and be mistaken for actual memories. We should remember that most Western practitioners of meditation adopt some technique of Oriental provenance; few of them are naive with regard to the possibility of reincarnation, and nearly all know that meditation may lead to the emergence of memories of previous lives. This makes them liable to interpret uncritically as memories of previous lives any fantasies that happen to develop during their meditation.

STRONG EMOTION

In a small number of cases known to me, adults have had apparent memories of previous lives that occurred during periods of strong emotion, such as grief. The case of Georg Neidhart seems to me the best example of this type. When Georg Neidhart, who lived in Munich, Germany, was still a young man, his first wife and daughter both died within a short interval. As a consequence, he fell into a depression that lasted several months. While in this condition, one day he suddenly began to see inwardly a series of scenes of what seemed to be a previous life. The scenes ordered themselves into a sequence of events, about which he made notes. Subsequently, he verified some of the details and found that others were plausible for the life of a man who had lived in Bavaria (northeast of Munich) during the twelfth century. A few other cases of this type have come to my attention, although none have been as strong evidentially as that of Georg Neidhart.

MISCELLANEOUS WAKING EXPERIENCES OF ADULTS

Some adult persons have had occur to them spontaneously, during a normal, waking state, "flashes"—or longer sequences—of what seem to be memories of previous lives. We cannot tell how common such experiences are because reports of them so far have depended on voluntary submission of accounts by the persons having them. These

spontaneous "flashes" pose the same problems of analysis as do all the
other types of evidence that I have mentioned: they are of little value
unless verified, and, even if verified, of little value unless we can
exclude normal sources of information for their content.[21]

SPONTANEOUS EXPERIENCES OF YOUNG CHILDREN

Apart from the dreams and nightmares, which often begin when
the subject is a young child, the subjects for all the types of evidence so
far discussed have been adults. By the time a person reaches adulthood, his mind has been filled with a wide variety of information from
many sources. Much of this information lies in obscure recesses of the
mind, and its possessor may not even be aware of having acquired it.
Yet it remains available to be tapped for fantasies about previous lives.
Such mobilization of unconscious memory stores is particularly likely
to occur when a deliberate effort is made to evoke previous life memories. I have described how this can occur in cases of hypnotic regression and during meditation; and it seems to occur sometimes also
when hallucinogenic drugs are taken.

The foregoing remarks will help readers to understand why I
value so highly the spontaneous utterances about previous lives made
by young children. With rare exceptions, these children speak of their
own volition; no one has suggested to them that they should try to
remember a previous life. And at the young age when they usually first
speak about the previous lives their minds have not yet received
through normal channels much information about deceased persons.
Moreover, we can usually make a satisfactory appraisal of the likelihood that they have obtained normally whatever information they
communicate about such persons. For the past twenty-five years I have
concentrated my attention on the cases of these young children, and I
feel justified in devoting almost all the remainder of this book to
them. In the next chapter I shall present twelve typical cases, the
subjects of which were all young children when they first spoke about
previous lives.

CHAPTER FOUR

Twelve Typical Cases of Children Who Remember Previous Lives

I shall now describe, in the most summary fashion, twelve representative cases of the reincarnation type. I have selected them from eight different cultures in which I have studied these cases. To help correct the widely held belief that cases of this type occur only among Buddhists and Hindus, I have included one case from the Tlingit tribe of Alaska, one from Lebanon, one from England, one from Finland, and four cases from the continental United States. (I have used pseudonyms for all five cases from the United States.)

In every case, the subject made statements about the life he claimed to remember while he was still a young child; and in every case one or several adult informants corroborated that he had made such statements at that age.

I have published detailed reports of six of these cases elsewhere; more detailed reports of the other six are planned for future volumes. [1]

THE CASE OF GOPAL GUPTA

Gopal Gupta was born in Delhi, India, on August 26, 1956. His parents were members of the lower middle class with little education. They noticed nothing unusual about Gopal's development in infancy and early childhood.

Soon after Gopal began to speak (at the age of between two and two and a half years), the family had a guest at their house, and Gopal's father asked Gopal to remove a water glass that the guest had used. Gopal startled everyone by saying: "I won't pick it up. I am a Sharma." (Sharmas are members of the highest caste in India, the Brahmins.) He then had a temper tantrum in which he broke some glasses. Gopal's father asked him to explain both his rude conduct and his surprising explanation for it. He then related many details about a previous life that he claimed to remember having lived in a city called Mathura, which is about 160 kilometers south of Delhi.

Gopal said that he had owned a company concerned with medicines, and he gave its name as Sukh Shancharak. He said that he had had a large house and many servants; that he had a wife and two brothers; and that he had quarreled with one of the brothers, and the latter had shot him.

Gopal's claim to have been a Brahmin in the previous life explained his refusal to pick up the water glass, because Brahmins would not ordinarily handle utensils that a member of a lower caste had already touched. His own family were Banias, members of the businessmen's caste.

Gopal's parents had no connections with Mathura, and his utterances about a life there stirred no memories in them. His mother did not wish to encourage Gopal to talk about the previous life he was claiming to remember, and at first his father felt indifferent about the matter. From time to time, however, he told friends about what Gopal had been saying. One of these friends vaguely remembered having heard about a murder in Mathura that correponded to Gopal's statements, but this did not stimulate Gopal's father to go to Mathura and verify what Gopal had been saying. Eventually, he went to Mathura (in 1964) for a religious festival, and while there he found the Sukh Shancharak Company and queried its sales manager about the accuracy of what Gopal had been saying. What he said impressed the manager, because one of the owners of the company had shot and killed his brother some years earlier. The deceased man, Shaktipal Sharma, had died a few days after the shooting, on May 27, 1948.

The manager understandably told the Sharma family about the visit of Gopal's father. Some of them then visited Gopal in Delhi and, after talking with him, invited him to visit them in Mathura, which he did. At the times of these meetings in Delhi and Mathura Gopal recognized various persons and places known to Shaktipal Sharma and made additional statements indicating considerable knowledge of his affairs. The Sharma family found particularly impressive Gopal's mention of an attempt by Shaktipal Sharma to borrow money from his wife; he had wished to give this to his brother, who was a partner in the company but a quarrelsome spendthrift. Shaktipal Sharma hoped to mollify his demanding brother by giving him more money; but his wife did not approve of appeasement, and she refused to lend her husband the money. The brother became increasingly angry and then

shot Shaktipal. The details of these domestic quarrels were never published and were probably never known to persons other than the family members concerned. (The murder itself was widely publicized.)
Gopal's knowledge of these matters, his other statements, and some of
his recognitions of persons known to Shaktipal Sharma convinced
members of the Sharma family that he was Shaktipal Sharma reborn.

Along with his statements about the previous life, Gopal showed
behavior that a wealthy Brahmin might be expected to show but that
was inappropriate for his family. He did not hesitate to tell other
family members that he belonged to a caste superior to theirs. He was
reluctant to do any housework and said that he had servants for that.
He would not drink milk from a cup anyone else had used.

Dr. Jamuna Prasad, who worked with me for many years on cases
in India, began the investigation of this case in 1965. I took up the
investigation in 1969, when I had interviews with members of both
families concerned, in Delhi and Mathura. I remained in touch with
the case until 1974.

Gopal never expressed a strong desire to go to Mathura, and after
he had been there in 1965, he never asked to return. For a few years
after 1965, he occasionally visited Shaktipal Sharma's two sisters, who
lived in Delhi. Then all contact between the two families ceased. As
Gopal became older, he slowly lost his Brahmin snobbishness and
adjusted to the modest circumstances of his family. He gradually
talked less about the life of Shaktipal Sharma, but as late as 1974 his
father thought that Gopal still remembered much about it.

Gopal's case seems to me a strong one with regard to the small
chance that he could have obtained normally the knowledge he had
about the life and death of Shaktipal Sharma. It is true that Shaktipal
Sharma belonged to a prominent family in Mathura, and his murder
was prominent news when it happened. However, the Sharmas and
the Guptas lived in widely separated cities and belonged to different
castes and economic classes. Their social orbits were totally different,
and I have no hesitation in believing members of both families who
said that they had never heard of the other family before the case
developed.

THE CASE OF CORLISS CHOTKIN, JR.

This case started with a prediction by an elderly Tlingit fisher-
man (of Alaska), Victor Vincent, who told his niece, Mrs. Corliss
Chotkin, Sr., that after his death he would be reborn as her son. He

showed her two scars from minor operations, one near the bridge of his nose and one on his upper back; and as he did so he said that she would recognize him (in his next incarnation) by birthmarks on his body corresponding to these scars.

Victor Vincent died in the spring of 1946. About eighteen months later (on December 15, 1947), Mrs. Chotkin gave birth to a baby boy, who was named after his father. Corliss Chotkin, Jr., had two birthmarks, which his mother said were exactly at the sites of the scars to which Victor Vincent had drawn her attention on his body. By the time I first examined these birthmarks in 1962, both had shifted, according to Mrs. Chotkin, from the positions they had had at Corliss's birth. Yet they remained quite visible, and the one on Corliss's back impressed me strongly. It was an area on the skin about 3 centimeters in length and 5 millimeters in width; compared with the surrounding skin it was darker and slightly raised. Its resemblance to the healed scar of a surgical wound was greatly increased by the presence at the sides of the main birthmark of several small round marks that seemed to correspond to positions of the small round wounds made by needles that place the stitches used to close surgical wounds.

When Corliss was only thirteen months old and his mother was trying to get him to repeat his name, he said to her petulantly: "Don't you know who I am? I'm Kahkody"; this was the tribal name Victor Vincent had had. When Mrs. Chotkin mentioned Corliss's claim that he was Kahkody to one of her aunts, the latter said that she had dreamed shortly before Corliss's birth that Victor Vincent was coming to live with the Chotkins.[2] Mrs. Chotkin was certain that she had not previously told her aunt about Victor Vincent's prediction that he would return as her son.

When Corliss was between two and three years old, he spontaneously recognized several persons whom Victor Vincent had known, including Victor Vincent's widow. Corliss's mother said that he also mentioned two events in the life of Victor Vincent about which she did not think he could have obtained information normally. In addition, he showed several behavioral traits corresponding to similar ones that Victor Vincent had shown: Corliss combed his hair in a manner closely resembling the style of Victor Vincent; both Corliss and Victor Vincent stuttered; both had a strong interest in boats and in being on the water; both had strong religious propensities; and both were left-handed. Corliss also had a precocious interest in engines and some skill in handling and repairing them; his mother said he had taught himself how to run boat engines. It is unlikely that Corliss inherited or learned this particular skill from his father, who had little interest in engines or skill with them.

After the age of about nine, Corliss made fewer remarks about the previous life he had seemed to remember earlier, and by 1962, when I first met him, he said that he remembered nothing about it. I met Corliss and his family three times in the early 1960s and once more in 1972. At the time of this last meeting, Corliss had almost completely lost the stuttering that formerly afflicted him; but he still stuttered when he became excited. His interest in religion had diminished, but he had maintained his interest in engines. During the Vietnam War he had seen combat as an artilleryman, and a shell bursting near him had damaged his hearing. Otherwise, when I last saw him in 1972, he enjoyed good health and was working contentedly at a pulp mill near his home in Sitka.

THE CASE OF MA TIN AUNG MYO

Ma[3] Tin Aung Myo was born in the village of Nathul, Upper Burma, on December 26, 1953. Her parents were U Aye Maung and Daw Aye Tin. When Daw Aye Tin was pregnant with Ma Tin Aung Myo, she dreamed on three occasions that a stocky Japanese soldier, shirtless and wearing short pants, was following her and saying that he would come to stay with her and her husband. Ma Tin Aung Myo first indicated that she might be remembering a previous life when she was between three and four. At that time an airplane flew over Nathul, and Ma Tin Aung Myo became frightened and cried. She continued to show a phobia of airplanes—for her fear of them amounted to that—for some years. On another occasion when she was about four, she was noted to be weeping, and when asked what was troubling her she said that she was pining for Japan. Thereafter, she gradually told about having been a Japanese soldier stationed in Nathul during World War II, when the Japanese army occupied Burma. Ma Tin Aung Myo said that she had been a cook and that an (Allied) airplane had come over the village, strafed it, and killed her.

Ma Tin Aung Myo also furnished a few other details about the life she claimed to remember. She said that she came from the northern part of Japan, where she had been married and had had children. She thought that she had had a small shop in Japan before she joined the army. She claimed that she had been killed during the Japanese retreat from Burma. (This would make 1945 the probable year of death of the concerned previous personality.) She described what the Japanese soldier had been wearing and doing when the strafing airplane came over and how he had tried to avoid being hit by its bullets. She said that he was struck in the groin and died immediately.

Ma Tin Aung Myo mentioned no proper names except that of Japan. She could not remember the names either of the Japanese soldier or of the place in Japan from which he had come. Consequently, we could not even begin to trace a Japanese person corresponding to her statements. They are, however, harmonious with events in Nathul as the Japanese army evacuated Upper Burma. Daw Aye Tin recalled that she had known and had even been friendly with a cook in the Japanese army who had been stationed there, but she did not know whether he had been killed there.

Ma Tin Aung Myo showed behavior unusual for her family but harmonious with that of a Japanese soldier. She did not like the hot climate of Upper Burma, or its spicy food; she preferred sweet foods and liked to eat fish half raw, although she did not try to eat completely raw fish, as do some Japanese people. She frequently expressed a longing to return to Japan and would sometimes lie on her stomach and cry disconsolately from (what she said was) homesickness.[4] She also expressed anger toward British and American people when they were mentioned in her presence.[5]

Ma Tin Aung Myo's most remarkable behavior was her extreme boyishness. She insisted on dressing in men's clothes and wearing her hair in a boy's style. This eventually led to a crisis at her school when the authorities there insisted that she come to school dressed appropriately as a girl. She refused; they were adamant; and so she dropped out of school at the age of about eleven. Her lack of education limited her choice of occupation, and when I first met her in 1974 she was earning only a meager income as a hawker of foods at the nearby railway station.

As a young child, Ma Tin Aung Myo had played at being a soldier. Whenever her father visited Mandalay, she would ask him to buy her a toy gun. Her three sisters and her only brother did not play at soldiers when they were young. Ma Tin Aung Myo also played football and caneball, both primarily boys' games.

Ma Tin Aung Myo's parents had had three girls before she was born. They therefore had hoped their next child would be a boy; but this does not mean that they encouraged Ma Tin Aung Myo to behave like one. Indeed, her mother strongly opposed her daughter's masculine mode of dress, although her father appears to have been more indulgent toward it. (He had died before I reached the case, and so I did not learn about his attitude directly from him.)

As Ma Tin Aung Myo grew older, she remained strongly masculine in her sexual orientation. She still dressed in men's clothes and had no interest in marrying a man. On the contrary, she said that she would like to have a wife. She obviously thought of herself as a man and disliked being considered a woman. When U Win Maung, my associate in Burma, addressed her with the female honorific "Ma," she asked him not to do so and requested that he call her "Maung" (the honorific for boys) or use no honorific for her whatever. During one interview, she told U Win Maung and me that we could kill her by any method we chose if we would first guarantee that she would be reborn as a man.

Ma Tin Aung Myo's family accepted her explanation of her case, namely that her sexual orientation derived from a previous life as a man; they similarly accepted much of her other unusual behavior as having been carried over from the previous life of a Japanese soldier.

This case is a good example of an unsolved case of the reincarnation type. Ma Tin Aung Myo made no detailed and verifiable statements that permitted identifying a particular deceased person whose life she seemed to be remembering. Nevertheless, her statements about the previous life were all plausible, and she showed a group of unusual behaviors that fully accorded with her claim to have been a Japanese soldier in a previous life. Whether such a case could have developed solely from the influence of her parents or as the expression of obscure motives on the part of Ma Tin Aung Myo herself are questions to which I shall return in a later chapter.

Ma Tin Aung Myo's case is one of claimed "sex change," and I shall discuss cases of this type (of which I have studied numerous examples) in chapters 5 and 9.

I met Ma Tin Aung Myo again in 1975, but have not met her since. However, U Win Maung (who has assisted me in Burma since 1970) met her twice more, in 1977 and 1981.

THE CASE OF SHAMLINIE PREMA

Shamlinie Prema was born in Colombo, Sri Lanka, on October 16, 1962. Her parents lived in Gonagela, a town about 60 kilometers south of Colombo, and Shamlinie grew up there.

Shamlinie's parents noticed that even before she could speak, she showed a remarkable fear of being bathed; she resisted with screams and struggling any attempt to immerse her in water. She also showed, while still an infant, a severe phobia of buses, and she cried whenever her parents took her on one, or even when she only saw one at a distance. These phobias puzzled her parents, although they surmised that they might have derived from traumatic events in a previous life.

After Shamlinie began to speak, she gradually told her parents, and other interested persons, about a previous life that she claimed to remember. This life had taken place in a nearby village called Galtudawa, about 2 kilometers from Gonagela. Shamlinie mentioned the names of the parents she said she had had there, and she often referred to her "Galtudawa mother." She also spoke of sisters and two school companions. She described the house of the previous life, the location and characteristics of which were quite different from those of the house in which her family was living. She described the death in the previous life in the following way. She said that she went to buy bread in the morning before going to school. The road was flooded. A bus splashed water on her and she fell into a paddy field. She threw up her arms and called "Mother." After that she fell into sleep.

A girl named Hemaseelie Guneratne, who had lived in Galtudawa, had drowned on May 8, 1961, in circumstances corresponding to Shamlinie's description. (She appears to have stepped back to avoid a passing bus and fallen into a flooded paddy field.) Hemaseelie had been a schoolgirl of just eleven years when she drowned. Shamlinie's parents were distantly related to the Guneratnes, but they had little acquaintance with them and had never met Hemaseelie. They remembered hearing about Hemaseelie's death and feeling sad about it at the time, but afterward they had completely forgotten the incident, and when Shamlinie first began to talk as if she remembered drowning in a previous life, they did not initially connect her statements with Hemaseelie's drowning. However, at about three years of age Shamlinie recognized one of Hemaseelie's cousins when she saw him in a street in Gonagela. More than a year later, she recognized one of

Hemaseelie's sisters, also in Gonagela. In the meantime, Shamlinie had been clamoring to be taken to Galtudawa, particularly to visit her "Galtudawa mother," and she compared her own mother unfavorably with the "Galtudawa mother."[6]

Shamlinie's father finally took her to the Guneratne home in Galtudawa. A large crowd gathered there when they learned that a child who claimed to have been reborn was visiting the village. The presence of many strangers may have inhibited Shamlinie so that she made fewer recognitions than she might have done in a more relaxed atmosphere. Shamlinie's father said that she had recognized Hemaseelie's mother, W. L. Podi Nona; but the Guneratnes remained doubtful about this. The visit, however, permitted verification of Shamlinie's statements, nearly all of which corresponded to facts in Hemaseelie's life. In addition, the two families exchanged information about the girls concerned and learned that Hemaseelie and Shamlinie had some traits in common, such as preferences for certain foods and styles of clothing.

I began to investigate this case in 1966, a few weeks after Shamlinie's first visit to Galtudawa. I could therefore interview the informants while their memories—both of what Shamlinie had said and done and of the life of Hemaseelie—remained fresh. In the following years, I made additional visits to both of the families in order to obtain further information about details, to test the informants for consistency in what they said, and to observe Shamlinie's further development. Apart from a few discrepancies in minor details, the informants gave concordant statements, and what they said in later interviews agreed with what they had said earlier.

After her first visit to Galtudawa, Shamlinie exchanged some further visits with the Guneratnes, but these gradually diminished over the ensuing years. The decrease in visits coincided with a gradual fading of Shamlinie's memories of the previous life. She stopped speaking spontaneously about it when she was between five and seven, and she appeared to have forgotten it entirely by the time she was eleven, in 1973; probably she had forgotten it even earlier. She had lost her phobia of water by the age of four and had become less afraid of buses by the age of eight; yet some slight fear of buses persisted even then. In all other respects, Shamlinie, when I last met her in 1973, was developing like an entirely normal Sinhalese girl.

Shamlinie's case seems to me to be another one of at least moderate strength with regard to the chance that she had obtained her knowledge of Hemaseelie's life by normal means. It had the undoubted weakness that the families concerned lived within about 2 kilometers of each other and had had a slight acquaintance before the case developed. In my judgment, however, the rare contacts the families had had could not explain Shamlinie's detailed knowledge of Hemaseelie's life or the unusual behavior that accorded with her statements about it.

THE CASE OF SULEYMAN ANDARY

Suleyman Andary was born in Falougha, Lebanon, on March 4, 1954. His family were Druses, members of a religion that derived from Islam. This religion has, however, separated so much from orthodox Islamic teachings that its members now regard it as separate. Reincarnation is a central tenet of the Druse religion.[7]

As a young child, Suleyman seemed to remember fragmentarily a few details of a previous life. Some of the information came to him in dreams. He recalled having had children and knew some of their names; and he remembered that he was from a place called Gharife and had owned an oil press there. Unlike most children subjects of these cases, however, he did not recall additional details until he was considerably older.

When he was about eleven, a particular episode appears to have stimulated further memories. He was living then with his paternal grandmother. His maternal grandmother came to the house and asked to borrow one of the Druse religious books. Suleyman refused her request rather curtly, asking her whether she did not have the book at her home. (He apparently did not stop to think that if she had had the book, she would not have come to borrow it.) His paternal grandmother overheard his rude handling of his other grandmother and asked him to explain his conduct. Suddenly, he remembered that he had had religious books in a previous life and that he had not allowed them to leave his house. Druses who have copies of their religious books almost venerate them and preserve them carefully at home; Suleyman's attitude, therefore, although impolite for a young boy, accorded well with what one might expect of an older Druse man.

After this incident, Suleyman made a more or less deliberate effort to retrieve further details of the previous life that he seemed to be remembering. He then recalled that he had been the mukhtar (headman) of Gharife. He also remembered the mukhtar's name, Abdallah Abu Hamdan, and other details of his life. Now, however, Suleyman became afraid of being teased if he told people that he had been a mukhtar in a previous life. His family and friends, he thought, would accuse him of arrogance or would deride him. So he kept his memories to himself for almost another two years. He then talked a little about them, at first with other children and later with adults.

Some of Suleyman's adult relatives proposed to take him to Gharife in order to verify what he was saying about a previous life there. Gharife is about 30 kilometers from Falougha, but in a different region of Lebanon. Although roads connect the two villages, it takes some effort and a special reason to travel from one to the other, as I found myself. With one exception, members of Suleyman's family had no connections with Gharife. One member was employed there temporarily, but he could not confirm from his own knowledge what Suleyman was saying about a previous life in Gharife. Later, this relative made inquiries in Gharife and managed to verify a few of Suleyman's statements. In the meantime, other persons had also confirmed the accuracy of some of these statements.

As usually happens in these cases in Asia, word about Suleyman's claims concerning a previous life spread to other persons. A cousin of his family met (in Saudi Arabia) some residents of Gharife and told them about Suleyman's statements. They confirmed that Suleyman's memories accorded with facts in the life of one Abdallah Abu Hamdan, who had owned an oil press and had been the mukhtar of Gharife for many years before his death—probably of heart disease—in 1942 at the age of about sixty-five. The Gharife residents who gave this information invited Suleyman to visit them. At first he refused, but then in the late summer and autumn of 1967 he went twice to Gharife.

Suleyman seemed shy and inhibited in Gharife. Abdallah Abu Hamdan's widow and two of his children were still living there, but Suleyman did not recognize them; nor did he recognize members of the family in photographs.[8] He did, however, recognize three other persons and a few places at Gharife. Perhaps the most important of these recognitions occurred when he pointed out an old road, no longer used and almost obliterated by 1967, for reaching the house where Abdallah Abu Hamdan had lived. However, the importance of Suleyman's case does not lie in his few recognitions. It derives instead from his statements about the previous life and from some unusual related behavior that he showed.

Before going to Gharife, or during his first visit there, Suleyman made seventeen statements about the previous life. These included the names of most of Abdallah Abu Hamdan's children and some other details of his life. His statements were all correct with two exceptions: he gave the name of Salim as that of one of Abdallah Abu Hamdan's sons, whereas Salim was his brother; and he said that Salim was blind, whereas a son of Abdallah Abu Hamdan named Naseeb was blind, but Salim was not.

I began investigating this case in March 1968 and continued working on it until 1972. I interviewed numerous informants in Falougha and Gharife. Suleyman later emigrated to Saudi Arabia, and I have not met him since 1972.

When he was still a young child, Suleyman comported himself like an adult. He preferred the company of adults to that of children, and even in a group of adults he tended to seat himself prominently among them as an important person might do. He objected if anyone scolded him, and when this happened he would say something like: "One doesn't scold me. I am an adult."

Suleyman's fears that other persons would laugh at him if they knew he claimed to have been a mukhtar in a previous life proved sound; his family and friends did tease him for this pretension, and they even nicknamed him "Mukhtar." This did not altogether displease him, especially as some members of the family seemed to use the nickname affectionately, as if to say: "We believe you." And indeed they did believe him after they had verified his statements about the life of Abdallah Abu Hamdan.

Suleyman also showed greater concern about religion than the other members of his family did. This accorded with Abdallah Abu Hamdan's strong interest in religion; toward the end of his life, he had become a sheikh, which meant taking vows to maintain a much higher standard of conduct than ordinary people aspire to.

I mentioned earlier that Suleyman did not wish to visit Gharife, and when he was first invited to do so, he refused. His family understood this better when, at Gharife, they learned of the tragedies in the life of Abdallah Abu Hamdan. Abdallah Abu Hamdan's children had given him little comfort; several had congenital deformities, one had emigrated to America, and another had had a poor relationship with his father. Then other events darkened the last days of his life. In order to help a friend, Abdallah Abu Hamdan had foolishly falsified a document that, as mukhtar of his village, he had to execute; when the government learned of his deception, he was dismissed from his office as mukhtar. Finally, he invested beyond his means in an oil press. The payments for this proved more burdensome than he had expected; and according to his wife, worry about his indebtedness brought on his final illness. No one could feel surprised, therefore, that anyone claiming to have Abdallah Abu Hamdan's memories would not rush over to Gharife.

As I mentioned, Abdallah Abu Hamdan died in 1942, twelve years before Suleyman's birth. If Abdallah Abu Hamdan had reincarnated as Suleyman, where had he spent the interval? Suleyman answered this question by saying that he had had an intermediate life of which he remembered nothing. This is the stock answer of Druses when an interval—even of so little as a single day—occurs between the death of an identified previous personality in a case and the subject's birth. Occasionally one may find some slender evidence of such intermediate lives, but usually they remain entirely conjectural. [9]

With regard to Suleyman's memories of the life of Abdallah Abu Hamdan, however, I do not think they derived from information he obtained through ordinary means of communication. The distance between the villages concerned in this case—30 kilometers—considerably exceeded that in Shamlinie Prema's case, although it was much less than that in Gopal Gupta's. Yet we should not measure accessibility only in kilometers. We must evaluate all the possibilities by which a subject could have obtained normally the information he had about the previous personality. Assessing it in this way I am inclined to rank Suleyman's case above that of Shamlinie, in which the two families concerned had had some slight acquaintance before her case developed. It is perhaps on the same level of Gopal's case. In the latter case there were greater geographical and socioeconomic separations between the families concerned than in Suleyman's case; but Gopal was remembering the life of a prominent man whose murder by his brother became a sensation, whereas Suleyman's memories related to a person about whose life and death little information had diffused outside his village.

THE CASE OF BONGKUCH PROMSIN

Bongkuch Promsin was born in the village of Don Kha in Nakhon Sawan Province, Thailand, on February 12, 1962. His father Pamorn Promsin, was principal of a school near Don Kha and therefore a person of some education, although having extremely modest financial means.

Soon after Bongkuch could speak coherently, and perhaps even before, he began to make references to a previous life, and he gradually unfolded details about it to his family. He claimed that he came from Hua Tanon (a village about 9 kilometers from Don Kha). He gave the name of the person whose life he claimed to remember, Chamrat, as well as the names of Chamrat's parents. He also described some objects that he had owned, such as a knife and a bicycle, and he referred to two cattle the family had owned. (Bongkuch's family owned no cattle.) Above all, he described how two men had murdered him at a fair that the villagers of Hua Tanon had held. The murderers had stabbed him in several places, taken his wristwatch and neck chain, and afterwards dragged his body into a field. (Bongkuch was about two years old when he communicated the foregoing details.)

Bongkuch said that after Chamrat's death he had stayed on a tree near the site of the murder for about seven years. One day when it was raining he had seen his (present) father and accompanied him home on a bus. Bongkuch's father later recalled that he had been over in Hua Tanon not long before his wife became pregnant with Bongkuch; he had attended a meeting there, and it had been raining.

His mother, Sawayi Promsin, had gone looking for bamboo shoots in the area where the murder had occurred before she became pregnant with Bongkuch, but I did not learn how long before her pregnancy. She said that she had not gone into the part of Hua Tanon where Chamrat's family lived. [10]

Pamorn Promsin had some acquaintance with schoolteachers of Hua Tanon through his professional work, but he had no relatives or social acquaintances there. He and his wife told me that they had never heard of the murdered Chamrat, who had been a mere youth at the time of his death. The news of a murder in a village like Hua

Tanon might have reached nearby villages, including Don Kha; on the other hand, the area had a high rate of murder, and one could not expect a resident of it to remember all the killings that had occurred. Moreover, Chamrat had been murdered more than ten years before Bongkuch talked about him. I think it likely that Bongkuch's parents had heard about Chamrat's murder, but had given it little attention and had quickly forgotten it.

Word of what Bongkuch was saying reached Chamrat's family, and some of its members came to see him in Don Kha. (He was about two and a half years old by this time.) Later, he went to Hua Tanon with members of his family. These visits led to the verification of nearly everything that Bongkuch had said about the previous life. My informants—and I myself, later—could not verify some of his statements about Chamrat's murder, such as the details of how he was stabbed; there had been no autopsy. One of the murderers had quickly fled, and the other, although arrested and tried, was acquitted for lack of evidence. Nevertheless, some policemen I interviewed recalled the murder rather well, and they confirmed as correct some of Bongkuch's statements about it, such as the names of the suspected murderers.

Reports of the case appeared in newspapers of Thailand in March 1965 and were sent to me by a correspondent. Dr. Sophon Nakphairaj (Director of the Government Hospital in Nakhon Sawan) made a preliminary investigation of the case in 1965. I began studying it in 1966. I interviewed members of both families concerned in Don Kha and Hua Tanon. I continued studying the case in the following years and last met Bongkuch and his parents in March 1980.

Bongkuch's unusual behavior attracted from the members of his family—and from me later—as much attention as his statements about the previous life did. During the period when he talked most about it, he exhibited what his family considered dirty habits, such as in his manner of washing his hands; and he used a number of words that his parents could not understand. He also showed a strong preference for foods that his family did not eat much or especially relish. It turned out that Chamrat's family were Laotians (whom the Thais consider less concerned about cleanliness than the Thais are) and that Bongkuch's strange words were Laotian. I do not wish to suggest that this is a strong case of xenoglossy (the ability to speak an unlearned language); nevertheless, no other members of Bongkuch's family used the Laotian words he spoke, and I think it unlikely that he learned them normally. (There were no villagers in Don Kha from whom he could have learned Laotian.) The foods Bongkuch enjoyed so much were ones, such as sticky rice, commonly enjoyed by Laotians; Thais sometimes eat these foods, but Bongkuch's food preferences were much more appropriate for Chamrat's Laotian family than they were for his own Thai family.

Bongkuch showed an unforgiving attitude toward Chamrat's murderers, and for years he threatened to take revenge on them when he could do so. He sometimes practiced beating on a post with a small stick that served as his imaginary weapon, while the post represented Chamrat's murderers, whose names he would call out as he did this.

Like many subjects of these cases, Bongkuch sometimes thought of himself as an adult imprisoned unwarrantedly in a child's body. At times he had what I call attacks of adulthood. He brushed his teeth like an adult (children do not ordinarily brush their teeth in Thailand), and on at least one occasion he asked the local barber to shave him. He ignored girls of his own age, but made advances to postpubertal young ladies, which they found startling and even alarming. One girl who came to visit the Promsins had planned to stay longer, but she departed precipitately after Bongkuch tried to fondle her. Yet Bongkuch was not exclusively a little lecher; sometimes he talked about joining the order of Buddhist monks and would ask for a monk's costume or fashion one for himself from cloth that was at hand. These two, somewhat opposite, aspects of Bongkuch's nature matched attitudes we can reasonably ascribe to Chamrat. At the time of his death, Chamrat had a girlfriend to whom he was more or less engaged; at the same time, he had a strong interest in religion and had expressed the intention of becoming a monk. (These are not incompatible interests; in Thailand many young men become monks for a few months or longer and then return to the life of laymen and marry.)

As Bongkuch became older, his memories of the previous life gradually faded. In his village, some other children teased him as "the boy with two lives," and this may have made him say that he had forgotten more of the memories than he actually had. At any rate, he stopped discussing his memories with other persons, and I think he had forgotten most of them by the time he was ten. His unusual behavior also diminished along with the imaged memories, and he gradually developed—so far as I can tell—entirely normally. In 1980, when I last met him, he was a young man of eighteen and was studying in a school in Nakhon Sawan. A final residue of Laotian behavior persisted in his continued fondness for sticky rice.

THE CASE OF GILLIAN AND JENNIFER POLLOCK

Gillian and Jennifer Pollock (identical twin girls) were born at Hexham, Northumberland, England, on October 4, 1958. When they were between two and four years old, they made several statements that suggested they remembered the lives of their two older sisters, Joanna and Jacqueline. On May 5, 1957, a crazed automobile driver had deliberately driven her car onto the pavement of a street in Hexham, where Joanna and Jacqueline were walking, and killed them both almost instantly. Joanna had been eleven and Jacqueline six when they died.

Grief from this tragedy numbed their parents, John and Florence Pollock. Mr. Pollock, however, was a strong believer in reincarnation (although his wife was not), and when Mrs. Pollock became pregnant early in 1958, he confidently asserted that the two deceased sisters were going to be reborn as twins. Despite medical advice to the contrary, he persisted, up to the time of the twins' birth, in saying that his wife would have twins. Their births then vindicated his seemingly rash prediction, at least about a twin birth. His conviction immediately received some further support, because he and his wife noticed that Jennifer, the younger twin, had two birthmarks that corresponded in location and size to two marks on Jacqueline's body. A mark on Jennifer's forehead, near the root of her nose, matched a scar that had persisted on Jacqueline's forehead after she had fallen and cut herself there; and a brown mark (nevus) on the left side of Jennifer's waist matched a similar (congenital) one on Jacqueline.

I mentioned above that between the ages of two and four the twins made a few statements about the lives of their deceased sisters. In addition, they recognized some objects, such as toys, that their sisters had owned or with which they had been familiar. Their parents later asserted that the twins could not have known about these objects normally; the Pollocks had never discussed the deceased older sisters with the twins, and the twins could not have seen the objects they recognized before the occasions when they did so. When the twins were less than a year old, the family moved away from Hexham, and the twins did not return until their parents took them there when they were about four. On that occasion, the twins spontaneously mentioned two places—a school and some swings in a park—before these were in their view. Although the twins had been taken to the park in their perambulator when they were infants—they had left Hexham when nine months old—their parents did not believe that they could have thereby acquired any normal knowledge about the school or swings in the park.

Gillian and Jennifer also showed behavior that corresponded to the behavior of their deceased older sisters. Jennifer was rather dependent on her older (twin) sister, Gillian, just as Jacqueline had been on her older sister, Joanna. When the twins learned to write, Gillian readily held a pencil between her fingers and thumb; but Jennifer grasped her pencil in a fist. Joanna had been able to write correctly for some years before her death, whereas Jacqueline (who was only six when she died) still persisted in holding a writing instrument in her fist.

I first investigated this case in 1964 and remained in touch with the Pollock family until 1985. Mr. Pollock's enthusiasm for reincarnation may diminish the strength of the case among persons who cannot believe that he and his wife (or some other member of the family) did not talk about the deceased sisters in front of the twins. In response to the suggestion that his conviction about reincarnation may have weakened and even vitiated the case, Mr. Pollock wisely replied that, although this objection has some merit, his openness concerning reincarnation enabled him to note and remember remarks and behavior of his twin daughters that most other Western parents would have ignored or laughed at. I shall return to this important point in chapters 5 and 8.

In 1978 I arranged for blood tests that would show, through analysis of the blood types and subtypes of Gillian and Jennifer and other members of the family, whether the twins' bodies derived from one or two eggs. The tests demonstrated that they are identical or one-egg twins; this means that they have the same genetic material. Since birthmarks of the type Jennifer had are sometimes hereditary, one would expect that if Jennifer's birthmarks were of genetic origin, Gillian would have similar marks. Because she does not have any, we may suppose that some biological aberration during the twins' gestation produced Jennifer's birthmarks, but this hypothesis would not account for their close correspondence in size and location to the marks on Jacqueline's body.

Gillian and Jennifer Pollock grew up to become normal young women. Long before that, they had completely forgotten, in later childhood, the memories they had had of previous lives. In my later meetings with them they were mildly skeptical about their own case. By this I mean that, not then having any persisting memories of the previous lives, they did not present themselves as offering evidence for reincarnation; but they did not deny the evidence their parents had obtained from observing them when they were young children.

THE CASE OF SAMUEL HELANDER

Samuel Helander was born in Helsinki, Finland, on April 15, 1976. When he was between one and two years old, he began to make some statements and recognitions that suggested he was remembering the life of his mother's younger brother, Pertti Häikiö. Later, Samuel showed some behavior that was unusual in his family but harmonious with Pertti's behavior. I investigated this case in Helsinki in 1978 and 1981; my informants were Samuel's mother and his maternal grandmother, who was also Pertti's mother.

Pertti Häikiö was born on June 8, 1957, also in Helsinki, and died there of severe, uncontrolled diabetes mellitus on June 10, 1975, when he was just eighteen years old. For some months before his death he had shown one of the prominent symptoms of uncontrolled diabetes—drinking large amounts of water—but no one at the time had realized how seriously ill he was before he fell into a coma and died. Pertti's mother, Anneli Lagerqvist (who had married again after divorcing Pertti's father), and his sister, Marja Helander (Samuel's mother), grieved severely after his death. When Marja was ten weeks pregnant with Samuel, she dreamed about Pertti. At the time she had been considering having an abortion, but in the dream she heard Pertti say to her: "Keep that child."

Samuel was only about a year and a half old when, upon being asked his name, he said that it was "Pelti." (At that time and for some time later, he could not pronounce the r sound of "Pertti.") Attempts to convince Samuel that his name was "Samuel" generally failed; he insisted that it was "Pelti" and later "Pertti." He was still saying that his name was "Pelti" at the age of six. He did not, however, refuse to respond or to come to his mother when she called him "Samuel."

Samuel made only a few direct statements about the previous life that he seemed to remember, and nearly all of these occurred in connection with his recognizing some person (often in a photograph) or object familiar to Pertti.

Photographs of Pertti taken when he was a child of under ten seemed often to stimulate Samuel's remarks; those taken when Pertti was older did not. On looking at one photograph Samuel remarked that he remembered how a dog had bitten him on the leg. A dog had bitten Pertti on the leg when he was a child of three, but Samuel had never been bitten by a dog and had never been told about Pertti's having been bitten. Nor did the photograph give any clue suggesting that he had been bitten.

On another occasion Samuel noticed a photograph of Pertti as a young child using a walker. He said that the photograph was of himself and that he had been in the hospital with his legs in plaster. When I was studying this case in Helsinki, I was shown the photograph that had stimulated this remark. It showed Pertti using a walker, and one might infer that he had injured his legs; but nothing in the photograph suggested that his legs had been in plaster, as they had been just before the photograph was taken. Pertti's legs had both been fractured in an accident when he was about four years old. When Samuel made his remark about this, he was himself between three and four years old.

Samuel's claim that photographs of Pertti were photographs of himself were not made only on the occasions that I have mentioned. The family had some of these photos in an album that they would occasionally look through, and each time Samuel saw Pertti's photograph he would say: "That's me."

When Samuel saw a photograph of Pentti Häikiö, Pertti's father, Samuel said: "This is my father." Because Anneli Lagerqvist's second husband was somewhat jealous of Pentti Häikiö, this photograph was ordinarily kept hidden, and she was certain that Samuel had never seen it before the occasion when he recognized it as that of "his father."

Samuel also identified several objects that had belonged to Pertti: a guitar, a velvet corduroy jacket, and an old watch. The hands had been lost from the watch, and it had been put away in a drawer full of junk; but when Samuel saw it he pounced on it, said it was his, and insisted on keeping it. Sometimes he slept with the watch under his pillow; at other times he placed it in a drawer under his bed.

Samuel never alluded directly to Pertti's death. He did, however, make two remarks suggestive of memories of events occurring after it. He said that he had been to a place where there were a lot of coffins and that some of them were open. (Samuel had never been taken to a mortuary, but Pertti's body was taken to one after his death.) Samuel also remarked on how much Pertti's mother (Samuel's grandmother) had cried after his death; however, he might have obtained this information normally or surmised it.

When Samuel was taken to the cemetery where Pertti had been buried, he looked at Pertti's grave and said: "This is my grave."

Samuel's mother and grandmother mentioned several items of unusual behavior on his part that accorded with similar behavior of Pertti. When Pertti was a young child, he had swallowed water while he was in a bathtub; this had frightened him, but he did not then develop a phobia of water. Later, when he was about fifteen or sixteen years old, he fell off a quay, through thin ice, and into the sea. He nearly drowned. After that accident he did have a phobia of water and would not go swimming. Samuel showed a marked phobia of being immersed in water. He especially resisted being bathed, and his grandmother said the struggle to give him a bath was a "nightmare."

When Samuel first began to speak, he called his parents by their first names: Pentti and Màrja. He also called his maternal grandmother, Anneli Lagerqvist, "Mother." He was definite about these identities and told Marja Helander: "You are not my mother." Samuel showed a strong attachment to Mrs. Lagerqvist, and when he was about two he tried to nurse at her breast. (He had already been weaned at that age, but Pertti had not been.) Samuel had stopped calling Mrs. Lagerqvist "Mother" by the age of five.

Pertti had had the pleasant habit at Christmas time of going around a room full of assembled members and kissing each person in turn. This seems not to have been a custom among other members of the family, and they were therefore surprised at the Christmas gathering of 1978 when Samuel, only two and half years old, went around the room and kissed each person present, just as Pertti had done.

Samuel also had two physical stances that resembled those of Pertti. Both had a habit of standing with one foot forward, often with a hand on a hip; and both tended to walk at times with their hands held behind the back. No other members of the family assumed such postures.

THE CASE OF ROBERTA MORGAN

I first learned about this case in February 1971, when the subject's mother, Mrs. Shirley Morgan, telephoned me at the University of Virginia from Minnesota, where she lived. She said that her daughter, Roberta, had several years earlier talked insistently about having "another mummy and daddy" whom she eagerly—it seemed almost desperately—wished to visit. Roberta had said that she (presumably in the previous life she seemed to remember) had promised this "other mummy and daddy" that she would go back to them, and she wanted to keep her promise.

Roberta had been born on August 28, 1961, and therefore in February 1971 she was nine and a half years old. She had begun to talk about the previous life when she was between two and two and a half years old. (But by 1971 she had long ceased to do so, for reasons that I shall describe later.) Mrs. Morgan explained that at the time Roberta was talking most about the previous life, she herself had not known anything about reincarnation and thought that Roberta was talking nonsense. Then later, through reading and reflection, it occurred to her not only that Roberta might have been remembering a real previous life, but that she (Mrs. Morgan) had failed in her responsibilities by suppressing Roberta when she talked about it. Mrs. Morgan then swung almost completely around to the opposite extreme, and in 1971 she became rather frantically preoccupied with how she might trace Roberta's previous family so that Roberta might visit them after all. She then decided to telephone me.

When Mrs. Morgan gave me the information that I have included in the preceding paragraphs, I asked her to write out for me an account of what Roberta had said concerning the life she appeared to be remembering. Mrs. Morgan did this, and she also answered further questions for me in subsequent letters. In July 1972, I visited Roberta and her mother at their home in Minnesota. (I did not meet Roberta's father during my visit.) Roberta was friendly with me, but by the time I met her she had completely forgotten about the previous life. Thus all my information about the case derives from Mrs. Morgan.

During our interview and in correspondence, she gave me the following information.

At the peak of her talk about the previous life, Roberta behaved "at times like an adopted child with full memory of her [previous] parents and their house." She said that her previous house was reached by going down a long road; it stood on a hill with no other houses nearby. Roberta further described the house and land that she said she remembered, but her mother could later recall little of Roberta's description except that the previous family had lived on a farm where there were horses and dogs. Once when she was about four, she was taken to a horse farm; she went directly to the horses and petted them. When someone asked her: "Aren't you afraid of the horses?" she replied: "No, I have been on horses lots of times." Roberta also spoke of an automotive vehicle that the previous father had owned. (It was not clear whether this had been a passenger automobile or a truck.) She would sometimes indicate a vehicle and remark: "There is a car [or truck] [like the one] that my Dad used to own."

Roberta said that her "other mummy and daddy" lived in the same town where she and her family were then living. (This was a different town than the one where I visited them.) On one occasion, Roberta was in a car with her mother and pointed to a road, saying that was where she lived; she indicated a dirt road that joined the highway. She wanted to go down the road to see the previous family. Her mother did not wish to do this, evidently because at this time she was not able to think that Roberta might be correct. Roberta reproached her mother for days afterward for not having taken her to the previous family when they had a chance to visit them.[11]

Roberta asked her mother to buy her toys similar to those she said that she used to have; when her mother said she did not know what these were, Roberta became annoyed at what she considered her mother's dullness. On other occasions, also, she scolded her mother for not remembering her (Roberta's) previous life, as it seemed to Roberta she should have done. (And yet Roberta did not claim that her mother had had a part in the previous life.)

Roberta evidently had clear visual images of the appearances of the previous parents. Referring to the previous mother, she told Mrs. Morgan: "You act like her, but she did not look like you."[12] Roberta favored the previous mother's style in various household tasks, including cooking. When her (present) mother prepared some new dish for dinner, Roberta would sometimes tell her parents that she had eaten it many times before. Once her mother cooked scalloped corn as a surprise for the family. When she placed this on the table, Roberta said: "I had that lots of times. Don't you remember, my other mother used to make it." She then referred to it by some name other than scalloped corn, but Mrs. Morgan later forgot this name. Mrs. Morgan asked Roberta how her "other mother" prepared the dish, and Roberta patiently explained her "other mother's" way of cooking it. Roberta also thought her mother foolish not to wash windows in the more efficient manner of her previous mother. She often intervened in her parents' conversations with remarks indicating familiarity with some topic or object of which, in her mother's opinion, she could have known nothing normally.

Roberta gave few clues to the period when the previous life took place. She did not, for example, refer to wearing clothes that obviously belonged to earlier fashions. Her familiarity with automobiles suggested that the previous life had occurred at least after they had become commonly owned by American farmers. She implied, more than she expressly stated, that the previous parents were still living and could be found if only her parents would apply themselves to the task.

Roberta showed some inclination to wear boys' clothes, and she complained of being a girl. She did not, however, state that she had been a boy in the previous life. Her requests for toys suggested that the person whose life she was recalling had died young, yet Roberta never said anything about how that person had died. In fact, she denied having died. When Mrs. Morgan once asked a direct question about this, Roberta replied: "I didn't die. I had to leave them [the other parents] for a while. And I told them I was coming back." She never said that she loved the previous parents, and, indeed, Mrs. Morgan thought that in a straight popularity contest between herself and the previous mother, she (Mrs. Morgan) would win, although barely. Roberta's pressure to return to the previous family appeared to derive more from her promise to go back to them than from ties of affection. Since, however, she never gave any names for herself or the family of the previous life, Mrs. Morgan had no way of tracing them, even if she had wished to do so at the time, which was far from being the case.

Mrs. Morgan and her husband were both Christians—she a member of the Assembly of God, he of the Roman Catholic Church; reincarnation had no place in the teachings of either of these religions. Mrs. Morgan knew nothing about reincarnation at the time Roberta began talking about a previous life; she was not prepared for such talk, and she was even less prepared for Roberta's demands to be taken to the "other mother" and for her constant, unfavorable comparisons of Mrs. Morgan with the "other mother." Every parent has a limit of tolerance for such assessments, and Mrs. Morgan reached hers after about six months of daily pounding by Roberta. She then began to punish Roberta every time she alluded to the previous life. This gradually brought Roberta's utterances to a halt (except for occasional lapses, such as the one that occurred when she was four and spoke about having ridden horses).

I do not know when Roberta actually forgot about the previous life. She may have remembered it for a time after her mother began punishing her for talking about it. To outward appearances, however, she remembered it less than her mother did in the years that followed her mother's efforts to suppress her memories. The matter continued to trouble Mrs. Morgan, latently at first and then openly. Finally, as I have explained, she became "obsessed"—that was her own expression—with the thought that she must trace Roberta's previous family and allow her to meet them. She began blaming herself also for not having allowed Roberta to speak freely about the previous life; she was sure that Roberta at that time could have stated some names that would have permitted verification of her memories.

Unfortunately, this change of attitude came too late. Roberta by this time was nine and a half years old, and she had given no additional clues to the identity of the previous family since her allusion to horses at the age of four; she never added proper names to what she had said earlier. Mrs. Morgan appears to have considered a search of farms with horses in the area of the Morgans' former home: this seemed impractical without some further clues that might have narrowed the area of searching. However, I do not understand why she did not try driving down the farm road that Roberta herself had indicated about six years earlier.

Soon after my visit to Roberta and her mother in the early summer of 1972, I lost touch with them and have been unable to trace them. I can say nothing therefore about Roberta's further development.

THE CASE OF SUSAN EASTLAND

I first learned of this case in 1968, when I received a letter from Mrs. Charlotte Eastland, who, having read about my research in a magazine, volunteered information about the statements and behavior of her daughter Susan. These suggested that Susan had memories, albeit fragmentary ones, of the life of her deceased older sister, Winnie. I exchanged letters with Mrs. Eastland during 1968 and early 1969, and in the summer of 1969, I visited her in her home in Idaho. There I also met Susan, the subject of the case, and Mrs. Eastland's older daughter, Sharon. However, I did not meet Robert Eastland, the stepfather of Sharon and Susan, who had also been, according to Mrs. Eastland, a witness for some of Susan's statements about the previous life.

Winnie was a lovable six-year-old girl who was hit by an automobile and fatally injured in 1961. Her sudden death devastated the members of her family. Her mother suffered grievously and found herself longing to have Winnie somehow back in the family. At this time, she had only the vaguest notions about reincarnation; she told me later that she had heard about the belief held by people in India that humans can be reborn as subhuman animals (which she considered impossible), but she had never heard of reincarnation in another human body.

Nevertheless, the family members had an idea that Winnie might somehow return to them. About six months after Winnie's death, her older sister, Sharon, dreamed that Winnie was coming back to the family. And when Mrs. Eastland became pregnant two years later, she dreamed of Winnie being with the family again. In 1964, when she was in the delivery room for the birth of her new baby, her first husband (the father of all her children) thought he heard Winnie's voice saying distinctly: "Daddy, I'm coming home." The baby, Susan, thus came into a family that had lost a girl just a few years earlier and that had some expectations that this same girl would be reborn among them. We have to remember these facts when we evaluate Susan's remarks related to Winnie's life.

When Susan was about two years old, she made several statements that seemed like references to the life of Winnie. When anyone asked her how old she was, she would answer that she was six (the age Winnie had been when she was killed). Her sense of being older than her actual age persisted at least up to the age of five, because at that time she insisted that she was older than her brother Richard, who was then eleven. Winnie had been more than three years older than Richard, so Susan's remark was correct for Winnie but obviously wrong with regard to her own age relationship to Richard.

Susan expressed unusual interest in two photographs of Winnie and said of them: "That was me." Mrs. Eastland thought that she might earlier have told Susan that the photographs were of Winnie; but she had not told Susan that she thought she (Susan) might be Winnie reborn. Susan not only identified the photographs as being of her; she insisted on having them for herself. She kept one hanging by her bed and carried the other around with her for weeks, sometimes repeating that it was a photograph of herself.

Susan never asked to be called Winnie, but on one occasion, when she could barely scrawl, she took a crayon and wrote letters on the kitchen door that spelled "WINNI." She omitted the final *E* of *Winnie,* and she laid the *I* on its side, instead of standing it upright.

During this same period, Susan frequently used the phrase "When I went to school," and she talked also about playing on the swings at school. Susan had not yet gone to school; she had played on a swing in the family's back yard, but not on one at a school. Winnie, on the other hand, had started school before she was killed, and she used to play on the swings at her school.

During Winnie's lifetime, Mrs. Eastland had a cookie jar that had a cat on its lid. She used to play a game with her children in which, when one of them wanted a cookie from the jar, she would ask the cat how many cookies the child could have. She would then imitate a cat by replying in a squeaky voice: "Meow, you may have one." (The number of allowed cookies varied with Mrs. Eastland's estimate of the child's needs and hunger.) After Winnie's death, Mrs. Eastland put the cookie jar away and forgot it; the jar remained packed away for several years. When Susan was about four, Mrs. Eastland brought it out and again filled it with cookies. Susan asked for a cookie. Without realizing that Susan would know nothing about the game with the cat on the cookie jar, her mother unthinkingly asked her: "Well, what does the kitty say?" Susan startled her by replying: "Meow, you may have one." Mrs. Eastland, in recounting this episode to me, wisely remarked that a child as intelligent as Susan might have inferred the answer; and I would add that she might also have obtained the reply from her mother by telepathy. Her spontaneous reply was nevertheless harmonious also with the interpretation that Susan somehow had access to Winnie's memories.

After this, Susan spoke of several other events in which Winnie had participated. She described an occasion when she and other members of the family had gone to a beach and had caught a crab, and she named family members present on this outing. Mrs. Eastland recalled that the family had gone to a beach in the state of Washington the year before Winnie's death. They had played in the surf and on the sand; they had found shells and dug for clams; Mrs. Eastland could not remember their catching a crab, however. Susan correctly named three of the four persons who had been present, but she included one person, her stepfather, who had not. Later, however, she corrected herself and said that Winnie's (and her) father had been present.

Susan also referred to playing in a pasture with her sister, Sharon; she said that she had been unafraid of the horses and that she had once walked under a horse. All this was correct for Winnie, who had played in a pasture with Sharon, was unafraid of horses, and had once walked under one.

Mrs. Eastland once asked Susan whether she remembered the little boy Gregory who had lived across the street from them. Susan replied: "Yes, I remember Greggy. I used to play with him." "Greggy" had been Gregory's short name; Mrs. Eastland had not mentioned it before Susan did.

Susan's mother also asked her if she remembered Uncle George, who had lived up the street from them. Susan could not remember what Uncle George's house looked like, but said that she remembered him and then added: "We used to stop and see him before going to school, and play awhile." This had been Winnie's custom; in fact, she had stopped to play at Uncle George's house on the day she was killed. I should add that Gregory and Uncle George lived in the town where the family lived during Winnie's life. Susan was born and had lived all her life in another, smaller town of Idaho.

Readers will have noticed that Susan's mother tried sometimes to stimulate her memories by asking questions about events that had occurred during Winnie's life. This sort of conversation carries some risk of inadvertently furnishing information to the child thus questioned; and it may encourage an identification with the dead person that would not have happened otherwise. Nevertheless, such questioning, if conducted by a person as vigilant and intelligent as Mrs. Eastland seemed to be, may arouse additional memories without lowering safeguards against normal communication.

Here is another example. Mrs. Eastland once told Susan that she (meaning Winnie) had lost some new shoes in a field. At this, Susan laughed and said that she had not cared about the loss of the shoes. Then she added: "And you had to go up to town and buy me some more." Such an incident had happened to Winnie, who had lost her only pair of shoes in a field.

I thought that by the end of 1969 I had learned all that I could about this case. However, when I was corresponding with Mrs. Eastland in 1977—in order to recheck some details and enquire about Susan's further development—I learned that Susan had recalled yet another incident in Winnie's life. My letter to her mother, which Mrs. Eastland told Susan about, evidently stimulated her to further recollections of the previous life. She then told her mother about a time when she (as Winnie) had accompanied her mother to a bowling alley. While her mother was bowling, Winnie was left in the area where food and candy were sold, but she kept running between this area and the place where her mother was. A boy who happened also to be there was running around with Winnie, and he kissed her. Mrs. Eastland remembered this incident well, especially because the boy's kissing Winnie had greatly annoyed her husband when she told him about it.

Susan never directly said anything like: "I was Winnie," or "I am Winnie." She came closest to such a statement when she claimed that the photographs of Winnie were of herself. She had memories that, in her mother's expression, seemed to be of "a long time ago." She remembered doing things that Winnie had done but that she (Susan) had not. However, Susan's memories of Winnie's life were not organized into a more or less coherent pattern, as are the memories of most other subjects of these cases. Put another way, we might say that although Susan had memories of a previous life, she seemed not to have an explicit idea that she had lived before.

Susan learned rapidly, so much so that Mrs. Eastland wrote in one of her letters to me: "Sometimes I feel when she learns something new that she knew it all the time and only had to be reminded of it."

Mrs. Eastland had noticed two features of personality in which she thought Susan and Winnie resembled each other. She said both were rather aggressive girls and well coordinated. She distinguished them in these two characteristics from her other daughter, Sharon, who, she said, was inclined to be timid and poorly coordinated.

Susan did not resemble Winnie physically, however. Winnie had had red hair and extremely dark eyes; Susan had blond hair and blue eyes. Susan and Winnie both had a rather heavy growth of hair on their backs. Their father had an unusual growth of hair on his back, but the other children did not. Susan also had a small birthmark on her left hip, which corresponded in location to the most serious external injury Winnie received when she was struck by the automobile and fatally injured. (I obtained a copy of Winnie's medical records from the hospital to which she was taken after the automobile struck her, and where she died.) No other member of the family had a similar birthmark.

This case is one of a considerable number of American cases in which the subject's religious background was not in any way favorable to the belief in reincarnation. Mrs. Eastland belonged to a Christian church that sternly denies the possibility of reincarnation. When I visited her, she told me that she thought her congregation might expel her from the church if they suspected that she found the idea of reincarnation attractive. She did find it attractive, although she also managed to continue conforming to her church in other doctrinal matters.

Mrs. Eastland assured me that up to the time of my visit to her in early summer of 1969, she had not told her children about her belief that Susan was Winnie reborn. She did tell them later that summer, however, perhaps in response to their understandable curiosity about the reason for my visit.

THE CASE OF MICHAEL WRIGHT

My investigation of this case, like that of Roberta Morgan's, began with a telephone call from the subject's mother, Mrs. Catherine Wright. A colleague talked with her first and found her distraught about some statements her son had made, which suggested—indeed had convinced her already—that he remembered the life of the boyfriend she had had before she married her husband. This friend, Walter Miller, had died in an automobile accident when the car he was driving ran off the road and crashed.

The idea of reincarnation did not perturb Mrs. Wright. On the contrary, she believed in it firmly and also believed in a wide variety of other paranormal phenomena. I will not digress to describe her personal psychical experiences, but I cannot neglect to mention them here and also what seemed to me a degree of related credulity that she showed. These might—in the view of some readers—diminish her reliability as a witness of her son's statements about a previous life. I myself have not formed this opinion, however; if I had, I would not offer a report of Michael's case, for which Mrs. Wright provided nearly all the testimony.

A reader may ask here, however, why, if Catherine Wright had such an open mind about psychical experiences, she had any need to telephone so urgently to the University of Virginia in September 1978. I did not learn the answer to that question until the following month, when I interviewed her in Texas. (Nearly all the information for this report derives from this interview and another one conducted a year later by my associate, Emily Williams Cook.) At the time of my interview, I learned that Mrs. Wright formed with her mother a two-person enclave (in her community) of believers in reincarnation. Her husband, I also learned, did not share her beliefs. In addition to this, Mrs. Wright knew him well enough to think he would not enjoy hearing about the pretension of his son to be his wife's former boyfriend reborn. She could readily imagine his recalling without effort or pleasure that he had succeeded in marrying her only because Walter Miller had died in an automobile accident. Was Walter Miller then not permanently dead, but invading now his successor's home?

In the event, Mrs. Wright's fears about her husband's reaction had little or no foundation. Between the time of her telephone call to us in September 1978 and my visit to her at the end of October, she braved her husband's expected wrath and told him about her conjectures regarding what Michael had been saying. She then learned to her surprise that he had already surmised that she might be thinking that Michael was the reincarnation of Walter Miller, and he seemed to take this in good part. I never learned enough about the relationship between Mrs. Wright and her husband to decide whether his unexpected knowledge of her opinion derived from telepathy between them or from some normal seepage of information from her to him that had occurred without her being aware of it.

To go back to Catherine Wright's boyfriend, Walter Miller, he was not quite eighteen years old when he died in the summer of 1967. A promising amateur artist and a popular high school student, he had looked forward to his senior year, which was to begin in the autumn. He and Catherine had known each other for about three years and had dated steadily with an understanding of being engaged, short of formally stating this. One night Walter attended a dance with a friend, Henry Sullivan, and he probably drank more alcohol than he should have. Returning from the dance, he appears to have fallen asleep at the wheel of his car and run off the road. Walter died almost instantly, although his friend emerged unharmed.

Catherine felt the death of her boyfriend keenly, but she rallied; and about a year later, in 1968, she married another boyfriend, Frederick Wright, who had earlier stood in second place. They had a daughter first, and then Michael was born. Before this happened, however, and a little more than a year after Walter's death, Mrs. Wright had a dream about him that would certainly have counted as announcing his rebirth if it had occurred to a prospective mother in most of the countries where these cases are frequently found. In fact, Mrs. Wright interpreted her dream as doing that. In it Walter said that he was not dead as people thought, that he would come back, and that he would draw pictures for her again. At the time of the dream and even after Michael's birth, which did not take place until 1975, Mrs. Wright thought that Walter would return as the child of someone else—perhaps, she mused, of his sister, Carole Miller Davis, who happened to be pregnant at the time of the dream. I mention this because the dream prepared Mrs. Wright in a general way for Walter's rebirth, but it left her with no expectation that he would reincarnate as her son.

Michael's birth and early development proceeded normally, although as an infant he apparently had some difficulty in breathing, which he later outgrew. He was about three when he began to show signs of having an unexpected knowledge of people and events. He startled his mother one day by uttering the name "Carole Miller." Catherine Wright had maintained some friendly contact with Carole Miller after Walter's death; but Carole had married ten years earlier, and Michael, who had met her only twice, had never known her except by her married name, Carole Davis.

The foregoing opening utterance by Michael did little to prepare his mother for his detailed narration, which followed, of the accident in which Walter Miller had died. After a false start in which he referred to a motorcycle, Michael corrected himself and said, according to his mother: "A friend and I were in a car, and the car went off the side of the road, rolled over and over. The door came open, and I fell out and was killed." Michael also added other details, although I am not sure whether he included these in his first account or stated them later. He said, for example, that the glass in the car had broken and that he had been carried over a bridge (after the accident). He also said that he and his friend had stopped (along the highway) and had gone to a rest room before they had the accident. Michael also mentioned the name of the town where the dance from which Walter Miller was returning had taken place.

Mrs. Wright knew that most of these statements applied correctly to Walter's accident, and a newspaper report (with a photograph of the mangled car) that she showed me confirmed her account of the main events of the accident. The impact of the crash threw Walter from the car, and he died almost instantly of a broken neck. The ambulance transporting his body went over a bridge near the site of the accident.[13] Mrs. Wright could not say whether Walter and his friend had stopped to use a rest room before the accident, and her sense of being an almost solitary believer in reincarnation in a community of nonbelievers prevented her from daring to broach the subject with the only person who could verify the detail. (This was Walter's companion, Henry Sullivan, who had survived the accident.) Nor did she approve my doing so; neither of us imagined that I could conceal the true purpose of any such inquiries I made in a small Texas town, even if I had been willing to do so, which I was not.

Michael made some further statements about matters within the knowledge of Walter, but outside his own, so far as his mother could tell. He knew some details about Walter's home and that of Henry Sullivan. Eventually, but only after questioning by Mrs. Wright, Michael gave out the last name of Henry Sullivan. He also stated (with a slight error) Henry's nickname.

Mrs. Wright's mother, Margaret Carpenter, participated in my interview with Mrs. Wright, and she corroborated her daughter's report of what Michael had said about the accident, which he had repeated in her presence. Unfortunately, we lack corroboration for Mrs. Wright's report of other details stated by Michael. When my associate Emily Williams Cook visited Michael's family, she briefly interviewed his father, Frederick Wright, but learned that he then remembered almost nothing of what Michael had said about the previous life. I do not know whether this ignorance derived from lack of attention to what his son had said or to his not having been present when Michael spoke about the previous life, which he often did with his mother.

I am far from satisfied with my understanding of this case, but I have thought it worth presenting because it illustrates features found in many American cases of the reincarnation type and in some cases of other countries. Its weaknesses lie mainly in the somewhat overeager attitude of Michael's mother toward her son's remarks and in our inability, for the reason stated earlier, to verify any of Michael's statements independently with Walter Miller's family or friends. Normally I do not publish a report of a case, if it has verifiable features, unless I can make independent verifications; but other considerations influenced me to set this rule aside in this instance. My grounds for doing this included certain strengths the case undoubtedly has. It developed in a subculture that I think we can fairly describe as hostile to the idea of reincarnation. Nor can one easily find any motivation within members of the Wright family to contrive, or even encourage, a case of this type with its poignant domestic triangularity.[14] In the fantasy world of those psychiatrists who assign motives as they wish, one could easily imagine that Mrs. Wright thought up the case to torment her husband or that Michael conceived it as a subtle torture for his parents. Maybe they did, but I do not believe it. We should not ascribe a motive for which we have no independent evidence, unless we can point to some gain from its expression. I fail to see that anyone profited from Michael's statements about the life of his mother's boyfriend. And the frantic nature of her first telephone call to us seemed evidence enough that she had no control whatever—at that time—over the psychological forces released in the case.

THE CASE OF ERIN JACKSON

I learned about this case when Erin Jackson's mother, Mrs. Marilyn Jackson, wrote to me about it in 1980. She told me that when Erin, who was born in a town of Indiana in 1969, was about three years old, she had spoken often about a previous life she seemed to remember. After exchanging several letters with Mrs. Jackson, I arranged to meet her and Erin at the town in Indiana where they resided. We had a long interview there in the summer of 1980. Erin's father did not participate in this meeting; according to Mrs. Jackson, he could have added nothing to what she remembered.

Mrs. Jackson herself had to remember events of some years back, because Erin had stopped speaking about the previous life when she was about four years old. Her references to it had continued for about a year only, a shorter time than that during which most subjects of these cases speak about the lives they seem to remember.

During the period when Erin talked about the previous life, she made frequent references to the time "when I was a boy" and "when I was called John." These allusions would form part of statements like: "When my name was John, we went to a lake and I floated my big boat," or "When I was a boy, we had a black dog and a white cat." Erin said she had a stepmother who loved her and treated her well and a brother called James. She recalled James had a strong preference for wearing black clothes and even wanted to wear black underwear.

Erin mentioned no place where this life had occurred, and she gave no direct indications of its period. She did, however, make frequent allusions to the ugliness of modern American highways with their billboards, telephone poles, and automobiles massed together. She sometimes muttered to herself about the loss of rural (and urban) beauty, and her mother overheard her making such remarks as: "It was lots better when there were horses. These cars are awful. They've just ruined everything." (The spoiling of the American countryside took several decades. We might say that it began around 1910 with Henry Ford's development of methods for mass-producing automobiles, which in turn led to the building of modern highways. If my appraisal is correct, Erin's remarks refer to a time before 1930, at least.)

In keeping with her conviction that she had been a boy, Erin wished to dress like a boy and engage in boys' activities. As soon as she became old enough to appreciate that boys and girls dressed differently, she insisted on wearing boys' clothes. When she began to learn swimming, her mother bought her two-piece bathing suits of which Erin regularly wore only the bottom part. To prevent this, her mother eventually bought her one-piece bathing suits. Erin seemed to feel humiliated when her mother insisted on her wearing a dress; she much preferred jeans and slacks. Even at the age of ten, when I met her, she was wearing a dress only about three times a year, and she required that such dresses as she did wear not have noticeably feminine features, such as lace or ruffles. She also wanted her hair kept short and allowed it to grow long only when she was about nine.

Erin had no interest in dolls representing humans, and if she was given such a doll, she would strip off its clothes and transfer them to an animal doll. Her favorite indoor activities were drawing, reading, and building with toy blocks. Among outdoor activities, she enjoyed swimming, climbing trees, and fishing. She expressed a strong wish to learn baseball, and she intensely wanted to become a Cub Scout; she became incensed when told that as a girl she was ineligible to join the Cub Scouts. Mrs. Jackson wrote me that Erin would sometimes say with a sigh: "I wish I were a boy. Why couldn't I have been a boy?"

Erin was a child of superior intelligence. Her mother said that she seemed to know how to read at the age of three, before anyone had taught her. She had a gift for drawing that I judged—after looking at some sketches she had made—unusual for a child of her age. She also composed poems that a much older person might have felt pleased to have written.

For a year Erin spoke frequently—on average, once a week—about the previous life. From the age of about four on, she began to talk of it less and less frequently and finally stopped altogether; by the time I met her, when she was nearly eleven, she seemed to remember little of what she had said when she was three or four years old. Slight traces of the memories remained, however, so that when I was talking with her mother, Erin sometimes intervened with comments concerning them. Her associated masculine behavior persisted for four or five years after she stopped speaking spontaneously about the previous life. Residues of this behavior still remained at the time I met her, but she was then moving toward normal development as a girl.

Erin's parents had a conventional Protestant Christian background; they did not believe in reincarnation at the time she began speaking about a previous life. Mrs. Jackson appears to have known almost nothing about the subject at that time. Later she read something about it and began to believe in reincarnation, but Erin's father remained a disbeliever. By 1980, Mrs. Jackson had read a few popular books on the subject, but no one could classify her as a propagandist for it. I do not think anyone can attribute this case to Erin's parents' having encouraged her to engage in fantasies about a previous life. Mrs. Jackson said that she showed a polite interest in what Erin said about the previous life and never ridiculed her when she referred to it; but neither did she encourage her to talk more than she did of what seemed to Mrs. Jackson at that time mere "fantasy." This last word she herself used to characterize her first opinion of what Erin had been saying about the previous life.

The foregoing summaries show some of the strengths and weaknesses of these cases, considered with regard to evidence for the subjects' having information about a deceased person that they could not have obtained normally. In later chapters I shall describe the methods I have used to investigate the cases and the ways in which I have analyzed and interpreted them. Before these chapters, however, I shall present next some observations of features that recur in large series of cases.

CHAPTER FIVE

CHARACTERISTICS OF TYPICAL CASES OF THE REINCARNATION TYPE

The twelve case summaries that I gave in the last chapter have given a provisional basis for outlining a typical case. Readers will probably have noticed, for example, that in at least seven of the twelve cases the death in the remembered previous life had been violent. (In two cases the cause of death was unknown.) In the present chapter I shall describe other recurrent features of typical cases [1] and also draw attention to the more important variations among them. First, however, I shall tell where the cases are found most abundantly and mention the social and economic backgrounds of the persons concerned in them.

WHERE THE CASES ARE FOUND

Persons who claim that they remember a previous life are easily found in certain areas of the world. These are northern India, Sri Lanka, Burma, Thailand, south central Turkey, Lebanon, Syria, West Africa, and the northwestern region of North America. I have also found and investigated many cases in Europe and North America (apart from the tribes of the northwestern region). I have found cases in South America as well, but much less abundantly than in the other countries and regions I have mentioned.

Tibet must at one time have been a country where many cases of this type occurred, if I may judge from their fairly common occurrence among the refugees from Tibet who now live in India. I have studied a few cases among these Tibetans, but the dispersal of family members and other firsthand informants makes their investigation unusually difficult.

I have reason to believe that cases could also be found easily in parts of Japan and in eastern Indochina (that is, Laos, Cambodia, and Vietnam). I have learned of some cases in these countries, and correspondents have told me that they think numerous cases could be found there if someone would look for them, which I have not yet done. I lacked time, not zeal, for this, and thought it better to concentrate my efforts on a smaller number of countries with the cultures of which I have gradually become at least somewhat familiar.

The most obvious aspect of the inventory of geographic locations that I have just given is the correlation between a high density of reported cases and a belief in reincarnation. I shall discuss possible interpretations of this correlation later. I wish to emphasize here, however, that cases also occur—and much more frequently than the average Westerner realizes—in Western countries, such as those of Europe and North America. Moreover, we have found some cases in Asia among groups of peoples who do not believe in reincarnation (for example, the Christians of Lebanon and Sri Lanka, and the Sunni Moslems of India).

I can say much more confidently where we can easily find cases than what their real incidence is. I can only investigate a case after someone has informed me about it, and there are many filters between the development of a case and news of it reaching me. There are several reasons for my not learning about cases promptly or not learning about them at all.

An unknown number of cases are quietly observed just within a small circle of family members and perhaps a few close friends. These are usually cases in which the subject is identified as being a deceased member of the same family reborn. I sometimes refer to these cases as "private cases." As I have continued my investigations and become better known to informants in various countries, more of them have taken me into their confidence and told me about private cases, even allowing me at times to investigate them thoroughly.

Another unknown number of cases are suppressed, even within the subject's own family. This is particularly likely to happen in cultures, such as those of Western countries, where the majority of people do not believe in reincarnation. The parents of the child subject of such a case may think he is talking nonsense or telling lies, and they often try to shut him up. A similar motive accounts for the suppression of cases among the Sunni Moslems of India and the Christians of Lebanon and Sri Lanka.

However, even in cultures with a strong belief in reincarnation, parents may sometimes not wish a child to talk about a previous life, and they may try to stop him from doing so. They may try to suppress him if they believe—as many persons in India and Burma do—that it is harmful and possibly fatal for a child to have such memories. In many instances also parents dislike either the content of what a child is saying or some features of the child's behavior that matches his statements. Thus if a child talks about a sordid murder in the previous life or if he claims to have belonged to a family markedly superior (or markedly inferior) to his own, his parents may try to stop him from talking about his memories.

We may nevertheless learn about suppressed cases when some informant breaks ranks, or when the subject simulates amnesia for the previous life while actually retaining his memories, which he later reveals to listeners more sympathetic than those he found in his own family. The case of the Thai monk Chaokhun Rajsuthajarn provides and excellent example of this. As a young child he had clear memories of the life of his own maternal uncle. His family fully accepted his statements as indicative of his being his uncle reborn; but he insisted on a certain adult status and, for example, addressed his mother familiarly as if she were his sister, not his mother. His family therefore took various measures to suppress his references to the life of his uncle, including some mild physical handling, such as making him dizzy by turning him on a potter's wheel.[2] To prevent any worse treatment, the boy pretended that he had forgotten the previous life, although he had not. When he grew up, however, he began to tell some other persons about his memories, and eventually he wrote and published in Thailand an autobiographical account of them.

If a case is not private and is not suppressed, I may learn about it through one of many associates and assistants who have helped me—often first as interpreters—in different parts of the world. In India, Sri Lanka, and Thailand, cases are reported in newspapers from time to time. In contrast, cases are rarely reported in newspapers in Burma, Turkey, and Lebanon. In India the newspapers tend to publish reports of cases only if they have some dramatic feature, such as the case of Gopal Gupta, which included the detail—attractive to many newspaper readers—of a man shooting his own brother, a prominent man of the community where they lived. The newspapers of Sri Lanka and Thailand are less discriminating and publish reports of a wide variety of ordinary cases, as well as ones having sensational features. In the early days of my investigations, I depended heavily on newspaper reports for my first information about a case. In recent years I have done this much less, because some of my associates and assistants have become adept at locating unpublished cases, and also because now informants for one case that we are investigating often tell us about others, which we then schedule for study as soon as possible.

I am confident that the incidence of cases is much higher than the number of reported ones.[3] I have learned this particularly through the labors of some of my associates and of the persons whom I call sub-agents; these latter are persons who, having become interested in this research, have kept a close watch for cases occurring in their vicinity. Pins on a map indicating cases known to us sometimes show dense clusters around the towns where these admirable scouts live.[4]

In 1978 two of my associates, David Barker and Satwant Pasricha, conducted a systematic survey of cases on a sample of persons living in a designated part of the Agra District in Uttar Pradesh, India. They found an incidence of nineteen cases per thousand inhabitants. We need similar surveys in other regions of India as well as in other countries.

THE SOCIAL AND ECONOMIC BACKGROUNDS OF THE SUBJECTS

In Asia most of the cases I have investigated have occurred among villagers of poor economic means and little education; but that is the condition of most Asian families, and so there is nothing remarkable about the backgrounds of the cases. I should add, however, that we also find Asian cases among prosperous and educated town and city dwellers. Further analysis of our data may reveal patterns in the social and economic circumstances of the families concerned in these cases that I have not yet discerned.

I shall venture one comment under this heading with regard to cases in the United States. (I refer her to cases other than those found among the tribes of the Northwest.) I have noticed that the informants for these cases (usually the mothers of the subjects) tend to be residents of small towns and villages and to have had little education beyond high school. They are likely to be Christians who are more attached to Christ's teachings than to the various doctrines of the churches founded in His name. And they are likely to read occasionally or regularly one or more popular magazines dealing with paranormal experiences or the "occult." In this way they may have heard of reincarnation and of my research. Such qualifications make these persons protestants in the original meaning of that word: they need no intermediary directing them in matters concerned with religious belief. Most of them can therefore allow a child to talk about a previous life without becoming alarmed.

THE RECURRENT CHARACTERISTICS OF THE CASES

A fully developed case has five major features. It begins with a person—usually an elderly one—predicting that he will be reborn (after he dies); he often indicates to which parents or what place he would like to return. He later dies, and then someone—not necessarily a member of his family—dreams about his returning to a particular family. The baby is born and is found to have birthmarks (or perhaps birth defects) that correspond to wounds or other marks on the body of the deceased person whose reincarnation was expected. Soon after the baby begins to speak, he makes statements—rudimentary at first and then more detailed—about the deceased person's life. Finally, the child behaves in ways that are unusual in his family but that informants say match behavior that the deceased person had shown or that might have been expected of him.

Thus the fully developed case has a prediction of rebirth, a dream, a birthmark or birth defect, statements about the previous life by the child, and associated unusual behavior.[5] However, few cases show all five of these features. Specific predictions about reincarnation occur rarely. Also, even when three or four of the other features occur in a case, some elements may appear much more prominently than others. I shall next consider each of these five features in turn.

Predictions of Reincarnation Made before Death

As I have just said, specific predictions about where a person will be reborn occur rarely in most of the cultures where we find these cases. However, they do occur with notable frequency in the cases of two peoples: the Tlingit of northwestern North America and the Tibetans. I found that in ten (22 percent) of forty-six Tlingit cases the concerned previous personality had stated premortem his choice of parents in his next incarnation.

Many Tlingits also express wishes for physical, and sometimes other personal, improvements in the next life. Such aspirations sometimes represent hopes more than predictions; yet a small number of cases do suggest the fulfillment in one life of wishes expressed in a preceding one. Tlingits also sometimes predict the appearance on their next body of birthmarks that will correspond to scars or other marks on their (present) body. They mention these to aid in the later identification of themselves as having reincarnated.[6]

The lamas of Tibet also often make predictions about their next lives.[7] Their predictions tend to be more subtle and allusive than those of the Tlingit; nevertheless, they also may tell, or make hints about, where they expect to be reborn. To such indications they may add others, such as that they will have a birthmark on a particular part of the body. However, obscureness in the hints dropped by a lama concerning the place and circumstances of his next incarnation may leave his surviving disciples puzzled about how to interpret the indications given for them to find the lama's successor incarnation.

Among the cases of other cultures, predictions of rebirth, when they occur, tend to be a feature of cases in which an elderly person says that he will be reborn in his own family. I have studied numerous cases of this type in Turkey and in India. In these countries cases of claimed reincarnation within the same family are exceptional; but when a child does recall the life of a deceased member of his own family, that person has often predicted his reincarnation within the family.

Announcing Dreams

In many cases, someone connected with the (future) subject has a dream in which a deceased person appears to the dreamer and indicates his wish or intention to reincarnate. The dreamer is usually a married woman and a potential mother for the next incarnation of the person who is to be reborn. Sometimes the woman's husband, another relative, or a friend may have a dream of this type. I call these dreams "announcing dreams" because they occur, with a few rare exceptions, before the birth, and sometimes before the conception, of the subject.[8] Five examples occurred among the twelve cases that I summarized in chapter 4.

Announcing dreams have been reported in all of the countries where we find these cases. They happen with greater frequency, however, among the Burmese, the Alevis of Turkey, and the tribes of northwestern North America.

We have found that among the Burmese the dreams tend to occur *before* the subject's conception; among the tribes of northwestern North America, on the other hand, they occur nearly always during the last month of pregnancy and especially within the last few days or hours before the subject's birth.

The dreams also vary in their form. Among the Tlingit the discarnate personality appearing in an announcing dream often conveys symbolically his intention to reincarnate. For example, in the dream he may walk into the house with his suitcase and deposit it in one of the bedrooms; or he may enter the parents' bedroom and lie down between them. In contrast, announcing dreams among the Burmese often represent the discarnate personality as *petitioning* to reincarnate in the family chosen. This suggests that the dreamer has the option to refuse such a request.

Amusing contretemps can occur in connection with such dreams. A Burmese wife whose husband was away from home on a long journey had a dream in which a deceased friend seemed to be asking for permission to be reborn as her child; she did not like this proposal and (in the dream) told him not to come to them. When her husband returned from his journey, he told her that he had dreamed of the same old friend and had told him (in *his* dream) that he (the friend) would be welcome to be reborn in their family. In due course a child (Maung Aung Than) was born who later made statements suggesting that his father's acceptance had prevailed over his mother's attempted veto. His mother accepted the situation with the good humor characteristic of the Burmese.

Much less frequent than announcing dreams are what I call departure dreams. In a dream of this type, a member of a deceased person's family—his widow perhaps—dreams that the deceased person indicates the family in which he can be found after his reincarnation.

Some instances have occurred in which a member of a deceased person's family has had an apparent communication from him in a dream *after* the birth of the baby in whose body he is thought to have reincarnated. In one such instance the mother of a man who had died dreamed that her son appeared to her and said: "Help! I have got myself in a poor family. Come and rescue me." She obtained sufficient information in the dream to trace the child, who (later) had memories of her son's life. In two other instances the presumed previous personality of an infant communicated in a dream (had by a member of the previous family) his dissatisfaction with the infant's situation. In one of these, the previous personality complained that the infant's father was drinking alcohol excessively; in the other, the previous personality alleged that the infant's mother was feeding him at her convenience rather than when he needed feeding, and this was making the baby hungry.

In most announcing dreams the dreamer recognizes the person appearing to communicate his intention of being reborn. In some, however, the dreamer cannot identify the person in the dream, but after the child's birth she may notice that her baby resembles in appearance the person appearing in the dream. For example, Necip Ünlütaşkıran's mother, before her pregnancy with him, dreamed about a man unknown to her who had several bleeding wounds. When Necip was born, he had prominent birthmarks that were later found to correspond to fatal wounds on the body of the man whose life Necip (also later) claimed to remember, but his mother had known nothing about this man or his murder when she had her dream.

In some dreams later related to a case, the connection between the dream and the subject appears to be tenuous or even only symbolic. Among the Sinhalese, dreams in which an identified person appears in a dream occur rarely, but the Sinhalese sometimes interpret dreams of snakes, elephants, and other animals as having some connection with a case that develops later. I myself attach little importance to such dreams, especially those given a significance only after other developments in a case.

The more common type of announcing dream, which occurs before the child's birth or even his conception, tends to lessen the value of other evidence that may emerge later in the case. Such a dream nearly always disposes the child's parents to act differently toward the child than they otherwise might have done, and they may influence the child to adopt the attitudes of the deceased person, even without being aware that they are doing so.

Birthmarks and Birth Defects

Many subjects of these cases have birthmarks or birth defects that correspond, according to the informants and other sources of evidence, to wounds (or other marks) on the body of the related previous personality. In some instances a correspondence occurs between an internal disease of the subject and a similar one from which the previous personality suffered.

Since I cannot examine the body of the deceased person figuring in one of these cases, I have had to rely mainly on the memories of his surviving relatives and friends for information about the location of the wounds, or other marks, on his body; and since these informants usually know the location of the birthmarks on the subject's body, a temptation may arise to harmonize the memories of the wounds with the observations of the birthmarks. (Even when I am confident they have not done this, I recognize that some critics may think they have.)

I have overcome this objection in about thirty cases by obtaining autopsy or other medical records of the wounds on the concerned deceased person. The authors of these reports obviously wrote them without any knowledge of the birthmarks on the subjects, and indeed before the related subject of the case was even born. Moreover, since these medical records have confirmed (with some exceptions) the other testimony, based on memory, that I had already obtained from informants in these cases, they justify my general confidence in that testimony.

Birthmarks and birth defects related to the previous personality seem to me to provide some of the strongest evidence in favor of reincarnation as the best interpretation for the cases. They are objectively observable (I have photographed several hundred of them), and for most of them the only serious alternative explanation that I can think of is a psychic force on the part of the baby's mother that influences the body of the embryo or fetus within her. However, this explanation, which is itself almost as mind stretching (for the average Westerner) as reincarnation, can be firmly excluded in about twelve cases in which the child's mother and father had never heard of the identified previous personality until after the child's birth.

Birthmarks and birth defects figuring in these cases have the additional importance of suggesting a psychic influence on the devel-

opment of a person's physical body. The considerable double importance of birthmarks and birth defects—as evidence of reincarnation
and as evidence of a psychic force on human bodies—has led me to
report a large number of cases having these features in volumes now in
preparation. Because these are still unpublished, it would be inappropriate for me to discuss further in this one the cases with birthmarks and birth defects.[9]

The Child's Statements about the Previous Life

Under this heading I propose to discuss the age and manner of
the child's speaking about the previous life and the common themes of
the statements the child makes. I shall also briefly mention recognitions attributed to the child of persons and objects familiar to the
previous personality.

Age and Manner of Speaking about the Previous Life. A child who is
going to refer to a previous life nearly always does so for the first time
between the ages of two and five. If a younger child has imaged memories of a previous life, as some have afterward claimed they had, he
nearly always lacks the verbal skills to express what he wants to say.
Even so, some subjects begin speaking about the previous lives before
their verbal skills have developed enough for adequate communication of the images in their minds.

Children starting to speak this early often mispronounce words
and use gestures to eke out a deficient vocabulary. It may take baffled
parents a year or more before their dull comprehension—as it seems to
the child—and the child's improving powers of speech provide an
intelligible picture of the life he is trying to describe. A few examples
will help to illustrate the early age at which the children begin to
communicate their memories. Imad Elawar (in Lebanon) wanted to
say that in the life he was remembering he had a double-barreled gun;
he held up two extended fingers to represent the two barrels of the
gun. When Kumkum Verma (in India) wished to tell her family about
the occupation of the previous personality's son in her case—he was a
blacksmith—she gestured to imitate the movements of knocking a
hammer on an anvil and of working bellows. Pushpa, another Indian
subject, wanted to say that her husband had a bicycle repair shop; she
lay on her back and with her legs in the air made the movements of
pedaling a bicycle.

An analysis that my associates and I carried out on 235 cases in India showed that the average age at which the child began to speak about the previous life he remembered was thirty-eight months. The average age of first speaking about the previous life was the same or close to the same in the cases of five other cultures that we analyzed; for example, it was thirty-eight months in a sample of seventy-nine American cases.[10]

A few children do not remember a previous life until they are older, or they do not tell other people about any memories they have until they are older. Some children, even in cultures where people believe in reincarnation, do not speak about what they remember for fear that their family and friends will tease or scold them. (Suleyman Andary illustrated such inhibitions.)

In general, I become doubtful about the value of a case as evidence of anything paranormal if I learn that the subject first had memories of a previous life in later childhood or adulthood. I recognize, however, that some subjects seem to have had significant memories for the first time in adulthood. In the majority of these cases (as I explained in chapter 3) the memories have first occurred either after an emotional shock, as in the case of Georg Neidhart, or during or after meditation, as in the cases of Pratomwan Inthanu and Uttara Huddar.

The children vary widely in the amount of detail included in their memories. Some remember little of the previous life; others could talk a volume about it. A boy of Delhi probably holds the record for paucity of such memories: he said that he was from Bombay and could remember a lot of smoke and people weeping. That was all. (His statement about a lot of smoke and people weeping could have derived from a scene at a cremation ceremony, but this was not verified.) At the other extreme of abundance of detail in the memories we find cases like those of Edward Ryall, Marta Lorenz, and Swarnlata Mishra. Edward Ryall wrote an entire book filled with extraordinary details; a few were inaccurate and some unverified, but most were correct. He had some of his memories in later childhood, but most of them even later. Legitimate questions can be raised about the source of the many accurate details he said were memories, but here I am considering only the *amount* of these. The father of Marta Lorenz (subject of a case in Brazil) wrote down 120 statements that she made about a previous life when she was a young child. Unfortunately, someone accidentally discarded his notes, and less than a third of what Marta had said was ultimately properly recorded. As for Swarnlata Mishra (of India), she claimed to have almost total recall. Although this was probably an exaggeration, and was certainly never tested, she did have many more memories than most subjects have had. Unfortunately— and this time the cause was my own inexperience when I studied Swarnlata's case—only a small portion of her memories were adequately recorded.

More subjects may belong to the class of those with abundant memories than we now realize. Unfortunately, we reach few subjects during the peaks of their speaking about the previous life; too often we meet them only later, by which time many details may have slipped away and left a smaller residue of fading memories, or perhaps no memories at all. Some children's parents say that they too have forgotten much of what their child said earlier. Be that as it may, in most cases that I have studied, the informants have remembered between five and fifty separate statements that the child has made about the previous life.

The children vary widely also in their desire and apparent need to talk about the previous life. Some, like Mallika Aroumougam, talk about the previous life only when some object or event reminds them of a similar feature of the previous life. Others cannot keep off the subject and become bores or worse. They talk about the previous life so incessantly, even after several years, that the other members of the family may crave a meal without having to hear once again about how much better the child's previous life was than his present circumstances are. The number of details in a child's memories may correlate poorly with his desire to talk about them. Mahes de Silva, for example, remembered only a few details about a previous life, but he battered his parents—especially his mother—with them until it became a wonder that they applied no measures of suppression to him. Other parents have been less forbearing.

The subjects also differ markedly in the forcefulness with which their memories impinge on them. Some use the present tense in their statements. They may say, for example: "I *have* a wife and two sons," or "My house *is* much bigger than this one." (They may talk in this way even after they have learned to distinguish past and present with appropriate words.) Other children make a point of distinguishing the two lives in their remarks. They will begin some reference to the previous life with a phrase such as: "When I was big . . . "

Sometimes the children act as if they have been snatched without warning from the body of an adult and thrust into that of a helpless child.[11] When Celal Kapan, a subject in Turkey, began to speak, almost his first words were: "What am I doing here? I was at the port." When he could say more, he described details in the life of a dockworker who had fallen asleep in the hold of a ship that was being loaded. Unfortunately, a crane operator who did not know he was there allowed a heavy oil drum to drop on him, killing him instantly. From the evidence of the case, one might say that this sleeping man regained consciousness in the body of a two-year-old child. These cases remind me of the case of a woman who had a stroke and became unconscious while playing bridge. When she regained consciousness several days later, her first words were: "What's trumps?"

What I have said above may have prepared readers for my now saying that the children show differing expressions of emotion when they speak about the previous lives. Some speak of them with detachment, as if they are referring to far-off things; but the majority show a continuing strong involvement with the remembered people and events. Some weep as they talk about the previous life; others angrily denounce murderers who ended it. Teasing adults and siblings have brought some subjects to tears by falsely telling them that a spouse, other relative, or close friend of the previous personality was ill or had died.[12]

Some of the subjects pass rapidly from complete absorption in the memories of the previous life to the usual behavior of a young child. For example, a boy may gravely talk about his wife and children one minute, and the next minute run off to play a child's game with his young brothers.

A few children become abstracted from their immediate surroundings as they talk about the previous life. They may talk about it to themselves. Sometimes they may appear to onlookers to be in a partial trance; but the word *trance* may be inappropriately strong, because these children can be readily brought back to awareness of their environment. Cases like that of Uttara Huddar, in which an apparently total change of personality occurs, are extremely rare.

Most of the children have their memories only in the waking state. However, I have studied some cases in which the subject definitely or probably had memories of the previous life during dreams or nightmares.[13] Also, some children have tended to talk about the memories more when getting ready to go to sleep (and perhaps already drowsy) or soon after awakening.

Although most of the children have communicated their memories in words only, perhaps supplemented with gestures, some have also made drawings in which they depicted persons and events of the previous life.

The children nearly always stop talking about the previous lives between the ages of five and eight, but some stop earlier and others later. A few subjects claim to preserve all their memories intact into adulthood; and a few others pretend they have forgotten everything, although they apparently still remember much. Parents often credit themselves with having arrested the flow of a child's talk about a previous life by various measures they adopted to "help" him forget. Yet the children appear to forget the memories at about the same age regardless of whether their parents have encouraged them to remember or have forbidden them to do so.[14]

The usual age of forgetting seems to coincide with the increased activity of a child outside the physical and social environment of his immediate family. Whether or not he goes to school, this is a period when a child can no longer manage life solely by controlling other members of his family; he must adapt to other, less indulgent persons. I believe this adjustment brings new experiences, the memories of which cover and seem to obliterate those of the previous life. Another occasion for the beginning of forgetting that the subject's parents often mention is his first visit to the family of the previous personality. Sometimes, after such a visit, what had seemed before to be a torrent of talk about the previous life dries to a trickle and soon afterward ceases.[15]

The attention given a child who talks about a previous life appears to influence how long he continues talking about it; this is how I interpret our finding that children who talk about the lives of identified deceased persons go on talking longer than do children who speak about persons who cannot be traced. Children who remember verified previous lives (solved cases) continue speaking about them to an average age of just under seven and a half years, whereas children having unverified memories stop speaking about the previous lives at an average age of under six. When the child's statements cannot be verified, members of his family tend to lose interest in them; and without any encouragement from surrounding adults the child may soon cease to mention his memories. In contrast, if the statements are verified—and especially if the child then has the additional attention of another family, that of the deceased person about whom he has been talking—he has incentives and stimuli to continue talking about the previous life.[16]

Although social factors seem important in bringing on the amnesia for the memories, they are probably less important than developmental ones within the subject himself. The onset of the amnesia coincides with the rapid development of verbal language and the associated loss of visual imagery in the child. Memories of previous lives appear to occur primarily (in the child's mind) in the form of visual images.[17] Then as the child acquires the ability to speak, he gradually finds words with which he tries to communicate the content of these images to his family. However, the development of language leads in most persons to a layering over of visual images, which gradually become less and less accessible. Even the ability to have visual images becomes greatly impaired in most persons as they leave early childhood. After that age, most ordinary persons have visual images only in dreams or when deliberately reminiscing; apart from poets and artists, few adults preserve an ability to think normally with visual imagery.

I cannot emphasize too strongly that—with some exceptions—a child who is going to remember a previous life has little more than three years in which to communicate his memories to other persons, and he often has less. Before the age of two or three he lacks the vocabulary and verbal skill with which to express what he may wish to communicate. And from the age of about five on, heavy layers of verbal information cover the images in which his memories appear to be mainly conveyed; amnesia for the memories of a previous life sets in and stops further communication of them.

The Principal Themes of the Memories The child's memories tend to cluster around events of the last year, month, and days of the life remembered.[18] Nearly three-quarters of the subjects claim to remember how the person of the previous life died, and they remember this detail more often when the death was violent than when it occurred naturally.

In addition to the mode of death of the previous personality and the events immediately preceding it, the subjects may recall a wide variety of persons and objects with which the previous personality had been familiar. Recency of association with the person or object (on the part of the previous personality before death) appears more important than length of association in influencing the subject's memories. For example, Sukla Gupta remembered numerous details of the married life of Mana (the previous personality of her case), but she had almost no recollection of the family in which Mana had spent nearly all her life before her marriage.

The subjects usually remember the names of the previous personality and of some members of his circle of family, friends, and enemies. In cases in which the previous personality has been murdered, the subject tends to recall the murderer's name. Here again, however, many variations occur—not only from one case to another within a culture, but among cases of different cultures considered as groups. For example, the children of cases in India, Burma, and Thailand tend to remember the name of the previous personality, but those in Sri Lanka and North America (apart from the northwestern tribes) do not.

I attribute the general deficiency in remembering names among subjects in Sri Lanka to a common reluctance on the part of the Sinhalese people to use proper names in their everyday living. They prefer to address each other by titles or relationships, rather than by proper names.[19] Since repetition strengthens memories, the failure to use proper names in the everyday activity of one life could lead to poor retention of them in another.

However, for the corresponding deficiency in the memories of American children (for proper names) we must find another explanation, because Americans show no reluctance to use names in their ordinary communications with each other. So far, we have not been able to find a satisfactory explanation. For a time I thought that American children who remember previous lives had fewer memories of any kind than similar children of other cultures; this would have meant that their failure to remember proper names was only one aspect of a general paucity of memories. However, a comparison of the number of statements American children made with the number made by Indian children failed to support this conjecture. Nevertheless, American children do not make as many *verified* statements as Indian children; and it is possible that many of their statements derive from fantasies with which they fill gaps in real memories. This question is one of many awaiting further research.

Most of the subjects have nothing whatever to say about events between the death of the person whose life they remember and their own birth. In their memories this period is usually a complete blank. Parmod Sharma, the subject of an Indian case, passed over this interval in a single sentence when he said: "I was sitting in a bathtub, and my feet have become small." (This was a reference to naturopathic tub baths that the man whose life he recalled had taken just before he died.)

Nevertheless, some subjects do claim to remember events that happened between the death of the previous personality and their own birth. These memories are of two types: of terrestrial events (chiefly in the previous personality's family) and of experiences in a discarnate "realm."

In the first type, the subject remembers events happening to living persons after the previous personality's death. It is as if the previous personality had somehow stayed near where he had lived and died and had monitored the activities of living persons while he was discarnate; in fact, some subjects claim that they did just that. I mentioned in chapter 4 that Bongkuch Promsin remembered that Chamrat's murderers had dragged his body into a field and that he (the then discarnate Chamrat) had stayed at a bamboo tree near the murder site until he saw Bongkuch's father. Disna Samarasinghe (a subject in Sri Lanka) remembered that the body of Babanona (whose life she recalled) had been buried near an anthill; the burial site had been chosen only after Babanona's death.

Veer Singh, the subject of another case, in India, claimed that after death in the previous life he had remained near the house of the previous family. As evidence of this he gave an account of the food consumed at family social occasions, such as weddings. There was nothing especially remarkable about his description of the food at the weddings, which is just as predictable as the conventional food served at Western weddings, although different. More impressive was his assertion that he had accompanied members of the family who went out of the house alone at night. This matched a dream that the mother of the previous personality (Som Dutt) in this case had had. She had dreamed that the discarnate Som Dutt told her that he was accompanying his older brother, who was slipping out of the house at night and attending fairs being held in the region. (Upon being asked, the brother acknowledged that he had been doing just that, but the other members of the family did not know it until the mother had her dream.) Veer Singh also showed knowledge of other private family matters occurring after Som Dutt's death and before Veer Singh's birth, such as lawsuits involving the family, a camel they had purchased, and children born during this interval.

The Thai monk, Chaokhun Rajsuthajarn, to whose case I referred earlier (in describing the futile efforts of his parents to suppress his memories), remembered that after dying in the previous life he had attended the funeral of the person whose life he recalled. At this time, he said, he had a sense of lightness and seemed to move easily from place to place. He thought that he was in charge of the ceremony and was receiving the guests; in fact, however, he was invisible to the participants, who went on with the ceremony with no suspicion of his presence.

Occasional subjects claim to have engaged in poltergeist activity while discarnate. Veer Singh said that he had broken the plank of a swing on which people were playing; and Tinn Sein said that he had thrown a stone at the man who later became his father (in the next incarnation).

The second, commoner type of memory of the period between death and presumed rebirth is that of another realm where the subject claims he sojourned—usually not knowing for how long—after death in the previous life and before his birth in the present one. Disna Samarasinghe gave a rather circumstantial account of her stay in such a place after the death of Babanona, the old lady whose life and death Disna remembered. The clothes one wore there were rich and elegant, she said, and they needed no washing. One could have food, which appeared when one wished for it, but there was no need to eat. She met a kindly "ruler," who eventually advised her to get herself reborn, but did not tell her where.

Subjects in Burma and Thailand (and occasionally elsewhere) who have memories of a discarnate realm may describe meeting in it a sagelike man who befriends them and later guides them to a family for their next rebirth. The Burmese monk Ven. Sayadaw U Sobhana, who (as a child) remembered a previous life, gave one of the fullest descriptions I have of a meeting with such a discarnate advisor. He recalled that the sage had brought him back to the village where the previous personality had lived, had taken him first to that person's house, and finally had led him to another house a few doors away and left him there; this was the house of Ven. Sayadaw U Sobhana's parents, where he was born.[20]

Recognitions. Subjects frequently claim that if someone would take them to the village or town of the previous life they would be able to meet and recognize persons (and also recognize places) they knew in that life. Reports of recognitions by the subject of persons, places, and objects with which the previous personality was familiar figure in the testimony of many cases. These recognitions usually occur when the child's parents take him to visit the previous family, or when members of the previous family who have heard about the child first come to visit him.

The informants for these cases attach much more importance than I do to such recognitions, which rarely occur under even partially controlled conditions. When the child meets members of the previous family, he is almost always surrounded by a number of persons varying from a few members of the families to a huge crowd. They frequently ask the child leading questions, such as "Do you see your wife here?", and the expectant stares of the encircling people toward the previous personality's wife may then make it impossible for the child to answer incorrectly.

I must add, however, that recognitions by the child under two types of circumstances deserve credit. First, a child may unexpectedly and spontaneously recognize someone he sees, for example, someone walking along the street. Corliss Chotkin, Jr. (whose case I summarized in chapter 4), thus spontaneously recognized a stepdaughter of Victor Vincent (whose life he was recalling). She was at the docks in Sitka, where Corliss happened to be with his mother. Corliss, suddenly noticing her, called out excitedly: "There's my Susie." In this instance, Corliss's mother was acquainted with Susie, although she had not noticed her before Corliss did. In the best of these spontaneous recognitions, the subject identifies someone who is completely unknown to any person with him. Ampan Petcherat, a subject of Thailand, spontaneously recognized on the street of the small town where she lived an aunt (Joy Ruang Gun) of Chuey, the boy whose life she remembered. Ampan's mother, who was with her, had not previously known Joy Ruang Gun. Another subject, İsmail Altınkılıç of Turkey, spontaneously recognized two ice cream vendors who came along the street outside his home. Members of İsmail's family probably knew these persons by sight, since they came into the area to sell ice cream; but they did not know their names, which İsmail stated. In the too few incidents of this kind, there can be no question of prompting by the subject's family members.[21]

Second, in a small number of situations, responsible adults have managed to control conditions so that persons the child might recognize were presented to him in a secluded and tranquil setting, and the only question asked was: "Do you recognize this person?" Gnanatilleka Baddewithana, the subject of a Sri Lanka case, made several recognitions under these conditions when her case was first studied (not by me). I did not witness these, but I have been present on a few other occasions of similarly controlled recognitions, including a later one by Gnanatilleka. For it, I brought to her house a friend of Tillekeratne, the boy—Gnanatilleka's was another case of sex change—whose life she recalled, and another person whom Tillekeratne had not known. Gnanatilleka, upon being asked whether she knew these persons, gave the name of the previous personality's friend (with a slight error, saying "Dora" instead of "Lora"), but did not recognize the other visitor. When asked where she had known the recognized visitor, she correctly gave the town's name (Talawakele); she might perhaps have inferred the name of the town from the circumstances of being asked to make this recognition, but not, I think, the name of Tillekeratne's friend.

On another occasion, without prior announcement I brought to a subject in Burma, Ma Choe Hnin Htet, a close girlfriend of the girl whose life Ma Choe Hnin Htet remembered. When Ma Choe Hnin Htet was asked whether she knew this person, she distinctly said the girl's name. However, Ma Choe Hnin Htet did not recognize (under similar circumstances, but at another time) the cardiac surgeon who had operated on the previous personality. (This girl had died during the operation.)

One other common feature of the recognitions deserves mention. Some subjects, after making a recognition that by itself is of no particular significance (perhaps because leading questions had been posed), make further pertinent remarks spontaneously. For example, they may mention a nickname the recognized person had had, or make some telling personal comment, such as "What has become of your teeth?"

Jasbir Singh (a subject in India) provided an example of the use of a nickname. When a man called Birbal Singh came into a room where Jasbir was, he spontaneously said: "Come in, Gandhiji." Someone present corrected him by saying: "This is Birbal." Jasbir replied: "We call him 'Gandhiji.'" Birbal Singh was in fact called "Gandhiji" because he had large ears and somewhat resembled Mahatma Gandhi. (The suffixed *ji* is a commonly used honorific in Hindi.)

Swarnlata Mishra (the subject of another case in India) recognized a friend of Biya (the woman whose life she recalled) and commented that he was wearing spectacles, which he had not done during Biya's life. Disna Samarasinghe (whose description of the discarnate realm I mentioned above) recognized a boy passing along the road outside her family's house. She said to her parents: "Do you know that child? This is the boy who stole my green gram." Disna's parents later learned that the boy in question was the grandson of Babanona (whose life Disna was remembering) and that as an infant he had eaten and spilled some gram that Babanona had been cooking and left unattended while she bathed.

The spontaneity with which many subjects state nicknames or make references to little, often long-forgotten episodes in the life of the previous personality seems to me one of the most impressive features of the cases. It damages the criticism sometimes put forward that the subjects (before these meetings) had crammed themselves (or had been crammed by their parents) with normally acquired information about the previous personality.

The Child's Behavior Related to the Previous Life

Subjects of these cases often show one or both of two types of behavior that are unusual in their families.

First, the child may show emotions toward the family of the previous life that are appropriate for the memories he claims to have. If the previous life was a happy one, and less often when it was not, he may ask—or even clamor—to be taken to see the surviving members of the previous family. When he meets them, he may show joy, familiarity, aloofness, or rejection; these reactions nearly always accord closely with what can be learned or conjectured about the previous personality's relationships with these persons.

The case of Ratana Wongsombat (in Thailand) provides an excellent example of a subject's discriminating responses to members of the previous personality's family. Ratana was overjoyed to meet Anan Suthavil, the daughter of the old lady, Kim Lan, whose life Ratana remembered; but she was indifferent, and later even inimical, toward Kim Lan's husband, to whom Kim Lan had barely spoken for the last years of their unhappy marriage. Gnanatilleka Baddewithana's behavior toward the family of the boy (Tillekeratne) whose life she remembered illustrated the same differrentiating capacity. Gnanatilleka was extremely friendly with Tillekeratne's sisters and with one of his schoolteachers; but she was almost offensively cool toward his brother. Tillekeratne had had a good relationship with his sisters, and had adored the schoolteacher, but he disliked his brother, who seems to have been unkind, perhaps even cruel, to Tillekeratne.[22]

The child's later attitudes and behavior toward the previous family depend to some extent on how its members receive him. In some cases the child wins total acceptance by the previous family; they invite him for visits and give him gifts or more substantial support.[23] In other instances, the previous family rebuffs the child, and the first visit becomes the last. This happens often—and for the most part only—when the family of the previous personality is much wealthier than that of the subject, and its members fear (unreasonably in my experience) that the subject and his family will mulct them.[24] In the majority of cases in which I have been able to make later observations, the two families have exchanged friendly visits for a few years and then have gradually ceased to meet as their lives developed in different ways.

The second type of unusual behavior consists of traits (such as fears, likings, interests, and skills) that are unusual in the child's family but that correspond to traits the previous personality was known to have had or could be reasonably conjectured to have had. The other members of the subject's family in such instances either show no similar traits or show them to a lesser degree; and the development of the traits cannot be attributed to any event the child experienced before the trait manifested.

Phobias related to the previous personality's mode of death have particularly impressed me. And they occur frequently. Among 252 cases in which the previous personality had died violently, we learned of phobias in 127 (50 percent). If the previous personality died of drowning, the subject is likely to show a phobia of water; if he died from being shot, the subject is likely to have a phobia of firearms.

The children with phobias frequently show responses that seem to be generalized from the original stimulus. Thus Ravi Shankar Gupta, who remembered being murdered by a barber, showed a phobia not just of this murdering barber (who was still around when Ravi Shankar was a young child), but of *all* barbers. A subject of Turkey (studied by Can Polat) who remembered the life of a man who had been killed by someone called Hasan had a phobia of everyone with the name *Hasan* (fairly common in Turkey).

Sometimes the child manifests a phobia before he has learned to speak and to explain the apparent cause of the phobia in the previous life. In summarizing the case of Shamlinie Prema, I mentioned that soon after she was born she had shown an extreme fear of being immersed in water when her mother tried to bathe her; when she became able to speak, she described how she had drowned in a previous life. Another, similar example occurred in the case of a boy of Sri Lanka, Lal Jayasooria. He visibly reacted to the appearance of policemen before he could speak, and he would hide from them as best he could; he later described a previous life as an insurgent.[25] (The police in Sri Lanka had suppressed an insurgency in 1971 with unnecessary violence.)

Likings for particular foods (and aversions to them also) form another large category of unusual behaviors the subjects show. I earlier mentioned Bongkuch Promsin's fondness—almost a craving—for sticky rice, a food to which his family was indifferent but which had been the favorite food of the youth, Chamrat, whose life Bongkuch remembered.

Individually, few of these behaviors are specific; many children show them and so do many adults. But collectively they become impressive, because the subjects often show a *syndrome* of behaviors that sets them apart from other members of the family but that characterized the person the subject claims to have been. The following examples will illustrate such groups of unusual behavior. Ma Tin Aung Myo showed masculine traits, a phobia of airplanes, play at being a soldier, and several "Japanese-like" behaviors; Sujith Lakmal Jayaratne manifested, when a young child, cravings for alcohol and tobacco and had phobias of trucks and policemen; Shamlinie Prema had phobias of buses and of being immersed in water, as well as having somewhat unusual tastes for particular foods; and Erkan Kılıç (of Turkey) showed a phobia of airplanes and a fondness for alcohol, and he played at running a nightclub. All these sets of behaviors were appropriate for the previous personalities concerned.

Subjects of a social class markedly different from that of the previous personality often show particularly vivid unusual behavior. Thus a child of poor parents who claims to remember having belonged to a wealthy, upper-class family may disparage and scold his parents for their poverty and their low-class habits. I mentioned earlier that Gopal Gupta shunned household work on the grounds that he had servants to do it. Another Indian subject, Bishen Chand Kapoor, looking contemptuously at the cheap clothes his family gave him, said that he would not give such clothes to his servants.

Conversely, a child remembering a previous life in a family of circumstances inferior to his own may behave in a coarse manner that members of his family find disagreeable. An Indian subject, Swaran Lata, who was born in a Brahmin family, remembered the life of a sweepress (a member of the lowest caste). She had many lovable traits, but her personal habits were (to her family) repulsively dirty, and she horrified her vegetarian family by asking for pork. Unlike the other members of the family, she willingly—almost eagerly—cleaned up the excrement of younger children. Some children who recall lives in inferior social circumstances also express pleasure and gratitude when they compare their situation with that of the previous life. For example, Anusha Senewardena (of Sri Lanka) was delighted with, and thankful for, foods like marmalade, which were ordinary in her wealthy family; she recalled the life of a poor village schoolgirl who had had only a bun for lunch, and had even had to share that with another child.[26]

Most of the unusual behaviors that I have described in this section exemplify the kind of memory that I described in chapter 1 as behavioral memory. The behavioral memories often persist longer than the imaged ones. When this happens, the child may continue to show some behavior (for example, liking particular foods) after he can no longer remember details in the life of the previous personality who had had similar behavior. For example, Bishen Chand Kapoor told me that he continued to eat meat (whenever he was away from his vegetarian family) many years after he had almost forgotten his earlier memories about the life of a person who had eaten meat. Ravi Shankar Gupta (of India), whose phobia of barbers I mentioned above, remained afraid of the murderers of Munna (the boy whose life he remembered) after he could no longer remember the origin of his fear (although he understood it from what other persons had told him).

In keeping with their remembered adult status, many subjects appear to their elders to be more mature than other children of their age. They adopt an adult demeanor and at times an air of condescension toward other children and even toward some adults.[27] After all, what else should we expect from a married man with a wife and children, even if he is a boy of only four? Some of these children may, however, also match rank with service; the mother of a young girl subject may find, for example, that she can trust this daughter with household responsibilities at a much earlier age than she can her other daughters.

One of the most interesting and most important types of unusual behavior shown by subjects is that usually observed in the children who say they were a member of the opposite sex in the previous life. (These are the subjects of what I call cases of the sex-change type or sex-change cases.) Most such children show (in varying strength) habits of dressing, ways of speaking, play, and other behavior appropriate for the sex of the life remembered. The cases of Ma Tin Aung Myo and Erin Jackson, which I summarized in chapter 4 illustrate such behaviors.[28]

The Interval between Previous Personality's Death and Subject's Birth

With the exception of a small number of outliers and cases with anomalous dates (which I shall briefly describe later in this chapter) the interval between the previous personality's death and the subject's birth is usually less than three years. The median interval varies from culture to culture and ranges from six months among cases in Lebanon to forty-eight months among Tlingit cases.[29] The median interval for 616 cases from ten different cultures was fifteen months.

There is a widespread subsidiary belief about reincarnation according to which violent death leads to a more rapid reincarnation than natural death. Our cases tend to support this idea. Among the pooled cases of northwestern North America (from which region our vital statistics are most reliable) there was a (statistically) significantly shorter interval between death and presumed rebirth in cases with violent death compared with those having a natural death. We obtained similar results in an analysis of cases in India.

THE ATTITUDES OF THE ADULTS CONCERNED
IN THE CASES

When parents (and other adults) hear a child talking about a previous life, their initial reaction depends on their convictions concerning reincarnation. The usual Western parents do not merely disbelieve in reincarnation; they do not even think it possible. For some such parents, a child who claims to remember that he lived before is susceptible to bizarre fantasies, if he is not indeed a monstrous liar. Such parents think chiefly of how they can limit the scandal if word gets around in their community that they have procreated such an abnormal child. The Western cases that have come to my attention have occurred in families in which the parents did not have this attitude or overcame it if they did.

In Asia and other parts of the world where people are hospitable to the idea of reincarnation, a case starts off on a better footing. In these regions parents of a child who talks about a previous life do not consider him to have lost his mind; they accept that he may in fact be having memories of a real previous life that he lived before being born in their family. However, parents in India and in Burma (but not, so far as I know, elsewhere in South Asia) consider that it is unhealthy and perhaps even fatal for a child to remember a previous life. This may lead them to suppress him. Apart from this, the child's parents take up positions toward his statements and behavior according to the *content* of what he says and the implications for their family life if he continues to talk about it and if what he says becomes generally known.

If the child is talking about a previous life that seems to have been ordinary, his parents may not trouble themselves much about the matter. Many of the lives talked about, however, have not been ordinary. For one thing, many have ended in murder, and the attitude of the murderers may have to be taken into account; they may still be in the neighborhood and dislike the subject's aspersions on them. Such a child's parents may thus think it expedient to silence him.

Many subjects of these cases reject their parents on the grounds that they are not their "real" parents; these, they say, live elsewhere and must be gone to or brought to the child. Such attitudes put a severe strain on even the most affectionate parents. No parent wants his child to reject him, and sometimes a negative reaction by the parent to the child's invidious comparisons increases the child's isolation in his family. Fortunately, in the places where these cases occur most often, the belief in reincarnation has provided a cushion against the child's rejection of his parents. Since the parents believe in reincarnation, they reason—with themselves and sometimes with the child—that some larger process has brought them (parents and child) together in a new family unit; even if the situation is not a happy one, it probably has some ultimate good purpose, they will say.

The children of poor parents who claim to have lived previous lives in luxurious upper-class homes pose another difficulty. Such a child's parents may find their initial tolerant amusement over his pretensions gradually displaced by a sense of vexation as the child continues to denigrate the hovel in which they live. I sometimes wonder whether the widespread superstition in India that a child who talks about a previous life is destined to die young may not have originated as a handy excuse for suppressing a tiresome child. Be that as it may, many parents do eventually resort to various measures of suppression. (I described some of them in note 2 of this chapter.) It may surprise readers to learn how many cases are suppressed in India for one reason or another. In a small series of Indian cases, 27 percent of the subjects' mothers and 23 percent of their fathers took some measures, often violent ones, to suppress the subject.[30] These are figures from cases we learned about; we have no knowledge of the frequency with which completely successful suppression prevents us from ever learning about cases so handled.

Parents do not suppress cases only in India. In other countries also they may disapprove of children talking about previous lives, and for a variety of reasons. Among the Tlingit of southeastern Alaska a child may start talking about a murder related to a quarrel between septs, and his parents, not wishing to start up an old clan feud that has been quiescent, may hush him up. When I was with the Igbo of Nigeria, I heard several times that parents consider it harmful for a child to talk about a previous life that ended violently.

Whether or not the parents have attempted to suppress the child, word of what he has been saying usually leaks into the community. The neighbors then begin to assess the merits and weaknesses of the case; sometimes they even hint maliciously at contrivance and exploitation on the part of the parents, and this may stimulate the parents to try to vindicate the child, something they can only accomplish by verifying what he has been saying. This fits the subject's plans, because he has usually been asking them to take him to the previous family. And so, with one of these several incentives, but most often because of either the child's importunity or their own curiosity, they nearly always try to locate the family to which the child seems to be referring.

The least important of all motives among the adults concerned in a case is that of converting other people to a belief in reincarnation. The simple villagers—among whom, for the most part, these cases occur—care not at all whether other persons share their convictions about reincarnation. Sometimes they themselves have had doubts about its reality, but even if a case has helped to relieve these doubts, this does not seem to fill them with missionary fervor to influence other people. (Critics who believe the contrary would find astonishing the skepticism that relatively uneducated villagers may show in appraising the claims of a subject to be a particular deceased person reborn.) Better-educated persons may express more interest in the relevance of a case to their traditional beliefs; some of them show an understandable satisfaction in thinking that a particular case confirms what their elders taught them to believe. Yet none of these persons (known to me) has tried to publicize a case for purposes of religious propaganda.

THE LATER DEVELOPMENT OF THE SUBJECTS

I have already mentioned that the children of these cases usually forget their memories—or at least stop talking about them—between the ages of five and eight. Most have completely forgotten the previous life by the age of eight, and many have done so at an even younger age. The behavioral memories tend to diminish as the imaged memories do; but, as also mentioned earlier, they sometimes continue for many years after the imaged memories have completely faded.

As the child forgets his imaged memories of the previous life, and his behavioral ones yield under the influence of new experiences, his further development is generally entirely normal. I have been able to follow into adulthood many subjects whom I first knew when they were young children. Some have married and now have children of their own. Nearly all have taken appropriate places in society and have no conspicuous features of behavior that might make them obviously distinguishable from their peers. This last remark includes the behavior of the subjects of sex-change cases who, when they were young, showed traits of the opposite sex. Most of them, as they grew older, accepted their anatomical sex. In this respect Ma Tin Aung Myo has been exceptional instead of typical.

Paulo Lorenz (of Brazil) was another exceptional subject of a sex-change case. He remembered the life of his sister Emilia, who committed suicide in young adulthood. Emilia had been masculine in her outlook, never married, and predicted that if she reincarnated she would be a man. Paulo Lorenz was markedly feminine when he was a young child, and, although he became more masculine in later childhood and adulthood, he never married. He too was a lonely, depressed person, and he committed suicide in his forties.

Rani Saxena (of India) was another subject of a sex-change case who intransigently retained some masculine attitudes into middle life. Although she had married and had children, she still used masculine verb forms (in her late thirties, when I knew her). Hindi is a language in which some verb forms identify the speaker's sex, and Rani's use of masculine verb forms communicated her continuing strong identification with a male lawyer whose life she remembered.[31]

A few other subjects have found the later path stony for reasons other than claimed sex change. Sometimes their difficulties seem to arise from their inability to leave the previous life behind and move ahead in the present one. Jasbir Singh, who was born in a Jat (low caste) family of India, remembered the life of a (high caste) Brahmin. As a young child he exhibited caste snobbishness toward his family that led him almost to starve, because he refused to eat their food, which he considered polluted. This in turn earned him beatings by his older brother. As he grew up he seemed to lose some of his sense of superiority, but, although he then ate his family's food, he still thought of himself as a Brahmin; for example, he tacked the Brahmin name of the man whose life he remembered onto his Jat family's name. When he became a young man, he had great difficulty finding employment that he considered appropriate for a person of his status. Eventually, one of my colleagues in India (who had studied Jasbir's case with me) found him a job, which Jasbir accepted; but our next news of him was that he had quit the job because of its menial nature, which he considered beneath the dignity of a Brahmin.

Occasionally, the subjects become so absorbed in the memories of the previous life that they fall behind in schooling. This happened to Parmod Sharma, another Indian subject. When he was a young child, he spent much of his time playing that he was managing a shop for selling biscuits and soda water. (This had been the occupation of the man whose life he remembered.) His mother told me that he spent so much time at this kind of play that he lost a year of school, and in scholastic accomplishment he never fully recovered from this. He later performed poorly in college, and when I last met him (he was then in his early thirties), he had a low-level clerical position with the government, one that seemed to me distressingly far below his natal capacities.

I am unable to say why behavioral memories persist for many years in some subjects but not in others. For example, against Jasbir's entrenched adherence to his identity as a Brahmin we could set Jagdish Chandra's happier development. Jagdish Chandra, who was born in a family of Kayasths (a middle-level caste), remembered the previous life of a Brahmin child; when he was young, he had marked Brahmin traits, but as he grew older he lost most of these, although a few persisted into his middle adulthood. I mentioned above three subjects of sex-change cases who continued to show some traits of the opposite sex in adulthood. In contrast to them, Ampan Petcherat, the subject of another sex-change case, showed masculine behavior in childhood but developed a normal feminine orientation in her teens and early adulthood. The different course of development in these subjects may be due to the different ages of the previous personalities when they died. Jagdish Chandra and Ampan Petcherat remembered the previous lives of young children, who perhaps had not lived long enough to develop hardened attitudes of Brahminism or masculinity, whereas such attitudes might have been developed by the adult previous personalities who figured in the cases of Jasbir Singh, Ma Tin Aung Myo, Paulo Lorenz, and Rani Saxena.

However, we must consider at least two other factors that may influence the fading or persistence of behavioral memories. First, the subject's parents may either indulge or oppose unusual behavior and accordingly affect whether it persists or not. Jagdish Chandra's father used the powerful weapon of laughter when his son assumed poses of superiority as a Brahmin, and he thereby probably contributed to Jagdish Chandra's giving up his Brahmin attitudes. On the other hand, the two families concerned in the case of Veer Singh (another Indian subject, to whose case I referred in describing memories of the period between death and birth) reacted in ways that prolonged the conflict he had about caste differences between the families. Like Jasbir Singh, Veer Singh was born in a Jat family and remembered the life of a Brahmin; this Brahmin was a child, Som Dutt, who had died naturally at the age of about four. Veer Singh exhibited Brahmin snobbery when he was young, but one might have expected him to lose this trait as he became older, on the grounds that Brahmin attitudes could not have been strongly developed in Som Dutt by the time he died. But Veer Singh's family allowed him to spend much time with Som Dutt's family, and while he was with them he naturally lived as a Brahmin. They, however, did not fully accept him, and as a consequence in early adulthood he was half-Jat and half-Brahmin in his attitudes.

Another factor that might contribute to the strength, and hence the persistence, of behavioral traits would be a series of incarnations under similar circumstances. A person who had, for example, six successive incarnations in male bodies before having one in a female body might have more difficulty in adjusting to life as a female than would a person who had had only one previous incarnation as a male. We could extend this principle to many other traits that may persist in unusual strength. Chauvinism of all varieties—social, sexual, religious, national—may derive some strength from repeated incarnations in the same type of body, the same circumstances, or the same country.

In the preceding paragraphs of this section, I have discussed the tendency of the outward circumstances of a life to consolidate habits. (In this I count the sex of a person's body as one of the outward conditions of a life.) I think it probable, however, that the most important factor in the persistence of behavioral traits that may be carried over from one life to another is inflexibility of attitude—the inability to adapt to different circumstances.

SOME VARIANT TYPES OF CASES

Before concluding this chapter, I shall refer to two types of cases that depart significantly from the "standard" case.

Xenoglossy

In chapter 3 I briefly referred to xenoglossy, the ability a few persons have demonstrated to speak a foreign language they have not learned normally. Authentic cases of xenoglossy contribute importantly to the evidence for human survival after death.[32] Xenoglossy does not, however, figure prominently in the ordinary case of the reincarnation type, even when the subject claims to remember a previous life as a person who spoke another language;[33] few subjects of this group appear able to speak the language spoken by the previous personality, although informants said that several of them learned that language (for example, English taught in an Asian school) more rapidly than their siblings did. A few other subjects of this group seemed to learn their mother tongue slowly and imperfectly, a condition I have called glossophobia.[34]

Cases with Anomalous Dates of Death and Birth

In a small number of cases, the subject was born *before* the person whose life he remembered died. (The intervals vary between a day or two and several years.) In a case of this kind, taken at face value, it would seem that the subject's body was fully made and presumably occupied by one personality before another one took it over. We may be talking here about a type of body theft, often called possession.

The quickest way to rid oneself of such awkward cases is to suppose that errors have been made in recording the dates, and in some cases vagueness about the exact dates supports this conclusion. I have satisfied myself, however, that in at least ten cases of this type we have obtained accurate dates and the anomaly remains.[35]

Having now summarized twelve typical cases of the reincarnation type and described what we have observed as recurrent features in a much larger number of cases, I shall next, in the following two chapters, describe my methods of investigating these cases and how I analyze and interpret them.

CHAPTER SIX

Methods of Research

I begin this chapter with a short history of the investigation of cases of the reincarnation type. Then I briefly mention some of my observations when I first began to investigate these cases in the early 1960s. Next, I summarize the principal improvements in methods of investigating the cases that I have introduced. This section leads to the main part of the chapter, in which I outline the methods that my associates and I now use. Because we now usually work in a team to which my associates contribute as much as I do, it is appropriate (in this section) to describe what *we* do rather than what I do.

THE INVESTIGATION AND REPORTING OF CASES BEFORE 1960

A few claims to remember previous lives have come down to us from ancient times. Of these, the most notable are those of Pythagoras[1] and Apollonius[2] (whom I mentioned in chapter 2), but few authentic details about their claims were recorded. The earliest account of a case that has features recognizably similar to those of the modern cases that I have studied is probably the Indian one (which I also mentioned earlier, in chapter 2) that the Emperor Aurangzeb investigated early in the eighteenth century.[3] Following it, I know of no similar case until that of Katsugoro, a Japanese boy of the early nineteenth century who remembered the life of a farmer's son.[4] And after Katsugoro's case, there was another long gap until the publication of summaries of six Burmese cases in 1898.[5]

Between 1900 and 1960 a number of cases (mostly in India) were reported in newspapers, spiritualist magazines, a French journal of psychical research, and separate books and pamphlets.[6] Because most of them were published as reports of a single case, or of a few cases only, it was easy to disregard each one as an unimportant aberration and to overlook the common features in the cases that would encourage closer examination of similar ones. In the 1950s I began to collect and compare the published reports of cases that I could find. Once I began to look for them systematically, I succeeded in finding forty-four that were reasonably detailed and appeared to be authentic. (I have since learned of additional case reports from this period.) In 1960 I published an article giving short summaries of seven of these cases, together with a discussion of several possible interpretations.[7] My main conclusion, which seemed a rather startling one at the time, was that the evidence these cases provided, defective as it was, appeared to justify careful investigation of any further cases of this type that might present themselves. I did not have long to wait. In 1961 I learned about a new case in India, received a small research grant to go there, and thus began my field investigations.

EARLY INVESTIGATIONS IN THE 1960s

Nothing had prepared me for the abundance of cases that I found in India when I first went there in 1961. The reports of the eighteen from India that I included among the forty-four analyzed in my first paper on this subject had been gathered over a period of about thirty-five years; and yet during my first five weeks in India I learned about no fewer than twenty-five cases. It immediately seemed clear to me that only a small portion of all the earlier cases had penetrated the barriers to communication and generated a published report. Since 1961 my colleagues and I have investigated more than 300 cases in India, and we still do not know what relation our sample bears to the total number of cases that occur there.[8]

There were other aspects of these cases for which I was unprepared as well. The published reports that I had studied were concerned almost exclusively with the statements a subject had made about the previous life; they sometimes alluded to pertinent recognitions that the subject had made, but only a few described the subject as showing behavior that was both unusual in his family and harmonious with what could be learned or conjectured about the previous personality. Accordingly, I found myself both surprised and impressed by what informants told me (in 1961) about the remarkable behavior of Jasbir Singh, whose case was one of the first I ever investigated. In the preceding chapter I mentioned that he had refused to eat his family's food on the grounds that he was really a Brahmin; and since Jasbir's family were Jats, their food and manner of preparing it were unacceptable to him.

However, my surprise over this and other unusual behavior I learned about did not lead me at once to make adequate inquiries: it took more years than I like to admit before I realized the significance of such behavior. It seems to me now, years later, that when we evaluate the cases, this unusual behavior, when it occurs, should receive at least as much study as the subject's statements, and possibly more. I shall explain my reason for this opinion later.

My 1960 review of the older reports drew attention to some recurrent features of the cases, such as the extremely young age of many of the subjects when they first began to speak about a previous life and the tendency for the apparent memories to fade as the child grew older. My early fieldwork with new cases in the 1960s confirmed the frequency of these features and soon began to show others, such as the high incidence of violent death among the persons whose lives the children subjects remembered.

The abundance of the cases and the repeated occurrence in them of certain features pushed me onto the piercing horns of a dilemma. Should I study a small number of cases intensely so that I could presume to say later what the most probable interpretation of each one was? Or should I study a large number of cases less thoroughly (although sufficiently to be reasonably confident of their authenticity[9]) in order to analyze them for recurrent features? In the second choice, the larger number would presumably allow for better-founded conclusions (provided not too many faulty cases gained admittance to the series through a lessening of vigilance). In the end, I was unable to discard either of these strategies and tried to adopt them both. As a consequence, I have much data from each of a small number of thoroughly investigated cases and less data (on each case) for a larger number of cases that I have studied more superficially.

I have now intensely investigated about 250 cases (in India and other countries) and at least another thousand less thoroughly, but yet sufficiently to consider them deserving of inclusion in our analysis of recurrent features. The remainder of the cases in the collection of the University of Virginia have been investigated by my associates and assistants or (in a few instances) by other persons in whom I have confidence, usually from direct acquaintance with them. We have also included in our series the now proportionately small number of cases whose reports (published between 1890 and 1960) first stimulated my interest in the prospects for this research.

PRINCIPAL ADVANCES IN RESEARCH METHODS SINCE 1960

A few of the best case reports from before 1960 bear comparison with the best we can offer today. For the most part, however, they fail to furnish sufficient information for a sound judgment about whether the subject could have gained his knowledge about the previous life by normal means. Too much in them is summarized; we are not told enough about the chronological order of events in the development of the case, about exactly what the subject said, when he said it, and to whom; and we are told little or nothing about who verified his statements. To remedy these problems the methods I have adopted emphasize the following procedures: interviews with multiple firsthand informants; recording who said what and when; evaluation of the credibility of informants; repeated interviews with the same informants to check for consistency of their reports and to study details previously missed; independent verification, whenever possible, of the subject's statements with informants who either knew the previous personality or had reliable information about him; and locating and copying all pertinent written documents, such as records of significant dates, hospital records, and reports of postmortem examinations.

These methods are not new; lawyers and historians have used them for centuries, and so have psychical researchers since their earliest days in the last quarter of the nineteenth century. We have some equipment, such as tape recorders, that they lacked; but we have not improved on their principles in the investigation of cases that seem to show paranormal processes.

My adaptations of these methods and the additions of some of my associates did not develop smoothly and effortlessly. It took years for us to design a reasonably adequate Registration Form on which we record the principal demographic features of the families concerned in a case and which also has an aide-mémoire reminding us of many details about which we should inquire. Also, in my early interviews my notes had deplorable gaps, as I did not at first appreciate the importance of recording what informants said verbatim or nearly so; and it was only around 1970 that we began systematically to record the questions we put to informants as well as the answers given.

I shall now describe the main features of our present methods, beginning with the interview, which is by far the most important of them. [10]

CURRENT METHODS OF RESEARCH

Methods of Interviewing

The Persons Interviewed. Our most important informant, if he will talk with us, is the subject of the case himself. Children vary greatly in their affability with strangers, and the interpreters with whom I have worked have varied also in their ability to help the children become comfortable and talk with us if they wish to do so.

Next to the subject himself, the parents are usually the main informants; and if the subject does not care to talk with us or no longer remembers the previous life, his parents become the most important informants. After the subject's parents, we like to hear the testimony of other persons involved, such as grandparents, siblings, neighbors, and other members of the community. We require that all the persons we interview be firsthand informants,[11] not busybodies merchandising tertiary fragments of information. (Unfortunately, such persons sometimes obtrude into interviews in Asia and Africa, where one can rarely find a private place to talk; and they have to be gently set aside.) Intelligent members of the community (other than members of the subject's family), such as village headmen and schoolteachers who have heard the subject speak about the previous life, often give valuable information. They are more detached from the case than the subject's parents and can listen to him with less emotion—whether of enthusiasm or vexation—concerning what he says. These persons often help us also to appraise the reliability of the principal informants, such as the subject and his parents. When someone tells you his opinion of another person, he generally tells you more about himself than about the other person; but he does tell you *something* about the other person, and I find that one informant can sometimes aid my assessment of the value of another one.

After we have recorded (usually in written notes, but sometimes on tape) what the subject and his family can tell us, we go to the family of the previous personality (if he has been identified) and begin a new, similar series of interviews with the members of that family and community.

In most cases we do not reach the scene of a case until after the subject and his family have met the family of whom he has been talking. However, if they have not identified this family, we try to do so ourselves whenever there seems a reasonable likelihood of success, and sometimes even when success seems unlikely but worth trying for. Thus, even when the child has not given much information about the previous family, we may search for a family corresponding to his statements. I think this effort justifies any time spent because, since we have already recorded what the subject has said, if we succeed, we shall add to the small number of cases in which we can firmly exclude the possibility that informants later misremembered what and how much the subject actually said before the families met. As I shall explain later, errors in the informants' memories seem to me now the most likely explanation for these cases other than reincarnation itself.

How the Interviews are Conducted. At the beginning of an interview with an adult informant (following appropriate introductions and explanations of what we are trying to do), we ask an open question or make a general request, such as: "Tell us how the case began," "What did you notice first?" or "Tell us everything you know about the case." We then record the first flow of whatever the informant says, without our interrupting—unless to check obviously irrelevant digressions. Afterward we go back to particular statements or events that the informant mentioned and ask for more details or clarifications. Then we turn to questions concerning matters that we consider important but that the informant may have omitted. Here we may work the informant onto unfamiliar ground; if so, we take pains to explain to him why we are asking certain questions, since he may not immediately understand their relevance.

Certain informants are too shy or too inarticulate to give a spontaneous narration. We try to help these persons—even at the beginning—by asking specific questions. Similarly, in the clarification phase of the interviews we often need to ask direct and even leading questions. I have no phobia of leading questions, but we do make a note of the fact whenever we ask one.

Most informants are unaware of the importance of the difference between firsthand testimony and hearsay; and many are not even aware that there is a difference. Consequently, some of our effort goes to telling (and reminding) the informant that he should say only what he has witnessed himself.

We never (or almost never) use secondhand testimony either for information about the subject's statements and behavior or for information about the previous personality. In general, we do not even listen to secondhand witnesses, although, as I mentioned above, they sometimes press themselves importunately on us and have to be sifted out from true eyewitnesses. Occasionally, however, we use information furnished by a secondhand informant as a guide to firsthand sources and in the appraisal of these.

How the Information is Recorded. We prefer to take notes instead of making tape recordings. The latter become filled with irrelevancies, and they miss many of the nonverbal features of the interviews. (We can note the more important of these in writing as the interview proceeds.) We can also review written notes more easily than a tape-recording when we need to learn quickly about possible omissions and discrepancies; it is sometimes important to note these before we leave the area of a case so that we can remedy the former and inquire about the latter on a second interview the next day. We do, however, like to record on tape whatever the subject himself tells us that he remembers about the previous life. In addition, we sometimes use tape recorders when an informant seems to have little time to give us or we ourselves become pressed to leave the site of an interview sooner than we wish. (Drivers of taxis and bullock carts have less interest in these cases than we have, and we must sometimes adjust to their needs.)

Whenever it is feasible, two members of our team take notes during an interview, and I have often been able to arrange for this, at least in recent years. When this is done, one assistant or colleague acts as the main interpreter (where one is needed); a second assistant makes notes in the language of the informant and, at the same time, monitors the accuracy of the first assistant's translation; and I make notes in English (or in French when appropriate) of both the questions put to the informant and the answers given. In the evening after the interviews (or sometimes later), we have often reviewed the two sets of notes for the day's work. When we do this, we note and discuss discrepancies and omissions and may decide that we need another interview to clarify doubtful matters. Sometimes I have compared the accuracy of my note-taking against a tape recording of an interview.

In the next chapter I shall discuss the difficulties involved in reaching the best interpretation for these cases. Here I wish to emphasize that by being meticulous about the accurate recording of what the informants tell us, I have tried to transfer to them responsibility for whatever imprecisions get into my reports.

I have to use interpreters for many interviews, and this raises the question of their competence and the possible influence of biases they may have on the information expressed and recorded. Probably some errors in translation have occurred from time to time, as I have noted (when I have detected them) in my detailed case reports. However, I do not think these have been numerous or damaging. In several different countries, I have been fortunate in having the same interpreters work with me for a decade or longer. They have become used to my methods, and together we have identified some of the words and phrases in the languages used that are particularly liable to faulty translation. Moreover, by recording the questions asked as well as the answers given, I can observe whether the interpreter is asking my questions or pursuing his own line of inquiry. The more experienced interpreters often think of better ways of phrasing a question than I have, and they may also suggest further questions to pursue a point that seems to them important. They have thus become collaborators more than assistants in the interviews. [12]

The Information Obtained during the Interviews with the Subject's Family. The information that we like to obtain falls into five main categories. These are: 1) what the child has said about the previous life; 2) what possibilities existed for normal communication of information to the child; 3) observations of any unusual behavior shown by the child that apparently relates to the previous life; 4) information about the mother's pregnancy with the subject and about the subject's early development; and 5) miscellaneous information about such factors as the subject's birth order in the family, appraisals of his intelligence, the social and economic circumstances of the family, and the attitudes of the adults concerned toward the case.

I mentioned above that we prefer to record the subject's own account of his memories, if he still has any and if he is willing to tell us about them. However, often the subject is too shy—at least initially—to talk freely with us; and sometimes the parents wish to tell their accounts before letting the child speak. In these cases, we ask the parents to tell us whatever they can about the child's statements concerning the previous life. I attach particular importance to their memories of the child's first, often half-articulate, communications. We particularly wish to learn what the child said spontaneously, as opposed to what he may have said in response to questions. And we try to separate what he said before the two families concerned in the case met, if they have met, from what he said afterward. Anything he said after they met—or even at the time of their first meeting—has much less value when we come to appraise the evidence that the child had knowledge about the previous life that he could not have obtained normally. Nevertheless, we do record these later statements by the subject as well as the earlier ones.

Some parents confuse their own inferences with the child's statements, and we have to pare away a crust of the former before we can reach the latter. Imad Elawar's parents made numerous inferences about his statements, and as his was one of the first cases I investigated, I was unaware at first that they had done this. A woman to whom Imad frequently referred and who they thought was a sheikh's wife turned out to be the previous personality's mistress. Imad's parents told me that he had mentioned a relative called Amin who was a judge and lived in Tripoli (Lebanon). In fact Imad had said only that Amin worked in the courthouse in Tripoli; on hearing this his parents promoted Amin to a judgeship, although he was a government official who happened to work in the courthouse building.

In 1986 I observed (in Sri Lanka) one of the most extreme instances of mistaken parental inferences I have ever known. The subject was a young girl, Wimalawathie Samarasekera. (She was called Wimala for short.) Wimala's mother told us that she had said that in the previous life her father had been a doctor whose name was Wijesekera, she had lived in Colombo 3 (a particular district of the city of Colombo), she had attended St. Thomas's College, and she had died in an automobile accident when her (previous) mother drove a car off the road into a drain. After patiently repeating requests to learn exactly what Wimala had said, we learned that she seemed to have a precocious knowledge of medicine (unusual for her family, which had no medical people in it) and she had mentioned the name Wijesekera; so her mother assumed that the previous father was a Dr. Wijesekera. Wimala had said she had lived in Colombo, and she had mentioned the number 3; her mother assumed that she was referring to Colombo 3, although she might just as well have been trying to give the number of a house in a street. Wimala had made numerous references to

"Baby Jesus," and this led her family (who were Buddhists) to think that the previous personality had been a Christian. It was an easy step to suppose then that the previous personality had attended a Christian school, St. Thomas's College; but Wimala had not said this. Finally, although Wimala had mentioned an automobile accident in which the previous mother had driven a car off the road into a drain, she had not said that she had died in this accident. Wimala's family thought it would be easy to find a family corresponding to her statements, and this might have been true if she had really said what they assumed she had said. In fact, she had given rather scanty specific information, and her case remains unsolved.

Eliciting information about possibilities for normal communication between the two families requires the most careful attention to detail and possibly needs more patience—on the part of both informants and investigators—than any other aspect of the investigation. The informants are usually unaware of the subtle opportunities that may exist for the normal communication of information; they sometimes expect us to accept their statements of not having previously known the other family as putting an end to the need for further inquiry on the topic. Yet from pushing these inquiries, we have sometimes found possibilities for contacts between the families that they themselves had overlooked.

For example, in the case of Pushpa (in India) I found that although the two families concerned in the case had never met, they had bought their vegetables at the same market, which was a place where the subject's family might have overheard talk about the gruesome murder of a Sikh girl by her husband, to which Pushpa referred in her statements. I do not think this happened, but it was a definite possibility.

In another Indian case, that of Sunita Khandelwal, I learned that the subject's uncle had had a slight acquaintance (through his business) with the father of the previous personality. The two families *immediately* concerned in this case lived in towns located about 250 kilometers apart, and each was being completely honest when they asserted that they had never even been to the other family's town, much less heard of that family's existence. However, the subject's uncle and the previous personality's father had met in connection with their businesses—both were jewelers—in the city where the previous personality had lived. (They had no social relationship.)

In a third Indian case (already mentioned twice), that of Parmod Sharma, I learned that the subject's uncle had sometimes bought biscuits at a shop in Moradabad (about 125 kilometers from where Parmod lived) that had been owned by the previous personality of this case and was still, when the case developed, run by members of his family.

In all three of these cases, I eventually concluded that the subjects' families had not learned normally about the details of the previous lives; but I had a stronger conviction about this after I had examined and reasonably excluded the possibilities that we discovered for normal communication between the families.

The information obtained about the subject's behavior falls into two categories. First, we learn everything we can about the child's manner of speaking about the previous life and about the circumstances that appear to stimulate his utterances concerning it. Does he show strong emotion when he speaks about the previous life? To what extent does he ask or demand to go to the family he seems to remember? Does he make comparisons between the present and previous families? Second, we learn of whatever observations members of the subject's family may have made about unusual behavior he has shown that seems related to his statements about the previous life. Such behavior, which I discussed in chapter 5, may include unusual fears, likings, aptitudes and skills, tastes for food or dress, or attitudes of humility or hauteur toward other persons.

We next compare the subject with his parents and siblings, so that we can try to estimate how unusual his behavior is in the family. We also search for models of it in his environment and for specific experiences that might account for it, such as a history of the child's having been burned that might explain a phobia of fire.

The Information obtained during Interviews with the Previous Personality's Family. When we meet members of the family the child has talked about, we ask them to evaluate the accuracy of all the child's statements about the previous life. His parents usually say that they have verified the most important of them and perhaps all of them, but I attach great importance to making my own independent verifications. On a number of occasions the parents have claimed that a child's statement was correct when it was not. (This can be innocent; during the usual excitement associated with the first meetings between the families, it is easy for participants to neglect or misunderstand details.) Occasionally also, informants for the previous personality's family may tell us about correct statements the child had made that the child's family had not heard or had not mentioned when they talked with us.

From the family of the previous personality we also learn what we can about his character. In doing this we often have to work against the almost universal tendency to magnify the virtues of the dead and diminish their vices. (Fortunately, many human attributes that pertain to these cases are morally neutral—deserving neither blame nor praise—and hence we can expect informants to report them candidly.) The deceased person's relatives may also tend to harmonize their reports of his personality with what they know about unusual behavior on the subject's part; and the subject's family may embroider their reports of his behavior in order to make it seem closer to that of the previous personality than it was. However, it is a mistake to think that the principal informants for these cases are always enthusiastic about them and therefore always trying to improve their reports of them. On the contrary, it is rare to find both families eagerly supporting a case; one or the other may—for various reasons—regard it negatively or with indifference, and sometimes both families do. And yet if both families do accept the case as authentic, they may unintentionally smooth out the wrinkles of discordance in their observations and reports to us. Here again, observers more detached from the case, such as neighbors, can often help us more than the persons closely associated with the subject and previous personality.

Written Documents

In the study of these cases, written records have particular importance, although they are unfortunately rare. They supplement memory and often correct it. Thus we try to examine (and copy if possible) diaries, horoscopes (for birth dates), hospital records, birth and death registrations, reports of postmortem examinations, and any other written or printed material that has recorded some detail before the case developed or has fixed it with more certainty than memory alone usually can. In a few cases the parents or other relatives of the subjects have written out their own accounts of what a child said while he was at the phase of talking most about the previous life, or soon afterward. These records are especially precious documents in the study of a case.

Psychological Tests

I have so far made scant use of psychological tests in the investigation of these cases. I should like to undertake or sponsor a systematic testing of subjects and compare them with a group of their peers matched for sex, age, and socioeconomic circumstances, but this has not yet been feasible.

In cases of the sex-change type, I have found that an extended Draw-a-Person Test may contribute helpful information about the subject's sexual identification.[13] The main information provided by the test comes from the child's selection, on free choices, of the sex of the person he draws and from the sexual characteristics of the persons represented in the drawings.

Second and Later Interviews

I tend to become absorbed in the interviews and may forget that the informants—especially busy housewives—often have other things to do. I nevertheless try, sometimes under the prodding of my associates, to end the interviews before the informants have become exhausted or annoyed. (Interviews of vexatious length do not seem to happen often, because the informants nearly always welcome us back warmly for further interviews.)

In any case, a period of withdrawal from the subject's family is desirable until we have interviewed informants for the previous personality's side of the case and reflected on the information already obtained. Moreover, after leaving the scene of an interview I invariably think of additional questions that I should have asked during it; sometimes I think of these questions only much later. If the questions thought of later seem important, they usually lead to further visits from me and my associates.

A published case report requires an orderliness that we cannot expect the informants to provide as they speak to us, often in gushing streams of uninterrupted talk; I have to sort out all the information obtained and arrange it as coherently as possible. The drafting of a case report frequently exposes additional questions that I failed to ask and thus may stimulate another interview.

I have other motives for returning besides that of obtaining information I should have obtained earlier. Later interviews enable us to check the consistency of what the informants say. This does not mean that inconsistencies are necessarily marked against them: they may have remembered some additional details after we left; they may have come to think differently about some they had mentioned earlier; or a more skillful way of putting a question the second time may elicit a more reliable answer. On second and later visits we can also sometimes meet informants who were away at our first visit. One may compare the accumulation of information about a case to the building up of a mosaic: many items, some seemingly insignificant in themselves, gradually fit together and allow a picture of the whole to be seen.

Questionnaires

During the course of these investigations, my associates and I have developed several questionnaires that have proven useful in focusing on particular aspects of the inquiries.

One of these questionnaires explores in detail an informant's beliefs about reincarnation, including such matters as when and how it may occur, to whom, and for what purpose.[14]

We use another questionnaire for making systematic inquiries about masculine and feminine behavior in cases of the sex-change type. And with a third questionnaire, we have tried to systematize the inquiries we make about the unusual behavior that so many of the subjects show in connection with their statements about previous lives.

Follow-up Interviews

In recent years we have given increasing attention to observing the further development of the subjects, and this provides us with still another reason for later visits. In the follow-up interviews we try to answer the following questions: Has the child stopped talking spontaneously about the previous life? If so, when did he cease to speak about it? What seemed to influence him to stop talking about it? Has he forgotten or has he just given up expressing what he still remembers? Does he continue to show unusual behavior related to the previous life, even if he appears to have forgotten his imaged memories of it? To what extent has his remembering a previous life influenced his relations with other members of his family and with persons outside it? Have the memories he had of a previous life helped or hindered his overall adaptation in the present one?

At the beginning of this chapter I explained that, when I first began to study these cases, I quickly found a large number of them; and they have continued to be abundant ever since. However, I also learned in that same early period that finding and investigating cases was far easier than deciding how best to explain them. In the next chapter I shall describe my approach to the analysis and interpretation of the information we obtain about the cases.

CHAPTER SEVEN

The Analysis and Interpretation of the Cases

In describing my methods for conducting this research, I mentioned my inability to choose between the thorough investigation of a small number of individual cases and a more superficial study of a larger number. If this indecision was unwise, it has at least led to our being able to analyze the cases in two ways. We can examine individual cases and try to find for each the best interpretation (or interpretations); and we can search a large series of cases for recurrent features and ask ourselves about the meaning of any that we find. I shall consider these two types of analyses successively; but before coming to them, I must first explain why I think we have data worth analyzing.

THE RELIABILITY OF THE TESTIMONY

I have already explained that, by giving careful attention to the identification and avoidance of errors in translation and to the careful recording of what informants say, I have tried to pass responsibility for the accuracy of the data to the informants. Only a small amount of our data derives from written sources,[1] and we cannot directly observe much in these cases ourselves.[2] We obtain at least 90 percent of our information by listening to the oral testimony of informants. The value of what we learn in this way depends on the accuracy of the informants' statements. This, in turn, means that we must evaluate the reliability of their memories and appraise whatever tendencies they may have to distort, in their communications to us, whatever they do remember. I shall here say something about the accuracy of the informants' memories, but shall defer until a later section of the chapter my discussion of motives on the part of the informants to distort the testimony.

We need to appraise an informant's ability to remember accurately events that happened days, weeks, months, and sometimes

years before the date of his telling me and my associates about them.
To what extent can we depend on testimony of this kind? Numerous
experiments have shown how extremely unobservant some persons
can be. Experiments that demonstrate this usually consist of staged
scenes, often violent ones, about which witnesses are asked to write
reports from memory later. Subjects in such experiments may completely fail to observe and remember important details, and they may
get others badly confused. Yet these same experiments also show that
witnesses may be wrong about some details but correct about others
and correct in reporting the main events they observed. Moreover,
since the main events, such as a staged scene of violence, did really
occur, the mixing up of details in reports about them cannot be used
to deny this. Lawyers recognize this in their appraisal of eyewitness
testimony of accidents; a witness may be wrong about which of two
automobiles involved in an accident had the right of way, but correct
in saying that both were speeding and that they crashed together.
Critics sometimes forget this point and suggest that an event about
which a witness muddled some of the details may never have occurred
at all.[3]

I have a further reason for discounting experiments in eyewitness
testimony as necessarily discrediting the reliability of the data in the
cases I have investigated. These experiments all require the observer
to notice and remember details about an event that occurred once and
during a few minutes only. A single occurrence and a brief duration are
features also of one type of evidence in these cases: the recognitions
often attributed to the subjects, which occur in a flash and one time
only. I am, therefore, not surprised—and have frequently mentioned
in my reports—that eyewitnesses of recognitions often disagree about
just what took place when a subject is said to have recognized a person
known to the previous personality in a case. The frequent occurrence of leading questions and other types of cueing of adults, as I
mentioned earlier, further reduces the value as evidence of most
recognitions.

However, other types of events in these cases are not analogous to
the staged scenes that have shown defects in eyewitness testimony in
such circumstances. For example, the subject of a case nearly always
repeats his statements about the previous life, often over several years
and frequently so often that he makes himself a nuisance in his family.
Similarly, the associated unusual behavior—of demanding specially

prepared food, cross-dressing, or whatever it may be—also usually continues over years, and often for even longer than the child's statements. These repetitions and prolongations of utterances and behavior tend to fix the memories of such events in the minds of those who observe them.

I do not deny that inaccuracies often occur, and the detailed case reports that I have published are sprinkled with notes about discrepancies in the testimony of different informants. My principal defense against such errors has been the use, whenever feasible, of two or several informants for the same event. In this way I think I have been able to understand many of the discrepancies. What is more important, however, I think I have obtained a satisfactorily accurate account of the main events of the case, even when informants have made mistakes about some details.

I should like to try to remove a common Western prejudice concerning informants' memories, which is that the memories of uneducated persons, such as Asian peasants, are worse than those of educated persons. I am sure this opinion is wrong. Accuracy of memory derives from many factors, but education has not been identified as one of these.

The foregoing remarks are only preliminary. I shall discuss further the reliability of the informants' testimony in considering different explanations for the individual cases.

However, before coming to these explanations I shall take up the important question of how we decide when we think we have identified the single deceased person to whom the subject's remarks could apply.

THE IDENTIFICATION OF THE CORRECT
PREVIOUS PERSONALITY

One of the first questions to settle about a case is whether the subject's statements have been verified or can be verified, if this has not already been done. In short, has a deceased person been found, or can such a person be found, the facts of whose life correspond to the statements (and also to the behavior) of the subject? In this respect the cases seem to fall into three groups.

First, there are cases in which the subject gives so little specific information about the previous personality, especially proper names of people and places, that no corresponding person can be traced. We sometimes forget that without our names we would not lose our identity, but other persons might lose their ability to identify us. Consider, for example, the difference in specification between "Sir William Robertson, a British general of the First World War," and "a soldier called Robertson." One could easily trace the first Robertson, but not the second one. Of the latter we do not even know whether he belonged to the British, Canadian, Australian, or United States armies, or for that matter, the French foreign legion; nor do we know during what period he may have lived. Unless we had some other narrowing clues we should probably not even attempt to trace such a man, because the inevitable result would be the discovery of many soldiers called Robertson, any one of whom might be the person we are trying to find. The case of a subject who could furnish no better identifying information about the previous life he seemed to remember would remain unsolved.[4]

However, if a subject of a case can precisely locate the previous life geographically and can state two or three other adequately specific details, we may solve his case, even though he mentions no personal names. I studied such a case in Sri Lanka in 1986. The subject, a boy called Sidath Wijeratne, stated no personal names, but he said that he had lived at Balapitiya, where he had dealt in fish and had owned a green Jeep. Balapitiya is a small coastal town about 100 kilometers from where Sidath lived. Only one person in Balapitiya owned a green Jeep, and he was a fish merchant. Sidath's few other statements about the previous life exactly fitted this man's life, and I consider the case solved.

The case of Dolon Champa Mitra is another that I consider adequately solved despite Dolon's inability to state personal names among her numerous statements about a previous life. She gave the name of the city, Burdwan, where she said she had lived, stated many accurate details about the life of a young man who had lived there, and eventually located the house of this man's family. Inside the house she made a number of recognitions, some of them under conditions that I consider satisfactory.

In the second group of cases, we achieve verification but some doubts remain about whether we really have found the right deceased person. In this group the subject furnishes enough specifying information to permit tracing a deceased person who fits his statements. The more specific and the more numerous the child's statements are, the more confident we can become that we have found the correct person; but for one reason or another, some doubt may linger.

Concerning the identification of the correct deceased person in the case of Indika Guneratne, I remained for several years in doubt. Indika, like Dolon, gave the name of the city of the previous life (in his case Matara, in Sri Lanka); but he mentioned only one other proper name, that of a servant called Premadasa. Fortunately, he referred to wealth and to owning elephants, details that narrowed the search considerably. Even so, seventeen details that Indika had mentioned applied correctly to two wealthy citizens of Matara who had owned elephants. Other items Indika had stated were incorrect for one of these men, but fitted the second; a clinching detail was his having had a servant called Premadasa, whereas the other candidate had not. Only a careful examination of both men's lives enabled me to feel confident about the one to whom Indika's statements applied and therefore to feel justified in considering the case solved.

I have mentioned the applicability of many of Indika's statements to two different men in order to show the trap into which unwary parents (and investigators) may fall if they think too quickly that a child's statements apply to a particular person when they may apply as well, or almost as well, to many other persons. I think that this sometimes happens when parents become too eager to achieve closure in considering to whom a child's statements about a previous life may refer.

We can sometimes observe such attitudes among the Druses of Lebanon. Although parents of subjects in India are usually in no hurry to look for the family about whom their child is talking—they may put this off until they can no longer tolerate the child's insistent demands to be taken to the family—parents in Lebanon seem often to feel pressed to find the family of the person about whom their child is talking; and this may lead to mistakes. So may an equally strong desire of many grieving Druse persons to find where a deceased family member has been reborn. It is important therefore to recognize cases in which the identification of the correct deceased person must remain in doubt.

In the cases belonging to the third group the subject has stated so many specifying names and other detailed information that we can confidently assert that his statements refer to one deceased person and could not refer to any other. The children of Burma seem particularly adept at establishing the identity of the person whose life they remember. They often state the name of that person together with the names of his spouse and parents and murderer, if there was one. Among my cases, however, the record for stating proper names is held, not by a Burmese child, but by Suzanne Ghanem of Lebanon. I recorded a (probably incomplete) list of fifty-nine items she had stated about the previous life that she remembered. Her statements included the names of twenty-three members of the family to which she referred and two acquaintances. Moreover, she placed all but one of these persons in their proper relationship to Saada, the woman whose life she remembered.

THE ANALYSIS OF INDIVIDUAL CASES

In considering individual cases we need to keep before us the question: Could the subject of the case have acquired his information about the previous life normally? If, in addition to his statements, the child shows unusual behavior apparently related to them, we also need to ask whether he might have developed such behavior as a result of imitating other members of his family or as a result of experiences he had since his birth.

When we ask the first of these questions, we can see immediately that in two large groups of cases the child's statements can rarely provide any evidence of paranormal processes; these are cases in which no person has been found whose life corresponds closely enough to the subject's statements (unsolved cases) and those in which the person identified as having this correspondence lived in the subject's family or close to where it lived ("same family" or "same village" cases). In unsolved cases the question rarely arises of our deciding that the child has information he could not have obtained normally, because his statements remain unverified[5]; and in the same-family and same-village cases we can almost never obtain convincing evidence that the child had not been exposed normally to the details of which he had knowledge. (Cases of these two groups may, it is important to note, have features other than the child's statements—unusual behavior or birthmarks, for example—that warrant our attention.)

I shall, therefore, in the remainder of this section, discuss the appraisal of cases in which the two families live in different communities and say that they had no previous acquaintance with each other before the case developed. We call these long-distance cases, but this phrase does not imply that we are measuring the value of a case only by the number of kilometers separating the families. In a country like India, for example, families living in neighboring villages, but belonging to different castes, may be more isolated socially than families of the same caste living a hundred kilometers apart.

Given, however, a case in which the two families concerned live in separated communities, we must assess possibilities for normal communication between the families concerned. There are several types of cases in which a child might seem to show unusual knowledge about a distant family, even though the knowledge had been obtained by some normal means.

The most obvious possibility for normal acquisition of the information is fraud. Hoax cases do occur from time to time. I have studied one case in India that was definitely a hoax (prepared by the subject) and have learned of two other faked cases, one in Israel and one in Lebanon.[6]

Perhaps I have been hoaxed in some cases without knowing this. I cannot deny that this may have happened, but I think it can only have happened rarely, if ever. My confidence in this assertion comes from familiarity with the circumstances and motives of the people among whom these cases are usually found. The average villager in Asia and Africa does not have time to devise and perpetrate a hoax. He sometimes begrudges the time we take for our interviews; a hoax and its related cover-up would take far longer. One can see no profit in money from a case and usually none, or only the slightest, in local fame. Moreover, with the multiple interviews that I usually conduct, a fraud would require the cooperation of numerous witnesses, any one of whom might forget his rehearsed lines or defect from the other conspirators. The child designated as subject of the case would also need to be drilled, because we have sometimes heard subjects repeat, more or less exactly, the statements their parents said that they had made. I have occasionally heard adults prompting children subjects, and although I strongly disapprove of this, it has never seemed to me to be more than an expression of the prompting adults' eagerness not to have the child let them down in front of strangers, when they know that the child could, if he would, tell the strangers (my associates and me) what they themselves have often heard him say.

If we can eliminate fraud, we should next consider gross self-deception in the development of a case. I have studied a few cases in which it appears that the entire case developed out of the wishes of the people concerned. In these cases the previous personality is typically a famous person of the community, the country, or the world. During our days of investigating cases in southcentral Turkey Reşat Bayer and I learned of no less than three Alevi children who were identified as being the reincarnations of President John F. Kennedy. The father of one of these children, Mehmet Alkan, had dreamed of President Kennedy a few hours before the birth of a son (in November 1965), and he named the son "Kenedi" (giving the name a Turkish spelling). In November 1967 Reşat Bayer and I met the two-year-old Kenedi, and his father told us that he was saying that he was President Kennedy. I am sure that Mehmet Alkan was unaware of the likelihood that he was imposing another identity on his son; this was not a hoax, even though Mehmet Alkan, and later Kenedi, picked up some kudos in their village. (President Kennedy was the best known and most highly regarded American president among foreign peoples since Franklin D. Roosevelt.) There is a sequel. In 1985 Can Polat learned of the case of Kenedi Alkan and met him. He was then a young man of about twenty. He firmly believed that he had been President Kennedy in a previous life. He claimed to remember a few details about Kennedy's life, such as that he had been rich, married, and had two children. He showed Can Polat a birthmark—on his chest, the wrong place for anyone claiming to be the reincarnation of John F. Kennedy. Cases of this type are relatively uncommon in my experience and I think they are fairly easy to expose.

If we exclude fraud and self-deception, as I think we can in nearly every case, we are still left with two other, far more subtle, ways in which observers may incorrectly credit a child with unusual knowledge of a person who had lived far away.

The first of these involves an unobserved transmission of the information to the child by persons who knew the previous personality. For example, a visitor from another community may come to the child's house when his parents are away, and, while the subject is playing unnoticed on the floor, the visitor may tell a servant of the family about a man who had been murdered where the visitor lives. The child could absorb this information and later incorporate it into a fantasied previous life. We can easily imagine variations of this process. The child's parents may themselves have learned about the deceased person and forget later that they had done so; in the meantime, however, the child may have obtained the information from the parents either normally or by telepathy.

A person who obtains some information normally and later forgets that he has done so is said to show "cryptomnesia" or "source amnesia." I consider the possibility of cryptomnesia in almost every case I study. The results of inquiries have occasionally surprised me. As I have penetrated a case more deeply, I have sometimes found that, even though the two immediate families were unacquainted before the case developed, they turned out to have one or more mutual friends; in other instances, they had more possibilities for indirect communication with each other than they had earlier realized. In the last chapter I mentioned three cases (those of Sunita Khandelwal, Pushpa, and Parmod Sharma) in which the two families concerned had had some slight contact with each other. I found no evidence in any of these cases that information about the previous personality had passed from one family to the other; but I could not decisively exclude the possibility that this had happened.

I am, however, sure that cryptomnesia is not the correct explanation for most long-distance cases. In the first place, in many cases in which I have pushed inquiries just as far as I did in the cases of Parmod, Pushpa, and Sunita, I have not found even the slight links between the families that I found in those cases. [7]

However, there are other objections to cryptomnesia as an explanation of these cases. First, I do not think a young child can assimilate from a single overheard conversation the information needed to compose a credible set of previous life memories. (I assume his exposure to the information occurred only once; otherwise, if it happened repeatedly, the child's parents would, I think, have known about it.) At the age when the subjects first talk about the previous life, they often lack the vocabulary they need for communicating the images they seem to have. It is doubtful, therefore, although not impossible, that such a young child could understand the words the average adult would use in describing, say, a murder that he had learned about.

A further objection to cryptomnesia as an explanation—at least for some cases—comes from the knowledge shown by some subjects of private affairs that were not known outside the previous personality's family and could not therefore have been disseminated as the publicly known details of a sensational murder might be. I have already given one example of such a private matter in chapter 4, where I mentioned Gopal Gupta's knowledge of Shaktipal Sharma's attempt to borrow money from his wife. Two other excellent examples figured in the cases of Swarnlata Mishra and Erkan Kılıç. Swarnlata mentioned an occasion when the previous personality in her case and another woman had gone to a wedding in a village (which she named), where they had had difficulty finding a latrine. Erkan Kılıç knew that a watch the previous personality in his case had given to a friend had tooth marks on it.[8]

My last objection to cryptomnesia seems even weightier than any of those I have already mentioned. These cases consist of much more than a display of information communicated in words, and any interpretation of them must include the unusual behavior that most of the children show in relation to what they say about the previous life. In the case of Pushpa, for example, let us assume that in the vegetable market she had heard talk about the fatal stabbing of the Sikh girl whose life she claimed to remember. This overhearing might explain the knowledge she had about the Sikh girl, but it could not explain her strong identification with that girl; and it could not account for her unusual interest in the Sikh religion (her family being Hindus), her phobia of knives, and her strong attachment to the family of the murdered girl. Such behavior is part of an entire role; it is an aspect of personality transcending mere verbal knowledge. One may argue that if Pushpa came to believe that she had been stabbed in a previous life, a phobia of knives would become part of that belief. One might similarly try to explain her other behavior as expressions of her strong conviction that she really had lived the previous life she claimed to remember. This interpretation, however, would leave the remaining question of why a child would take on the identity of a murdered girl in the first place.

Although I think cryptomnesia an improbable explanation for the cases, I cannot say the same of *paramnesia*, which is the technical word for distortions and inaccuracies in the informants' memories. I think that if I were going to coach a critic of these cases, I should advise him to concentrate on whatever evidence he can find of the unreliability of the informants' memories.

To understand how paramnesia may occur, or at least one way in which it may occur, we need to consider again a child's first utterances about a previous life that he seems to remember. Let us suppose that his parents, hearing him make a few statements, begin to give them a coherence that they may not have had. They think of the sort of person about whom the child might be talking. Then they start searching for such a person. They find a family having a deceased member whose life seems to correspond to the child's statements. They explain to this family what their child has been saying about the previous life. The second family agrees that the child's statements might refer to the deceased member of their family. The two families exchange detailed information about the deceased person and about what the child has been saying. From enthusiasm and carelessness, they may then credit the child with having stated numerous details about the identified deceased person, when in fact he said very little, and perhaps nothing specific, before the two families met. In this way a myth of what the child had said might develop and come to be accepted by both the families. How far will such an explanation take us?

It certainly seems the best one for some cases. I mentioned above that the strong desire of many Druse persons to trace a deceased person into a new incarnation or to learn a living person's past identity may lead them to close prematurely the question of identification in a case. When a Druse dies, his family nearly always wishes to know where he has been reborn; and when a Druse baby is born, *his* family nearly always wishes to know who he was in his previous life. Thus, the eager family of an infant barely speaking may meet the equally eager family of a deceased person whose members are still grieving for him. It would be surprising if two such families did not sometimes incorrectly agree on slender evidence that they had made the right match of infant and deceased person, when they had not done so. Later, they could honestly believe the child had said much more about the previous life before the two families met than he had said. The additional details thus accreted to the case would give it an appearance of having stronger evidence than it had.

Nevertheless, when we test this explanation in many cases, including some Druse ones, it seems inadequate. First, it could not apply to those cases in which someone had made a written record of what the child had said *before* his statements were verified and before the two families concerned had met. In such cases, we know that the child really did say before the families met what they later said he had said. Unfortunately, these cases are still few (1 percent of all cases) compared with the large number in which no such record was made.[9]

In other cases, however, my associates and I have reached the scene of a case within a few weeks or months of the first meeting between the families concerned, [10] and probably the informants' memories had faded little during this interval. In other instances this meeting has taken place after the child has been talking about the previous life for a year, or maybe several years. Throughout this period the typical child has repeated many times his main statements about the previous life. I have already said that this repetition would tend to fix what the child had been saying firmly in the minds of listening adults, and it seems unlikely that these memories would be much altered by meeting the other family. Serious distortions in remembering what the child said in most such cases would require the informants to have more impaired memories than there is any evidence of their having. The defect, moreover, would have to affect more than one person, because for most cases several informants have corroborated each other (with some discrepancies about details) as to what the child said before the two families met.

One may argue nevertheless that motives for shaping the case in a particular way may be strong enough to produce distortions in memory of the magnitude required. There is no doubt that such motives occur in some cases. The parents often wish their child's statements about the previous life proven correct; a confirmation of their accuracy would vindicate the family against doubts that gossiping neighbors may have expressed. And as I have mentioned, a family that has lost a loved member may show faulty judgment in appraising a child's statements, out of a wish to believe that the deceased member has returned to life, if not with them, at least in another family.

Against cases of these types, however, we can set as many more in which the families concerned either are indifferent to the case or adopt negative attitudes toward it. I have already pointed out that many parents find the child's statements uncongenial for one reason or another. They may believe it can harm him to remember a previous life; they may fear they will lose him to the other family; they may be reluctant to have anyone verify statements the child has made about another life that was, compared with theirs, lived either in very poor circumstances or in very prosperous ones; or they may dislike any encouragement of behavior that they find unattractive in the child and that verification of his statements might enhance. [11]

For their part, the members of the previous personality's family may be less ready to endorse the case than we might expect on the basis of their beliefs and their grief, considered alone. I have already mentioned that some of them (particularly wealthy persons) are afraid that the subject's family means to exploit them. Others dread discreditable revelations that the subject may make about their family. Still others—paradoxically perhaps—fear that exposure to the subject will reawaken the grief they continue to have for the deceased person.[12]

For these diverse reasons it often happens that one or the other of the families concerned feels no wish to have the subject's statements verified. Such persons would tend to minimize, not exaggerate, the child's accuracy. In sum, paramnesia, whether from ordinary forgetfulness with the passage of time or from motivated distortion of memories, may affect the accuracy of some informants' reports and may occasionally account for an entire case; but I do not think it an adequate explanation for most cases.[13]

Fraud, cryptomnesia, paramnesia: these are the three main explanations we can offer for these cases that do not suppose some process, such as telepathy or survival of death, that is regarded as paranormal in Western societies. The word *paranormal*, as I explained in chapter 1, refers to concepts that are not yet assimilated into Western science. Before discussing these paranormal explanations, I shall briefly evaluate one more normal explanation that is frequently advanced for these cases. I refer to "inherited memory" or "genetic memory."

When the interval between the death of the presumed previous personality and the subject's birth is sufficiently long, the subject could be a descendant of the previous personality and could, in principle, inherit memories of his life. The detailed images that most of the subjects of these cases describe far exceed the kind of memory that is usually credited to inheritance. When we use the phrase *inherited memory* or the word *instinct,* we are usually thinking about spiders that spin webs and birds that build nests without being taught to do so. Our concept of such instinctive behavior does not usually suppose that the spider or the bird has conscious images of previous webs spun and nests built. Such activities are better subsumed under what I call behavioral memories. However, perhaps the communicating sounds of animals, like the songs of birds, have some faint resemblance to the imaged memories of past events that the subjects of these cases demonstrate. If this is so, we could allow that the subjects *might* inherit imaged memories as well as behavioral ones.

There remain, however, graver objections to genetic memory as an explanation for most of these cases. First, the interval between death and birth is usually extremely short and rarely more than five years. [14] A subject born in a different family just a few months or years after the previous personality's death could not possibly be a descendant of the previous personality.

Furthermore, genetically transmitted memories could never include the memory of an event that occurred after the conception of the previous personality's children through whom the memories might descend. It follows that memories of a person's death could not be transmitted genetically; and yet the majority of the children of these cases remember—even when they remember little else—how the previous personality died. It may help the reader to consider here the case (summarized in chapter 3) of Mary Magruder, who had a recurrent nightmare of being chased by an American Indian who seemed intent on scalping her. I said earlier that we might explain her case by inherited memory; but there is an essential condition for the use of this interpretation. If the girl attacked by the Indian escaped her pursuer, and later had children, they might have inherited the memories of her ordeal and these might have continued to pass down to later descendants until they reached Mary Magruder. However, if the Indian caught and killed her, such memories would not have descended through any of her children already born. [15]

Turning now to explanations that include some paranormal process, I recognize three principal ones that deserve attention: extrasensory perception, possession, and reincarnation. I explained in chapter 3 that we have almost no independent evidence for reincarnation apart from the cases that I have investigated, and so I would not accept it as the best explanation for any case until I had eliminated, so far as I could, all other explanations, normal and paranormal. I shall therefore first discuss extrasensory perception and possession.

During the first years of my research on these cases, I took extrasensory perception more seriously as a plausible explanation for them than I do now. I still consider it an important possibility, but I no longer give it the weight that I formerly did.

I have two main reasons for this change of opinion. First, the children subjects hardly ever show, or have credited to them by their families, any evidence of extrasensory perception apart from the memories of a previous life. I have asked hundreds of parents about such capacities in their children. Most of them have denied that the child in question had any; a few have said that their child had occasionally demonstrated some form of extrasensory perception, but the evidence they provided was usually scanty. I cannot understand how a child could acquire by extrasensory perception the considerable stores of information so many of these subjects show about a deceased person without demonstrating—if not often, at least from time to time—similar paranormal powers in other contexts. [16]

In addition, as I have said more than once already, a case nearly always includes more than the verbal statements that the child makes about the previous life. For one to several years, and sometimes for much longer, most of the subjects show behavior that is unusual for their families, but that matches what we could learn or reasonably infer about the behavior of the previous personality.

Many of the subjects respond with strong emotion and in appropriate ways to stimuli related to the previous personality. For example, İsmail Altınkılıç clapped with joy when he learned that the murderers of the man whose life he remembered had—after particularly lengthy legal proceedings—been judicially hanged. I mentioned earlier that other subjects, for example, Imad Elawar and Sukla Gupta, were brought to tears by the mere mention of some untoward event in the life of a person of whom the previous personalities in their cases had been fond. One may suppose that individual emotions may be communicated by extrasensory perception, and indeed there is evidence for this; but much more is at issue in the behavioral responses that I am discussing. The child shows a syndrome of behaviors that in the more developed instances amounts to a facsimile of the previous personality's character. (In chapter 5 I gave some examples of such syndromes.) We have no grounds for thinking that processes of paranormal cognition can reproduce, in effect, an entire personality transposed to another person. Experimental parapsychology certainly offers no evidence for extrasensory perception of the kind required; and other types of spontaneous cases only rarely offer parallels. [17]

Leaving aside the question of the incommunicability by paranormal processes of a complex group of behavioral responses, the subject's imitation of another person requires a strong motive on his part. In most cases, however, we cannot find any such motive. The unusual behavior of the subject, as I have shown, frequently embroils him in conflict with his family without bringing him any concomitant benefits. Nor can I find in most of the subjects' parents any reason why they should wish to impose a different personality on their child, assuming they had somehow obtained the necessary information—whether normally or by extrasensory perception.

In the paragraphs above I have supposed that the extrasensory perception invoked in this explanation would occur between the subject of the case and living persons who knew the previous personality. (He might need some supplementary clairvoyance for reading obscure documents not easily accessible that sometimes figure in the cases.) The variant of paranormal cognition known as retrocognition supposes no living agents as the source of the subject's information; instead, he draws this from a hypothetical "universal memory" on which all events are somehow inscribed. However, retrocognition has the weaknesses, when applied to these cases, of other forms of extrasensory perception. For example, it does not explain why the subject shows such a remarkable paranormal talent only in one situation: that of seeming to remember a previous life.

I come now to possession. For several centuries the idea that a discarnate personality might influence or "possess" a living person has been unfashionable in Western intellectual circles; but from time to time this idea has been proposed as an explanation for cases suggestive of reincarnation.[18] Possession seems to me an important alternative explanation for the cases with anomalous dates (of death and birth), to which I briefly referred in chapter 5. There are also some cases, such as those of Ravi Shankar Gupta and Sujith Lakmal Jayaratne, in which the subject's mother was two or three months pregnant when the previous personality died. If we believe that conception and embryonic development require the association of some discarnate mind or soul with the developing physical body, we could also subsume these cases under possession.

However, I do not favor the interpretation of possession for the standard cases suggestive of reincarnation, and this for several reasons. First, the concept of possession fails to account for the almost universal amnesia that overtakes the subjects between the ages of four or five and seven or eight. Why should all possessing personalities quit their victims when the children are at about the same age? Second, the frequent stimulation of the subject's memories by visits to the family and community of the previous personality seems better explained by mental associations than by possession. Third, the subjects are usually ignorant of changes that have taken place in people and buildings since the previous personality died; I should have expected a possessing discarnate personality not to be omniscient, but to be more aware of such changes than the subjects are. Fourth, the interpretation of possession fails to account for the occurrence of birthmarks and birth defects apparently related to previous lives. Whatever the origin of these, they clearly antedate the subject's birth; and if we say that possession starts at conception, or even during embryonic life, I fail to see how the concept differs from that of reincarnation. I have already explained that I wish to say little here about the cases with birthmarks and birth defects, and I hope this also excuses me from saying more at this time about possession. I shall therefore turn to a discussion of the merits of reincarnation as an interpretation for these cases.

Reincarnation, as I said earlier, is the last interpretation we should accept for the cases, and we should adopt it only after we have eliminated all the alternative explanations, for each of which we have some independent evidence. All the cases that I have investigated have some flaws, and some have many. Moreover, their blemishes are of different sorts. Of some cases it can be said that I reached the scene too late, by which time important memories had faded or become distorted. In others, one can imagine some previously overlooked connection between the families concerned. In still others, one can discredit the testimony because I observed some prompting of the subject by an adult or found important discrepancies in the testimony. One may ask, nevertheless, how reasonable such criticisms are and to what extent they cover all the cases. When we do this we find that judgments about them depend greatly on the initial stance the person judging adopts toward reincarnation. A person who already believes in reincarnation will probably overlook flaws in the evidence or minimize them; a disbeliever, on the other hand, may magnify them and justify rejecting all the cases because of them. The situation resembles that of different persons regarding a bottle containing some wine. Some may say that the bottle is half full, others that it is half empty. [19]

This is not a situation without hope of resolution. Further investigations may provide evidence pointing more definitely toward the correct interpretation. For example, we may find more cases in which someone has made a written record of the subject's statements before they are verified. I do not think I could have been more eager to find such cases or more disappointed that we have so far found so few. Still, there may be further steps we can take in this endeavor.[20]

More objective data will come also from the further investigation of cases with birthmarks and birth defects, and perhaps from some other types of cases, such as those of the sex change type and those occurring among twins. (I shall say more about these types of cases in chapters 8 and 9.)

I may have a duty here to say what interpretation of the cases I myself favor. I have no preferred interpretation for all the cases, and I do not think any single one of them offers compelling evidence of reincarnation. Yet I can say that I think reincarnation is, for some cases, the best interpretation. I am not claiming that it is the only possible interpretation for these cases, just that it seems the best one among all those that I have mentioned.[21]

I have already disclaimed any expectation that this book by itself will convince any reader that reincarnation may occur. My more modest hope is that it will lead some readers to study my earlier books in which I have given detailed case reports. If you, the reader of this book, should turn to my others, I exhort you to give your attention unstintingly to the details of the cases. "More details. More details. Originality and truth are found only in the details," Stendhal has one of his characters exclaim.[22] I agree, with the addition that details provide more than just the interest of the cases; they contain the key to their interpretation.

After you have read my detailed case reports, I do not think you will say that there is *no* evidence for reincarnation, although you may certainly say that you find what we have unconvincing. If you reach that point, I think it fair to ask you: "What evidence, if you had it, *would* convince you of reincarnation?"

THE ANALYSIS OF LARGE SERIES OF CASES

In chapter 1 I mentioned the value of examining large numbers of cases, and I quoted Kant approvingly as having said that although individual cases raised doubts in his mind, he found his doubts lessened when he considered all the cases together. I shall now discuss this point at greater length and with regard to the cases of children who remember previous lives.

More than a century ago, Whately stated the advantages of searching for concurrent testimony from different witnesses of the same events:

> *It is manifest that the concurrent testimony, positive or negative, of several witnesses, when there can have been no concert . . . carries with it a weight independent of that which may belong to each of them considered separately. For though, in such a case, each of the witnesses should be even considered as wholly undeserving of credit, still chances might be incalculable against their all agreeing in the* same *falsehood.*

In the above passage Whately referred to the value of separate concurrent testimonies concerning the same event. As he pointed out, however, the principle applies equally well to separate testimonies concerning different, but similar, events:

> *The remark above made, as to the force of concurrent testimonies, even though each, separately, might have little or none, but whose* accidental *agreement in a falsehood would be extremely improbable . . . may be extended to many arguments of other kinds also . . . . E. G. If any one out of a hundred men throw a stone which strikes a certain object, there is but a slight probability, from that fact alone, that he aimed at that object; but if all the hundred threw stones which struck the* same *object, no one would doubt that they aimed at it.*[23]

Writers of an earlier generation of investigators sometimes used a different metaphor to describe the combined strength of a series of cases. It was, they said, like that of a faggot of sticks; the sticks may all have individual weaknesses, but these weaknesses are in different parts of the sticks, and when all are bound together in a faggot, it has a greater strength than any individual stick.[24] (Some critics have said that a chain with a weak link, which for these cases would be eyewitness testimony, offers a more appropriate analogy.)

Applying the faggot principle to the present cases, we can search large numbers of them for similar features. To the extent that we find such recurrences we shall gain confidence in the authenticity of the cases taken as a whole. The concordance in the accounts of widely separated informants (having no communication with each other) points to some natural phenomenon as responsible for the similarities in the cases. We can thus delineate a standard case or type.[25] Individual cases may deviate more or less from the standard one, but we may suspect as inauthentic any case that departs too far from the range found in cases judged to be genuine.

The study of large numbers of cases has another value no less important than that of assisting us to detect inauthentic cases. By establishing a type of case, we can relate its features to knowledge we have of other processes and to cases of other types; and these comparisons may eventually lead to our understanding the processes involved in the newly identified type.

Here I must add another warning. The haphazard ways in which information about cases reaches me—which I hope I have fully exposed—tell us that the cases I have studied may not be representative of all naturally occurring ones. However, we are entitled to ask whether the cases we have are unrepresentative in important ways or only in unimportant ones, and I shall address this question later.

I have already mentioned (in chapter 5) several of the recurrent features of the cases, such as the usual ages of the child's first speaking and of his no longer speaking spontaneously about the previous life. Here I shall mention some other recurrent features.

The first of these finally explains why, as I mentioned in the Preface, I have used masculine pronouns in referring to the subjects of the cases: the majority are males. In a series of 1,095 cases, 62 percent of the subjects were male and 38 percent female. We have found a similar lopsided proportion of males (66 percent) to females (34 percent) among the previous personalities. With one exception, this difference occurred in the cases of all cultures.[26] I discuss possible reasons for it in chapter 10.

One of the most interesting, and potentially most important, of the recurrent features is the high incidence of violent death among the previous personalities of the cases. We found that among 725 cases from six different cultures, 61 percent of the subjects remembered previous lives that ended in violent death.[27] This incidence far exceeds the incidence of violent death in the general populations of the countries where these cases occurred. But we need to ask whether it might arise from biases in the reporting of cases to us. Violent deaths attract more attention than natural ones, and our informants may have remembered longer and better the cases in which violent deaths figured than those in which the previous life recalled had ended naturally.

We were able to study indirectly the influence that violent death might have on the reporting of cases through a comparison of two series of cases in India. The cases of the first series were collected unsystematically over a period of about twenty years. Entry into this series depended on the casual, unforced memories of informants who for one reason or another notified one of my associates or me about a case. There were 193 cases in this series. The 19 cases in the second, much smaller, series were detected during the systematic survey in the Agra District (which I first mentioned in chapter 5). Informants were selected randomly and asked to search their memories for any case of the reincarnation type they could remember. In the larger, unsystematically collected series, the incidence of violent death in the previous life was 49 percent; in the smaller series it was only 35 percent. The difference suggests that some of the high incidence of violent death in our series may be due to informants' remembering cases with violent death more than they remember those with natural death; however, an incidence of 35 percent violent deaths still far exceeds that in the general population of India, which (for the comparable period) was less than 7 percent.[28]

The high incidence of violent death in these cases seems therefore to be a natural feature, not an artifact of reporting. It seems likely that one or more circumstances of violent deaths make them more memorable than natural ones. This is further suggested by another of our results. We have found that in solved cases with violent deaths 94 percent of the subjects mentioned the manner of death, whereas when the death had occurred naturally only 52 percent of the subjects mentioned it.

The prominence of violent death among the cases of all cultures in which I have investigated these cases seems to me one of the most important features of the data. I shall resume its discussion in chapter 10 when I consider factors that may make some lives more memorable than others. I shall also discuss it further in connection with unsolved cases, which form the remaining topic of this chapter.

The unsolved cases differ from the solved ones in three features.[29] First, the subjects of unsolved cases remember the name of the previous personality much less often than do the subjects of solved cases. This is not independent of the failure to solve the case, because, as I explained earlier, finding a person corresponding to the child's statements requires that he state at least some proper names, and when he fails to mention the name of the person whose life he claims to remember, it becomes more difficult to solve the case than when he does.

The second difference between solved and unsolved cases also seems to have a simple explanation. The subjects of unsolved cases stop talking about the previous lives they remember much earlier than do the subjects of solved ones. The former stop talking about the previous lives at an average age of under six years, whereas the latter go on speaking about them until an average age of almost seven and a half years. In chapter 5 I attributed this difference to the greater attention and encouragement to speak that other persons give the subject of a solved case. In contrast, the parents of a child who makes unverified statements about a previous life can rapidly lose interest in what he is saying, and so he tends to stop speaking about it. Also, the subjects of solved cases nearly always exchange visits with the other family, and these visits would tend to keep the subject's memories in his consciousness and thereby postpone their fading.

Third, the subjects of unsolved cases tend to remember the death in the previous life as violent much more often than do the subjects of solved cases. Among solved cases a verified violent death occurred in 51 percent of the cases, but 91 percent of the subjects of the unsolved cases said the death they remembered had been violent. The question arises of whether the subjects of unsolved cases may be imagining a violent death. Since what they say is not verified, they may be narrating nothing but fantasies; but it is also possible that some subjects of this group have had vague memories of a real previous life, which they have embellished with a fantasy of a violent death.

Perhaps, however, the subjects of unsolved cases are not fantasizing. Instead, they may be remembering real previous lives, but with less verifiable detail (and perhaps also more errors) than the subjects of solved cases. Although, as I have explained above, unsolved cases differ from solved ones in three important features, they resemble the solved ones in three other features. The subjects of unsolved cases begin to speak about the previous life at the same age as do those of solved cases; and they mention the manner of dying in the previous life and show phobias related to the death just as often as do the subjects of solved cases. These similarities suggest that the unsolved cases belong to the same species, or at least to the same genus, as the solved ones.

Returning for a moment to the group of cases as a whole—solved and unsolved ones—72 percent of the subjects remembered the previous personality's manner of dying, but only 63 percent remembered his name. Among solved cases (in which the mode of death was ascertainable) 94 percent of the subjects remembered the mode of death when it was violent, but only 52 percent remembered it when it was natural. Among solved cases 76 percent of the subjects remembered the previous personality's name. It appears, therefore, that if reincarnation occurs and a person dies violently and reincarnates with only a few memories of the previous life, the violent death is more likely to figure among those memories than the person's name. This development repeated in numerous cases might partly account for the much higher incidence of remembered violent death among unsolved compared with solved cases. (I am not suggesting, however, that it is the only factor contributing to this important difference between the solved and unsolved cases.)

This concludes all I can say at present about the analysis of large numbers of cases. In previous publications I have sometimes called the recurrent features that we have identified in the cases of all cultures (so far studied) by the somewhat grandiose and possibly misleading term *universal*. I have not meant to imply by this word that the identified features occur in every case, but they are found with a high frequency in the cases of every culture that we have so far examined for them. Other features of the cases vary from one culture to another much more than do the ones I have mentioned in this chapter. I shall describe some of these culture-bound features in the next chapter.

Before ending this chapter, however, I wish to raise the question of how we should explain the recurrent features of the cases that I have just reviewed. It seems impossible that the similarities in the cases from widely separated cultures arose from knowledge the informants had of cases in cultures outside their own. Reports of cases published in the newspapers and magazines of Asia and Africa are nearly always confined to local cases. I cannot recall ever having read in India, for example, a report of a case in Sri Lanka or of having read in Sri Lanka a report of an Indian case. Some of the informants have a little information about one or two cases of their own country other than the one for which they are furnishing information. They have learned about these either through oral communication in their community or from reading reports of other cases in a magazine or newspaper. But there have been no publications of data from large series of cases that the average Asian informant for these cases could have read. Thus the informants have no model to which they might try to make a case conform, either to accord with their own beliefs or perhaps to suit what they think I would like to hear.[30] If, however, they are not conforming their accounts to others, we are warranted in believing that they are describing a natural phenomenon.

CHAPTER EIGHT

Variations in the Cases of Different Cultures

In this chapter I shall consider two aspects of the relationship between the cases and culture: variations in the incidence of reported cases in different cultures and variations in their features in different cultures. These topics are not completely independent, but I think it appropriate to discuss them separately.

VARIATIONS IN THE INCIDENCE OF REPORTED CASES IN DIFFERENT CULTURES

I have emphasized that we know something about the incidence of *reported* cases, but almost nothing about the real incidence of cases. Nevertheless, even within the group of reported cases we can find important differences from culture to culture. I have also said that cases are reported much more frequently in cultures having a belief in reincarnation than in those without it. Anyone doubting this has only to compare the abundance of cases among the Druses of Lebanon with their scarcity—near absence, I could say—among Christians of Lebanon in neighboring villages, or even in mixed villages where Druses and Christians live almost side by side. Similar differences occur in the incidence of reported cases among the Christians and Buddhists of Sri Lanka and among the Hindus and Moslems of India. Cases do occur among the Moslems of India (as they occasionally do among Christians of Lebanon and Sri Lanka), but only with extreme rarity.

The most obvious explanation for these differences is that culture facilitates the development of cases. I agree with that, because if parents believe that reincarnation is possible, they will allow a child to talk about a previous life without thinking him mad. But cultural influences can lead to the suppression of cases just as much as to their promotion, and we cannot ask why so many cases occur in Southeast

Asia, parts of western Asia, and West Africa without also asking why so few occur in Europe and North America. Parents who disbelieve in reincarnation may have just as much influence over their children as those who believe in it.

There must, however, be factors other than the acceptance of reincarnation that lead to the development of more cases in some parts of the world than in others. What might they be? If we assume for the moment that the influence of reported cases known to us is approximately proportional to the real incidence of cases in different parts of the world, we cannot account for the different incidences on the basis of a simple connection between belief and the occurrence of cases. If there were nothing more to be considered, we should expect a much higher incidence of cases in Western countries where, on average, more than 20 percent of the population believe in reincarnation. Although I believe more cases are suppressed in the West than in Asia, I do not believe that the much lower frequency of cases in the West derives only from more suppression there than in Asia. (We have seen that approximately 25 percent of cases in India are suppressed, and yet the cases occur abundantly there.)

We are led, therefore, to conclude that the countries and cultures where the cases are found abundantly must have some other important factor that facilitates the development of cases. Or perhaps there are several such factors.

The peoples where the cases frequently occur have (in general) these features in common (in addition to the belief in reincarnation):

a. They remember the dead more than we do in the West. Living persons consider dead ones as being still present, active, and capable of intervening in terrestrial affairs; it is thought that they need our help and we need theirs.

b. They also remember living persons more than we do in the West. Family ties are stronger and more obligatory. When one of them becomes mentally ill, the family consolidates with the patient against the illness; in the West the family of a mentally ill patient tends to extrude him from its circle of amity. Not surprisingly, the rate of recovery (and duration of recovery) from serious mental illness, such as schizophrenia, is markedly higher in underdeveloped countries compared with highly industrialized ones.[1] We might even regard the corruption that often dismays the modern Western visitor among these peoples as a form of family assistance.

To abandon corruption and supersede it with loyalty to a larger group, say the community or nation, may weaken family ties.

c. Their concept of causality embraces many more events than do concepts of causality in the West. They have no idea that corresponds to Western ideas of "chance," "luck" and "randomness." Instead, events always happen because someone—be he good or evil—wishes them to happen or has deserved that they should happen. This feature pertains particularly to illness. Traditional healers, shamans, and other persons having similar roles would lose their clientele rapidly if they announced that a disease was just bad luck or happened by accident. Always they will say it is due to sinfulness on the part of the afflicted person, failure to worship ancestors properly, jealousy of others who have invoked malignant spirits against him, and numerous other *personal* reasons—but not chance.[2]

d. They believe more than do Western persons that distantly separated persons can communicate with each other. Thus, telepathy and related experiences that Western persons designate as paranormal they regard as normal, even though unusual. They often regard dreams as truth-telling and believe that the living can sometimes meet the dead in dreams. The concept of privacy as we know it in the West has hardly begun to develop in the countries of which I am speaking. This may reflect poverty and overcrowding more than choice. Be that as it may, if there is no shutting out of other persons from your normally conducted affairs, perhaps this helps you to be more open to telepathic communications in which other persons reach into your mind without the use of the normal senses.

e. They value verbal skills less than we do in the West; they may thereby preserve mental imagery better.

f. Time passes differently among them. A Westerner may find the lack of "time sense" among Asians and Africans vexatious; but they may think his clock-ridden punctuality pathetic.

g. Among these peoples there is less to be done, or at any rate, less sense than in the West that one must be doing something all the time. This gives more time for reflection and perhaps allows memories—of the present life as well as of any past ones lived and remembered—to come into consciousness.

These factors seem to me to favor the kinds of experiences that we in the West consider paranormal—not just memories of previous lives, but many other types of related experiences: telepathic impressions, poltergeists, apparitions, and others. I am not one to lament the loss of past simplicities, but everyone who thinks about these differences should ask himself whether the West may have lost as well as gained in making its technological advances.

I may not have identified the critical factors that account for the more abundant occurrence of cases in some parts of the world compared with others. Some of my readers may think of other distinguishing features. I shall be satisfied concerning this matter if I have thwarted an intention to say casually that the belief in reincarnation alone is a sufficient explanation for the different incidences of reported cases in different countries. There must be more to be learned about the causes of these differences.

If I am correct, however, in delineating the features I have mentioned as important, they do not by themselves suffice to produce large numbers of children who remember previous lives any more than does the unaided belief in reincarnation. Most of the people living in vast tracts of Asia, Africa, and Latin America have the same beliefs and attitudes that I have described, and yet they have few cases. They, however, do not believe in reincarnation; it is not part of orthodox doctrine among either Sunni Moslems or Christians. In sum, the occurrence of frequent cases seems to require *both* the belief in reincarnation *and* some other factor or factors; neither, alone, is sufficient to generate numerous cases.

Before leaving this topic I shall mention two other factors that may be in play. First, it is possible that, if reincarnation occurs, the belief in reincarnation itself may be carried over from one life to another. In chapter 1 I discussed the concept of behavioral memory as applied to cases of the reincarnation type. In that chapter I also alluded to the possibility of our having subliminal cognitive memories that we have carried over from previous lives, and I gave the example of knowing how to speak a language. Later, in chapter 5, I said that strongly held attitudes—such as about being a woman, a Frenchman, a Moslem, or a white person—might be reinforced by similar existences in successive previous lives. Here I wish to add to these examples that of beliefs, including the belief in reincarnation itself. This could be carried over from one life to another and become stronger with each incarnation in a culture favorable to it. It would not need to be remembered explicitly, only as an intuition; it could pass from one life to another as a mental set or frame to which other, more distinct memories could be related. If a child is born with a belief in reincarnation carried over from a previous life, he has at hand a conceptual scheme into which he can fit any imaged memories of a previous life that he also happens to have. On the other hand, a child who does not have such a framework may reject any imaged memories he has of a previous life and, in effect, suppress himself.

I know that something like self-suppression of apparent memories of a previous life does sometimes occur, because some Western subjects have told me that as young children they had clear mental images of scenes and events in some other time and place, but that at that age they could not understand what significance these images might have. They ignored (and concealed) them, but did not forget them. Years later, they read for the first time about reincarnation and then thought that perhaps the puzzling images of scenes and events they had had when much younger could have been memories of a previous life.[3]

Second, the interval between death and reincarnation may be shorter in countries having a high incidence of reported cases than it is where cases are reported less often. We find hints of a longer interval than occurs in Asia in the cases of Western Europe and North America, but we still have too few verified Western cases to justify a stronger assertion about this possibility.

VARIATIONS IN THE FEATURES OF CASES IN DIFFERENT CULTURES

In the last chapter I mentioned several features that occurred in the cases of all cultures where I have studied them. The incidence of these features does vary somewhat from one culture to another. On the whole, however, the variations are slight; otherwise I would not have dared to describe these features as "universal." In some other features we find much greater differences from culture to culture, and I shall now describe some of these.

One such feature is the frequency with which the subject and previous personality of a case belong to the same family. (As I mentioned earlier, I call these same-family cases.) Cases of this group form the majority of all solved cases in Burma, in Thailand, among the nontribal cases of the United States, among the Igbo of Nigeria, and among the Tlingit of Alaska. They occur much less frequently in India, Lebanon, Sri Lanka, and Turkey.

Among same-family cases of the Tlingit, I found a distinctive feature: the way in which the two persons concerned in a case are related. In about 75 percent of the cases they are related on the side of the subject's mother. This accords with the matrilineal organization of Tlingit society; a Tlingit derives through his mother, not his father, both his membership in one of the tribal moieties and that part of his status that he inherits.[4]

Among the same-family cases of the Igbo of Nigeria, on the other hand, I have found the opposite type of relationship between the subjects and previous personalities of the cases. The Igbos have a patrilineal society—so much so that preliminary genealogies sent to me from Nigeria frequently show no women whatever. In keeping with this, I found among forty-three Igbo same-family cases that subject and previous personality were related on the father's side in thirty-two (74 percent) cases and on the mother's side in only eleven (26 percent) cases.[5]

In Burma women have a social status almost equal to that of men, and among Burmese same-family cases the subject and previous personality are related with about equal frequency through the subject's mother or father.

Announcing dreams also occur with markedly different frequencies in the cases of different cultures. They are common among the cases of the Tlingit and other tribes of northwestern North America, in Burma, and in Turkey. They almost never occur among the Igbo or in Sri Lanka and Lebanon. An announcing dream is more likely to be remembered if the dreamer recognizes the person in the dream. It is possible that in a country like Sri Lanka, where there are almost no same-family cases, persons may have had announcing dreams in which someone completely strange to them appeared; the person was not recognized, and the dream was therefore quickly forgotten.[6] The cases of India support this interpretation. In that country I have learned of announcing dreams only, without any exceptions that I can remember, in same-family cases.

The absence of announcing dreams in the cases among the Druses of Lebanon accords with the Druse belief that reincarnation occurs instantly at death. Druses do not believe that a soul or mind can exist incorporeally prior to the Day of Judgment; and so they do not believe in the possibility of discarnate souls. A deceased Druse could not participate in an announcing dream, because he has, in the Druses' view, already been reborn in an infant's body.[7]

The foregoing topic leads naturally to that of variations found in different cultures in the interval between the death of the previous personality of a case and the subject's birth. Among the cases we have examined, this interval varies from only a few hours to twenty years or more, although the median interval (among 616 cases in ten cultures) is fifteen months.[8] In accordance with this wide variation, the members of most cultures believe that no fixed duration exists for the interval between death and rebirth.

The Druses and the Jains (of India), however, believe that the interval *is* rigidly fixed for everyone. They assert that a soul cannot exist unattached to a physical body, but they differ in the beliefs they hold about when a deceased person becomes associated with his next physical body. For Jains, this occurs at the moment of the conception of the next body, and they therefore expect always to find an interval of approximately nine months between the death of a person whose life a subject remembers and the birth of that subject. Our collection of cases contains too few Jain cases to permit our saying that they always fit the Jains' expectation.[9]

The Druses, on the other hand, believe that when a physical body dies, its associated soul becomes immediately attached to a newly born physical body, that is, to the body of an infant just delivered from its mother. The Druses acknowledge no exceptions to the rule, and if an interval—even of a day—occurs between the death of the previous personality and the subject's birth, they assume that an "intermediate life" filled the gap, even if the subject does not remember it. Such a life would have been that of a person—usually a young infant or child—who died at an age corresponding to the length of the interval. Occasionally, Druse subjects have slight memories of such intermediate lives, but most of them have none whatever.

Subjects of other countries, particularly India, sometimes claim "intermediate lives" and may narrate detailed, but usually unverified, memories of them. Examples occurred in the cases of Swarnlata Mishra, Gopal Gupta, Pushpa, and Manju Tripatti. All these intermediate lives are unverified.

I am inclined to think that Swarnlata remembered a real previous life, because she demonstrated recitative xenoglossy that seemed to derive from the intermediate life she remembered. On the other hand, I believe that Gopal Gupta's claimed intermediate life (in London, England) is at least partly a fantasy, which he first communicated in response to a direct question about what had happened (to him) during the eight-year interval between the death of Shaktipal Sharma (the previous personality in his case) and his (Gopal's) birth.

I remain in doubt about the best interpretation for the intermediate life described by Manju Tripatti, who lived in Kanpur, Uttar Pradesh, India. She remembered the previous life of her paternal aunt; her memories of it included some verified details, although these were of little value evidentially because Manju might have learned normally about her aunt. Manju was not born until twelve years after the aunt's death. She said that during this period she had been reborn far away in Srinagar, Kashmir. She described scenery and other features, such as the houseboats, that one might see at Srinagar, and she gave enough details about this life so that members of our team made two separate efforts in Srinagar to solve the case; but we all failed. Manju's memories of an intermediate life may have been all fantasies; or they may have been a mixture of some real memories of a previous life supplemented with fantasies, as I think some other unsolved cases are.

Pushpa said she had been the son of a temple priest during the approximately four years between the death she remembered in the (principal) previous life and her birth; she stated no verifiable details about this intermediate life.

This brings me to another feature in which cases of different cultures show marked variations. I refer to memories of experiences the subjects claim to have had in a discarnate state between death in the previous life and rebirth. In chapter 3 I mentioned that such memories may be either of terrestrial events occurring after the previous personality's death or of experiences in a discarnate realm, and I gave some examples of these types of memories.

The recall of intermediate terrestrial events occurs sporadically in the cases of all cultures. The event of which the subject claims later to have knowledge is often the funeral or some feature of the burial of the deceased person whose life he remembers.[10] An event occurring in the subject's family just prior to his conception may also figure in these memories.[11]

Claimed memories of experiences in a discarnate realm also occur sporadically in the cases of all cultures, but they occur much more frequently in Burma and Thailand than elsewhere. [12] Why this should be so, I cannot say. At one time I attributed it to the fairly widespread practice of meditation in Burma and Thailand. Buddhist meditation is said to clarify the mind and—incidentally, but not as a goal in itself—to facilitate the recall of previous lives, including sojourns in a discarnate realm. However, the previous personalities of the subjects who have had these memories have not all been meditators; nor were they all exemplary characters.

I also think it unlikely that the high incidence in Thailand and Burma of claimed memories of a discarnate realm has a necessary connection with Theravada Buddhism. Theravada Buddhism is the dominant religion in Burma and Thailand, but it is dominant also, if somewhat less so, in Sri Lanka, and few subjects there claim to remember anything of the interval between death and rebirth.

Still another variation between the cases of different cultures occurs in the claims about rebirth in the body of a nonhuman animal. The Buddhists and Hindus of South Asia believe that humans may be reborn as nonhuman animals and then again as humans, and I have occasionally learned of claims to remember a previous life as a nonhuman animal. (I discuss this topic in a section of chapter 10.) I have never learned of a case of this type outside South Asia, unless we consider as exceptions one or two vague secondhand reports that I heard in Turkey. [13]

I come finally to what seems to me the most important variation in features of the cases of different cultures, that in the incidence of cases of the sex-change type. The proportion of such cases varies greatly between cultures; it ranges from 50 percent of all cases among the Kutchin (Athabaskan) of the Canadian Northwest Territories to the complete absence of such cases in Lebanon, in Turkey, and among the tribes of southeastern Alaska (Tlingit) [14] and British Columbia (Haida, Tsimsyan, and Gitksan). The incidence in other countries falls between these extremes. For example, it is 3 percent in India, 9 percent in Sri Lanka, 13 percent in Thailand, 15 percent in the United States (nontribal cases), and 28 percent in Burma.

When I question informants of countries where sex-change cases occur, they tell me that sex change from one life to another is possible; but when I question informants of cultures where such cases do not occur, they tell me that it is impossible. (Sometimes they state their opinions with some asperity, as if I ought to know without having to ask.) I must admit that occasionally informants of the regions where sex-change cases are not found have shown a momentary hesitation before they pronounced emphatically against the possibility of sex change. I do not know what could have made them waver, because it is in the highest degree unlikely that they could ever have seen a sex-change case or even have heard of one until they met me.

In all but one of the cultures where sex-change cases occur, girls who remember previous lives as males occur three times as often— still considering *reported* cases—as boys who remember previous lives as females. Since this lopsided ratio appears so consistently, it might almost be regarded as one of the "universal" features of the cases, although one restricted to cultures where sex-change cases are found.[15]

It is easier to detect variations among the cases in different cultures than to interpret them. I shall offer two possible interpretations without meaning to suggest that no others could exist. In considering these interpretations I shall use the sex-change cases as my example, partly because of their importance and partly because I have much more data about this type of variation among the cases than about other culture-bound variations. To introduce what I shall say, I shall take the reader back across some ground already traversed.

Cultures are set apart not only by their social and economic practices, but by the beliefs that the members of a culture share. Belief or disbelief in reincarnation is a distinguishing aspect of some cultures. The various groups believing in reincarnation have developed different subsidiary beliefs about how it occurs and about what can and cannot happen in connection with reincarnation. (Christians should find nothing surprising in this if they remember that among persons trying to follow the teachings of Jesus Christ some believe in the Immaculate Conception and others do not.) The larger belief and the associated subsidiary beliefs form part of the cultural heritage passed from adults to children at each generation. Although instruction in religious beliefs begins in childhood, it continues through the later years of childhood and beyond. Some adults—and some children also—reject the religious beliefs of their elders and convert to other beliefs. The majority, however, accept uncritically the beliefs that are inculcated during their childhood instruction and frequently repeated to them later. By the time most people come to die they have fairly hardened concepts about what does or does not happen to a person at death; and they tend to reject as unsound or positively wrong concepts that differ from those they accept. A person may even stigmatize as "impossible" some experience or claim that seems discordant with his beliefs. Among Western persons, I have encountered numerous examples of this attitude with regard to reincarnation itself, but it also appears often among persons who believe in reincarnation and who have fixed ideas about how it occurs. For example, Jains to whom I have mentioned the birthmark cases find these laughably absurd; with their belief that a soul instantly enters a new physical body at the moment of death, they cannot accept that a mark on a new body might somehow derive from a corresponding wound on a dead one. Similarly, Druse parents might deride a child who claimed to have lived a previous life as a member of the opposite sex. (This is an imaginary example; I have never heard of a Druse child who claimed to have had a previous life as a member of the opposite sex.) Strong measures would not be needed to suppress such a child; children can take hints as well as adults, and sometimes better. Just as a Christian child may suppress glimpses he thinks he has of a previous life, so a Druse child might conceal, and subsequently entirely forget, memories he had about a previous life as a person of the opposite sex. In this way no cases of the sex-change type would appear in a culture, and their absence would tend to strengthen the belief in the culture that sex change could not occur from one life to another: in short, that it is impossible.

The foregoing explanation may adequately account for the absence of sex-change cases among the Druses. They form a rather compact group—socially; they are somewhat dispersed geographically now—and printed scriptures embody the essential elements of their beliefs. However, we cannot say the same for the Alevis of Turkey and the tribes of northwestern North America, who do not believe in the possibility of sex change. The former probably and the latter certainly have no written codification of their beliefs; their religions are transmitted orally. Moreover, the tribes of northwestern North America are spread over thousands of square miles of British Columbia and Alaska. They have had no paramount chief or universally sanctified shaman whose particular beliefs became promulgated as a truth for all to believe in. No one has paddled up and down the channels and rivers of Alaska and British Columbia telling his tribal neighbors that you cannot change sex from one life to another.

This being so, the question arises of whether the belief that sex change is impossible has been transmitted by means of reincarnation itself. I suggested earlier that, if reincarnation occurs, the belief that it occurs may be carried over from one life to another. Now I am suggesting that beliefs about how reincarnation occurs and what may happen from one life to another may also be carried over from one life to another.

In short, premortem beliefs, held tenaciously enough, may influence postmortem events, including the circumstances of the next incarnation.[16] Such beliefs may resemble posthypnotic suggestions and be implemented with the same compulsion. If a person dies believing that he cannot in another incarnation become a person of the opposite sex, perhaps he cannot, even if he can reincarnate.

We can consider further the sequence of possible events if, say, a woman dies and is reborn as a man in a culture, such as that of the Tlingit, with a strong belief in the impossibility of sex change. In the first incarnation as a Tlingit man, the subject of this imagined case might preserve subliminal memories of the previous life as a woman, and, even if he had no imaged memories of that life, he might remain open-minded with regard to the possibility of sex change. After several successive lives as a man, however, the memories of the life as a woman would probably become more and more remote and correspondingly less and less influential on the man's attitudes toward sex change in later incarnations. Ultimately, he might come to feel deeply from within himself that sex change was impossible, even though he might otherwise have some inclination to question the prevailing beliefs of Tlingit culture.

The possibility that beliefs can act as powerful releasers and inhibitors of experiences after death and in another incarnation has far wider applications than any it may have for the sex-change cases. I shall consider a few of these in later chapters.

CHAPTER NINE

The Explanatory Value of the Idea of Reincarnation

In chapter 6 I mentioned my surprise on first learning about the unusual behavior that most of the subjects of these cases showed and that seemed to correspond with behavior that the previous personalities were reported to have shown or might have been expected to manifest. I only gradually realized the importance of such unusual behavior for the evaluation of paranormal processes in the cases. It took me even longer to appreciate that these behavioral components have another value, in addition to their contribution to the evidence of reincarnation. I refer to the possibility that reincarnation, if it occurs, may explain unusual behavior of types not adequately accounted for by current understanding in psychology and psychiatry. Beyond this, reincarnation may even help to explain some presently puzzling biological and medical phenomena. In this chapter I propose to review ways in which I think reincarnation may help our understanding of unsolved problems in psychology, biology, and medicine.

Before I come to the specific matters that I believe the idea of reincarnation can help us to understand better, I have to ask my readers to make an additional assumption. (I have already asked you, for the purposes of this chapter, to assume that reincarnation does, in fact, occur.) This is that, although only a small number of persons have imaged memories of events in previous lives, many other persons may have behavioral memories derived from a previous life without having any imaged memories that might explain why or how they acquired such behavior.

A few of the cases I have already mentioned may have prepared you for this assumption. I refer to instances in which a subject continued to show behavior (such as a fondness for particular foods) related to the previous life after he had lost the imaged memories of that life. However, you may defer accepting this assumption until after you have considered the examples I shall present in this chapter. I shall take these (with rare exceptions) from the cases of subjects who had *both* imaged memories of a previous life (usually verified ones) *and* related unusual behavior. If you think it reasonable to consider the unusual behavior of these subjects a type of behavioral memory accompanying their imaged memories, you may also consider favorably the possibility that other persons have behavioral memories without having any imaged ones.

UNUSUAL BEHAVIOR OF CHILDHOOD

In considering the examples of unusual behavior that I shall now describe, you should understand that, in general, the following conditions pertain to the behavior in question. (I think it necessary to say "in general," because I have not always been able to make my inquiries related to the behavior as thorough as I wished.) First, the behavior is unusual in the subject's family; other members of the family do not show it at all or show it to a much smaller degree than does the subject. Second, I have not learned of any (postnatal) experience the subject has had that could explain the behavior; nor have I learned of any model in his family or neighborhood whom he might have imitated in acquiring the behavior.

Phobias of Infancy and Early Childhood

In earlier chapters I have described, with examples, some of the phobias that we find in these cases. I mentioned also that some subjects show a phobia before they have learned to speak and can explain it (as derived from a previous life) to their parents. Furthermore, some subjects continue to have the phobia after they have forgotten the imaged memories of the previous life that seemed to explain it.

The phobias commonly relate to the mode of death in the previous life. They occur as often in subjects with unverified memories as in those without. Ma Tin Aung Myo, whose case I summarized in chapter 4, offers a good example of a subject with unverified memories who had nevertheless a marked phobia—in her case, of airplanes. Phobias may even occur in subjects who have no imaged memories whatever. In such instances the phobia may be combined with one or more other features of the case to support a judgment that a particular deceased person has been reborn. Derek Pitnov, a Tlingit of Alaska, is an example of such an assessment. He had no imaged memories of a previous life, but he had a birthmark in a particular location that matched a fatal spear wound his great-great-granduncle had received; and he had a lifelong fear of bladed weapons.

Although most of the phobias in these cases relate to the instrument of the previous personality's death, some subjects show phobias of the place where the death occurred or of places resembling it. Süleyman Zeytun, a subject in Turkey, had memories of a man, Mehmet Coşman, who had drowned. Süleyman was afraid of water in general; but he was especially afraid of the place at the River Seyhan (in south central Turkey) where Mehmet Coşman had drowned. Necati Çaylak, another subject in Turkey, showed a marked fear when (as a young child) he was asked to cross a bridge at which the man whose life he remembered had been killed in an automobile accident. Ravi Shankar Gupta similarly showed a phobia of the place where the child whose life he remembered had been murdered.[1]

Not all subjects who remember previous lives that ended violently have corresponding phobias. Gopal Gupta, who remembered being shot in a previous life, had no phobia of guns, and Bongkuch Promsin, who remembered being stabbed, had none of knives or daggers. However, we find a similar unevenness in the occurrence of phobias following accidents and injuries that occur within a person's present life (if I may use that expression to make a distinction). Some persons seriously injured in a vehicle (or by one) never go near another, whereas other persons may ride comfortably in one at the earliest opportunity after the accident. Perhaps some of the differences in responses to injuries and other traumas of this life may result from varying experiences in previous lives. If a person drowned in a previous life and then nearly drowned in this life, he might be more likely to develop a phobia after the near-drowning than would someone who had no history of drowning in a previous life.

Some deaths seem to involve more suffering than others, and the amount of suffering as death approaches and arrives may influence whether or not a phobia develops. However, I have found that phobias occur after a variety of modes of death. For example, among forty-seven cases in which the previous personality drowned, a phobia of being immersed in water occurred in thirty (64 percent); and a phobia of snakes occurred in nine (39 percent) of twenty-three cases in which the previous personality had died of snakebite.

Child psychiatrists know that many children have phobias that neither the psychiatrists nor the children's parents can explain. These phobias do not derive from any known trauma or imitate a similar fear in a family member. Some psychiatrists attribute otherwise inexplainable phobias to a symbolic displacement of a fear of some person onto another person, an animal, or an object. Freud's case of Little Hans, who had a phobia of horses, provides an example of such tortuous reasoning. Freud believed that Little Hans's fear of horses masked a terror of his father; but Little Hans had had frightening experiences with horses, which were enough to account for his fear of them without invoking any other explanation. [2]

If we confine a search for the traumas stimulating phobias to this life, we shall probably fail to explain many of them, and we should look elsewhere for the causes of these. Although a few phobias of childhood may have a symbolic significance, we should consider the possibility that a relevant trauma may have occurred in a previous life. [3]

Unusual Interests and Types of Play in Childhood

When a child shows some unusual play activity (or other expressions of unusual interests), psychologists and psychiatrists commonly attribute this to imitation of his elders or to a need to express covertly feelings and attitudes that he cannot verbalize. For example, playing at being a soldier may provide a child with an acceptable way of expressing aggression. Playing at being a doctor enables a child to identify with an older member of the family, the child's father perhaps, who is a doctor. Many children show early in life an interest in the work they later take up as adults. Among great musicians one can find numerous examples of parental influences that seem to explain adequately the early expression of interest and skill in music. For example, the fathers of Bach, Mozart, Beethoven, Brahms, and Elgar were all musicians. But Dvořák's father was a butcher, Delius's a businessman, Mendelssohn's a banker (albeit a cultured one), and Handel's a barber-surgeon. The case of Handel seems particularly instructive. His father opposed Handel's interest in music, which he showed in early childhood. His mother gave him no effective support, and although an aunt encouraged him, her influence seems insufficient to have counteracted by itself the stern opposition of Handel's father. The family had no known ancestors with an interest in music.

The prison reformer, Elizabeth Fry, showed in youth the piety and concern for "the lower classes" that later became her life's work. Florence Nightingale, the founder of modern nursing, expressed her later vocation in early childhood by doctoring her dolls. Both of these women developed and pursued their special interests against the traditions and inclinations of their families.

Some persons of outstanding accomplishment have announced in childhood what they intended to do when they grew up. For example, Heinrich Schliemann, who excavated Troy, said when he was less than eight years old that he was going to find Troy. Jean-François Champollion, the founder of Egyptology, expressed an interest in this subject when he was still a child; and according to his recollections later, he had determined to decipher the Egyptian hieroglyphics when he was not yet twelve. Michael Ventris, who deciphered Linear B, the script of the Mycenaeans, purchased and studied a German book on Egyptian hieroglyphs when he was only seven, and when he was fourteen he vowed to try to decode the then undeciphered Mycenaean writing.

Among saints who have given early evidence of their life's work, St. Catherine of Siena was unusually precocious, although not unique. In early childhood she played at being a hermit and fasted and scourged herself; at seven she solemnly dedicated her life to Jesus. St. Catherine's father was a dyer of Siena, and although he and his wife were pious persons and did not oppose their daughter's religious vocation, nothing in their lives can adequately explain her development as a saint.[4]

The expression early in life of interests that are unusual in a child's family does not occur only among persons who later distinguish themselves. We find ordinary children of ordinary parents showing interests that differ from those that might be expected in someone from their environment. Several examples of such persons have been brought to my attention. One of them showed a fascination with watches and a competence in repairing them that had no basis in any influence from his family. Another, who was raised in the interior of the United States, had a fascination for the sea and ships, although other members of his family did not have the slightest interest in seafaring. A third child of this group was a white American boy who showed an unsual partiality toward American natives. He liked to wear their tribal dress, and in any controversy dividing natives and white persons he invariably sided with the natives. No member of his family shared his enthusiasm for native Americans, and his attitude made him somewhat of an outsider. None of these children had any imaged memories of previous lives.

Current theories of personality cannot adequately explain the interest in their later vocations that the persons I have mentioned showed both at an early age and against the indifference or opposition of their families. It seems to me appropriate to consider the possibility that these interests derived from previous lives, even though none of the persons had any imaged memories of such lives.

In support of this suggestion, I can cite children from the cases I have studied who *did* have such imaged memories and who also showed early some unusual interest that seemed to derive from the remembered previous life. Corliss Chotkin, Jr., was one such child, and I mentioned in chapter 4 the interest that he had in engines, something that he evidently did not acquire through inheritance or from imitating his father, who had little or no interest in engines.

The children (usually girls) who remember the previous lives of persons with strong religious interests frequently show a precocious piety. This behavior may manifest itself in a family whose other members are also devout, as in the case of Ratana Wongsombat; but sometimes, as in Disna Samarasinghe's case, the child belongs to a family whose other members regard religion with indifference or distaste.[5]

Less amiable traits may also appear in the behavior of some children. In two instances children who remembered previous lives as thieves engaged in picking pockets and other larcenies.

Many subjects have expressed in their play the vocation of the previous personality. Wijanama Kithsiri regularly opened a play shop when he came home from school; and Parmod Sharma's mother grumbled that he had squandered a year in playing at having a tea and biscuit shop. Both of these subjects remembered lives in families of shopkeepers. Ma Tin Aung Myo (whose case I summarized in chapter 4) and Bajrang B. Saxena played at being soldiers when they were young children; they remembered the lives of soldiers. Vias Rajpal, who remembered the life of a doctor, used to pretend to take the temperatures of his playmates and listen to their chests. Daniel Jirdi, who recalled the life of an automobile mechanic, would lie under his family's sofa and make believe that he was under a car that he was repairing. Lalitha Abeyawardena, who remembered the life of a schoolteacher, assembled her playmates in the form of a class and used a stick to point toward an imaginary blackboard in front of which she would play at teaching.[6]

Judith Krishna, who as a young child remembered the life of a sweepress (in India), gathered twigs, which she put together in the form of a broom (of the type used by sweepers), and with this she would sweep out her family's compound. I mentioned earlier another young Indian girl, Swaran Lata, who remembered the life of a sweepress; she had particularly dirty habits, but she cleaned up the excrement of the younger children of the family with seeming pleasure. Both these last two subjects were daughters of middle-class parents in whose families the behavior of a sweeper was as unexpected as it was unwelcome.

Subjects of these cases may also express in play an addictive habit of the person whose life they remembered. For example, I have known two children who remembered the lives of alcoholics and in their play gave amusing demonstrations of how a drunken person staggers around and collapses. One of these children was Sujith Lakmal Jayaratne, whom I have already mentioned in connection with the phobias he had of trucks and policemen.

Other subjects have relived in play how the previous personality died. Ramez Shams, who remembered a life that ended in suicide (by shooting), used to enact the motion of shooting himself; another child, Maung Win Aung, who recalled a suicidal death by hanging, had the habit of playing with a rope around his neck in a seeming enactment of hanging himself. Three other subjects who remembered previous lives that ended in suicidal drowning used to play at drowning.

In some cases, a subject has given dolls or play objects the names of the previous personality's children.[7] I have sometimes asked Western parents from where their children derived the names they gave their dolls. Often the source of the names is obvious, but when it is not, I think it worth considering that the child may have given to the dolls the names of persons who figured in a previous life that the child subliminally remembered.

Unusual Aptitudes and Untaught Skills of Early Childhood

A few subjects have shown in early childhood some unusual aptitude or untaught skill. Corliss Chotkin, Jr., whom I mentioned in the preceding section, had more than an interest in engines; he seemed to know how to repair them without having been instructed in this.

Susan Eastland's mother said that Susan sometimes seemed to know, without being taught,[8] how to do things she had not done before.

I must note, however, the scantiness of evidence that child prodigies derive their skills from practice in previous lives. To the best of my knowledge no child prodigy in the West has ever attributed his skill to a previous life, and few of Asia have done so. However, I have studied two subjects in India who were said to have recited in childhood lengthy passages of scriptural verses they had never learned (in childhood) and who remembered the lives of devoutly religious persons who had learned the scriptures thoroughly. By the time I reached these cases, one subject was a young woman, and the other was a middle-aged woman. In view of their ages, it did not seem feasible to me to try to learn exactly either what scriptures they had recited without instruction when they had been young children or what normal exposure to the scriptures they might earlier have had. However, the careful study of similar cases when the subjects are still young children might provide support for the idea that child prodigies have studied and learned their skills in previous lives.

Addictions and Cravings

Some subjects have surprised and amused their elders by requesting—even demanding—an intoxicant, such as alcohol, tobacco, or cannabis derivatives. They claimed to remember previous lives in which these substances solaced them, and they saw no reason why they should not resume their use. Their tastes for the intoxicants seemed in no instance explicable by imitation of their parents, who, so far as I could learn, either did not take the drug demanded by the child or, if they did, did not approve of a young child's doing so.[9]

Temperament

Psychologists use the word *temperament* to designate features of a person's behavior that remain more or less constant throughout his life regardless of particular stimuli. With a musical metaphor we could say they are the ground bass above which the various melodies are played. One dimension of temperament is the general level of physical activity. Another is the persistence with which one pursues some undertaking despite interruptions. A third is irritability or the tendency to lose one's temper readily in response to a frustration.

Students of temperament have found that infants even a few days old show marked differences in this respect; indeed some expressions of temperament, such as the level of activity, may manifest and be observed in fetuses. The causes of differences in temperament have received comparatively little study, and no expert claims full understanding of them; some experts admit to bafflement about the differences. [10]

In several cases I have investigated, informants emphasized similarities of temperament—such as a high level of physical activity or a quick temper—in a subject and in the person whose life the subject claimed to remember. Imad Elawar and Disna Samarasinghe were said to have quick or "hot" tempers that corresponded to similar features in the persons whose lives they remembered.

Precocious Sexuality

Some subjects of these cases when still young children have overtly expressed sexual interest in the wife, mistress, or girlfriend of the previous personality. Others have made precocious sexual advances to members of the opposite sex who resembled the partners of the previous lives. I have found this type of behavior only in subjects who remembered the previous life of a person who died during the usual years of maximal sexual activity, that is, youth and young adulthood.

In chapter 4 I described behavior of this type in Bongkuch Promsin. [11]

Gender-Identity Confusion

The children who say they remember previous lives as a member of the opposite sex nearly always show, when young, traits that are characteristic of the claimed former sex. They may reject, or act as if they rejected, the anatomical sex of their bodies. A girl, for example, may assert that she is a boy and insist on dressing in boys' clothes, playing boys' games, and being addressed as a boy would be. [12]

I have followed some of these children into their teens and young adulthood or later. The majority gradually accept their anatomical sex, give up cross-dressing, and become normal in all respects. A small number, however, have not adapted so well; they have remained fixed in the gender role of the sex of the previous life and usually are correspondingly unhappy.

In summarizing the case of Ma Tin Aung Myo I mentioned the obduracy with which she insisted—even in adulthood—that she was

a man, not a woman. In chapter 5 I mentioned another subject of a
sex-change case, Rani Saxena (of India), and described her tenacious
persistence in using masculine verb forms when speaking Hindi. I
shall now give some additional information about her case. She remembered the previous life of a prosperous lawyer of Benares. She was
born in Allahabad in a family remotely connected with that of the
Benares lawyer, but of much more modest resources. From an early
age she had detailed accurate memories of the lawyer's life in Benares.
(A reliable firsthand informant told me that she once recognized a
person unknown to her, but well known to the deceased lawyer, by his
voice alone and before she had even seen this man; she was in a room of
a house he visited, and she heard him speak before she saw him.)

Despite her strong masculine orientation, Rani was ultimately
married by an arrangement of her family, according to the Indian
custom. Rani's unusual behavior made it impossible for her family to
find an economically satisfactory husband for her, and after her marriage she lived in desperate poverty. She bore two children and brought
them up as a good mother, albeit a somewhat reluctant one. The
Benares lawyer had selfishly exploited women, and Rani believed that
God had put her in a female body so that she could experience life as a
woman. However, she showed an ambivalent attitude toward her situation. On the one hand, she said that she could see God's justice in putting her into a female body and obliging her to live in a clay hut; on the
other hand, she also still thought of herself as fully and properly male,
and she pined for the rich life in Benares that she still remembered.

Cases such as those of Ma Tin Aung Myo and Rani Saxena resemble those that Western psychiatrists label "gender-identity confusion" or "gender dysphoria." Some investigators of this condition have
incriminated a biological factor (such as Klinefelter's syndrome) but
cannot thereby explain all cases. [13] In some cases the parents, having
hoped for a child of a particular sex but having obtained one of the
opposite sex, have guided the child—sometimes unconsciously—to
assume the sexual identity they wished for the child. Yet this explanation also does not fit all cases of gender-identity dysphoria. [14] Some
patients with this condition have exonerated their parents from any
responsibility for it. A male patient may say, for example, that from
early childhood, almost as soon as he could think, he thought he
should have been in a female body; and he may specifically remember
that his parents disapproved of his attempts to dress in girls' clothes or
otherwise behave like a girl. [15]

The common occurrence of some gender-identity confusion among the subjects of sex-change cases that I have studied allows me to suggest that perhaps the condition of other persons afflicted with gender-identity confusion (and also homosexuality) derives from previous lives as members of the opposite sex. As I said at the beginning of this chapter, this might occur even when the person concerned has no imaged memories of a previous life.

Differences between Members of One-Egg Twin Pairs

In my collection of cases there are thirty-six pairs of twins; one or both of these twins has remembered a previous life. In about two-thirds of the pairs, one twin has remembered more about a previous life than the other. In some instances only one of the twins has had memories of a previous life; and sometimes this twin has said that the other twin was with him or her in the previous life, even though the second twin has not remembered this.

In twenty-six of the cases of twin pairs a previous personality was satisfactorily identified for both twins. (Among the other twin pairs one or both of the twins' cases remained unsolved.) Among the twenty-six solved cases, the previous personalities had had a familial (sometime marital) relationship in nineteen cases and had been friends or acquaintances in the remaining seven cases; in no instance had the previous personalities been strangers.

In chapter 4 I gave an illustration of these relationships in the summary of the case of Gillian and Jennifer Pollock, who remembered the lives of their own older sisters, Joanna and Jacqueline. Similarly, Ramoo and Rajoo Sharma, twins of India, recalled previous lives as twin brothers in another village. In a third case, Ma Khin Ma Gyi and Ma Khin Ma Nge (of Burma) recalled the previous lives of their own maternal grandparents. Ma Khin Ma Gyi was thus claiming to have been a man in her previous life, and she showed (as a young child) cross-dressing and some characteristics of her grandfather.

Sivanthie and Sheromie Hettiaratchi (both females) remembered the previous lives of two young men who had been close friends and homosexuals. (These twins were thus both subjects of sex-change cases, and, as in most other such cases, they both showed strong masculine behavior.)

In their relationships with each other, the twins who remember previous lives often adopt attitudes consonant with those of the previous personalities. Thus, Gillian Pollock acted toward Jennifer like an older sister, and Jennifer was correspondingly dependent on Gillian. (Joanna, with whom Gillian identified, had been five years older than Jacqueline.) Similarly, Ma Khin Ma Nge fussily dominated Ma Khin Ma Gyi, just as her maternal grandmother had tried to control her husband.

Two Burmese twins, Maung Aung Cho Thein and Maung Aung Ko Thein, remembered the life of the owner of a rice mill (a woman) and that of a rice farmer who had brought his paddy to this mill. The behavior of the twins (who are almost certainly of the two-egg type) toward each other reflected the somewhat haughty demeanor of the wealthy female millowner and the deferential attitude of the paddy farmer. We found this kind of dominant/submissive relationship in all eleven of the twin-pair cases for which we had sufficient information about the roles and behavior of the subjects and previous personalities.

Identical or one-egg twins [16] provide an excellent opportunity for separating genetic factors from environmental ones as causes of various individual differences, abnormalities, or diseases. Investigators of behavior and mental illness have given special attention to one-egg twins who were separated soon after birth and reared apart. [17] To simplify slightly, behavioral differences between such twins are attributed to the influences of their separate environments, and similarities are attributed to their common genetic material. In general, whether they have studied one-egg twins reared together or those reared separately, investigators have emphasized their similarities rather than their differences. Reincarnation may contribute to an understanding of both.

Let us consider first the similarities between one-egg twins reared apart. They have been said to develop schizophrenia more readily than do two-egg twins reared apart. Many psychiatrists believe this concordance reflects genetic factors that underlie such behavior, although they have not asserted this without challenge, and the matter is still debated. [18] I suggest that the similar behavior of one-egg twins (whether reared apart or reared together) may derive, at least in part, from their having had previous lives together; in these they might have developed similar habits and attitudes that persisted when they reincarnated. If two men who have been criminals together die and reincarnate as one-egg twins, we should not be surprised if both become criminals again.

Now let us turn to the differences between one-egg twins, especially those reared together. Like identical twins reared apart, they have identical genetic material. Dissimilarities in their behavior may derive from differences in the attitudes of their parents toward the individual twins. For example, one twin is sometimes appreciably smaller and weaker than the other, and this twin is likely to evoke solicitude, or perhaps some other special attitude, not shown to the other twin. Investigators have also attributed the differences between one-egg twins reared together to their not having had exactly the same environment in the uterus. It is suggested, for example, that after the division of the single egg from which the two embryos developed, one embryo received a better blood supply (or was otherwise favored). An explanation of this type is invoked in cases of one-egg twins when one has a birth defect and the other does not. As an example of this we may consider cleft lip, which is a birth defect occurring in about one baby of every 2,000 born. The marked difference in the concordance for cleft lip between one-egg and two-egg twins provides strong evidence of a genetic factor in this birth defect. Among two-egg twins, if one twin has a cleft palate, both have the condition in 8 percent of cases; but among one-egg twins, if one has the condition, both have it in 38 percent of cases. However, as nearly two-thirds of one-egg twins do *not* show this concordance, some other factor besides the genetic one must be responsible when cleft lip occurs in only one of the twins.[19] It is for these cases that some investigators invoke the explanation of a deficiency in the blood supply to one twin or some other local uterine abnormality during the embryonic development of the lips.

Yet perhaps differences in the uterine environment of the two embryos do not tell the full story of the dissimilarities between one-egg twins. In addition to variations in blood supply before birth and differences in the attitudes of their parents toward the twins, a third factor may be in play: behavioral memories from previous incarnations. I can illustrate this possibility with a case of one-egg twins that I studied in Sri Lanka.

The twins, Indika and Kakshappa Ishwara, look somewhat alike, although they would not be as easily confused with each other as are many one-egg twins. However, I know that they are one-egg twins from tests (of blood groups and subgroups) carried out at the University of Virginia with blood drawn from the twins and members of their family, which I brought with me when I returned from one of my visits to Sri Lanka.

From their early childhood Indika and Kakshappa manifested markedly different behavior, which I shall describe below. When they became able to speak, Indika gradually narrated details of a previous life that he said he had lived in another town of Sri Lanka, located about 50 kilometers from where the twins were born. The life he recalled was that of an innocent, studious schoolboy. Indika stated a number of names and other unusual details that permitted tracing a family to which he seemed to be referring. Members of this family confirmed that almost everything Indika had stated about the previous life was correct for a young boy they had lost. At the age of thirteen, this youth had developed a serious (evidently infectious) disease and died within a few days. (The records of this boy's admission to the hospital where he had died had been destroyed by the time I instigated a search for them.)

At about the time Indika began to talk about the previous life he remembered, the twins' family asked Kakshappa whether he also remembered a previous life. He said that he had been an insurgent. (In chapter 5 I mentioned that Sri Lanka had a serious insurgency in the spring of 1971, and the army suppressed it with considerable loss of life.) The other members of the family thought that Kakshappa's claim to have been an insurgent was amusing, and they ridiculed him, so that he stopped talking; they thus learned almost nothing more about the life he said he remembered. Before Kakshappa's family unintentionally suppressed him, he had not given enough details to permit verification of the previous life to which he had been referring. He had, however, mentioned the name of one town that figured in the life of the insurgent about whom he had tried to talk. This town was well known to have been a center where the insurgents had gathered, and some of them had been killed there. It is also only a few kilometers from the town where Indika said that he had lived.

Indika was a gentle, bookish sort of boy. He had a definite dignity and expected respect from others that seemed more appropriate for the life he remembered than for the circumstances of his family, since the previous family in his case was more prosperous than his own. Kakshappa, on the other hand, could fairly be described as "tough." His talk was likely to focus on guns and bombs, never on books; indeed, he resisted going to school (when he first went). He also showed a pervasive fear, and he ran away and hid from strangers, behavior that reminded observations of the way the Sri Lanka insurgents of 1971 tried to conceal themselves from the police until they were ready to strike. It is possible that once Indika and Kakshappa had spoken about the two quite different previous lives they remembered, they became cast by their family in two roles to which they then tended to conform more and more. This might have led to some further polarization of their behaviors and of informants' reports about them. Although this may have happened to some extent, it seems reasonable to suppose that some of their disparate behavior expressed behavioral memories from the different previous lives that they remembered.[20] In 1982, when Indika and Kakshappa were just ten years old, I met them again and learned that the differences in their personalities had become much less marked. For example, Kakshappa was enjoying school and doing almost as well there as Indika was. However, in a dispute Kakshappa was inclined to resort to violence, whereas Indika was not.

Before leaving the subject of twins, I wish to mention the opportunity for further investigations along these lines provided by cases of conjoined (often called Siamese) twins. An early investigator of twins, Newman, observed that members of Siamese twin pairs tend to differ in personality even more than do the members of ordinary (separated) one-egg twin pairs. Chang and Eng, the original Siamese twins, who lived in the middle of the nineteenth century, showed vivid differences in personality. Chang was inclined to be cross and irritable; Eng, good-natured. Chang drank alcohol, often excessively (especially in their later years), whereas Eng was a teetotaler. What one liked to eat, the other detested.[21] Since members of a Siamese twin pair, like members of other one-egg twin pairs, have identical genetic material and since, even more than separated one-egg twins, they also have closely similar environments, we might expect the members of conjoined twin pairs to resemble each other more than do members of separate one-egg twin pairs; but they do not. Although neither Chang nor Eng ever said anything suggestive of memories of previous lives, I conjecture that the marked differences in their personalities may have arisen from their having had different behavioral memories (for example, of drinking alcohol or not drinking it) that derived from previous lives.

Child-Parent Relationships

In earlier parts of this book I mentioned, with examples, the frequent desire expressed by the subjects of these cases to visit the previous family. I suggested various motives for this longing, such as a wish to be again with the spouse of the previous life or concern about the welfare of the previous personality's young children. Here I shall discuss another motive for the child's wanting to be with the previous family. This is the strong conviction some subjects have that their previous parents were better than the parents now available to them. They sometimes distinguish the previous parents from the inadequate substitutes with whom they find themselves by giving the former some descriptive title, such as "my real parents." I earlier described such attitudes in my summaries of the cases of Shamlinie Prema and Roberta Morgan.[22] Even when the subject's parents provide well for him—both materially and emotionally—he may long to be again with his "real parents." The wish to see the other parents may derive in such cases from some residual attachment to the parents of the previous life or a concern about their welfare.

From whatever motive it may arise, a child's repeated references to other parents, his frequent comparisons between them and his parents, and his often-expressed wish that he be allowed to go to the other parents may result in the alienation of the child from his family. The degree of such estrangement naturally depends upon the duration of the child's references to the "real parents," the noisiness of his demands to meet them, the starkness of the comparisons he makes, and—not least—his parents' tolerance for all this unpleasant behavior.

If reincarnation occurs, friction between a parent and child may derive from another type of relationship in the child's previous life. I refer to cases in which a child claims that, in the previous life he remembers, he was equal or senior in age to a parent.[23] He may, for example, say that he was his mother's grandfather and, what is more important, behave as if he still is. What follows from this behavior may depend, at least in part, on the mixtures of kindness and selfishness that characterized the grandfather's attitude toward his granddaughter and hers toward him.

A strained relationship may also occur between a subject and one parent if the subject claims to have had a special relationship in a previous life with the other parent. In chapter 4 the case of Michael Wright illustrated this possibility; I also mentioned there (in note 14) three cases in which the subject claimed to have been the first spouse of one of his or her parents. The case of Taru Järvi in Finland produced many awkward moments. She claimed to have been her mother's first husband in her previous life, and she made some effort to rid her family of her father on the grounds that she and her mother did "not need him."[24]

In a few cases the subject has claimed to have had in the previous life a relationship with a parent, not of blood ties with affection, but of animosity and even of hatred.[25] I have so far published only one detailed report of such a case, that of Zouheir Chaar of Lebanon. He remembered the life of a man who quarreled bitterly with Zouheir's mother over rights to irrigation water. Each had accused the other of stealing the precious water. Observers of Zouheir's case thought it included some justice for both Zouheir and his mother. Almost as soon as Zouheir could speak, he began to accuse his mother of stealing water from him. His mother handled his attacks adroitly, and over a few years Zouheir's rancor gradually abated.

In Zouheir's case he stated the basis for his grievance, and his mother could remember the quarrels about the irrigation water, even though she did not admit to having been in the wrong. In other cases, however, a child may show unprovoked animosity toward a parent without giving any reason for it. If this happens in a culture favorable to the idea of reincarnation, the parent can respond constructively through believing that the child's hostility perhaps derives from a previous life rather than from any wrong the parent has done to the child. In contrast, Western parents unfamiliar with the concept of reincarnation may find themselves nonplussed and hurt by a sulky or unaffectionate child whom they cannot remember offending or mishandling. In some instances of this type, the parents may well have overlooked some deficiency in their handling of the child; and yet in others it may be worthwhile for them to consider the possibility that attitudes from a previous life (or lives) have been brought into the present relationship without either parent or child having any imaged memories of the earlier shared experiences that generated the attitudes that now perplex them.

For many years some psychiatrists blamed certain serious mental illnesses, such as schizophrenia, on mishandling or rejection by the parents of the patient when he was a young child. In thus condemning the parents, these censors overlooked how successfully many of the parents of a schizophrenic patient had raised other children. They also ignored the frequent observations of the patients' mothers that a child who later became a patient had behaved differently, almost from birth, compared with his siblings. He would not, for example, relax and cuddle up to the parent when picked up. Child psychologists and psychiatrists now recognize that children differ in their responses to their parents at birth and even before they are born; but the origin of these differences is usually assigned to a genetic factor or to events during gestation. I think we should look still farther back for the origins of at least some of the impaired relationships—and some of the good ones also—between parents and their children.

Apparently Irrational Aggression

If I am right in suggesting that reincarnation may help to explain some aspect of the relations between parents and children, it may also help to improve our understanding of behavior in relations outside the family. I am thinking here of apparently irrational antagonisms shown by some persons toward other persons or toward whole groups of persons. The high incidence of violent death among the previous personalities in these cases has given excellent opportunities for studying the apparent carryover from one life to another of attitudes of vengefulness, such as might be expected of a victim for his murderer. As we might predict from what we know of people's reactions toward experiences in one life, some subjects show forgiveness toward the persons who they say murdered them in a previous life and others do not. Several children subjects have spoken openly about revenging themselves on the assailants of the previous life when they became big enough to do so. In chapter 4 I described how Bongkuch Promsin would beat a post in anger and call out the names of Chamrat's murderers as he did so. As such children become older, their vengefulness usually recedes, and a more tolerant attitude toward the previous personality's murderer succeeds it.

When a subject does show an attitude of vengefulness, his animosity may extend to the entire group of which the previous personality's assailant was a member. The subject may show antagonism toward, say, all policemen, all Bedouins, or all Moslems.[26]

From adverse generalizations about vocational, tribal, and religious groups, it is only a short step to hatred of entire nations and races. Perhaps the obvious normal source for the transmission of such attitudes from one generation to successive ones suffices: I am thinking here of the manner in which children may learn at a parent's knee to take his enemy as theirs. From such oral transmission, presumably, Southerners hated Yankees, Frenchmen hated Germans, and Mac-Donalds hated Campbells throughout decades or centuries. But international and interclan animosities may not be transmitted solely by the telling of tales to children. If reincarnation occurs, the hatred that a person killed by a member of another nation may feel toward all people of that nation might be carried over into his next life. I know of no verified case that exactly illustrates the process I am conjecturing; but certain unverified Burmese cases offer some support for it. I refer to those cases—of which we now have twenty—in which a Burmese child has remembered a previous life as a Japanese soldier killed in Burma during World War II. (Ma Tin Aung Myo, whose case I summarized in chapter 4, is an example.) Many of these children had traits that are unusual in Burmese families, but characteristic of Japanese persons, especially Japanese soldiers.[27] Some of these subjects showed a special interest in Japanese persons who occasionally came to Burma when the subjects were children; and a few were reported to become angry when British or American persons were mentioned in their presence.

OTHER ABNORMALITIES THAT REINCARNATION MAY EXPLAIN

Abnormal Appetites During Pregnancy

Many women experience unusual cravings or aversions for particular foods during pregnancy. A few pregnant women have noted other changes in their feelings and behavior from those that they believe are normal for themselves.

Extensive physiological and anatomical changes occur in a pregnant woman. In addition, her relations with the people around her necessarily become altered, especially those with her husband and her children, if she has any. A pregnancy may bring unusual joy and well-being; but it can also bring discomfort, anxiety, and even dread. The vast biochemical and psychological changes that accompany the smoothest of pregnancies may account for most of the unusual appetites that pregnant women have noted in themselves. I should therefore not have included this topic here if I had not learned of some cases in which pregnancy cravings or aversions on the part of a subject's mother corresponded to the subject's later appetitive preferences and, in some instances, to similar preferences reported by informants for the previous personality of the case.

In the case of Bongkuch Promsin (summarized in chapter 4), the mother of Chamrat (whose life Bongkuch remembered) had had, during her pregnancy with Chamrat, the same craving (for a special type of noodles) that was later shown by Chamrat, by Bongkuch's mother during *her* pregnancy with Bongkuch, and by Bongkuch himself.[28]

Maung Myint Tin (a Burmese subject whose case U Win Maung studied) remembered the previous life of an alcoholic, and he himself showed a strong craving for alcohol when he was young. Pertinent to the present topic was his mother's report that for the first four or five months of her pregnancy with Maung Myint Tin she had had an almost overpowering desire to drink alcohol herself; she only controlled this with great effort during the latter part of her pregnancy.

A few of the subjects' mothers have also reported having noted during their pregnancy with the subject other changes from their accustomed behavior. Disna Samarasinghe's mother was one of these. She said that during her pregnancy with Disna she felt unusually devout and wished to hear monks chanting more than she ordinarily did; Disna, as a young child, was remarkable for her precocious piety, and she remembered the previous life of a woman who had meditated much. Ornuma Sua Ying Yong's mother found she was unable to gamble at cards during her pregnancy with Ornuma, although ordinarily she relished this activity. Ornuma showed unusual piety as a young child; among her expressions of this trait, she strongly objected to her mother gambling at cards and made herself tiresome with her interferences among her mother's circle of cardplayers.

A Tlingit informant told me about different experiences she had had when pregnant with her four children. During three pregnancies she was strongly interested in music and each of the children born of these pregnancies was musical. During her fourth pregnancy she was not especially interested in music, but cooked and sewed—more than usual, I understood; the child of this pregnancy was not musical but was interested in cooking and sewing.

I obtained all the reports of these changes in behavior *after* the births of the subjects (and after the cases had developed), although in some instances the mother's husband (and subject's father) corroborated her statements about her altered behavior. I should also emphasize that reports of cravings or other unusual changes in the mother during pregnancy occur in a small percentage of cases only; in most cases when I enquire about them the mother (or other informant) reports that she noticed nothing of the kind when she was pregnant with the subject.

My informants may have modified their reports of the mother's cravings or other changes in order to harmonize them with observations of the child's later behavior. We could also suppose that the child had received encouragement from his mother to accord his behavior with her pregnancy experiences. Furthermore, it is possible that the mother's abnormal appetite was communicated paranormally to her fetus and impelled in it a similar appetite that persisted after birth. This may have happened in one case: The subject's mother reported having had pregnancy cravings that later corresponded to food preferences of the subject, but these cravings did not correspond to any appetites the previous personality of the case was known to have had.

My observations about certain behavioral changes in pregnant women are merely preliminary. However, I think that they justify further investigations, which should include prospective studies of the relationship between pregnancy cravings (or other behavioral changes in a pregnant woman) and subsequent behavior shown by the child born from the pregnancy. In the meantime, we can continue to entertain the possibility that a personality who is going to reincarnate may sometimes impose on a pregnant woman some of his appetites and attitudes.

Left-handedness

The use of one hand in preference to the other appears to derive much from social training; adults who prefer using the left hand are far less numerous than are children who do. Childhood training appears, therefore, to favor preferential use of the right hand, and many persons who have inclined in early life toward left-handedness gradually adapt to equipment, tools, and other objects that favor right-handed persons.

Some left-handedness appears to be congenital; it has, at any rate, been observed early in infancy. This and other evidence suggests a hereditary factor in the occurrence of left-handedness. However, when the trait occurs in two or more members of the same immediate family, it may be difficult to separate the influence of a genetic factor from that of imitation of a left-handed parent by a child. Perhaps in some cases we should invoke both a genetic factor and the influence of imitation.

Hand preference is a type of skilled behavior. Threading a needle, for example, is a skill, and doing so better with one hand than with the other is a further specialized development of the basic skill. It seems likely that hand preference—whether of the right or the left hand—gives an advantage; presumably it enables us to do better something like threading a needle that we would not do so well if we did not "allow" one hand to practice the action more than the other and thus become more expert than either hand would be if both practiced the action equally. If this is so, we might expect that a person would carry over a hand preference from one life to another, and I have found a small amount of evidence suggesting this. My associates and I have obtained information about ten cases in which the subject was left-handed and the previous personality was also said to have been left-handed.

I should mention that in two of these ten cases, I also obtained conflicting testimony concerning whether the previous personality had been left-handed; and in two other cases the subjects' statements have not been verified, so we have only their statements that the previous personalities of their cases were also left-handed. Moreover, in five of the cases, the subject and previous personality belonged to the same (immediate or extended) family, and in these cases we cannot exclude a genetic factor. (Corliss Chotkin, Jr., was one of these subjects.)

It seems legitimate to ask why everyone does not use his right hand preferentially. This is another way of asking how left-handedness started and what causes it to persist. I am far from daring to offer a comprehensive answer to these questions, but we do have grounds for some conjectures related to reincarnation. In the first place, a right-handed person who loses his right arm or hand usually adapts to his new condition and becomes left-handed. This is what the great British admiral Lord Nelson did. He was wounded at the battle of Santa Cruz de Tenerife in 1797, and his right arm was amputated. Afterwards he learned to write passably well with his left hand.[29]

Presumably, someone like Lord Nelson who became left-handed by necessity would, if he were reborn, have a congenital disposition toward left-handedness. (In this suggestion I assume that the hand that was more practiced at the time of death would become dominant in the next incarnation.) I know of only one case that directly supports this conjecture. It is that of a young girl in Burma, Ma Khin Sandi, who was identified as the reincarnation of her maternal grandmother. Ma Khin Sandi was left-handed, but her grandmother was not; nor was anyone else in the family. However, the grandmother had a stroke with paralysis of her right arm for the last several months of her life; and I conjecture that a behavioral memory of a useless right arm may have led Ma Khin Sandi to use her left arm preferentially.

Three other cases in Burma touch on the question of how left-handedness may develop. In all three of the subjects of these cases, several fingers of both hands were congenitally deformed or completely absent. These birth defects, according to the statements of the subjects and other informants, corresponded to slashing wounds of the fingers (made with swords) that the three previous personalities received just before they were killed. It happened that in each of the subjects the right hand was more deformed, and hence less useful for holding objects, than was the left. These three subjects were, therefore, left-handed. They all told me that they had been right-handed in their previous lives. (I could not verify these statements, although I did verify other details of what these subjects said about the previous lives they remembered.) If a future child should claim to remember the lives of one of these subjects (after they die), I should expect that child to be left-handed.

Birthmarks and Birth Defects

In chapter 5 I mentioned the importance of those cases in which the subjects have birthmarks and birth defects. I also explained my reasons for not entering into the details of this topic in the present volume. I have included it here, however, because birthmarks and birth defects belong in any inventory of biological problems that reincarnation may help to elucidate.

The Uniqueness of the Individual

The uniqueness of the individual[30] is a topic of never-ending interest and conjecture. We often speculate about the origins of physical and personal traits in members of our families and in our friends. We may say casually that a daughter in a family received her blue eyes from her grandmother and her stubbornness from her grandfather. In the informal conversations in which remarks of this type occur, the speakers assume the inheritance of a wide variety of physical characteristics and behavioral traits. If we wish to explain some unusual quality that occurs in a member of a family with no known other member having it, we may attribute the quality to inheritance from some distant ancestor, even an imaginary one.

Geneticists tell us that an individual's uniqueness (at birth) derives mainly from the random distribution of chromosomes that occurred during the formation of his parents' gametes (sperm and egg) before his father's sperm began its journey to his mother's egg that it fertilized. The parents' chromosomes derived before that from a similar random sorting into their parents' gametes (germ cells) before they were conceived. According to this view, our uniqueness arises from the randomly sorted chromosomes dealt to us from among the chromosomes that were dealt to our parents from among the chromosomes dealt to them, and so on back forever. Ultimately, the unique combination of qualities each of us has is a matter of chance, just as is a hand in a card game that we may be dealt after someone has shuffled the cards.

If there were no evidence suggesting that reincarnation may occur, I should probably be content with the idea that our innate capacities derive from the chance shuffling of genes. As there is some evidence, however, it is possible that an individual's uniqueness derives not exclusively from his genetic makeup but also (at least in part) from experiences of predecessor personalities in previous lives. I have to admit immediately that an advocate of reincarnation must also make assumptions in accounting for most specific instances. It will, however, be worth mentioning some examples; if they are not as good examples as we might wish, they can at least illustrate what we might look for in future research.

Some of the children whose cases I have studied show combinations of traits that are unusual in their families but can be understood as deriving from the experiences of a *single* previous life. Disna Samarasinghe showed an unusual piety and also a precocious knowledge of household chores, such as cooking and thatch weaving; these corresponded with traits in the person, Babanona, whose life she claimed to remember. Similarly, Lalitha Abeyawardena, when she was a young child, played at being a teacher and, like Disna, showed an unusual interest in religious practices. Nilanthie, the woman whose life she claimed to remember, had been a schoolteacher and a person of renowned devoutness.[31]

Are there, however, any instances in which we can plausibly claim that different traits manifested in one life may have derived from two or more previous lives? Unfortunately, we have few examples of subjects making credible claims to remember more than one life; and we have even less evidence of more than one previous life being verified. I can, in fact, think of only two examples that may illustrate the point I am trying to make, and in each of these the second life remains unverified. For what they are worth, however, I shall refer to combinations of traits that occurred in two subjects who each claimed to remember two previous lives, one verified and one unverified.

Swarnlata Mishra (to whose case I have earlier referred briefly) made many statements that proved correct for the life of a woman called Biya, who had died in 1939, nine years before Swarnlata's birth in 1948. Biya had been married and a mother of children before her death. I think it reasonable to suppose that Swarnlata's strong tendency to care lovingly for other persons derived from Biya's experiences as a wife and mother. (This suggestion does not deny that Swarnlata's mother provided a model for such behavior.) Swarnlata also claimed to remember a short "intermediate" life that she said she had lived in Sylhet, which is now in Bangladesh. She claimed that in this life she had learned the Bengali songs and dances that she performed without being taught to do so. Although I have not verified the life in Sylhet, it is certain that neither Biya nor Swarnlata, living as they did in areas of central India where Hindi is spoken, could have learned Bengali songs and dances; so it seems reasonable to suppose that if Swarnlata had had a previous, "intermediate" life in Sylhet, she learned the songs and dances during it. (Bengali is the predominant language of Sylhet.)

Parmod Sharma remembered two previous lives. One of these, that of a successful businessman named Parmanand, was verified. We might trace to this life a precocious acumen in business matters that Parmod showed. Parmod also remembered an earlier (unverified) life as a *sannyasi*, or holy man. Both Parmod and Parmanand were notably religious persons compared with other members of their families; it seems reasonable to suppose that this trait in Parmod may have derived originally from the previous life as a sannyasi and been strengthened during the life of Parmanand.

THE LIMITS OF GENETICS AND
ENVIRONMENTAL INFLUENCES

I cannot make the explanatory value of reincarnation seem more attractive by pointing out the defects of the two explanations that now dominate attempts to understand human personality: genetics and environmental influences. I have already said that I regard the idea of reincarnation, not as replacing established knowledge in genetics and from studies of environmental influences, but as supplementing that knowledge. However, zealots for both genetics and environmental influences have made claims (for their favorite ideas) that are far more extravagant than any I am making for reincarnation; and some of their readers—as well as some of mine—may believe that more has been proven for these causes than has been.

The claims made for a genetic contribution to schizophrenia provide a good example of the large gap between such claims and the data said to support them. Investigators of the genetics of mental disorder have presented the case for a genetic factor in schizophrenia so convincingly that some textbooks of psychiatry teach it as an established fact. Cited investigations compared the incidence of schizophrenia in different persons and groups of persons with special attention to their genetic closeness to each other and to the similarities or differences in their environments. The main support for the idea of a genetic factor in schizophrenia in recent years has come from comparisons of twins (of both types) reared together and apart; from comparisons of the different incidences of mental illness in the children of schizophrenic parents adopted away from them (and hence presumably free from any noxious parental influence on their development) and in adopted children whose parents were not schizophrenic.

These kinds of investigations contain numerous sources of potential error. To begin with, schizophrenia is not a disorder for which we have as yet any objective indicator, such as measurements of blood sugar provide for the diagnosis of diabetes mellitus. Different psychiatrists sometimes disagree in their appraisal of the same patient, even when they have an opportunity to examine him at the same time. Such unreliability of diagnostic assessment may well be greater when the psychiatrists cannot examine the patients, but instead use hospital or other records and histories furnished by other persons. (This has happened in many of the criticized investigations.) Moreover, the lack of precise definition of schizophrenia encourages loose criteria of inclusion, so that persons identified as having "borderline disorders" or "schizophrenia spectrum disorders" have been accepted into a series.

In twin studies errors may arise in the determination of zygosity (although these are much reduced by examinations of blood groups and subgroups). The appraisers of psychiatric status may not always be as ignorant of the twins' zygosity as they should be, which is: completely "blind." Further errors can arise in assessing the environments of twins who are ostensibly raised apart or together. Sometimes twins said to have been raised apart have been found to have been raised by different members of the same family; in such instances the twins continue to meet each other to the point where it is doubtful whether their environments could be regarded as significantly different. A further source of error occurs in the tendency for social agencies (and families themselves even more so) to select adoptive parents from the same social stratum as the biological parents, which tends to bring about a similarity between the environments in which two twins ostensibly separated are raised. Another source of error works in the opposite direction. Parents who wish to adopt a child must be unusual in some respects, such as in not having a child of their own and in having an unusually strong desire to be parents. A child adopted away from his family may on this account alone receive an upbringing quite different from that of a child remaining with his biological parents.

Critics who draw attention to these sources of error do not minimize the difficulties in investigations of this type; they only insist that published reports of investigations have failed to show that the investigators have surmounted the difficulties. We still have no evidence for a genetic factor in the causation of schizophrenia. This is not to say that no such factor may exist, only to deny that it has been satisfactorily identified. Perhaps the amount of work lying ahead of geneticists in this field can be best demonstrated by drawing attention to the results of recent studies of twins. The best of these studies show a higher concordance of schizophrenia among monozygotic compared with dizygotic twins; but they also show a high *discordance* among monozygotic twins (who have the same genetic material). In fact, the co-twin of a monozygotic twin judged schizophrenic is more likely to be judged normal than otherwise.[32]

Even if all could agree that biological relatives have a higher incidence of a given abnormality—let it be obesity, schizophrenia, or criminality—this would not convince me that a genetic factor was the best interpretation of the data. In discussing similarities between one-egg twins I suggested earlier in this chapter that habitual criminals in one life might, if reincarnation occurs, find themselves linked as twins and repeat similar criminal behavior in a later life. In the same way obesity in several members of a family may not derive only from a genetic tendency to large bulk; it could also derive from familial habits of overeating that began in previous lives. Even alleged genetic factors in schizophrenia (if substantiated) remain open to alternative interpretations. The responses to stress that tragically unfold in the illness we call schizophrenia may derive from a combination of inflexibility toward changing situations and a tendency to blame other persons for one's hardships; such attitudes are spread within families, and if members of a family having them have lived previous lives together and reincarnate together, we should expect them to manifest the same or similar behavior and to suffer the consequences in mental illness. All that is familial is not necessarily genetic. Nor is it necessarily environmental, and I turn to this interpretation next.

If advocates of genetics as an explanation of differences in human personality have overstated their claims, so have proponents for the effects of environment, especially during the early years of life. For at least two generations clinical psychologists and psychiatrists enunciated the doctrine that the experiences of the first few years of life were crucial to the formation of human personality and, by implication, to the later occurrence or absence of mental disorder. In fact, this belief has a much longer history than that of either psychoanalysis or behaviorism, but the adherents of these two doctrines committed themselves to it along with their otherwise radically different claims to explain everything about human personality. It is curious that adherents of both psychoanalysis and behaviorism accepted with unusual dogmatism—even for them—the only concept that they held in common: that of the ineradicable influence of experiences during the first few years of life.

By the 1950s cracks had begun to appear in the edifice of theory and practice built on this assumption, for it has proved to be no more than that. Particularly damaging to claims about the primary importance of the early years of life has been the publication of reports of some children who have been neglected or mistreated during those years, but whose later development in a different environment has been normal. Careful observation failed to demonstrate the irreversible damage to the personality that doctrine had predicted. A further source of difficulty for believers in the primacy of early experiences arises from marked differences in intelligence and other aspects of personality between monozygotic twins reared together. The environmental influences that could bring about the observed differences have not been identified. It is merely supposed that they are too subtle to have been detected so far, and investigators are now hunting for what they optimistically call microenvironmental influences. The very word *microenvironmental* seems incongruous in relation to the macroscopic differences in personality that are to be explained. It betrays a fixed belief that what you are looking for must be where you are looking.[33]

Developmental psychologists have also pushed their investigations farther and farther back toward the days and weeks immediately after birth, and they have even begun to consider the influence of an infant's experiences during gestation. The results of these investigations also have not always conformed to expectations. For example, it has been found that infants show a wide variety of individual behavior almost immediately after birth[34] that cannot readily be accounted for by any identified experience they had before birth, or after birth and before the first appearance of the behavior.

The advocates of genetics and of environmental influences have in common that each thinks of the other party as the only adversary; claims are made and faults are found by members of both groups without any awareness that a third explanation for the gaps in knowledge awaits further examination.

CHAPTER TEN

Some Further Questions and Topics Related to Children Who Remember Previous Lives

In this chapter I shall consider some questions that are frequently asked, or that should be asked, about the cases that I have investigated. I have considered other important questions in previous chapters, but the miscellaneous group to which I shall now turn includes questions as important as any already discussed.

REINCARNATION AND THE POPULATION EXPLOSION

The present human population of the world amounts to approximately five billion persons. Since the end of the eighteenth century, when the modern rise in population began, world population has probably trebled. It continues to increase at a rate that has made some persons otherwise interested in reincarnation doubt whether there could be enough minds to animate all the human bodies that may soon exist.

Persons who raise this question seem to make the gratuitous assumption that there must be a perfect correspondence between the number of physical bodies that have existed and can exist and the number of human minds animating them. There are, however, other assumptions and speculations that one might make on this subject. One would be that new individual human minds are created as needed and attached to human bodies. Another is that human minds may split or duplicate so that one mind can reincarnate in two more bodies; the Eskimo, the Igbo of Nigeria, the Tibetans, the Haida of Alaska and British Columbia, and the Gitksan of British Columbia all believe this.[1] Still another possible assumption is that minds presently incarnated in human bodies have been promoted from previous incarnations in nonhuman bodies; Hindus and Buddhists believe this, and I shall discuss the belief in the next section.

Even if we make the first assumption I mentioned above—that of a close numerical matching between human minds and human bodies—we do not need to reject the idea of reincarnation solely because of the huge increase in population that has occurred during the past two centuries.

A somewhat conservative estimate of the number of human beings who have lived on the earth since recognized humans became distinguished from their hominid ancestors yields the figure of eighty billion.[2] This allows us to think that each of the five billion persons presently alive may have had, on average, sixteen incarnations; but this calculation involves the further assumption that the interval between death and rebirth has remained fixed, whereas it is just as likely to have fluctuated from time to time. There may have been periods when few minds were incarnated and many more were existing in a discarnate state, waiting for a terrestrial incarnation, or perhaps hoping to avoid one.

If we could take the cases already investigated as representative of the population as a whole, we might believe that the rate of reincarnation could not increase much. As I explained in chapter 5, the interval between death and presumed rebirth varies widely, but the median interval among 616 cases was only fifteen months. However, these cases may not be representative for several reasons, to one of which—the high incidence of violent death among them—I have already referred. Another reason is this: The short interval between death and presumed rebirth may have contributed to the development of a case. In the analyses we have made so far, we have found no correlation between the length of interval between death and presumed rebirth and the abundance of memories that the subject of a case expressed. If, however, memories fade with time in a world of discarnate minds—as they do in our familiar one—we would rarely find cases having verified memories when the interval was greater than the outer limits found in the cases presently known to us, which is (with a few rare exceptions) about twenty-five years. If reincarnation were to be delayed for longer periods than that, memories might attenuate markedly, and no identifiable cases from such incarnations would occur for our epidemiological studies. It therefore remains possible that for a major portion of all existing minds the interval between death and rebirth is longer—perhaps much longer—than what we have found in the cases that have come to our attention so far. This in turn means that many discarnate minds may be awaiting reincarnation and could thus contribute to an even greater increase in the world's population than we have seen during the last two centuries.

With a mere two thousand cases providing data, I am embarrassed to engage in the speculations of this section concerning billions of human beings who have all disappeared without a trace. I excuse myself because so many persons have raised the question of the population's increase with me, and I think I should show that I have given it some attention.

IS THERE ANY EVIDENCE FOR REINCARNATION AMONG NONHUMAN ANIMALS?

Hindus and Buddhists believe that nonhuman animals reincarnate and, further, that humans may reincarnate as nonhuman animals if they merit this by misconduct. After the demerit has been expiated in an incarnation as a nonhuman animal, another incarnation as a human may occur. These concepts may seem to burn away any remaining difficulties that the population explosion poses, since there exists a large reservoir of nonhuman animal minds presumably ready for, or working toward, incarnation in human bodies. Some difficulties would remain, however, because Buddhists and most Hindus believe that killing animals is wrong and likely to bring on the punishment of rebirth as a nonhuman animal; assuming the belief to be correct, one might therefore expect a balance of numbers to be maintained between human and nonhuman species.

In chapter 8 I discussed the apparently circular relationship between the belief in reincarnation and the occurrence of cases suggestive of reincarnation: the belief facilitates the development of cases, and the cases tend to strengthen the belief. However, I pointed out that the belief alone does not account for the occurrence of cases more frequently in some regions than in others, and I offered some speculations about other factors that may potentiate paranormal processes, including memories of previous lives. The present topic provides additional evidence that a belief alone is insufficient to generate cases. If it were, we should find in South Asia just as many claims of nonhuman animal rebirth as we find claims of human rebirth. In fact, claims of nonhuman animal rebirth are exceedingly rare in South Asia, and almost completely absent elsewhere. Having overcome an initial prejudice against such cases, I have conscientiously recorded notes of whatever anyone wished to tell me about them, and I still have notes about fewer than thirty cases of claimed nonhuman animal rebirth altogether. Most of them have as their subject a human who has said that he had an incarnation as a nonhuman animal. Sometimes such an animal life occurred as an "intermediate" life between another human life and the subject's present one. As an example of this I summarized in note 13 of chapter 8 the case of Ma Than Than Aye.[3] Occasionally, informants designate a living animal as the reincarnation of a deceased human. (A dream provides the basis and usually the only support for such a conjecture.)

The cases of claimed lives as nonhuman animals can, in the nature of things, offer little evidence of the kind that we have found in the ordinary human cases, and most of them provide no evidence whatever—merely the subject's unsupported claim that he had such an incarnation.

WHY DOES NOT EVERYONE REMEMBER A PREVIOUS LIFE?

I have put the heading of this section in the form of a question that persons having some acquaintance with these cases frequently ask. We cannot, I need hardly say again, even begin to answer the question. We have no evidence that everyone has had a previous life from which memories might derive. We may, however, make the assumption—for the purpose of considering this topic—that if one person reincarnates, everyone does so or may do so, even though most people remember nothing whatever about any previous lives they may have had. We can then reverse the question and ask what we know about circumstances that appear either to facilitate or to inhibit the occurrence of memories that seem to be authentic. We can try to discern in them recurrent features that will give us hints at least of why some children have memories of a previous life, although most do not. In this section I shall attempt to do this. With as little repetition as I can manage, I shall gather together some pertinent information and interpretations from previous chapters and introduce some new ones. I shall consider in order the following topics: what lives are most likely to be remembered; what kinds of persons, if they reincarnate, are most likely to remember a previous life; and what other circumstances seem to assist or to block the emergence of memories.

The Lives Most Likely to be Remembered

I have already discussed (in chapter 7) the high incidence of violent death among the deceased persons figuring in these cases. I said that in 725 cases from six different cultures, 61 percent of the previous personalities had died violently. I have also explained why I believe that the high incidence of violent death in the cases reflects a real factor in the generation (and fixation) of the memories and not merely an artifact in the reporting of the cases.[4]

The circumstances that usually accompany a violent death deserve attention no less than the violence itself. Violence is usually accompanied by extreme physical suffering, except when a victim loses consciousness almost instantly from an injury to the head or neck. In addition, violent deaths are nearly always sudden and unexpected.[5] In wartime soldiers die violently, but they expect that this may happen to them, whereas persons who die in private murders, village tumults, and vehicular accidents do not expect to die at the time they do. We should also remember that young persons die violently more often than older ones; a violent death is usually an early one. Therefore, when we appraise the effects of a violent death on a person who experiences one and apparently survives to have memories of it, we must take account not just of the violence as such, but of all the associated elements, such as the accompanying physical suffering, the unexpectedness of the death, and its prematurity.

For all the prominence of violent death in these cases, it must take more than a murder (or another type of violent death) to start a case. I say this because unless our cases are much more underreported than I think they are, the incidence of cases is far below that of violent death among the peoples where we find cases. In other words, of all the persons who die violently, only a handful have lived lives that a subject of one of these cases later remembers. I shall return to the question of what makes some lives ending in violence more memorable, so to speak, than others. Before doing that I shall mention some subgroups within the nearly 40 percent of previous personalities who died naturally.

When we examine the previous personalities who died naturally, we can distinguish several groups among them. Although we have not yet made a quantitative analysis of the numbers in each of these groups, I believe that together they would comprise the majority of the previous personalities dying natural deaths.

One group of these deceased persons who died naturally did so suddenly, that is, within twenty-four hours of being apparently well or not expected to die in the near future. Sunil Dutt Saxena, the subject of a case in India, remembered the life of a man who died this rapidly when he was in his early sixties. On the morning of the day he died, he seemed well and had attended to some business normally. Toward noon he became ill, and he was dead by early evening, probably of a heart attack.[6]

Another group of the deceased persons figuring in these cases who died natural deaths were those who died young, by which I mean under the age of twelve. We must interpret this observation cautiously, because the countries of Asia where the cases are found most abundantly have a high mortality in childhood compared with countries of the West. Even so, I think that among all the deceased persons figuring in the cases, children form a group that is out of proportion to the numbers of children (compared with the numbers of adults) who die in the countries where I have studied these cases.[7]

Still another group were those of persons having what I call "unfinished business."[8] The best examples are mothers who died leaving infants or young children needing care.[9] Also in this group are some persons who had debts to pay (or to collect) when they died.

In another group of cases we can characterize the previous personalities as engaged in "continuing business." Typical examples of this group were prosperous businessmen intently absorbed in their businesses and in the accumulation and spending of the wealth associated with these. A retired person, no longer ambitious to earn more money, could not qualify for membership in this group, but an active businessman could.[10]

If we now consider these five groups of persons who died either suddenly (whether violently or naturally), in childhood, with unfinished business, or with continuing business, we can see that all their lives ended in a state of incompleteness. At the time of death they might all, for different reasons, have felt entitled to a longer life than the one they had had, and this in turn might have generated a craving for rebirth, perhaps leading to a quicker reincarnation than that among persons who died replete with life, so to speak, and at its natural end.[11]

When we examine individual cases, we can often find two or more of the factors I have mentioned occurring at the same time. For example, some of the previous personalities who died violently also were young children at the time they died, and some of the persons with unfinished business died violently or naturally but suddenly.[12]

The Kinds of Persons Most Likely to Remember a Previous Life if They Reincarnate

In the preceding section I described types of lives, especially those having unusual circumstances at the time of death, that the subjects of these cases seem frequently to remember. We have seen, however, that people living the lives and dying the deaths of the types described are much more numerous in the general population than are the cases. Therefore, other factors influencing the remembrance of previous lives must be sought for.

One might ask: What sort of a person, if he died and reincarnated, would be most likely to remember a previous life? Unfortunately, I can say little in response to this question.

Perhaps the most obvious category of persons likely to remember a previous life might be that of persons with unusually good memories. The most obvious questions, however, are the most often overlooked, and I have given attention to this one only recently. I can, nevertheless, mention two pertinent cases in Lebanon that I happened to be studying at the same time. One is the case of Suzanne Ghanem, to which I referred in chapter 7 in connection with the large number of proper names (of the previous life) she had been able to state. Suzanne also stated an equal number of other details, making her one of the leading subjects with regard to the total number of details of the previous life recalled. I enquired about the memory of Saada (the previous personality of Suzanne's case) and learned that she was recognized in her family as having had an unusually good memory, especially for the names of people. The subject of the other case, Said Zahr, was making statements that his father thought referred to the life of a well-known Druse sheikh. One of the sheikh's sons learned about the case, made some study of it himself, and took me to meet the subject and his family. The sheikh had been an eminent person and greatly venerated. Much about him was common knowledge among the Druses; moreover, a family's prestige would mount if its members could say that the sheikh had been reborn among them. For these two reasons the sheikh's son adopted an attitude of extreme reserve toward the case and could not shake a suspicion that the subject's father had coached his son, although there was no direct evidence of this. At one point in our discussion of the case, I commented on the paucity of the subject's statements; he seemed to remember extremely little about the previous life. To this the sheikh's son replied: "That might be a feature in favor of the case's authenticity; my father had a very bad memory." If we assume that the case was authentic and best explained by reincarnation, we could say that if the sheikh's memory had been even worse than it was, he would have remembered nothing at all in his next incarnation.

However, it is not enough simply to have a good memory in this life in order to remember a previous one. Otherwise, we should have expected some of the great mnemonists to have remembered previous lives, and there is no hint even that any of them did.[13] We might then turn to other mental qualities that might facilitate remembering a previous life. The mental clarity that accompanies the serenity of spiritual development may be such a factor.

In chapter 3 I referred to the longstanding belief in Buddhism and Hinduism that spiritual development, through meditation and meritorious deeds, clarifies the mind and enhances memory. The *tulkus* of Tibet are said to remember the previous lives of spiritually evolved lamas. These lamas had led, for the most part, fairly ordinary monastic lives, and nearly all of them had died naturally. One might say of them that, although the events of their lives were not memorable, the persons who had lived these lives were remarkable and may have carried the mental clarity they attained by their spiritual practices into another incarnation.

I mentioned in chapter 5 that I have little direct experience with cases among Tibetan lamas, and I cannot testify from firsthand knowledge to the claims made on behalf of any individual *tulku*. However, I have studied a few cases of children in other cultures who remembered the previous lives of persons who had been unusually pious and generous. Some of them had meditated, others had not; all had died natural deaths. The subjects of these cases themselves often showed precocious piety and generosity when they were young children, thereby suggesting that they had behavioral as well as imaged memories of the previous personality's spirituality. I earlier mentioned, in other connections, Disna Samarasinghe and Ratana Wongsombat, who were outstanding examples of this small group of subjects.[14]

Among the cases involving pious previous personalities, the interval between death and presumed reincarnation was just as short, on the average, as it was in the cases with violent deaths or with natural deaths associated with the circumstances I mentioned that might lead to an early rebirth. Therefore, the lives of the pious previous personalities may have been remembered because, for presently obscure reasons, the interval between death and birth was short in these cases.

Other Circumstances That Seem to Facilitate or Inhibit the Occurrence of Memories of Previous Lives

I have already emphasized the warming or chilling effects that parents may have on a child who has memories of a previous life that he would like to express if anyone is willing to listen. I have also mentioned the possibility that the belief in reincarnation may itself be carried over from one life to another. To a child born with such a belief, any memories that he may have of a previous life will make sense; to one born without it they will not.

In some cases we can identify a mental shock as possibly stimulating or suppressing memories. I have already mentioned (in note 15 of chapter 8) the effect on a man who reincarnated of beginning to think that he was now in a girl's body, and I suggested that the shock of this realization might evoke additional memories and thus account for the lopsided ratio of girls who recall previous lives as men compared with boys who recall previous lives as women.

Shock may account for another lopsided ratio that we have found among our cases in India. A substantial number of Indian subjects recall previous lives in socioeconomic conditions distinctly different from their own. (We call these promotion cases and demotion cases.) Among these subjects two-thirds recall better material conditions and only one-third recall worse conditions.[15] A critic knowing little of India and eager to subsume these cases within a familiar psychological theory may suggest that unhappy Indian children imagine previous lives in better circumstances as a solace for the squalid conditions in which they find themselves. Several facts point away from this interpretation, however, and suggest that the correct one may lie elsewhere. First, although promotion cases are fewer than demotion ones, they do occur, and in considerable numbers. Some of them are as authentic as corresponding demotion cases, and they require explanation just as much as do those involving demotion. Second, a child obtains no credit for remembering in India a previous life in better circumstances than his own; on the contrary, he will be judged to have done something sinful (in a previous life) that earned the demotion. Third, any comfort from the fantasy of having been rich is more than canceled in most demotion cases by the trouble the subjects bring on themselves through their boasting, refusal to eat the family's food, complaints about their poverty, and other alienating behavior. Fourth, attributing such a motive to the subject does not address the question of how some of these children obtained correct information about someone unknown to other members of their families.

If we decide that we cannot account for all the facts of demotion cases as due to wish-fulfilling fantasies, we are free to consider other possibilities. I suggest that dim, slightly emerging memories of a previous life under better material conditions may act as a shock that brings additional memories into the child's consciousness.

If a mild shock can stimulate memories, perhaps a greater one can inhibit their emergence. Such a suppressing shock may occur when a child with a Burmese body begins to think that he had been a Japanese, European, or American in a previous life. It may also occur when an Indian child thinks that he previously lived in England or when a Turkish one thinks that he lived in Lebanon or Libya. I have learned of no child recalling a previous life in a country other than his own who has furnished sufficient information to permit verification of his statements. Such children seem to remember the vague outlines of such a life and often the details of how it ended, but nothing more. The important issue here may be, not the crossing of international boundaries as such, but changes in the circumstances of living, often broadly described as culture. However, cultural differences within one political unit may sometimes be greater than those between neighboring areas of different countries. For example, the Alevis (still mainly Arabic speakers) of Adana and Hatay in Turkey have more in common with Alevis (and other Arabs) of Syria than they have with Turks in Istanbul. It is not surprising—according to the explanation that I am offering here—that among five cases of children from south-central Turkey who have remembered previous lives in Istanbul, we have not verified a single one.

Anthropologists have some familiarity with an experience called culture shock, which refers to the stress often produced in a person who moves from one country to another, where the customs are markedly different. If reincarnation occurs, some persons may undergo culture shock because of a change from a life in one country to a life in another.

The preceding review shows adequately, I think, that several, or perhaps many, factors enter into the development and expression in a child of memories of a previous life. If there is, however, a typical formula for such an occurrence, I would describe it as having the following features: The preceding life should be that of a man of middle-class status who lived in a country with a strong belief in reincarnation; and he should die violently or, failing that, suddenly. The child having the memories of this life could be a boy or a girl, but it should be born in the same country and culture as that of the deceased man; and its parents should be poor, but nevertheless familiar enough with the belief in reincarnation of their country so that they can listen to the child without rebuking it.

IS REINCARNATION A UNIVERSAL EXPERIENCE?

I have already deprecated this question. I regard it as completely unanswerable now and in the foreseeable future. I am not going to attempt any generalization about billions of human beings based on the data of 2000 cases, not all of which, we must remember, provide good evidence that reincarnation occurs. The most I will say on this point is that if reincarnation does occur at all, it may well be something that everyone experiences; but we cannot know this.

We can, however, prove false some generalizations that have been made from the cases. I have heard it said, for example, that only persons who die violently reincarnate and that other persons do not. This is wrong, because some of the cases in which natural deaths occurred have evidence suggesting reincarnation that is just as strong as that in any case I have studied with a violent death.

IS IT A HELP OR A HINDRANCE TO REMEMBER A PREVIOUS LIFE?

Even to pose this question requires one to ask others: "Helpful or harmful to whom?" and "Helpful or harmful at what stage of life?"

Many of the children subjects of these cases suffer miserably because they feel separated from the families to which they think they really belong; they may make wounding remarks that provoke reprisals and lead to their being isolated within their own families. Such children can then be truly alone: physically separated from the "real" (previous) family and socially separated from their own (present) family. Their parents are in no better situation. A child they wanted has turned against them and declared them not his real parents, but unworthy substitutes. If we think only about the turmoil of conflicting loyalties in which most of the subjects of these cases find themselves between the ages of two and five, we cannot say that remembering a previous life is beneficial to anyone concerned. Apart from this, the memories themselves are more apt to be of unpleasant events than of enjoyable ones. Murders and other crimes dominate the memories, not scenes of love and friendship, although there may be some of these too.

In later life the advantages of remembering a previous life may outweigh the disadvantages. Some of the subjects have used their memories as a means for improving present conduct, rather as one may study the questions on an examination one has failed in order to pass the next test. Moreover, those who remember any previous life, whatever its content, may acquire from the experience a sense of detachment from present troubles that only a longer view of an individual's destiny can confer.[16] Some subjects of these cases have had no fear of death and have offered reassurance about it to their elders. For example, a recently bereaved visitor to the home of Marta Lorenz sorrowfully remarked: "Oh, dear. The dead never return." To this Marta replied: "Don't say that. I died also and look, I am living again." Another subject, Ma Than Than Aye, said, as her father was dying: "It is a happy release for him. There is no cause to be sorrowful. Death is not strange at all. We all must die too." She did not weep.

WHY DO MORE BOYS THAN GIRLS REMEMBER
PREVIOUS LIVES?

As I mentioned in chapter 7, boys appreciably outnumber girls (in a proportion of approximately three to two) among the subjects of the cases of (nearly) all the cultures so far analyzed. I think there are several reasons for this uneven ratio in the sexes of the subjects.

When we compared the cases with violent and those with natural deaths in the previous lives, we found the preponderance of boy subjects far greater in the former group (where boys outnumber girls by more than two to one) than in the latter one. This presumably derives from the greater tendency of men than women to kill each other and to otherwise die violently. However, the cases with natural death also show a marked preponderance of male subjects in India, Turkey, and Alaska (among the Tlingit). We found almost equal numbers of male and female subjects in the cases with natural death of Thailand, Sri Lanka, and Lebanon. Only in Burma did female subjects outnumber males among the cases with natural death.

Some of the preponderance of male subjects may result from parents suppressing and concealing female subjects so that their cases are not proportionately represented in the sample we can study. In many countries of Asia a girl is generally expected to remain inconspicuous, at least until her marriage, and the publicity associated with being the subject of a case can seem to damage her chances of being satisfactorily married. I have known of one case suppressed for this reason, and I believe there have been others.

Among the Igbo, male cases occur much more frequently than female ones, and this, I think, reflects the dominance of males in their society. The Igbo have much more interest in studying who a male child might have been in a previous life than in learning about the previous life of a girl.

I mentioned earlier (in note 15 of chapter 8) the possibility that men's lives have more memorable events than women's, and to the extent that this is so it may contribute to the preponderance of male subjects.

I do not think the foregoing explanations—even taken together—adequately account for the greater number of male compared with female subjects, which remains one of the many features of these cases that require further investigation.

WHY ARE NOT MORE LIVES THAN ONE REMEMBERED BY SUBJECTS?

In answer to this question, I should say first that a small number of subjects do claim to remember more than one previous life. However, the second life remembered is nearly always an intermediate life about which the subject furnishes few details, so that it remains unverified.[17] (I mentioned four of these in chapter 8.) I have so far found only one case (that of Pratomwan Inthanu) in which a subject remembered two previous lives with sufficient detail so that they could both be independently verified. I think this is what we should expect if the memories of previous lives, like other memories, tend to fade with the passage of time.[18]

Four cases in our collection suggest that such fading does occur from one life to another. In these, the subject remembered the life of a person who (according to informants of his family) had himself remembered a previous life; but the subject had no recollection of the more anterior life.[19]

When memories become ordinarily inaccessible they are not necessarily obliterated. Under unusual circumstances they may again come into consciousness; a case in India that Satwant Pasricha and I studied suggests this. I referred in chapter 8 (note 9) to the subject of this case, Ram Prakash, in discussing the fixed interval between death and birth that is part of the Jain teaching about reincarnation. Ram Prakash recalled verified details about the life of a man, Shev Behari Jain, who had died not long before Ram Prakash's birth. However, unlike most of our subjects, Ram Prakash also claimed to recall two more previous lives that he said he had lived before the one as Shev Behari Jain. (Ram Prakash did not give enough details about either of these other two lives to permit our finding persons corresponding to his statements about them. In addition, the life farthest back would presumably have occurred about a century ago and would be exceedingly difficult to verify.) Of interest in the present context is that our informants among the surviving members of Shev Behari Jain's family had never heard him mention either of the two lives that Ram Prakash said he had lived before he had been born as Shev Behari Jain. Unfortunately, I have no other case like this one that could help us with its interpretation. One possible explanation is that Ram Prakash added two fantasied previous lives as embellishments to the verified one that he really did remember; but there seems no obvious motive for him to have done this. On the contrary, he might have diminished his overall credibility with his family and with that of Shev Behari Jain by claiming to remember additional previous lives that were (probably) unverifiable. Perhaps Shev Behari Jain remembered these other two previous lives when he was a young child, but, like other subjects, forgot them when he became older. This would account for his widow and children not having heard of them. Finally, perhaps special conditions existed in Ram Prakash's family that facilitated his recalling three previous lives, even though Shev Behari Jain had not recalled any.

CHILDREN WHO REMEMBER LIVES THAT ENDED IN SUICIDE

Twenty-three of the approximately 2,000 subjects remembered the lives of persons who had killed themselves. Four of these deceased persons had accidentally shot themselves (two when they grasped a loaded gun by the barrel and it discharged, and two while cleaning a loaded gun). Two others had killed themselves rather than be killed by police or soldiers who were about to capture them. The remaining seventeen persons took their own lives when a social situation, such as a bankruptcy or thwarted love affair, seemed to them worse than death.[20]

If we regard reincarnation as the best interpretation for these cases, they disprove the belief expounded in some religions that persons who commit suicide live in Hell for centuries or even for eternity. They also offer for a person considering suicide the thought that it would not end his troubles but only change the location of their occurrence.

Several of the subjects of this group of cases had phobias of the instrument of the suicide, such as guns or poison. The memory of the suicide did not necessarily extinguish the inclination to suicide. For example, three of the subjects, when frustrated as children, made threats of committing suicide to their parents; a fourth actually killed himself in middle life; and a fifth told me that he would probably commit suicide if he found himself in a situation he judged intolerable. On the other hand, another subject (of an unverified case) told me that the memories of a suicide in a previous life had deterred her from killing herself.

OBSTACLES TO BELIEVING IN
THE POSSIBILITY OF REINCARNATION

I devoted chapter 2 to the belief in reincarnation. I do not propose to write another full chapter about disbelief in it, but the topic deserves at least a section of a chapter. I disclaim any aim in what follows at converting readers to a belief in reincarnation. I wish only to draw attention to a group of obstacles that seem to me often to hinder the open-minded appraisal of the cases of children who remember previous lives. The hindrances that I propose to discuss are: the unfamiliarity in the West with the idea of reincarnation; the assumption that our minds (and memories) are in our brains and cannot possibly also exist elsewhere; the belief that we cannot conceive what life after death would be like; and the preference many persons seem to have for not wishing to accept the personal responsibility for their destinies that reincarnation suggests they may have.

Lack of Familiarity with the Idea of Reincarnation

Neoideophobia (a word of my coinage meaning "fear of new ideas") afflicts humans worldwide. "One of the greatest pains to human nature is the pain of a new idea." [21] We tend to shun the unfamiliar and to prejudge it unfavorably before we examine evidence bearing on it. "To believe fully in some phenomenon one has to be accustomed to it." [22]

Here I should mention that the idea of *any* survival of human personality after death is unfamiliar (if expressed in concrete terms) to most educated persons of the West. (In chapter 1 I mentioned that reincarnation is only one form that survival after death might take.) Whereas five centuries ago disbelief in survival after death was almost nonexistent in Europe (and might even be punished with death), to-day belief in survival is the eccentric view. The belief in life after death has been steadily eroded by the successes of science concentrated on the easily manageable problems of the physical world. Statements scientists make about these carry weight to persons who cannot have experienced the events described, whereas those made about the phenomena we now call paranormal do not. Few persons have personally experienced an earthquake and yet few doubt that earthquakes occur; in contrast, most educated persons doubt the "reality" of apparitions, even though it is possible that more persons have seen apparitions than have been in earthquakes. The former have been authenticated by the collective judgment of scientists; the latter, not yet. Thus, further acceptance of the idea of life after death awaits the accomplishment of more research that may bring stronger evidence and eventually win a majority vote among scientists—the only test of truth reached by the route of scientific method.

Among the different types of evidence bearing on the question of life after death, that suggesting reincarnation has two additional handicaps. The first is the remoteness, in geographical terms, of most of the evidence from the Western persons who read about it. Interested colleagues have repeatedly told me that a case in Virginia, Yorkshire, or the suburbs of Paris would be vastly more credible than one in Sri Lanka, Burma, or Lebanon. There are three points to be made in connection with this objection. First, I have studied cases in Virginia, Yorkshire, and the suburbs of Paris, and I believe that we could investigate others in these places as well as elsewhere in the West, if only we knew how to identify them and to persuade the persons concerned to share their information with us. Second, Western skepticism about the authenticity of a case in an "undeveloped country" shows an arrogance that derives from the West's few centuries of political ascendancy in the world. No one has shown that we should believe a witness in South Asia less than one in Europe or North America. Third, there are probably important factors in the beliefs and circumstances of the countries where the cases occur abundantly that facilitate their development—apart from the belief in reincarnation. In chapter 8 I sketched my own ideas about these factors and suggested that the economic development of the West had wrought profound changes in mental processes and attitudes that are not well-recognized and not all gains.

A second handicap for acceptance of the idea of reincarnation among Western persons lies in the ways in which most Western persons have become familiar with it. Westerners who either adopt the idea of reincarnation or at least consider it worth serious study have nearly all learned about it—directly or indirectly—through popular writings on Hinduism and Buddhism, including variants of the teachings of theosophy. I have tried in chapter 2 (and also in chapter 8) to separate the primary belief in reincarnation from the encrusting secondary beliefs that have been deposited on it in different cultures.

Yet undoubtedly the greatest obstacle to acceptance of reincarnation among educated Westerners lies in the firm belief most of them have that persons are nothing but their physical bodies. Disbelief in one thing may derive from hardened belief in another, and a strong conviction can even neutralize perceptions and other kinds of evidence. A story tells of an uneducated American farmer who, at the insistence of some friends, once visited a zoo and came to an enclosure in which a camel lived. After staring at the camel for a long time, he turned and walked away murmuring to himself: "There ain't no such animal." Thus can beliefs triumph over experiences.

I observed a more immediately relevant example of this during a meeting with a full-blooded Tlingit who had a prominent birthmark on his neck just beneath his jaw. He told me that this birthmark, and other evidence, had convinced his mother that he was her uncle reborn; the uncle had died when he had been shot in the neck at the site of my informant's birthmark. In addition, my informant had two grandchildren who claimed to remember previous lives with not contemptible evidence. However, he had been trained and ordained as a

Presbyterian minister, his educators had taught him what to believe, and he told me, with an attitude of inerrancy, that he did not accept the idea of reincarnation. The Gospel did not teach it and that settled the matter for him.

Probably many aspects of reincarnation seem unfamiliar and hence improbable to Westerners, but the difficulty of imagining oneself getting younger may exceed in importance most other facets of the concept. It is not easy to picture ourselves getting older, although most of us can do this with some effort, because we observe the process of aging in our parents before we see it in ourselves;[23] however, "younging," which is what we would do if we reincarnate, seems particularly strange.[24]

The difficulty most persons have in thinking of themselves becoming younger may derive partly from misconceptions about the importance of physical size. Although we know that an acorn can give rise to an oak tree, we may not readily understand that the qualities of a large tree can be compressed into something the size of an acorn. This difficulty may come from thinking that only a large organism can accommodate all the information of many kinds that a human personality has when he dies. How can all that information, we wonder, be packed into the body of a tiny infant, or—more marvelous still—into that of an embryo? Such reasoning shows a blunted imagination. In the first place, there are no grounds for thinking that, if reincarnation occurs, a person carries *all* his knowledge over from one life to another, and in the next chapter I shall express doubts about this. Even more important, however, is the unlikelihood that minds—although they have spatial properties—are restricted to the size (and capacities to store information) of brains.

The children subjects of the cases I have studied often do not have the difficulties in conceiving the changes in age and size that most adults have. Some of them when young have remembered what it felt like to be old, feeble, and ill. Disna Samarasinghe recalled being toothless in old age and having to use a stick for walking. Pratima Saxena remembered a terminal illness (of pulmonary tuberculosis) with cough, fever, and fecal incontinence. Some of the children have commented on the change in their bodily size (since death in the previous life), and although most have done so uncomplainingly, others have shown impatience to be big once again.[25]

I mentioned earlier the importance of familiarity with a phenomenon for believing in it. Simple acquaintance with the idea of reincarnation, however, does not suffice for the fair appraisal of evidence for it. I can emphasize this best by mentioning the opinions about this research that some academic colleagues in the West and some in Asia and Africa express when they first learn of it. They tell me—if not explicitly, by hints and smiles—that I am wasting money. However, the two groups give opposite reasons for this judgment: those in the West think reincarnation is impossible; those in Asia and Africa think it a fact beyond need of demonstration.[26] None of the persons making these summary judgments has had any knowledge of concrete cases from the evidence of which they might modify their opinions. If this book has any central purpose, it is that of urging readers to judge the merits of a belief or a disbelief in reincarnation only after studying the evidence offered by children who claim to remember previous lives. This evidence—I say once again—is not in this book.

Brain and Mind

Most scientists today, and certainly nearly all neuroscientists, believe that our minds (and hence also our memories) are nothing but manifestations of the working of our brains. This assumption seems to receive much support from the effects on our mental processes produced by injuries to the brain or milder interferences with its functioning. I do not need to cite the evidence for this from neuropathology and from surgical operations on the brain, such as those that damage the temporal lobes, although that is often impressive; a high fever or one or two drinks of whisky will suffice to convince a doubter. Humble neuroscientists acknowledge that they have only begun to show in detail that brain processes can fully account for mental ones; but they optimistically believe that they or their successors will work out all the details to their own and everyone else's satisfaction. They assume, in an act of faith, that no other solution to the relationship between brain and mind will be found; hence, none other is worth considering.

However, we are not all pledged to the received opinion of most neuroscientists on this matter. Hippocrates said that "to consciousness the brain is the messenger."[27] In modern times Bergson was perhaps the first philosopher to express the same idea.[28] Within the last two decades a small number of psychologists and philosophers, and even a few neuroscientists, have begun to question whether we can fully explain the mind (and memory) in terms of brain functioning.[29] Some scientists are now beginning to regard the brain as an instrument of the mind just as the piano is an instrument for a pianist's expression of music.[30]

I cannot review the unmanageably extensive literature on this subject. To simplify the few remarks I shall make about it, I will reduce the possibilities I consider to two. The first is that what we call minds (or mental functions), including all our subjective experiences, are nothing more than an aspect of the activity of our brains. This view, which has various subtypes, is monism. (Some persons prefer to call this concept physical monism or physicalism in order to distinguish it clearly from the opposite concept—the monism of idealists, such as the Vedanta philosophers of India.) To monism is opposed the view that minds and brains interact during life, but are fundamentally different; this is dualism. I make no issue of our needing brains for the effective expression of our minds (in most circumstances) during our present life. I want instead to consider whether a living brain is essential to the existence of a mind. Arguments and evidence indicating the insufficiency of brains to explain all mental phenomena will tend to support dualism; and so will evidence of the survival of someone's mind after the death of his physical body. This book is mainly about the second type of evidence. Here I shall briefly discuss what I regard as five difficulties to an acceptance of monism (or physicalism), apart from evidence of the survival of minds after death.

First, what we know of brains cannot explain consciousness. The scientists and philosophers who call themselves monists tell us that consciousness is only an epiphenomenon of the working of our brains. This assertion remains to be validated. It would be more fitting to acknowledge the primacy of consciousness itself. We all experience it, and all our knowledge occurs in it. "Mind is the first and most direct thing in our experience; all else is remote inference."[31] Without consciousness we could not observe brains or imagine anything about them, including the probably false idea that their workings and nothing else produce consciousness. The study of our brains may clarify why when light waves of a particular length reach our eyes we have the sensation of blueness; but blueness remains an irreducible experience of consciousness. An understanding of consciousness may ultimately explain brains, but brains will never explain consciousness; and I do not think anything else ever will.[32]

In the foregoing I do not intend to deny what I have already stated—that what we experience in consciousness varies with the state of our brain. Nor am I asserting that all our mental activity is conscious. Far from it; I believe the simile of an iceberg for the conscious and unconscious parts of the mind not merely trite but absurd. Instead of the iceberg's one-ninth, I should think less than one-thousandth of a person's mind is normally accessible to his consciousness.

Second, our present knowledge of brains cannot explain the features of our mental images. No arrangement of neurons in the brain is circular like our experience of seeing a circle. The experience of seeing a circle, or a square, or almost any other shape, does not correspond to the spatial arrangement of neurons. In technical terms, the data of our perceptions and the arrangements of neurons in the brain are not isomorphic. (I am not saying, however, that brains play no part in our recognition of shapes during ordinary consciousness.)[33]

Third, our present knowledge of brains provides no satisfactory account of memory. (I am speaking here only of memory for events in one life, not about that for those in a previous life.) Neurophysiologists have suggested that experiences modify the brain and leave traces in it that later events may stimulate in a way that leads to recall of the original event in the experience that we call memory. This sounds plausible in the abstract, but its weaknesses become apparent when we ask how the traces are activated in the almost infinite variety of circumstances for which they, or some of them, are available.[34]

Fourth, mental events occur in a space that is different from the space familiar to us in our everyday lives as well as from the physical space that physicists describe. The image of a bear that we may hold in our minds (in the absence of a live bear) has spatial dimensions, and we can locate the bear in our minds at a distance from an also imagined river and a salmon in the river at which the bear may seem to lunge. We cannot, however, speak intelligibly about the distance between such an imagined bear and its imagined surroundings, on the one hand, and, on the other, any object that we locate perceptually in physical space.[35] A person's physical body is in physical space, his mind in his mental space.

It is not obviously true that the minds of two different persons exist in the *same* mental space just as their bodies exist (at different locations) in the same physical space. If it is true, as I believe it to be, we are not ordinarily aware of the fact; our minds are usually protected from the intrusion of other persons' thoughts in our part of mental space. However, on rare occasions the barriers weaken, and we experience telepathy or some other kind of paranormal communication. That the mental spaces of the persons participating in telepathy are somehow linked does not necessarily mean that they are in the same mental space, but I am inclined to think that they are.

Fifth, our understanding of brains does not explain telepathy and other paranormal phenomena. It is conceivable that a still undiscovered organ of the brain will some day be shown to facilitate telepathic communication,but this alone would not take us far. We should still have to explain the close correspondence between images in the minds of two persons who experience a telepathic communication. It may be said in objection to this point that we cannot explain telepathy without brains either. I agree with that, but how does the absence of an explanation in terms of other phenomena justify ignoring the evidence of telepathy?

I think those persons are mistaken who believe—or, if they do not believe, pretend—that telepathy and kindred phenomena are not subversive of the opinions most scientists today have about the nature of human personality. If materialism—I am speaking of the philosophical kind, not the economic one—were true, telepathy should not occur; but it does occur, and so materialism must be false.[36]

The acceptance of this conclusion should not await the development of a theory that will accommodate the facts of telepathy to the rest of scientific theory; instead, the assumptions of materialism should be abandoned to accommodate the facts of telepathy. I believe that after the next scientific revolution, dualism will regain the dominant position it held for centuries in the West and still holds in most of the rest of the world. I also agree with a statement that a prescient psychologist made many years ago: "The phenomena of telepathy are . . . not an alternative to survival after death, but a virtual guarantee of it."[37]

The data from observations of paranormal phenomena—going, I need hardly say, far beyond the small amount presented in this book—require a radical revision in present concepts of the relation between mind and body. Many other scientists are aware of this prospect, and the knowledge has caused some of them to challenge the credibility of testimony concerning paranormal phenomena. Scientists who choose this defense seem to occupy the high ground, because attempts to observe the phenomena under controlled conditions have so far produced (for the most part) only marginal effects that require statistics for their demonstration; and experimental results are exasperatingly unrepeatable at will.[38] Furthermore, scientists like myself who point to the seeming abundance of paranormal cognition in spontaneous cases must also ask their readers and listeners to share their confidence in human testimony about past events. Still, we cherish our assumptions also, and most of us remain confident that we shall ultimately obtain stronger evidence that will lead other scientists to change their minds. There is also the possibility—more to be hoped for than expected—that enough scientists will first change their minds and begin to consider more favorably the abundant evidence of paranormal phenomena that is already available.

I am aware that, having said that minds are not brains but users of brains, I have not said of what minds consist; nor can I say. I can, however, conjecture that they consist of some nonphysical substance. Let us call this substance "mind-stuff" until we know more about it. It is, in Schrödinger's happy metaphor, "just a little bit more than a collection of single data (experiences and memories), namely the canvas *upon which* they are collected."[39]

Can We Conceive a Life after Death?

Under this heading I should first remind you that nearly all the world's great religions—and many not so great ones also—have included in their teachings or their associated mythology some idea of a life after death. To the average educated Western person these ideas often have little appeal. They are either vague, such as the concept of "eternal bliss," or they seem to express nothing but a wish for the best of the present life to continue, perhaps improved and amplified; the Tlingit is apt to picture an orgy of salmon in the next world, just as the Viking thought of enjoying his kind of feasting in Valhalla.

When an educated Western person says that a life after death seems inconceivable to him, he is usually expressing his disappointment with the kinds of concepts I have just mentioned and also his conviction that there could be no life without our familiar physical bodies. However, several Western philosophers and psychologists have suggested some particular features that a postmortem life without our physical bodies might have.[40] These proposals are extrapolations of established knowledge, but they are not works of science fiction. We have some information on which we can ground conjectures. In the first place, a few subjects who have remembered previous lives with verified details have also said that they remembered events occurring in a realm of discarnate beings, of which they, at that time, were one.[41] (I have already referred to these and cited some examples in chapter 5.) To the information they have furnished, we may add that from persons who have lucid dreams[42] and persons who have approached death and then recovered or escaped.[43] I think we may also use in our conjectures the (admittedly small) knowledge we now have about circumstances and processes of telepathy.[44] Here then are some ideas about what life after death may be like.

Without the sensory organs of a physical body, perceptions after death would certainly differ from what we are accustomed to while alive; but they would not necessarily cease. Persons who nearly die and then recover report having had perceptions—some of them not greatly different from their ordinary ones—even though their physical bodies were ostensibly unconscious and sometimes thought to be actually dead, although they were not. Their sensory experiences, which seem to be had from a position in space different from that of their physical bodies, are not mediated by normal processes of the sensory organs.

Thoughts after death might consist of images much more than do those of our familiar waking world, since they might be less enriched (and also less encumbered) by words. In this feature, thinking after death might resemble that of young children and that of dreamers. The world of the after-death state would be an "imagy" one—to use Price's word—but it would not be an imaginary one or any less real than is a dream world to a dreamer.[45]

In the postmortem world, as in dreams, memories of some past events might be more accessible than they are in our ordinary condition. The memories that might come into consciousness after death would not necessarily be only those on which one would like to dwell. A review of one's life and one's conduct in it may occur, and I earlier mentioned (in note 22 of chapter 2) Patanjali's teaching that a subconscious dread of this review may account for the almost universal fear of death. Plato's Socrates was also thinking of judgments and destinies in a life after death when he said that a good man need not fear death.[46] At present, however, we have almost no evidence from the children who remember previous lives for the occurrence of such a life review; only a few of the subjects have referred to anything of this sort.[47] Such a review, often called "panoramic memory," does often occur in (Western) persons who approach death and recover from an illness or escape from a danger that seemed life-threatening. In a series of such cases that a colleague and I studied, 27 percent of the persons had experienced such a review of past events.[48] Since some of these persons (although by no means all) were considered dead or almost dead before they recovered, we may conjecture—but certainly cannot assert— that persons who actually die also scan the events of the life just ended. If so, they may afterward forget the details of the review, as Patanjali suggested.

The postmortem world that I envisage would, therefore, derive much of its content from the premortem thoughts of a person inhabiting it. It would reflect both the culture in which he had lived and the personal experiences and attitudes that he had had. It would be pleasant or painful according to the kind of life that the inhabitant had lived before dying.

We do not need to think of discarnate personalities as being completely isolated in this postmortem world. They might meet other discarnate personalities. They might communicate with each other through processes similar to those of telepathy between living persons. The biologist and philosopher Hans Driesch, whose works I mentioned earlier, put this succinctly: "The means of communication that are normal for a dead person are 'paranormal' for a living one."[49] If this is so, the communications and associations would take place mainly between persons who had a close relationship with each other before death. It follows, I think, that after death we could not get in touch with anyone who happened to interest us just by willing this. It is more likely that, according to our attachments and conduct during life, we would associate after death with persons of attainments similar to our own. If we have been loving, we might find ourselves among loving persons, particularly those we have especially loved ourselves; if we have been odious, we might find ourselves among other hateful persons.

Discarnate personalities inhabiting the realm that I am imagining may have some possibilities for monitoring events in our familiar terrestrial world and, much more rarely, for communicating with living people. In chapter 5 I gave some examples of subjects who made correct statements about events in the previous family that occurred after the previous personality's death and of which the subject could not have learned normally, so far as I could tell. Other subjects have remembered that while they were in a discarnate state they were able to appear visibly to living family members and friends of the previous personality they remembered having been, and other persons have sometimes confirmed these manifestations. For example, Maung Yin Maung and Chaokhun Rajsuthajarn remembered being seen as apparitions after death in the previous life and the Venerable Sayadaw U Sobhana remembered experiences as a discarnate personality that corresponded to those in the dreams of two living persons; the living persons who were the percipients in these apparent interactions between the two realms confirmed the subjects' accounts. The cases I have studied include many other instances of discarnate personalities being seen in what I call announcing dreams; but only rarely does a subject like the Venerable Sayadaw U Sobhana remember that, as a discarnate personality, he manifested in the dream of a living person.

Certain other cases of apparitions provide additional examples of the occasional communication of a discarnate person to family and friends who are still living. I am thinking of apparitions occurring months or sometimes many years after the deceased person's death. An apparition of this type is likely to be seen during a period of distress or crisis for the percipient, and this temporal coincidence suggests that the discarnate person has somehow kept in touch with the affairs of still living members of his family. These postmortem apparitions occur much less often than the death-coinciding ones of which I gave examples in chapter 1; but enough authentic cases have been reported so that they should be regarded as a class of apparition deserving much further study.[50]

Dying persons sometimes have visions of deceased persons who seem to have come to help the dying person through the transition of death. It is possible to explain some of these deathbed visions as deriving from the wish of the dying person to be reunited with loved persons who died earlier; and yet in a number of well-documented instances the dying percipient had not known that the person figuring in the apparition had died, and neither had the persons around him.[51]

The discarnate world may be a lawful one, but its laws may differ from those with which we are familiar in our present lives. Time may pass differently and physical space be superseded. The thought of someone may lead to being with that person instantly, so that "now" would equal "here."[52]

If anyone asks where this discarnate realm is located, I reply that it exists in the mental space that we all occupy now, while we are associated with our physical bodies.

To sum up, I am suggesting (while far from pretending to be the first person to do so) that the universe has at least two realms: a physical one and a mental (or psychical) one. These interact. During our familiar lives, association with our physical bodies restricts the actions of our minds, although perhaps also enabling us to have experiences that we cannot have without physical bodies. After death, unencumbered by our physical bodies, we would at first exist exclusively in the mental realm. Later, some persons or perhaps everyone in that realm may become associated with new physical bodies, and we would say that those who did this had reincarnated.

I conclude my comments on this topic by emphasizing the speculative nature of what I have adumbrated. I want only to show that a life after death is conceivable, not to insist on the details of the one I have tried to describe. These conjectures, however, have one priceless advantage over the "one world" hypothesis about the universe to which materialists adhere: they do not require us to ignore the evidence for telepathy.

Individual Responsibility versus Chance in Personal Destiny

I approach the topic of this section with some fear that I shall be guilty—or thought to be guilty—of moralizing or even being preachy. I should like to avoid these faults. However, reflection on the many arguments in favor of reincarnation and on the evidence for it, imperfect as it is, has made me ask whether there may exist irrational—as well as rational—impediments to believing in it. If so, one irrational objection against it may be the burden of responsibility for one's individual destiny that reincarnation imposes. Reincarnation is a doctrine of hope, to be sure; it suggests that a person can profit in a future life from the efforts he makes in this one. The hope becomes fulfilled, however, only through personal effort, and this may be more than most persons can accept. Passivity lies deep within humans as we now are. We can observe this easily without referring to the possibility of reincarnation. Many sick persons let themselves be cured to death with prescription drugs rather than modify the way they live—by eating and drinking alcohol less and smoking tobacco not at all. In the social sphere a thousand will vote for legislation to correct the fault of his neighbor for every ten who will say, as I believe Beethoven did: "Lord, cease not to labor at my improvement," and for every one who, with Beethoven, will actually labor himself at self-improvement. If a person cannot accept responsibility for the outcome of one life, he will not welcome being asked to assume it for two or more lives. Nevertheless, it remains true that, as Baudelaire wrote: "There can be no progress—real moral progress, I mean—except within an individual person and by the individual himself." [53]

The average Westerner seeks to avoid personal responsibility for his condition and conduct in a variety of ways. Christianity has offered a selection of escapes ranging from the idea of predestination to that of atonement for all our sins by Christ's death on the Cross. Modern science offers the concept of chance, but that idea began with gamblers and insurers, not with scientists. Already in the eighteenth century Gibbon could write (with some complacency, it seems to me): "When I contemplate the common lot of mortality, I must acknowledge that I have drawn a high prize in the lottery of life. . . . the double fortune of my birth in a free and enlightened country, in an honourable and wealthy family, is the lucky chance of an unit against millions." [54] The metaphors used to express the concept of chance vary from time to time; and I mentioned in chapter 9 that in its modern guise, the uniqueness of an individual person is said to derive, for the most part, from the random sorting of chromosomes into the germ cells of the person's parents. We use and have used many other names for the same concept: accident, luck, fate. Whatever the label, the idea serves to spare the person using it from even a share of responsibility in what happens to him. I believe that most Westerners find the idea of chance somewhat appealing; and to the extent that they do so, they may think that of reincarnation uncongenial. [55]

Some persons find unattractive the thought that chance is the governing force in their life; and yet they may still wish to avoid personal responsibility for it. For two generations now, Western psychiatry and psychology have soothed this group with assurances that all their troubles come from the defects of their parents or from the aggregate of everyone else—what we call society.

You may say that reincarnation cannot be repugnant to everyone, because millions of persons in South Asia and elsewhere believe in it. To this I reply that most South Asians believe in reincarnation without realizing—not to say practicing—its full implications. Indeed, they may apply the doctrine of karma as a means of evading responsibility instead of accepting it; by attributing a current misfortune to misconduct on the part of a remote predecessor personality, one can avoid a need for reform of one's present behavior. Moreover, few Hindus and Buddhists have confidence that the virtuous conduct their religions enjoin will suffice by itself to bring them what they want in life. Hindus appeal to a pantheon of intervening gods; the Buddhists of Sri Lanka swarm to the god Kataragama and bribe him to save them from an impending calamity; those of Burma frequently invoke help from the spirits they call nats; and those of Thailand install a miniature house for guardian spirits near their own house.

A monk of the Ramakrishna order, Swami Muklyananda, once remarked to me: "We in India know that reincarnation occurs, but it makes no difference. Here in India we have just as many rogues and villains as you have in the West." Speaking of the masses he was probably right; but I think he was wrong if he meant that the belief in reincarnation makes no difference for an individual person who accepts all that it entails.[56] However, it may be easier for a camel to go through the eye of a needle.

CHAPTER ELEVEN

Speculations about Processes Possibly Related to Reincarnation

If reincarnation is a universal phenomenon, as in the last chapter I suggested—but did not assert—that it may be, we look at it through a frosted window when we try to understand it by means of presently available cases. I hope that I have sufficiently emphasized in previous chapters how much the sample of cases I have studied must deviate from the lives of general populations. If reincarnation occurs, therefore, we can expect to learn from these cases only a little about factors involved in it and only for certain unusual groups of people; we can say almost nothing about reincarnation as it may affect most persons. However, believing that a crude sketch has more value than a blank page, I shall offer the following speculations unapologetically.

I shall consider the following topics: If reincarnation occurs, what reincarnates? Why is a person born in one family instead of in some other one? How can a discarnate personality who is about to reincarnate influence the physical body of the next incarnation? Does conduct in one life influence the circumstances of another one?

WHAT IS IT THAT MAY REINCARNATE?

Even if we knew what constitutes a whole personality in a living person we could not say from the evidence of any case that a whole personality had reincarnated. We can only point to certain aspects of the subject's personality that may derive from a previous life. To do this we should first try to explain along normal lines (by which I mean present knowledge of genetics and environmental influences) as much as we can of what the child says and does. Any residue of behavior not thus explained may derive from a previous life or previous lives. This line of inquiry should indicate what aspects of personality may reincarnate. We have seen that in a fully developed case the subject has imaged memories of events in a previous life; behavioral memories corresponding to habits, attitudes, and other residues of experiences in that life; and, in some instances, birthmarks and other abnormalities on his physical body that correspond with wounds or other marks on the previous personality.

These diverse elements are not, however, unconnected like pieces of washed clothing and linen hung on a line to dry. They belong to a unified being just as do the individual organs of our physical bodies. (There may be a confederacy within the unity—just as individual organs comprise a body—but there is unity nonetheless.) We can easily see the connections between the several elements in actual cases. For example, a boy who claims he has a wife and children in another village wants to go and see them; another boy who remembers the life of a doctor likes to play at being a doctor; and a third who describes being shot to death points to a birthmark that he says derives from the shooting and expresses an intention of taking revenge on the murderer. In short, we see not a group of isolated memories like a cabinet of tape recordings, but evidence of purpose. I mentioned earlier (in chapter 1) that in order to believe that someone had survived death we require evidence not only of memories of that person but of a continuation of his purposes. This we can find abundantly in the cases.

In the presumably reincarnated person the three elements I have mentioned—imaged memories, behavioral memories, and physical traces—associate inextricably, and I cannot imagine their not also being together during the period between terrestrial lives. This suggests that they exist (or a representation of them exists) on an intermediate vehicle of some kind, perhaps with other elements of which we still know nothing.

I propose to call the vehicle that carries a person's mental elements between incarnations a *psychophore*.[1] I know nothing about how the constituents of the psychophore are arranged, but I presume that it changes if a discarnate personality has experiences and does not remain idle. Presumably also the process of reincarnation modifies the psychophore. The wizened body of an old man differs greatly from the fresh but tiny one of a baby who, when he can speak, will remember the old man's life. The old man had many imaged memories; the baby may have these too, but if he has, they have usually dwindled to a small residue by the time he learns to speak and begins to tell about them.[2]

The behavioral memories have also shrunk, and what were skills in one life may become (with rare exceptions) mere aptitudes in another. As for the wounds of our old man—supposing, for example, that he was hacked to death with a sword—they too have healed. The marks on the body in which he reincarnates do not (usually) bleed, but the baby may have a hand missing where one of the old man's hands was struck off before he was knocked unconscious and died. The wounds on the old man therefore do not persist unchanged; instead, they act like a template, and, as part of the psychophore, they subsequently influence the form of the new physical body with which the psychophore becomes associated in its next incarnation.

Although I have adopted the phrase *previous personality* for a person whose life the subject of a case remembers, I have avoided saying that a *personality* can reincarnate entire, because no evidence suggests that it can. Instead, what may reincarnate is an *individuality* that derives from the immediately previous personality and also from personalities previous to that one.[3] The personality comprises all the outwardly observable psychological attributes a person has at any one time; the individuality, on the other hand, comprises these together with residues from earlier experiences of the present life and from other incarnations of the same series. Our individualities thus contain much that our personalities never reveal and much also that is inaccessible to the conscious parts of our minds except in unusual circumstances.

The history of the foreign languages that I have learned illustrates the distinction between personality and individuality. At one time I could speak Spanish well enough to conduct interviews in it during a visit to Argentina, where I studied some cases in 1962. I have not since endeavored to maintain my ability to speak Spanish, although I can still read (with help from a dictionary) the occasional letters I receive from Spanish-speaking correspondents; and I can just manage an elementary reply written in Spanish. For all practical purposes, however, my Spanish has gone—but only from my personality, not from my individuality. Were I to try to speak Spanish again I would learn it more easily than I did when I first learned it. In contrast to my neglected Spanish, I have maintained a fair competence in both French and German. They are still part of my personality—my working self, so to speak. At my death, however, I expect that my ability to speak these languages will also become part of my individuality; and if I reincarnate, the result of my efforts at learning foreign languages will be, not the ability to speak them, but a facility for learning the ones I have studied and spoken in this life—or, it may be, in earlier lives. So may it also be, I believe, with any other skills that I may have, whether intellectual, muscular, or moral. And this thought will encourage me to learn something new—to play the clarinet perhaps—in old age.[4]

I mentioned in chapter 9 that we have almost no evidence to warrant our thinking of reincarnation as an explanation of child prodigies and that no Western child prodigy has ever claimed to remember a previous life. However, I also mentioned (in chapter 5) that behavioral memories apparently derived from a previous life sometimes persist in a subject long after he has lost the imaged memories about the circumstances (in the previous life) in which the behavior was learned. Something similar may occur from one incarnation to another. Thus if a person has acquired skill in music, mathematics, or some other activity in one life, he may show evidence of it in another, despite his having no imaged memories of the previous life in which he acquired the skill.

WHY IS A PERSON BORN IN A PARTICULAR FAMILY?

In the cases of several peoples—the Burmans, the Igbo, and the tribes of northwestern North America, for example—the two personalities concerned in a case are almost always members of the same immediate or extended family. One can conjecture that if reincarnation occurs in the same family (or between two acquainted families), some psychic force has brought this about by attracting the discarnate personality to the family of its next incarnation.

How does this occur? It happens, I think, because all shared experiences leave mental traces within us and produce psychic connections between the persons concerned. I suppose further that the longer an association between two persons lasts, and the greater its intensity, the stronger the connections between them become.[5] When a need arises—as in a life-threatening situation—and when the psychic connections are strong enough, a telepathic communication may occur between persons who are geographically far removed from each other. Often the communication results in only an impression or intuition that something untoward has happened to the other person; but sometimes the communication generates a perception so vivid and detailed that the percipient experiences what we call an apparition of the distant person, and I gave examples of this in chapter 1. The two persons involved in an experience of this type are, we can say, attuned to each other; but their connection exceeds in complexity the resonance of two instrumental strings tuned so that when one is plucked the other also vibrates. Telepathic impression and apparitional experiences include a capacity for proper localization. Somehow the dead or dying person finds the other person with whom he has a psychic connection. That person and no one else receives the communication (except in the rarer cases of collective apparitions).[6] With some similar directional capacity, I suggest, a discarnate personality finds its way to the parents of the next incarnation.

In chapter 1 I mentioned that case studies of telepathic impressions and apparitions have shown that these experiences occur between husbands and wives as much as between parents and children. Likewise, in the same-family cases of the reincarnation type, the two persons concerned may be related through marriage as well as by blood.[7] Familial relationships, however, have in them nothing intrinsically binding. If we usually have more and stronger psychic links with members of our family than with other persons, this is because we spend more time with them, especially the times of strong emotions that, in my view, have more adhesive power than weak emotions. Some persons have stronger ties with friends than with members of their families. Accordingly, we find a number of telepathic and apparitional experiences in which the persons concerned were close friends, although they were not related. They rarely occur between strangers.[8] Similarly, we have reincarnation-type cases in which the previous personality had a special fondness for the subject's parents, although he was not related to them.[9]

In some cases a person has chosen parents for his next incarnation before he dies. (The Tlingit and the Haida are particularly inclined to do this.) Probably openly stating such a wish intensifies the affection it expresses; but the affection must have existed earlier in order for the person to express it, and surely many tacit attachments have as great a strength as those spoken about aloud.

Animosities also seem to bind. I have already mentioned some cases in which a subject remembered the previous life of a person who had quarreled with, or had even been injured or killed by, one of the subject's parents. (In chapter 9 I summarized the case of Zouheir Chaar, who remembered the life of a man who had quarreled seriously with Zouheir's mother.)[10]

It appears that guilt or a sense of indebtedness may also act as an

attractive force in these cases. In a small number of them—all Burmese—the subject remembered a debt that the person whose life he
recalled owed to a member of the subject's family. In these few cases
the debt in question usually seemed small to me, even trivial; but a
devout Buddhist who believes that he must pay for everything—now
or later—could die with a burden on his conscience that might bind
him to the creditor and lead to rebirth in the creditor's family.[11]

In some cases one cannot distinguish the role of friendship from
the other motives for a discarnate person's apparent attraction to a
particular family. The mother of Maung Myint Tin, whose case I mentioned in chapter 9 when describing pregnancy cravings, was the ap-
preciated purveyor of country-style liquor to the man whose life
Maung Myint Tin remembered. Maung Myint Tin showed, even before he could speak, the previous personality's fondness for alcohol;
and the convenience to him of his mother's abundant supply of alcohol
seemed to observers a sufficient explanation for the previous personality's apparent rebirth as her son.

I have so far been considering the factors that may enter into
reincarnation in a particular family when the previous personality and
the subject's family are related, friendly, or in some way acquainted. In
considering other cases I have less to say about why a child was born in
one family rather than in another. Indeed, I should acknowledge immediately that for the majority of long-distance cases I have no clues
whatever as to why the subject was born in his family. Nor have the
informants for the cases; when I ask them for their thoughts about the
matter, they usually attribute the child's birth in their family to karma
(if they are Hindus or Buddhists) or to God (if they are Christians or
Moslems). A child (the subject) was born among them, and they do
not bother themselves much about why. Despite my informants' inability to say anything specific on this question, I think I can discern
three factors that seem relevant to such cases.

First, in a few instances in which the families denied any acquaintance before the case developed, I nevertheless learned that there
had been some relationship between them. This was sometimes of a
commercial kind, but with harmonious tones. In one case of this type
in India, Ram Tirath, the subject, recalled the life of a man who had
grown vegetables, which he had hawked in the region where the subject's family lived. He remembered selling vegetables (in the previous
life) to his mother, and he further claimed that the man whose life he

remembered had, shortly before his death, inadvertently left a pannier of vegetables at the home of his (the subject's) mother, where he had been selling vegetables.

Another Indian child, Juggi Lal Agarwal, said that in the previous life he remembered he had been a farmer who had sold grain to the subject's father. The latter was a wholesaler of grain in a large town, Sirsaganj, which was located 70 kilometers from where the farmer lived. Juggi Lal further claimed to remember that his father had always treated the farmer fairly. (Farmers in India expect sharp practices on the part of dealers to whom they sell their grain.) He further recalled thinking to himself that, when he died, he would like to be reborn in the family of the grain dealer. I verified the most important particulars that Juggi Lal had stated concerning the farmer's life, but not those about the previous personality's relationship with the subject's father. The latter candidly admitted that he could not recall—from among many customers—the farmer his son claimed to have been in the previous life; and the farmer's family, although they knew that he had taken his grain to sell in Sirsaganj, could not say to which dealer he had sold it there. Despite these deficiencies, and because I verified the subject's main statements about the previous life, I credit as plausible the subject's explanation for his birth in his family instead of in another one.

A second type of explanation emerging in a few long-distance cases is a claim by the subject of some connection with his family in still another previous life, one more remote than that of his principal memories. For example, Swarnlata Mishra, who remembered two previous lives—one verified and one not—said that in yet another life she had been with one of her sisters. Sukla Gupta also said that in a life anterior to the one about which she had most memories she had been with members of her (present) family. Manju Bhargava said that she had been born in her family because her older sister Uma was already there; Manju said they had been together in a previous life. In these cases the members of the subject's family have only rarely reported to me any confirmatory memories of such shared prior lives.[12]

I have designated by the word *geographic* a third factor that sometimes seems to govern the selection of a particular family for the birth of a subject. The evidence for it occurs in two groups of cases.

In the first of these groups the subject is born far from where the previous personality of the case lived, but at or near the place where he died. The Burmese children who have claimed to remember previous lives as Japanese soldiers killed in Burma during World War II belong to this group. Two of these subjects, Ma Khin San Tin and Ma Khin San Yin, were twin girls who remembered having been brothers (not twins) in the same (Japanese) army unit, and they said that after their deaths (during the British advance near Pyawbwe, in April 1945) they had tried to be reborn in Japan, but had failed, and so had returned to the site of their deaths in Burma; they were born in a village near Pyawbwe, less than 100 meters from where they said they had been killed. (There had been a Japanese army entrenchment at that site.) This case remains unsolved, as do those of the other Burmese children claiming to have been Japanese soldiers killed in Burma.

However, informants have reported the same kind of sequence in verified cases. In one of them a woman who lived in Tatkon (Upper Burma) was traveling by train from Tatkon to Mandalay when she suddenly had what appears to have been a heart attack. She was taken off the train for medical care near a town called Thalun and died there soon afterward. The subject who remembered her life and death, a boy called Maung Win Aye, was born in Thalun. The subject's mother had gone—along with other curious persons—to see the laid-out body of the stranger who had died so unexpectedly in Thalun, and she had even helped to prepare the woman's body for her funeral. She became pregnant with the subject soon afterward. We may interpret this case as resulting from the normal communication of information between Maung Win Aye and his mother. We may also say that a telepathic communication occurred between them, either when Maung Win Aye was a fetus or after his birth. However, a third possibility remains, which is that the discarnate personality of the woman who had died had stayed near her physical body and became attracted to the subject's mother when she went to the railway station to see the body; she then reincarnated as Maung Win Aye.[13]

In several cases the subject was born at a place to which the previous personality's body had been carried after his death. A subject in Burma, Maung Aye Kyaw, remembered that he had been shot in the previous life and his body had been thrown into a small river. Maung Aye Kyaw recalled that in his discarnate state he had followed the body as it drifted downstream. Some miles below the place of the murder, the floating cadaver became stuck against the pilings of a small dock near a house on the bank of the river. A woman of the house noticed the body in the water and called some men, who pushed it back into the stream, causing it to be carried farther down the streams to the Irrawaddy River; soon afterward the woman became pregnant with Maung Aye Kyaw, who, when he could speak, narrated these details.

The case of Awdesh Mishra resembled that of Maung Aye Kyaw in the apparent circumstances of the subject's conception. Awdesh's family lived at a place called Kamalpur, which is in the Sitapur District of Uttar Pradesh, India. When Awdesh began to talk (at the age of two and a half years) about a previous life, he said that he had been called Hanne Lal and that after his death his body had been thrown into a river. He (as a presumably discarnate personality) had then seen his mother bathing in the river and attached himself to her. Awdesh said that he was from Faizabad, which is about 140 kilometers from Kamalpur. However, his mother had gone bathing in a river at a place called Ayodhya, which almost adjoins Faizabad, and Awdesh was born just nine months after she had been to Ayodhya. Awdesh's father did not go to Ayodhya, which suggests that the discarnate Hanne Lal followed her back to Kamalpur and took advantage of her next sexual relationship with Awdesh's father. When Awdesh's statements were verified, it was found that a man named Hanne Lal had lived at Faizabad, where he had died of plague. His family having deserted him—presumably from terror of infection—other persons had thrown his body into a nearby river.

In a similar case in Turkey, the subject, Yusuf Köse, was born in Ödabaşı, a village that is north of Antakya (in the province of Hatay) and between İskenderun and Antakya. Yusuf said that in his previous life he had lived in a village 20 kilometers south of Antakya. He also recalled that the person whose life he remembered had been returning from İskenderun to his village when he had been murdered at another village some 10 kilometers north of Ödabaşı (in the direction of İskenderun).

The question arose of why Yusuf was born in Ödabaşı rather than in the village of the previous personality, in the village where the murder had occurred, or, for that matter, in any other village of the world. The most likely answer to this question came out when I learned the history of the murdered man's corpse. The murderer had cut off the victim's head, and although this had happened during a particularly lawless time in Turkey, the villagers where the murder occurred found the severed head and body an encumbrance and a possible source of embarrassing inquiries by the police. They therefore quietly carried the body and head to the next village in a southerly direction and left them there. The residents of that village did not want the body and head either, so they moved them along to the next village farther south. In this way, the head and body eventually arrived at Ödabaşı. There a man saw it, and, deploring the selfish negligence shown in the other villages, he arranged for the body to be buried. Head and body were assembled and decently interred. Soon afterward the wife of this pious man gave birth to Yusuf.

In another case illustrating the geographic factor, the subject, Lalitha Abeyawardena, was born in a small town about 20 kilometers southeast of Colombo, Sri Lanka. When she began to talk of a previous life, she claimed to have lived at a place some 50 kilometers away, to the north of Colombo. Her family had no connections with that region. The investigation of this case showed that the person whose life Lalitha recalled had died in a hospital in Colombo and her body had been buried at the village north of Colombo where she lived. I learned, however, that two of the deceased woman's brothers lived in the small town where Lalitha had been born; one of these was her favorite brother, and he lived on the same road as the subject's family, just about 200 meters from them. I also learned that at the time the deceased woman had died, and for some years afterward, there were no women of childbearing age in either of her two brothers' families. If we favor reincarnation as the best interpretation of the case, it appears that the woman whose life Lalitha remembered may, after her death, have wanted to be near her brothers, perhaps with a view to being reborn among them, but had instead got herself reborn in a neighboring family.

I mentioned earlier that most cases among the Igbo of Nigeria are of the same-family type, but the Igbo recognize a type of case that they characterize as "enemy" cases. The subject of such a case remembers a previous life of a member of another group that came to the subject's village in a raid and was killed there. Through bungling—as it would seem to the Igbo—he got himself reborn in the raided village instead of back home among his own people.

A geographic factor also seems identifiable in another group of cases. In these, the subject's future mother or father had gone to the place where the previous personality of the case had died. The case of

Bongkuch Promsin illustrates this occurrence. In chapter 4 I mentioned that Bongkuch's father had been to the area of the previous personality's murder not long before Bongkuch's mother became pregnant with him. Bongkuch said that he (in the discarnate state) accompanied his father back to his village in a bus.[14]

If we extend the physical distance we consider, we can plausibly identify a geographical factor in many other cases. The majority of the subjects of cases in which the two families are not related or acquainted speak of a life that was lived within a radius of 25 kilometers from the subject's home. To be sure, in a few cases much longer distances separate the two families: it was 500 kilometers in Jagdish Chandra's case and 175 kilometers in Indika Guneratne's. These cases are exceptional. Most subjects, even of long-distance cases, are born much closer to the community where the previous personality lived. The two families can therefore be said to belong to the same geographical area so defined.

In sum, nearly all the cases I have investigated show one or another of the following circumstances: the previous personality was a member of the subject's family, or the two families were acquainted and often good friends; the previous personality died near where the subject was born, or members of the previous personality's family had some connection with the subject's community; the subject's father or mother visited the previous personality's community or place of his death shortly before (or perhaps soon after) the subject was conceived; or the subject and previous personality lived within 25 kilometers of each other.

The cases suggest that if—for whatever reason—a discarnate personality is to be reborn as the child of particular parents, physical distance is no impediment. For example, Ma Win Myint, the subject of a case in Burma (where she was born), was identified as the reincarnation of an Englishman who had lived in Burma but died in London, England. In the Turkish case of Adnan Kelleçi, the previous personality was a member of the Turkish army's contingent fighting in Korea (during the Korean War) when he was killed; but the subject was born in Adana, Turkey. The subject of an Indian case, Vinita Jha, who was born in Delhi, remembered the previous life of a girl who was strangled in London. Her case is unsolved, but Vinita (as a young child) made correct statements about London and showed marked "English" behavior. Suzanne Ghanem was born in Choueifate, Lebanon, and remembered the life of a woman, Saada, who had gone to Richmond, Virginia, for cardiac surgery and had died there.

Much of what I have said so far about the factors governing a person's birth in one family instead of in another may lead to the impression that the persons concerned participate in the process passively. No doubt this is true in most cases. So far as we can tell, the attraction of the discarnate personality to a particular family seems almost automatic, as if involuntarily activated by the ties of love (and occasionally of hate) that I have mentioned.

However, volition appears to enter into some cases. We would have to reckon with it as a possible factor in those cases in which a person had selected before his death the family for the next incarnation and in which a child later furnished evidence of having memories of that person's life.

The announcing dreams, especially the petitionary ones, also suggest that a discarnate personality has chosen the family for his next incarnation. In a few announcing dreams one senses even a determination on the part of the discarnate personality for rebirth in a particular family. In one Haida case a deceased person appeared in the dream of a potential mother and grumbled to her about being kept waiting to reincarnate. In chapter 4 I described how Samuel Helander's mother had a dream in which her brother Pertti (whose life Samuel later remembered) urged her not to have an abortion. A parallel case, that of Rajani Sukla, occurred in a family of India. A daughter of the family was killed in an accident. Later, her mother had a dream in which the daughter seemed to announce her wish to be reborn to her. Rajani's mother, however, did not wish to have another child and induced an abortion. The deceased child appeared again in a dream and rebuked the mother for not letting her reincarnate. Eventually, the mother consented and gave birth to Rajani, who later remembered the life of her older sister.

In another case, that of Maung Thein Htoon Oo in Burma (studied by U Win Maung), the subject's mother had two announcing dreams. In the first of these a deceased member of the family (a woman) placed a bag of money under the mother's pillow. In the second dream the same woman appeared to be astride a horse on which the subject's parents were also riding. The dreamer interpreted her dreams as indicating the deceased woman's intention to be reborn as her baby. At about the same time, a cousin of the deceased woman also dreamed that the same woman appeared to him. In his dream, the woman explained that she could not live with *his* family because they were too noisy.

One can explain the dreams I have just described as derived from the wishes and beliefs of the dreamers. I think, however, that they hint at an initiative on the part of at least some discarnate personalities in the selection of a family for another incarnation. Some of the dreams show also a desire for rebirth, and even a zest and craving for it.

WAYS IN WHICH A DISCARNATE PERSONALITY MIGHT INFLUENCE THE PHYSICAL BODY OF THE NEXT INCARNATION

The philosopher McTaggart, who eloquently endorsed the idea of reincarnation, considered the relationship that a soul might have with the physical body in which it reincarnated. He suggested an analogy between hats and their wearers, and if the reader finds this dated because hats are now out of fashion, he can adapt the analogy to clothes in general. McTaggart wrote:

> *In walking through the streets of London, it is extremely rare to meet a man whose hat shows no sort of adaptation to his head. Hats in general fit their wearers with far greater accuracy than they would if each man's hat were assigned to him by lot. And yet there is very seldom any causal connection between the shape of the head and the shape of the hat. A man's head is never made to fit his hat, and, in the majority of cases, his hat is not made to fit his head. The adaptation comes about by each man selecting, from hats made without any special reference to his particular head, the hat which will suit his particular head best.* [15]

If we now consider embryos, we should first note that they are made abundantly, and the question arises of whether a discarnate personality can select (or even produce) the embryo that fits him the best and avoid becoming attached to all the rest. A further question is whether a discarnate personality can also modify the embryo selected, just as a wearer may make some adjustments, by padding or stretching, to a hat that he has purchased. I think it premature to say much here about the second of these possibilities, because I have not yet published most of the evidence bearing on it; I shall present it in the books on cases with birthmarks and birth defects that I am now preparing.

The Possibility of Selecting One Embryo from among Those Available

What I have said so far about the tendency for the two families concerned in a case to have either personal or geographic connections suggests that a discarnate personality progressing toward reincarnation becomes attracted—perhaps impelled—toward a particular family, either because of previous ties of affection and friendship with that family or because of the geographical factors I have mentioned. Given an attraction between a discarnate personality and potential parents, the reincarnating personality appears obliged, in most cases, to take whatever body the parents can provide. In this respect, McTaggart's analogy with hats and their wearers proves unhelpful, because any pair of parents has a small range of bodies available for reincarnating persons. Most parents cannot offer as wide a selection of bodies for their children as hatters can of hats for their customers. If a discarnate person is, let us say, strongly attracted to a family with Huntington's chorea, sickle-cell anemia, hemophilia, or some other disease that in medical terms is prominently or entirely due to a disease-producing gene, he may have to take his chances on acquiring a body with that gene. If, for example, the person is to become, on reincarnating, the son of a woman who is a carrier for hemophilia, the chances are one in two that the baby boy will have hemophilia. (Such a mother could bear unaffected girls, although half of them would be carriers of the gene that produces hemophilia.)

Notwithstanding my conviction about the helplessness of the average incarnating person concerning the selection of his body (once his parents have been selected), occasional cases do suggest that some selection process may occur. We find such evidence among the cases of the sex-change type and of twins.

Cases of the sex-change type afford the best data for speculating about this subject. Suppose that a person, before he died, had expressed a wish to change sex in his next incarnation.[16] The sex of an embryo and of the body into which it will develop is determined by the type of sperm from the father that fertilizes the mother's ovum. When the fertilizing sperm carries a Y chromosome it will become a male; when it carries an X chromosome the embryo will become a female. Since half the father's sperm contain a Y chromosome and half an X chromosome, the chances should be equal that any embryo will be male or female. In the situation we are considering, the discarnate personality might become associated with an embryo of the right sex by influencing one of two events. It could try to guide a sperm with the right chromosome toward a ripe ovum, and perhaps prevent sperms with the wrong chromosome from reaching an ovum; or it could try to eliminate fertilized ova (and early embryos) of the wrong sex while waiting for one of the right sex to be conceived.

A male is more likely to be conceived if coitus occurs one or several days before ovulation than if it occurs at ovulation.[17] (However, the reverse is true in the practice of artificial insemination.[18]) Y chromosome-carrying sperms are more motile than X chromosome-carrying ones,[19] but the viscosity and other qualities of the fluids in which the sperm are swimming may reduce or cancel this advantage. Physiological changes in the woman being inseminated can apparently affect the penetration of the two types of sperms differently. I suggest that a discarnate personality might influence a potential mother telepathically and cause psychosomatic changes in her that would increase or decrease the chances of a male conceptus. However, this seems to be an undependable means of assuring the sex of one's next body.

As for the second plausible intervention, many fertilized ova are carried away in the next menstruation or, slightly later, in a miscarriage. The mother may remain unaware that she has had a miscarriage and perhaps think she only had a menstrual flow that was later and heavier than usual.[20] A discarnate personality might induce such early expulsions until an embryo of the desired sex for the next incarnation had been fertilized. It would then allow that one to continue developing.

Since on average half the conceptuses would be male and half female (or nearly so), the discarnate personality would need to monitor them when sex change was to occur and also when it was not. This last point is important, because sex-change cases are unusual, even in countries where their incidence is relatively high (for example, 28 percent in Burma), and in some countries, such as Lebanon and Turkey, it does not occur at all, so far as we can judge from the cases available for study. Thus, it would require more vigilance to avoid sex change than to have it happen.

If a discarnate personality cannot influence the fertilization of an ovum by the kind of sperm required to produce a conceptus of a particular sex and also cannot bring about abortions of conceptuses undesirable from its point of view, it may still have a say in the sex of its next body by a third method: that of waiting until a conceptus of the correct sex develops in the mother's uterus and becoming associated with it. A few cases suggest that this may occur. I refer to those in which the parents of a child who had died expect and want it to return to them. If such a child has distinctive marks, or if its parents mark or mutilate its body (as some parents in Africa and Asia do), the parents will look for corresponding birthmarks or birth defects on a later-born child. They will think that a child who has such identifiers is their deceased child reborn.[21] In some such families other children may be born between the death of the marked child and the birth of the one who is identified as the deceased (and marked) child reborn. Sometimes (but not always) these other siblings are of the opposite sex to that of both the deceased child and the one thought to be its reincarnation. This suggests that the reincarnating personality held tenaciously to its sex and somehow waited until a body of the same sex became available. However, other children of this group—apparently more flexible in matters of sex—have seemed to reincarnate in bodies of the opposite sex.

Some of the cases of twins contribute to the plausibility of these conjectures. I mentioned earlier that in most of the twin cases I have studied, one or both of the twins remembered a previous life in which the two previous personalities had had some close association with each other. They had usually been members of the same family, good friends, or closely associated in some other way. This observation suggests that in these cases two discarnate personalities had impulses to reincarnate at the same time or were otherwise attracted to do so. It seems likely that the mentioned previous association had something to do with the birth of twins instead of two births of singletons.

We have no case in which two persons, before dying, said that they would be reborn as twins and afterward seemed to provide evidence that they had done so. However, we do have one case in which we have some evidence of a plan conceived by a discarnate personality to be reborn as a twin with a village friend. The principal subject of this Burmese case (studied by Daw Hnin Aye) is Maung Kyaw Myint Naing, and his mother, during her pregnancy with him and his twin brother, dreamed that a deceased relative called Maung Than Aung said that he wished to be reborn as her son and was bringing a companion (unnamed in the dream) with him. Not long after this dream she became pregnant and gave birth to the twins (probably monozygotic, because she had only one placenta). When Maung Kyaw Myint Naing later spoke about a previous life he recalled that during his life in the realm of discarnate personalities he had invited one U Saing to come along with him and be reborn at the same time. He said U Saing was staying as a discarnate personality near the house in the village where he had lived. Maung Kyaw Myint Naing's twin has had no memories of the life of U Saing.

Discarnate personalities who wish for the close companionship of life as twins may simply wait until twin embryos become available to them. However, it is also possible that the discarnate personalities themselves bring about the development of twin bodies in the same pregnancy. If they do this, they may either separate a fertilized ovum (zygote) into two genetically similar, but independent parts (one-egg twins) or bring two ova into position for almost simultaneous fertilization by two different sperm (two-egg twins).[22]

I shall next consider cases in which an incarnating personality may have had some influence on whether his body does or does not have a particular disease or infirmity. I shall consider this possibility with the example of a disease that is clearly transmitted genetically: sickle-cell anemia. I choose it also because many West African people consider it to be associated with a particular type of reincarnation.

The genetics of sickle-cell anemia are well understood. When a man and his wife are each carriers (heterozygotes) of the S gene responsible for the abnormal hemoglobin in this disease, we can predict that, on the average, one-quarter of their children will be homozygotes and suffer from sickle-cell anemia. This is a serious condition, and many children die from it in infancy. The large families in West Africa have a high infant mortality to which other diseases contribute as much as does sickle-cell anemia. The Igbo and many other West African tribes believe that repeated deaths of infants in the same family are not the deaths of different personalities; instead, they are said to result from successive brief incarnations of the same personality, who is born, stays for a few months or years, dies, is reborn, dies once more, and is again reborn. (Several such cycles may occur in one family.) Although the African languages have special names for these children (it is *ogbanje* in Igbo), the concept is best described in English by the term "repeater children."[23]

West African parents suffer distress from the frequent deaths of infants and children in their families, and their grief has mixed with it elements of anger over the early loss of economically important children. Not surprisingly, therefore, they have evolved a belief according to which repeater children belong to a league of discarnate conspiring spirits who have pledged themselves to reincarnate and die prematurely just to harass their parents. Parents may suspect a child who is physically ill, or even one who is frail, of being a repeater child. They may then take measures to separate the child from the band of (discarnate) child spirits who are trying to entice it to die and join them. They may call in an *ogbanje* doctor, and he may cut the child's palm or perform other rituals to prevent the child from dying. If such a child nevertheless dies, the parents may mutilate its corpse. For example, a group of Igbo living in Awgu (in Igboland, Nigeria) often amputate the end of the deceased child's left little finger. As they (or a native doctor) do this, the parents may exhort the soul of the deceased child not to return to them unless he intends to remain and grow up to be a useful member of the family. After this, the parents await the birth of the next child, and they will be pleased if they find at its birth that the tip of its little finger is missing. They then recognize the child as the reincarnation of the dead child whose body they mutilated. They welcome him back, and supposing that he has resigned or been ejected from the league of repeater children, they expect him to be healthy and to survive into adulthood.[24]

The foregoing is less digressive than it may have appeared to be. Let us now consider the hypothetical case of an Igbo personality who is destined, for whatever reason, first to have an incarnation as a person with sickle-cell anemia and then, after dying in that incarnation, to be reborn into the same family, but without sickle-cell anemia. What are the options of this discarnate personality? The sickle-cell gene is not located on the X and Y chromosomes, so the previous personality does not seem to have available the possibility of blocking fertilization by an S gene-carrying spermatozoon. This *may* be possible, but we do not know of any physical mechanism for it. It would seem that if a discarnate personality trying to reincarnate is to become associated with a physical body having sickle-cell anemia, it must somehow identify a homozygotic embryo, which would occur on average in one out of every four fertilizations of an ovum in the intended mother. For the later incarnation, when he is *not* to have sickle-cell anemia, he would associate himself with either of two other types of embryos—

those that would be carriers only and those that would have normal genes for the hemoglobin affected in sickle-cell anemia. The latter would be the easier of the two tasks, since, again on average, three out of four embryos would be healthy with regard to sickle-cell anemia.

In order to influence the selection of an embryo, the discarnate personality would need somehow to learn what sort of embryo was being conceived (or had been conceived already)—that is, one with or without the S gene for sickle-cell anemia. I speculated above, when discussing twins, that two discarnate personalities may manipulate two ova of one woman so that both are fertilized by spermatozoa almost simultaneously or, alternatively, that they may divide a zygote (fertilized ovum) into two equal halves at a critical stage of its development.

If we can legitimately conjecture feats of this order, we should be able to imagine a discarnate personality capable of selecting or avoiding an embryo that will develop into a physical body having sickle-cell anemia. The paranormal knowledge required is not greater than that shown by a few extraordinary living persons.[25] However, I am not saying that a discarnate personality moving, for example, toward an incarnation with sex change and without sickle-cell anemia consciously processes information about an embryo and makes a rational decision thereby. I am only trying to state the problem confronting him, not pretending to know how it is solved. I suppose that few persons (if any), suddenly dying, think to themselves: "I must appear to my wife and tell her I am dying." Most apparitions happen automatically, so far as we can tell.[26] In the same way, I am suggesting, a discarnate personality becomes pulled toward the parents of the next life and then pulled toward a particular conceptus or embryo they provide. Levels of mental activity far deeper than those that regulate the digestion of our supper in our stomach, our ordinary breathing, and the healing without scars of all our superficial wounds must govern these processes.

For the question of whether a discarnate personality could influence a woman potentially a mother, we can begin by drawing on some substantial knowledge. At least we know that mental events can profoundly affect the physiology of a woman's reproductive tract. Has there ever lived a woman who, during her lifetime, never experienced some alteration of her menstruation stimulated by stress? This is doubtful. However, psychological experiences can produce much more extensive changes in a woman's reproductive organs than a mere delayed or skipped menstruation. An extreme manifestation of such influence occurs in the condition of pseudocyesis, or false pregnancy. A woman afflicted with this disorder, who believes she is pregnant when she is not, may stop menstruating for a lengthy period of imagined gestation. Further, she may show enlargement of her abdomen and breasts and even changes in the hormones concerned with reproduction.[27] All these physical changes melt away when the woman is finally made to realize—often after many months—that she is not pregnant.

We also have some evidence indicating the blocking of pregnancy by psychological factors within a fertile woman. The wife of an apparently infertile couple often becomes pregnant after she and her husband have adopted a child; this suggests that she (and her husband) overcame some inhibition against having children that had physical effects on her (or perhaps their) fertility. The Trobrianders engage freely in premarital sexual intercourse, but they strongly disapprove of a pregnancy occurring before marriage. They use no physical measures of birth control, and abortion among them is rare or absent. Yet the Trobrianders have an extremely low incidence of premarital pregnancy. These facts suggest a psychophysical inhibition of pregnancy among their unmarried girls.[28]

Another line of evidence for the influence of psychological factors on reproduction comes from studies of "overripeness" of the ovum before it is fertilized. This may be a factor in some birth defects, and emotional stress seems to be one of its causes.[29]

We need also to consider whether we have any grounds for believing that a discarnate personality could influence either a mother-to-be or spermatozoa and zygotes directly, to the extent required for the changes that I have described. The evidence from pregnancy cravings and aversions that I earlier described—although certainly not strong evidence—suggests that discarnate personalities may influence the physical condition of a mother. The records of psychical research also provide a few examples of mediums who have manifested the physical symptoms that discarnate persons had experienced when they were dying.[30] If a discarnate personality can influence a woman to the extent that these instances suggest, it is only a short step to imagining that one could affect the retention or rejection of a zygote or embryo in her reproductive tract.

How a Discarnate Personality Might Influence the
Development of an Embryo

The cases whose subjects bear birthmarks and birth defects corresponding to wounds or other marks on the previous personality suggest that a discarnate personality may do more than select an embryo with which it will be associated in a new incarnation; it may also modify the development of that embryo during its gestational period.

I explained earlier that I do not wish to enter into further details about the cases with birthmarks and birth defects in the present volume. Therefore, I shall here only promise to return to this topic in another book or a later edition of this one.

THE INFLUENCE OF CONDUCT IN ONE LIFE ON THE CIRCUMSTANCES OF ANOTHER INCARNATION

I have already emphasized that many peoples of the world who believe in reincarnation do so without linking it to their moral values. One might almost say that the idea of such links is a peculiarity of Hinduism and Buddhism. But, since most Westerners know Hindu and Buddhist concepts much better than those of such groups as the Druses, the Alevis, the Tlingit, and the Igbo, most of them who believe in reincarnation have unthinkingly adopted the Hindu-Buddhist concept of karma, according to which our conduct in one life determines the circumstances we shall find in a later incarnation, although not necessarily the one immediately following a particular deed or misdeed.

In the cases that I have investigated, I have found no evidence of the effects of moral conduct in one life on the external circumstances of another. When I examine the cases that include the feature of a marked difference in socioeconomic status between the families concerned, I can discern no pattern indicating that the vicious have been demoted in this respect and the virtuous promoted. Subjects born in materially poor circumstances who have remembered previous lives in prosperous circumstances have sometimes brooded over the difference and concluded that they had earned demotion by the sins or crimes of the previous life they remembered. Rani Saxena, whose case I summarized briefly in chapter 9, belonged to this group, and so did Bishen Chand Kapoor, another Indian subject. I have already alluded to some aspects of his case, but I have not yet described its most distinctive feature.

Bishen Chand was born to poor parents and remembered the life of a rich young man. This young man, Laxmi Narain, had shot and killed another man whom he saw coming out of his (Laxmi Narain's) mistress's apartment. Afterward, Laxmi Narain hid for a time and arranged for the bribing of legal officers and the hushing up of the case against him. He died a natural death a few years later. When Bishen Chand was a child, he used to boast of this murder and of how he (as Laxmi Narain) had escaped punishment for it. His childhood behavior was that of the spoiled rich young man that Laxmi Narain had been. He rebuked his parents for their poverty and demanded better food and clothes, which they could not afford. Later, his attitude changed. It gradually occurred to him that he might have been born the child of poor parents because of the murder Laxmi Narain had committed. (The memory of this murder persisted long after Bishen Chand's other imaged memories of the previous life had faded.) Bishen Chand became a reformed person, and his later life—when I knew him—showed no trace of the violent behavior that Laxmi Narain had manifested when he murdered a man.

A few other cases have similarly stimulated observers to consider whether conduct in one life may influence circumstances in another. The case of Zouheir Chaar of Lebanon provides another example. In chapter 9 I described how the man (Jamil Adnan Zahr) whose life he remembered had quarreled with his (Zouheir's) mother over the sharing of irrigation water. Zouheir was a Druse, and I have already explained that the Druses do not believe that conduct in one life affects the circumstances of another. Nevertheless, observers of Zouheir's case saw irony and a warning in his birth as his mother's son. In considering his case, the Druses would not say that he had been born as the child of his mother because of any misdeed on the part of either of them; but Zouheir's father told me that he thought the animosity between them had somehow acted as a factor bringing them together again when Jamil Adnan Zahr reincarnated as Zouheir Chaar.

The foregoing cases and a few others offer the only hints I have found for the working of a process such as retributive karma. Even these cases, however, provide no evidence for such a process. The explanations offered by the subjects (and other persons) for the different circumstances of two apparently linked lives may amount to nothing more than a rationalization of the differences. Nevertheless, persons committed to the idea of retributive karma may try to save it, despite the lack of supporting evidence, in one of two ways. They may say that a publicly visible criminal had some outweighing private virtue, such as selfless affection given to his family, and that this earned him an advance to a higher material position. Similarly, a person who outwardly acted like a saint may have practiced secret vices that brought about demotion in his next incarnation. If these explanations seem insufficient to cover all cases, proponents of retributive karma may suggest that the effects of misconduct need not occur until many lifetimes after the life in which a person showed it. These are irrefutable explanations but also unsupportable ones. I cannot see any way in which to study them empirically.

Although the cases provide no evidence for a process like retributive karma, this does not mean that conduct in one life cannot have effects in another. Such effects, however, would not occur *externally* in the material conditions of successive lives, but *internally* in the joys and sorrows experienced. In this respect—and in it alone, I think—the cases provide hope for improvement in ourselves from one life to another. The subjects frequently demonstrate interests, aptitudes, and attitudes corresponding to those of the persons whose lives they remember. These similarities occur not only in matters of vocation but also in behavior toward other persons, that is, in the sphere of moral conduct. One child counts every rupee he can grasp, like the acquisitive businessman whose life he remembers; but another gives generously to beggars, just as the pious woman whose life she remembers did. One young boy aims a stick at passing policemen, as if to shoot them as did the bandit whose life he remembers; but another solicitously offers medical help to his playmates in the manner of the doctor whose life he remembers.

The children just mentioned, however, did not all remain set in the attitudes of the previous lives, and I have had the pleasure of hearing about, and occasionally observing, the development of different habits in some of them. In these evolutions we see the effect of new environments perhaps; but I think we also see the inner growth of personalities, accomplished only by the self working on itself. There is a deep truth in a remark made by Friar Giles, one of St. Francis of Assisi's close companions: "Everything that a man doeth, good or evil, he doeth it to himself."[31] There is then—if we judge by the evidence of the cases—no external judge of our conduct and no being who shifts us from life to life according to our deserts. If this world is (in Keats's phrase) "a vale of soul-making," [32] we are the makers of our own souls.

Saints, who are the geniuses of morality, tell us and show us that serenity accompanies selfless conduct toward others, by which I mean conduct without expectation of any gain for oneself except that of serenity. A statement (possibly apocryphal) attributed to Pythagoras embodies this wisdom. He is said to have written to a friend: "You complain of being treated unjustly. Console yourself. Real unhappiness lies in acting unjustly."

If anyone seeks to improve himself, he may feel a need for better models than the persons around him provide. He may wish for the advantage of being born as the child of saints instead of criminals or the morally mediocre. This would be the best of promotions in circumstances from one life to another. Is there any evidence that it can happen? I should say very little. However, the bonds of families and communities, which link so many of the persons concerned in these cases, are not ineluctable. Although the majority of the cases show connections of family, community, or region between the child subject and the person whose life he remembers, a few cases show a tie of friendship. These suggest that we can sever old familial relationships and make new ones in the next life, as we can in this one.

That is all I can say about evidence we have of the effects in one life from causes in a previous one; and I may have said too much. I think it appropriate to end this book with an acknowledgment of our ignorance, even with an emphasis on it. Although the study of the children who claim to remember previous lives has convinced me that some of them may indeed have reincarnated, it has also made me certain that we know almost nothing about reincarnation.

Appendix

Notes

References

Index

Appendix: References to Detailed Reports of Cited Cases

In the following list the cases are cited according to the alphabetical order of the subjects' *first* or given names. Honorifics that have sometimes been used in the text (especially for Burmese subjects and for monks in Thailand) are not used in this list.

The following abbreviations are used for frequently cited sources.

Twenty cases	*Twenty Cases Suggestive of Reincarnation;* see Stevenson, 1974a
CORT 1, 2, 3, 4	*Cases of the Reincarnation Type,* vols. 1–4; see Stevenson, 1975a, 1977a, 1980, 1983a
BMBD	Volumes in preparation of reports of cases whose subjects have birthmarks and birth defects

Detailed case reports are planned for some of the cases annotated as "Unpublished."

Subject's Name	Reference to Detailed Case Report
Adnan Kelleçi (Turkey)	Unpublished
Alexandrina Samona (Italy)	Delanne (1924); Stevenson (1960)
Alice Robertson (U.S.A.)	Unpublished
Ampan Petcherat (Thailand)	CORT 4
Anusha Senewardena (Sri Lanka)	Cook, Pasricha, Samararatne, Maung, and Stevenson (1983a)
Arif Hamed (Lebanon)	Unpublished
Asha Rani (India)	Unpublished
Aung Ko Thein and Aung Cho Thein (Burma)	Unpublished
Aung Myint (Burma)	Unpublished
Aung Than (Burma)	BMBD
Awdesh Mishra (India)	Unpublished
Aye Kyaw (Burma)	BMBD

Subject's Name	Reference to Detailed Case Report
Bajrang B. Saxena (India)	BMBD
Bishen Chand Kapoor (India)	CORT 1
Bongkuch Promsin (Thailand)	CORT 4
Celal Kapan (Turkey)	BMBD
Cemil Fahrici (Turkey)	BMBD
Cevriye Bayrı (Turkey)	CORT 3
Chaokhun Rajsuthajarn, *see* Rajsuthajarn (the Venerable Chaokhun)	
Charles Porter (U.S.A.; Tlingit)	*Twenty cases*
Choe Hnin Htet (Burma)	BMBD
Corliss Chotkin, Jr. (U.S.A.; Tlingit)	*Twenty cases*
Daniel Jirdi (Lebanon)	Unpublished
Derek Pitnov (U.S.A.; Tlingit)	*Twenty cases*
Disna Samarasinghe (Sri Lanka)	CORT 2
Dolon Champa Mitra (India)	CORT 1
Edward Ryall (England)	Ryall (1974)
Erin Jackson (U.S.A.)	Unpublished
Erkan Kılıç (Turkey)	CORT 3
Faruq Faris Andary (Lebanon)	CORT 3
Gamini Jayasena (Sri Lanka)	CORT 2
Georg Neidhart (Germany)	Neidhart (1956)
Gillian and Jennifer Pollock (England)	BMBD
Gnanatilleka Baddewithana (Sri Lanka)	*Twenty cases*
Gopal Gupta (India)	CORT 1
Hair Kam Kanya (Thailand)	CORT 4
Henry Elkin (U.S.A.; Tlingit)	*Twenty cases*
Hmwe Lone (Burma)	BMBD
Husam Halibi (Lebanon)	Cook, Pasricha, Samararatne, Maung, and Stevenson (1983a)
Ichtyake Alamuddin (Lebanon)	Unpublished
Imad Elawar (Lebanon)	*Twenty cases*
Indika and Kakshappa Ishwara (Sri Lanka)	BMBD
Indika Guneratne (Sri Lanka)	CORT 2
Ishwar Godbole (India)	Unpublished
İsmail Altınkılıç (Turkey)	CORT 3

Subject's Name	Reference to Detailed Case Report
Jagdish Chandra (India)	CORT 1
Jasbir Singh (India)	*Twenty cases*
Judith Krishna (India)	Unpublished
Juggi Lal Agarwal (India)	BMBD
Kenedi Alkan (Turkey)	Unpublished
Khin Ma Gyi and Khin Ma Nge (Thailand)	Stevenson (1977b)—brief summary only; a detailed report will be included in BMBD.
Khin Sandi (Burma)	BMBD
Khin San Tin and Khin San Yin (Thailand)	Unpublished
Kumkum Verma (India)	CORT 1
Kyaw Myint Naing (Burma)	Unpublished
Lalitha Abeyawardena (Sri Lanka)	CORT 2
Lal Jayasooria (Sri Lanka)	Unpublished
Laure Reynaud (France)	Delanne (1924); Stevenson (1960)
Mahes de Silva (Sri Lanka)	CORT 2
Mallika Aroumougam (India)	*Twenty cases*
Manju Bhargava (India)	Unpublished
Manju Tripatti (India)	Unpublished
Marta Lorenz (Brazil)	*Twenty cases*
Mary Magruder (U.S.A.)	Unpublished
Michael Wright (U.S.A.)	Unpublished
Mounzer Haïdar (Lebanon)	CORT 3
Mu Mu (Burma)	BMBD
Myint Thein (Burma)	BMBD
Myint Tin (Burma)	BMBD
Nasır Toksöz (Turkey)	CORT 3
Nawal Daw (Lebanon)	Stevenson (1974c)
Necati Çaylak (Turkey)	CORT 3
Necip Ünlütaşkıran (Turkey)	BMBD
Nirankar Bhatnagar (India)	BMBD
Om Prakash Mathur (India)	BMBD
Ornuma Sua Ying Yong (Thailand)	CORT 4
Parmod Sharma (India)	*Twenty cases*
Paulo Lorenz (Brazil)	*Twenty cases*

Subject's Name	Reference to Detailed Case Report
Prabhu (India)	Sunderlal (1924); Stevenson (1960)
Prakash Varshnay (India)	*Twenty cases*
Pratima Saxena (India)	BMBD
Pratomwan Inthanu (Thailand)	CORT 4
Pushpa (India)	Pasricha and Stevenson (1977)
Puti Patra (India)	CORT 1
Pythagoras (Greece)	Iamblichus (1965)
Rabih Elawar (Lebanon)	CORT 3
Rajani Sukla (India)	Unpublished
Rajul Shah (India)	CORT 1
Rajsuthajarn (the Venerable Chaokhun) (Thailand)	CORT 4
Rakesh Gaur (India)	Pasricha and Barker (1981)
Ramesh Sukla (India)	Unpublished
Ramez Shams (Lebanon)	Unpublished
Ramoo and Rajoo Sharma (India)	CORT 1
Ram Prakash (India)	Pasricha and Stevenson (1977)
Ram Tirath (India)	BMBD
Rani Saxena (India)	Unpublished
Ranjith Makalanda (Sri Lanka)	*Twenty cases*
Ratana Wongsombat (Thailand)	CORT 4
Ravi Shankar Gupta (India)	*Twenty cases*
Roberta Morgan (U.S.A.)	Unpublished
Ronald Mapatunage (Sri Lanka)	Unpublished
Ruby Kusuma Silva (Sri Lanka)	CORT 2
Said Zahr (Lebanon)	Unpublished
Salem Andary (Lebanon)	CORT 3
Sampath Priyasantha (Sri Lanka)	BMBD
Samuel Helander (Finland)	Unpublished
Sanjiv Sharma (India)	BMBD
Sayadaw U Sobhana, *see* Sobhana (the Venerable Sayadaw U)	
Semih Tutuşmuş (Turkey)	BMBD
Shamlinie Prema (Sri Lanka)	CORT 2
Shanti Devi (India)	Gupta, Sharma, and Mathur (1936); Stevenson (1960)
Sidath Wijeratne (Sri Lanka)	Unpublished
Sivanthie and Sheromie Hettiaratchi (Sri Lanka)	BMBD
Sleimann Bouhamzy (Syria)	*Twenty cases*

Subject's Name	Reference to Detailed Case Report
Sobhana (the Venerable Sayadaw U) (Burma)	CORT 4
Soe Ya (Burma)	Cook, Pasricha, Samararatne, Maung, and Stevenson (1983a)
Som Pit (Thailand)	BMBD
Sujith Lakmal Jayaratne (Sri Lanka)	CORT 2
Sukla Gupta (India)	*Twenty cases*
Suleyman Andary (Lebanon)	CORT 3
Süleyman Zeytun (Turkey)	CORT 3
Sunil Dutt Saxena (India)	CORT 1
Sunita Khandelwal (India)	BMBD
Susan Eastland (U.S.A.)	Unpublished
Suzanne Ghanem (Lebanon)	Unpublished
Swaran Lata (India)	Pasricha and Stevenson (1977)
Swarnlata Mishra (India)	*Twenty cases*
Taru Järvi (Finland)	Unpublished
Than Than Aye (Burma)	Unpublished
Thein Htoon Oo (Burma)	Unpublished
Thiang San Kla (Thailand)	BMBD
Thusari Wijayasinghe (Sri Lanka)	Cook, Pasricha, Samararatne, Maung, and Stevenson (1983a)
Tin Aung Myo (Burma)	CORT 4; Stevenson (1977d)
Tinn Sein (Burma)	BMBD
Tin Tin Myint (Burma)	CORT 4
Udho Ram (India)	Unpublished
Uttara Huddar (India)	Stevenson (1984)
Veer Singh (India)	CORT 1
Vias Rajpal (India)	Unpublished
Vinita Jha (India)	Unpublished
Warnasiri Adikari (Sri Lanka)	CORT 2
Wijanama Kithsiri (Sri Lanka)	CORT 2
Wijeratne (Sri Lanka)	*Twenty cases*
William George, Jr. (U.S.A.; Tlingit)	*Twenty cases*
Wimalawathie Samarasekera (Sri Lanka)	Unpublished
Win Aung (Burma)	Unpublished
Win Aye (Burma)	Unpublished
Win Myint (Burma)	Unpublished
Win Shwe (Burma)	Unpublished

Subject's Name	Reference to Detailed Case Report
Yin Maung (Burma)	CORT 4
Yusuf Köse (Turkey)	BMBD
Zouheir Chaar (Lebanon)	CORT 3

Notes

PREFACE

[1] **The Meaning of *Karma***

The Sanskrit word *karma* means "action." By extension, it has come to mean also the effects of an action and, more particularly, the effects of moral conduct, especially an effect that occurs in a life after one in which the associated cause has occurred. The doctrine of karma in Hinduism and Buddhism includes many kinds of causes and effects, but popular usage focuses on appropriate retribution for the causative behavior. For example, a man born blind may be supposed to have gouged out the eyes of someone else in a previous life.

[2] **Pronouns Indicating Gender**

I have retained the use of the generic "he," because I find the obsessive use of sexually neutral language hobbling to readers while contributing little to overcome unfairness toward women. Also, in connection with the cases, I have usually used masculine pronouns because it happens that the majority of the children who claim to remember previous lives are males. I discuss possible reasons for this lopsidedness in chapter 10.

CHAPTER 1: INTRODUCTION

[1] **Verified Statements by Subjects**

In addition to making verified statements, the children sometimes make incorrect ones also; and some children of the same general group make nothing but unverified statements or no statements at all. I shall be considering these variations in the cases later.

[2] **Total Number of Cases Investigated**

The University of Virginia's collection of investigated cases suggestive of reincarnation now includes slightly more than two thousand cases. The number of cases in the collection is slowly increasing as my associates and I continue our investigations. At the same time cases already in the collection are sometimes dropped from it, if, upon reexamining their data, we develop doubts about their authenticity.

[3] **Possible Modes of Survival after Death**

Ducasse (1951) and Thouless (1979) have described some of the different ways in which a human personality might conceivably survive physical death.

[4] **Scientists' Disbelief in Life after Death**

A survey showed that whereas 67 percent of the general public believe in a life after death, only 16 percent of scientists do (Gallup, 1982).

[5] **Different Types of Evidence for Survival after Death**

Other evidence bearing on the question of life after death comes from investigations of apparitions, deathbed visions, near-death experiences, out-of-the-body experiences, and some mediumistic communications. I published a short review of this evidence (Stevenson, 1977c). Gauld (1982) has written a full-length book reviewing the evidence, and Thouless has also reviewed it (Thouless, 1984).

[6] **Criteria of Personal Identity**

Philosophers at least from the time of John Locke (1947/1690) have discussed the criteria of personal identity. During the past three decades books and chapters of books devoted to it have proliferated. An incomplete list of these would include Ayer (1963), Lewis (1973, 1978), Madell (1981), Penelhum (1970), Perry (1975), Rorty (1976), Shoemaker and Swinburne (1984), and Vesey (1974). It says something about the isolation of the kind of studies that I am describing in this book—or perhaps the isolation of modern philosophers—that I have read through fifteen inches of books by modern philosophers on personal identity (those just cited and others) without coming across more than three references to the data of paranormal phenomena. (I define this last phrase later in this chapter.)

However, several modern philosophers have considered the definition of personal identity in relation to the data from investigations. Ducasse (1951, 1961) wrote cogently on the subject and so did Broad (1958, 1962). They both considered the topic with regard to the possibility of reincarnation.

Also pertinent are an article by Wheatley (1965) and several articles included in two anthologies concerned with the relationships between philosophy and paranormal phenomena (Thakur, 1976; Wheatley and Edge, 1976). (These anthologies also include chapters not directly concerned with the questions of personal identity and survival.)

Murphy (1945), in one of his papers on the evidence of survival of human personality after death, insisted that evidence of persisting memories would not, by itself, satisfy his criteria for believing that a personality had survived death. He required, in addition, evidence of some intelligent purpose.

[7] **Lack of Change in Personality Soon after Death**

This phrase may seem to go around the question of whether we do survive bodily death. Some of the evidence suggesting that we do derives from apparitions and mediumistic communications (to which I shall refer later in this chapter), and these manifestations often include indications that, although the condition and circumstances of a person change greatly immediately after death, the person's character (or personality) does not.

[8] **Apparitions and Their Interpretation**

Readers wishing to study accounts of apparitions may find them in Gurney, Myers, and Podmore (1886), MacKenzie (1971), and Tyrrell (1953). Gauld (1982) and MacKenzie (1982) have reviewed the different interpretations of apparitions, and so have I (Stevenson, 1982).

[9] **Vitalism**

The concept of vitalism is particularly associated (in modern times) with the ideas and writings of Hans Driesch (1908, 1914). Driesch began his professional life as an embryologist and ended it as a philosopher. His experiments in embryology convinced him that the development of an organism from a fertilized ovum could not be adequately explained by current or future knowledge of chemistry and physics. He opposed a mechanistic explanation of the problems of morphology and said that they required for their solution the inclusion in all living organisms of some unifying and directing element, for which he adopted Aristotle's word *entelechy*.

Driesch became keenly interested in psychical research and was elected president of the Society for Psychical Research in 1926–27. His small book *Psychical Research* (Driesch, 1932/1933) still rewards study. Gruber (1978) published a sympathetic review of Driesch's ideas concerning biology and psychical research.

Other scientists besides Driesch have advanced ideas similar to his, not necessarily calling them vitalism (Hardy, 1965, 1966).

[10] **Conjoined Twins Going through a Door**

Jackson (1966) made this remark.

[11] **Descartes and Bacon on Psychical Research**

Descartes published his comment on what we now call telepathy in *Les principes de la philosophie* (Descartes, 1973/1644, p. 501). Bacon's suggestions for experiments can be found in *Sylva sylvarum* (Bacon, 1639, p. 210), published after his death.

[12] **Terms Used in Considering Paranormal Phenomena**

Glossaries of terms used in psychical research can be found in Grattan-Guinness (1982); Thalbourne (1982); White and Dale (1973); and Wolman (1977).

[13] **Telepathy and Clairvoyance**

In the remainder of this book I shall not usually make a distinction between telepathy and clairvoyance. Some investigators have emphasized the difficulty of showing that telepathy could occur, because a person's paranormal awareness of another person's thoughts might happen solely through the first person's clairvoyant knowledge of the second person's brain processes. However, I consider the term *telepathy* important, if only because it serves to remind us that the person about whom information is obtained paranormally may play just as important a part in the communication as the person obtaining the information does. Ample evidence of this derives from experiments (Schmeidler, 1961a, 1961b) and spontaneous experiences (Stevenson, 1970b).

[14] **Introductory Books on Paranormal Phenomena**

I can recommend several fairly short but comprehensive introductions to the field: those by Grattan-Guinness (1982), Heywood (1974/1971), and Murphy (1961). I also recommend Wolman (1977). Despite its title, Wolman's book cannot be easily carried in the hand. It is much longer than the books just mentioned and written for technically more advanced readers; yet it is packed with reliable information.

[15] **Four Autobiographical Accounts of Telepathic Experiences**

The percipients in these four cases have described their experiences in the books listed under their names in the References.

[16] **Trustworthy Witnesses of Paranormal Cognitions**

Many other equally trustworthy persons have recorded experiences similar to those I have cited. One encounters accounts of their experiences not infrequently in biographies and autobiographies, such as Stanley's and Brougham's. Prince (1928) collected many reports of similar experiences in a valuable anthology.

The large number of eminent persons competent in other fields of human endeavor who have testified to personal experiences of paranormal phenomena raises one of two important questions, depending on how we interpret their claims. On the one hand, if they are (correctly) judged to have been outstandingly competent in their chosen professions and yet mistaken in their reports of their apparently paranormal experiences, we should try to understand why on these occasions they fell so far below the standards they otherwise reached; on the other hand, if they were as competent in reporting these experiences as they are judged to have been in their main professional endeavors, we have to understand why other scientists have segregated their opinions on paranormal experiences as being valueless while continuing to respect their views on matters concerned with their fields of acknowledged expertise.

Furthermore, for scientists who believe in paranormal cognition, personal experience appears to be the predominant means of reaching such belief. A survey by McClenon (1982) of scientists' belief in extrasensory perception showed that few who believed that it can occur did so as a result of studying the books and journals of parapsychology; far more reached their belief because of having themselves had personal, convincing experiences.

[17] **Chance and Death-Coinciding Apparitions**

Details of this analysis may be found in H. Sidgwick and Committee (1894) and also in Broad (1962).

[18] **Agnes Paquet's Case**

The full report is in Sidgwick (1891–92).

[19] **Correspondence of Details between Vision and Distant Event**

Bergson (1913) made precisely the same point in his presidential address to the Society for Psychical Research. The case he cited was that of a woman who, at the moment of her husband's death, saw him killed in battle with many of the particular details of the event.

With characteristic common sense, Dr. Johnson made the same point a century and a half earlier when, talking with Boswell about ghosts, he said:

> Sir, I make a distinction between what a man may experience by the mere strength of his imagination, and what imagination cannot possibly produce. Thus, suppose I should think that I saw a form, and heard a voice cry, "Johnson, you are a very wicked fellow, and unless you repent you will certainly be punished;" my own unworthiness is so deeply impressed upon my mind, that I might imagine I thus saw and heard and therefore I should not believe that an external communication had been made to me. But if a form should appear, and a voice should tell me that a particular man had died at a particular place and a particular hour, a fact which I had no apprehension of, nor any means of knowing, and this fact, with all its circumstances should afterwards be unquestionably proved, I should, in that case be persuaded that I had supernatural intelligence imparted to me. (Boswell, 1931/1791, p. 246)

[20] **Rarities and Reports that Seem Incredible**

The quotation is from Bacon's *The Advancement of Learning* (1915/1605, p. 29).

[21] **The Case of the Blue Orchid of Table Mountain**

I have published details of this case (Stevenson, 1964). MacKenzie (1966) probed it further and published a report of it with some additional information. (The blue flower in question was not in fact an orchid, but at the time I published my report of the case I thought it was.)

²² **Surveys of Psychical Experiences**

Details of such surveys can be found in the reports of Palmer (1979), H. Sidgwick and Committee (1894), and West (1948).

²³ **Flaws in the Testimony of Spontaneous Cases**

Two types of reports of spontaneous cases have been published: those of investigated cases and those of uninvestigated ones. The investigation of a case involves (minimally) questioning the informants through correspondence or (preferably) personal interviews about details of the experience and the related events. The latter should then be verified by the investigator from some independent source, not accepted on the unsupported statement of the percipient. Uninvestigated cases that find their way to publication have usually been accepted at face value from a letter submitted to a research center without further enquiry.

Investigated cases offer two advantages over uninvestigated ones. First, the interviews (or, failing that, repeated exchanges of letters) permit the detection and elimination of cases that are inauthentic or that have an obvious normal explanation. Such cases, accepted into a series of uninvestigated ones, contaminate the series to a degree that one cannot assess, and they may damage the value of conclusions drawn from the series. Second, uninvestigated cases can rarely provide a complete picture of a case. The informant is usually the percipient, and he (or she) may ignore or minimize the experience of the agent. This imbalance can lead to faulty conclusions, such as Rhine's (1981) that agents are unimportant in extrasensory perceptions.

I should add, on the positive side of uninvestigated cases, that some series of them show features that we find in investigated cases; and this tells us that the inclusion of some inauthentic cases and biases from failure to study all aspects of a case may not always vitiate a series.

To study reports of investigated cases, a reader must usually go to the specialty journals of psychical research where they are published individually or in small groups. However, several collections of investigated cases have been published independently or separately from official society publications. These include volumes by Gauld and Cornell (1979; poltergeists); Gurney, Myers, and Podmore (1886; mainly apparitions); MacKenzie (1971, 1982; apparitions and ghosts); Stevenson (1970b; telepathic impressions); and Tyrrell (1953; apparitions). My published reports of the children who claim to remember previous lives are based entirely on investigated cases.

Among collections of uninvestigated cases the following deserve attention: Green (1960, 1968b); Prasad and Stevenson (1968); Rhine (1961, 1981); and Sannwald (1959a, 1959b).

²⁴ **Hallucinations of Widowhood**

Rees (1971) published a survey of such experiences.

²⁵ **Normal Explanations for Apparent Psychical Experiences**

I have discussed this subject, and given relevant references about it, elsewhere (Stevenson, 1983c).

²⁶ **The Themes of Love and Death in Psychical Experiences**

Gurney, Myers, and Podmore (1886) noted these features in their book on (mainly) apparitional experiences. Later series of cases have confirmed the high frequency of a loving relationship between percipient and agent and of death (or a serious illness or accident) as the theme of paranormal communications (C. Green, 1960;

Prasad and Stevenson, 1968; Saltmarsh, 1934; and Stevenson, 1970b).

[27] **Posthypnotic Suggestions**

In the latter part of the nineteenth century, Bernheim (1947/1889) published excellent examples of posthypnotic suggestions, and his work still merits study. Bernheim found that when he pressed and, so to speak, bullied the subjects of posthypnotic suggestions, some of them could remember that their bizarre posthypnotic behavior derived from Bernheim's instructions to them while they were hypnotized.

[28] **The Concept of Behavioral Memories**

Bergson (1959/1896) and Butler (1961/1877) showed the importance of behavioral memories. Penfield (1975) suggested that the main function of a brain is to learn sequences of automatic behavior, which the mind, using the brain as an instrument, initiates when it wills to do so.

CHAPTER 2: THE BELIEF IN REINCARNATION

[1] **Voltaire**

The sentence cited occurs in Voltaire (1960, p. 366).

[2] **The Geographical Distribution of the Belief in Reincarnation**

Information about some of the different beliefs in reincarnation may be found in the following sources:

> Islamic sects of western Asia: Makarem (1974) and Stevenson (1974b/1966 and 1980)
>
> African tribes, particularly of West Africa: Besterman (1968), Deschamps (1970), Noon (1942), Parrinder (1956, 1970), Stevenson (1985), L.-V. Thomas (1968), Uchendu (1965), and Zahan (1965)
>
> Brazil: Stevenson (1974b/1966)
>
> Trobriand Islanders: Malinowski (1916)
>
> Central Australia: Spencer and Gillen (1968/1899)
>
> Ainu: Munro (1963)
>
> Northwestern North America: de Laguna (1972), Slobodin (1970), and Stevenson (1966, 1974b/1966, and 1975b).

From somewhat fragmentary evidence, it seems likely that other American Indians besides those of northwestern North America also at one time believed in reincarnation and that some of them still do. (For example, Radin [1926] published a statement by a Winnebago Indian who claimed to remember two previous lives.) However, these groups certainly did not preserve the belief so long or so vigorously as have the tribes of the northwestern region of the continent. Missionaries of Christianity have not had contact with the latter groups for as long as they have with natives farther east and south.

[3] **Schopenhauer**

I have taken this quotation, which I have translated, from p. 395 of Schopenhauer's *Parerga und Paralipomena* (1891).

[4] **Surveys of the Belief in Reincarnation in North America**

Details may be found in Gallup Opinion Index (1969) and Gallup (1982).

[5] **The Belief in Reincarnation in the Ancient Scriptures of India**

Further information will be found in R. E. Hume (1931), Radhakrishnan (1923), Smart (1964), and Zaehner (1962).

[6] **Apollonius's Meeting with Iarchus**

Philostratus (1969/1912) in his *Life of Apollonius* gives an account of this meeting.

[7] **Common Origin of the Belief in Reincarnation in Greece and India**

Keith (1925) marshaled arguments showing the insubstantiality of much alleged evidence used to support the belief that the ancient Greeks borrowed concepts from the Indians and that the Indians borrowed some from the Greeks. Parallel concepts provide no evidence of borrowing or even of a common origin. It remains possible, however, that both the Greek and Indian concepts of reincarnation did derive from a common origin. Ruben (1939) suggested that this source may have been an early form of shamanism in central Asia.

[8] **Spread of Information between Asians and North American Tribes**

I have elsewhere reviewed the evidence, which is neither abundant nor strong, of contact between Asians and North American tribes in protohistorical times (Stevenson, 1974b/1966, pp. 217–19). Buddhist ideas *may* have reached the inhabitants of Alaska before the coming of Europeans in the eighteenth century. It seems unlikely, however, that they had an important influence on the concept of reincarnation among the tribes of northwestern North America.

[9] **The Alevis of South Central Turkey**

I have had to write "seem to have no scriptural authority" because I have not been able to learn of one. My informants in Turkey have sometimes shown a distressing mixture of ignorance and evasiveness when I have questioned them about the basis of their beliefs. Perhaps they thought me an infidel, unworthy of sharing a knowledge of their religious books. If so, they concealed the texts, but not their belief. The Druses of Lebanon and Syria show a somewhat similar attitude. Most of them talk uninhibitedly about their belief in reincarnation; but an outsider may not examine their holy books. Still, I know that the Druses have such books; I do not know that the Alevis do.

The Koran provides only feeble support for a belief in reincarnation. Like the Bible, it contains some ambiguous passages that lend themselves to interpretation as supporting the idea. I have elsewhere cited such verses in the Koran (Stevenson, 1974b/1966 and 1980). I have also described the belief in reincarnation among the Alevis of south central Turkey (Stevenson, 1970a, 1980).

[10] **Belief in Reincarnation among the Igbo**

I have described elsewhere the belief in reincarnation among the Igbo (Stevenson, 1985).

[11] **Schopenhauer's Conviction about Reincarnation**

Schopenhauer (1908) may not have arrived at his conviction about reincarnation only through philosophical reasoning; he had, for his time, an extensive knowledge of Hinduism and Buddhism, the scriptures of which were then being translated and studied in Europe.

[12] **Philosophers Who Have Endorsed the Idea of Reincarnation**

Anthologists of books on reincarnation frequently cite David Hume with the implication that he also believed in reincarnation or at least thought that it made sense. The sentence usually cited in this connection occurs in his essay "On the Immortality of the Soul," where he wrote: "The Metempsychosis is therefore the only system of this kind that philosophy can hearken to" (Hume, 1854, p. 553). In the immediately preceding passages of the essay, Hume had pointed out that because (nonhuman) animals resemble humans in many ways, we cannot say that humans have souls without allowing that animals also have them. His statement about metempsychosis then follows. (He seems to have used the word *metempsychosis,* as it properly should be used today, to refer to the rebirth after death of the soul of any animal, human or otherwise, in any other animal body.) Anyone who reads Hume's essay in its entirety, however, will acknowledge that he did not believe in the existence of a human (*or* animal) soul, much less in its survival of bodily death. As Boswell (1970) testified, Hume died tranquilly confident of his own mortality.

[13] **Plato's References to Reincarnation**

In addition to the argument in the *Meno,* Plato expounded the idea of reincarnation in other works, notably *Phaedo, Timaeus, Phaedrus,* and the *Republic.*

The quotation for the *Meno* is from pages 91–92 of the edition cited in the list of references (Plato, 1936).

[14] **McTaggart and Ducasse on Reincarnation**

Of all the modern philosophers who have given attention to the idea of reincarnation, McTaggart (1906) and Ducasse (1951, 1961) seem to me the most lucid and most persuasive. McTaggart made no reference to specific memories of previous lives, and he apparently believed that we could have none. However, he thought that a person could learn lessons from one life that he could bring to the next one, even though he brought to it no cognitive information—imaged memories, in my terminology—of the previous life. Ducasse, a generation later, encouraged the investigation of cases and followed reports of them with keen attention.

[15] **The Belief in Reincarnation among the Eskimo**

References to the belief in reincarnation among the Eskimo may be found in Birket-Smith (1959/1936), Boas (1964/1888), Hughes (1962), and Swanton (1908).

A person able to speak the Eskimo language of Greenland can understand the Eskimo language of Alaska without much difficulty. This suggests that the language changed little after the ancestors of the present-day Eskimo spread across the northern tundra. Perhaps the belief in reincarnation (found among the Eskimo of Greenland and Alaska, as well as those in between) also descended from a single locus of belief. And, as I mentioned earlier, the belief might have come from Asia with the ancestors of the present Eskimos.

[16] **Belief in Reincarnation Deriving from Claimed Memories of Previous Lives**

Peris (1963) in an essay on Pythagoras, suggested that the belief in reincarnation and the claim that at least some persons can remember previous lives may be of equal antiquity. Pythagoras provides an obvious example of this relationship, because he taught reincarnation and he also claimed to remember his own previous lives. Similarly, the Bhagavad Gita (of the *Mahabharata*), composed between 200 B.C. and 200 A.D., couples the belief in reincarnation with a claim to remember previous lives (Prabhavananda and Isherwood, 1944). In it Krishna tells Arjuna:

You and I, Arjuna
Have lived many lives.

I remember them all:
You do not remember.

Still another example occurs in Buddhism: the Jataka tales purport to narrate the Buddha's previous lives as remembered by him. As Peris (1963) pointed out, in all these examples we are concerned with a claim to remember previous lives on the part of a god or great sage; we seem a long way from the idea that ordinary men might remember previous lives. Nevertheless, the examples mentioned contain the germ of the idea that memories of previous lives come with spiritual discipline and attainment.

An inquirer may reasonably ask how memories of a previous life would be assimilated by someone who had no prior concept of reincarnation. Indeed, in a later chapter I shall argue that a person who has such memories may reject them unless he also carries over from a previous life a conceptual framework on which to attach them. Perhaps then the establishment of a belief in reincarnation requires two factors: imaged memories of a previous life by oneself or by someone in whom one has confidence and a belief (or intuition) that reincarnation may occur.

[17] **Early Cases of the Reincarnation Type in India**

In the sixteenth century, Tulsi Das, the translator of the *Ramayana*, claimed to remember a previous life, but we have so little information about his assertion that I cannot describe it as a case. In the eighteenth century, the Mogul Emperor Aurangzeb, although he was a fanatical Moslem who did not believe in reincarnation, showed that he was willing to examine facts that conflicted with his beliefs. He called the witnesses of a case to him and interrogated them in the manner of a modern investigator (Stevenson, 1974b/1966, pp. 15–16). The next Indian case known to me occurred in the early years of this century. Sunderlal (1924) published a report on it.

[18] **The Cathars**

Information, such as we have, about the belief in reincarnation among the Cathars, can be found in the works by LeRoy Ladurie (1975), Madaule (1961), Nelli (1972), Niel (1955), and Runciman (1947). LeRoy Ladurie gave one account of a claim by a Cathar to remember a previous life (or, more accurately, three lives, including two as nonhuman animals).

[19] **"Whoever believes that man's birth is his beginning. . . ."**

Schopenhauer (1908, 2:558).

[20] **Intimations of Reincarnation**

I have deliberately used the word *intimations* because I think Wordsworth's "Ode: Intimations of Immortality from Recollections of Early Childhood" illustrates what I am trying to describe.

[21] **Review of One's Life after Death**

Persons who approach death and recover sometimes report seeing scenes of their life flash through their mind. Some authors refer to this experience as "panoramic memory" because, for some persons, the memories seem to be all laid out at the same time. Information about the experience can be found in Greyson and Stevenson (1980), Heim (1972/1892), Noyes and Kletti (1977), and Stevenson and Greyson (1979).

Two further points require noting here. First, the modern reporters of panoramic memories (during experiences near death) do not describe the review as unpleasant. Second, few children who claim to remember previous lives include among their memories the experience of a review after death of the previous life they claim to remember. The cases of Shanti Devi, Nasır Toksöz, and Ishwar Godbole are exceptional; they said that they had experienced a life review at the end of the previous lives they remembered.

If reincarnation occurs, we may have many other subliminal memories of previous lives without having imaged memories that would explain them. I have described some of these as behavioral memories, but I mentioned earlier that we may also have subliminal cognitive memories derived from previous lives. Plato's *Meno* (mentioned above) was an attempt to demonstrate these. We could regard the boy geometer of the *Meno* as the subject of a case who had no imaged memories but had subliminal cognitive ones that he could apply in working out a geometrical problem. This was obviously the way in which Plato's Socrates regarded the boy.

[22] **Reasons for Fearing Death**

Persons who believe that death entails oblivion often fear death and try to avoid it, even when their lives have become miserable through illness and, in the opinion of other persons, "not worth living." Patanjali's (1953) explanation of the fear of death may cover such cases, but another explanation may also apply. During our lives we become strongly attached to the stream of consciousness that we think of as "I." Its cessation forever seems repugnant and something to be struggled against. A person who believes that his "I" will in some way continue after death can more readily abandon his physical body when it no longer serves him well.

Yet we must not say that fear of death always betrays selfishness. The dying often grieve for their survivors as much as the survivors do for the dying (Aldrich, 1963). And the children who remember lives with "unfinished business" (whose cases I shall mention further in chapter 10) help us to understand that some persons wish to live longer in order to continue helping others.

[23] **The Tibetan Pattern of Reincarnation**

Bell (1931) and Snellgrove and Richardson (1968) described the development of the system of *tulkus,* who are said to be the successive incarnations of advanced lamas.

[24] **Conversion of Hindus to Islam in India**

Spear (1965) described the several motives influencing Hindus (and Buddhists) to convert to Islam. Some were converted forcibly. Some sought political rewards under the Moguls. Many, exposed to the preaching and example of the Sufis, concluded that Islam was a superior religion. A large number of low-caste and outcaste Hindus (and Buddhists) escaped into Islam from the oppressions of Brahmans.

[25] **Loss of the Belief in Reincarnation among the Ismailis**

I have given sources for this statement elsewhere (Stevenson, 1980).

Shifts in the beliefs concerning reincarnation among the Ismailis deserve further study. I have been told that the modern Ismailis of East Africa believe in reincarnation. If this is correct, it suggests that their forebears, who lived (for the most part) in western India, may have come under the influence of Hindus, which influence encouraged them to persist in the belief when their coreligionists of western Asia abandoned it.

[26] **Belief in Reincarnation among the Celts**

Evans-Wentz (1911) found evidence of the persistence of the belief in reincarnation among the Celtic inhabitants of Scotland, Wales, and Ireland in the early years of this century.

Julius Caesar remarked on the belief in reincarnation among the Gauls whom he studied. About their priests, the Druids, he wrote: "The cardinal doctrine which they seek to teach is that souls do not die, but after death pass from one [body] to another; and this belief, as the fear of death is thereby cast aside, they hold to be the greatest incentive to valor" (Caesar, 1917, p. 339).

[27] Belief in Reincarnation among the Vikings

My sources for this statement are Davidson (1964) and Ker (1904).

[28] The Council of Nice in A.D. 553 and the Disapproval of the Teaching of Reincarnation

Some details about the teachings of Origen concerning reincarnation and their later condemnation may be found in Prat (1907, 1911). See also Daniélou (1955).

[29] Decline in the Belief in Reincarnation among the Eskimo

I published a brief account of this survey in a short report on the belief and cases related to reincarnation among the Eskimo (Stevenson, 1969).

[30] "It was believed according to ancient lore. . . ."

The quotation is from Ellis (1943, p. 139).

[31] Variations in the Belief in Reincarnation

In my volumes of case reports (Stevenson, 1974b/1966, 1975a, 1977a, 1980, 1983a), I have included chapters or other introductory sections describing the variations among the beliefs about reincarnation in the different countries where I have studied cases suggestive of reincarnation. Readers can find additional information on this subject in Stevenson (1966, 1975b, and 1985) and Parrinder (1956).

[32] Belief in Reincarnation among the Shiite Moslems

The Druses of Lebanon and Syria and the Alevis of Turkey hold the beliefs described in this paragraph (Stevenson, 1980).

Obeyesekere (1968, 1980) distinguished "primitive" and "ethicized" types of belief in reincarnation. According to him, persons who hold the primitive type of belief do not link their moral values with the process of reincarnation; those who hold an ethicized belief in reincarnation do. Obeyesekere cited the Trobriand Islanders and the Igbo as examples of peoples holding the primitive type of belief; Hinduism and Buddhism provide obvious examples of the ethicized type. Obeyesekere was incorrect, however, in asserting that the outcome of ethicizing the belief in reincarnation must be a doctrine like the concept of karma developed in Hinduism and Buddhism. The Druses have coupled their moral values with their ideas about reincarnation without reaching any concept of that kind.

[33] Belief in Reincarnation among the West Africans

Further information will be found in Parrinder (1956), Stevenson (1985), and Uchendu (1965). My article on the belief in reincarnation among the Igbo of Nigeria contains references to earlier discussions of the same topic.

[34] Belief in Reincarnation among the Tlingit

I have summarized the Tlingit concepts of reincarnation elsewhere (Stevenson, 1966; 1974b/1966).

[35] Choice for the Next Incarnation

Cases among the Tlingit of apparent success in premortem selection of the parents for the next incarnation include those of Corliss Chotkin, Jr., and William George, Jr.

[36] **Concept of Reincarnation in Plato's** *Republic*

The relevant passage occurs in the account of the experience of Er in the tenth book (Plato, 1935). Elsewhere, in the *Phaedrus* and the *Timaeus,* Plato gave a somewhat different account of the process of reincarnation and suggested that conduct in one life could affect circumstances in another retributively.

CHAPTER 3: THE TYPES OF EVIDENCE
FOR REINCARNATION

[1] **"Past-Life Readings"**

Eight persons have independently read my own purported previous lives. Not a single one of these readings has agreed with any of the others. Lest it be thought—fairly enough—that they might have described different but not incompatible lives, I will mention that several of the readings placed me in different countries *during the same periods of time.* The persons who gave me these readings had varied backgrounds and occupations. For example, one was an Indian swami, another an American sensitive, and another an Austrian housewife. So far as I could tell, they had nothing in common but honesty and an unshakable conviction in their own powers to do what they claimed to do.

A few seers may have had the ability to obtain information paranormally about other persons' previous lives. In chapter 2 I mentioned Iarchus, who made statements about a previous life of Apollonius of Tyana that accorded with Apollonius's own apparent memories.

I do not reject as impossible the rare occurrence of persons who can authentically read other persons' previous lives. I do insist, however, that most persons who have claimed to be able to do this have not had such powers and have deceived themselves as well as other persons.

[2] **Increased Accuracy of Memory during Hypnotic Age Regression**

True (1949) demonstrated increased accuracy of recall during hypnosis of details of childhood compared with recall during a normal or "waking" state. Reiff and Scheerer (1959) were not able to replicate True's results in full, but they did find improved recall during hypnosis in response to different questions from the ones True had asked. However, O'Connell, Shor, and Orne (1970) could not fully replicate Reiff and Scheerer's results.

Barber (1961) wrote a useful summary and critique of experiments to test improved memory during hypnotic age regression.

[3] **Errors in Recall during Hypnosis**

Orne (1951) showed that ostensibly age-regressed subjects often confabulated when they could not remember information about their childhoods that they were asked to furnish. Accurate and inaccurate memories were mixed and presented without the subjects' being aware of the mistakes they were making. The subjects sometimes "borrowed" memories of events in later childhood (or even later in life) and incorrectly placed these in the period of the ostensible age regression.

Putnam (1979) and later Zelig and Beidleman (1981) showed that when hypnotized (but not regressed) subjects were asked leading questions about an event they had witnessed, they made more errors during hypnosis than in their normal waking state.

Many years ago Stalnaker and Riddle (1932) observed that subjects could recall more items during hypnosis than they could in their normal state, but when hypnotized they also included more inaccuracies among the items recalled. Dywan and Bowers (1983) have reported similar observations.

⁴The Influence of Suggestions in Inducing Previous-Life Fantasies

Baker (1982) showed that the hypnotist's positive or negative suggestions could markedly influence whether or not previous-life fantasies occurred.

⁵Versailles during the Crusades

Bloxham (1958) published this case of hypnotic regression to a "previous life."

⁶Records of Births, Deaths, Marriages

Church records of such events as marriages and deaths and those of land tenure and for certain taxes have existed for centuries in some European countries. But the recorders often left gaps. Fire, damp, war, and negligence have led to the loss of many old parish records. Civil registration of births, deaths, and marriages did not begin in England and Wales until the 1830s, and in Germany until the 1870s. Reliable civil records in the United States also date only from the mid-nineteenth century and, for some states, later, I would not say that someone did not exist before 1850 because we could find no contemporary record of him; but he could not be *proved* to exist without such a record.

⁷Normal Sources of Information in Hypnotically Induced "Previous Personalities"

Dickinson (1911) published one of the most thoroughly worked-out cases showing the emergence into consciousness of information acquired normally many years earlier without the subject's consciously remembering that she had obtained it. The case, that of "Blanche Poynings," is one of communication through automatic writing, but it illustrates well the remarkable ability of the subconscious levels of the mind to organize normally acquired information into a coherent personality. The subject of this case had almost certainly read in childhood a novel in which occurred almost all of the many details incorporated in the constructed "Blanche Poynings." In a session held after those at which "Blanche Poynings" had communicated, Dickinson asked the subject about sources of information for "Blanche Poynings," and she then remembered having seen (and probably read) a historical novel *Countess Maud,* that included all the correct details of the communications from "Blanche Poynings."

Several psychologists have traced the ingredients of hypnotically induced "previous lives" to information the subjects had acquired normally, through reading (sometimes years earlier), without having consciously remembered that they had obtained the information. Examples of such cases can be found in the reports of Björkhem (1961), Kampman (1973, 1975), Kampman and Hirvenoja (1978), and Zolik (1958, 1962).

When a person learns some information, forgets that he has done so, but later shows knowledge of the information, he is said to show *cryptomnesia* or *source amnesia.* I have reviewed this topic elsewhere (Stevenson, 1983b). I also discuss it further in chapter 9 of this book.

⁸The Case of *The Search for Bridey Murphy*

"A lie can go half way round the world before the truth has got his boots on." For this reason, many uninformed persons mistakenly think that cryptomnesia has been shown to be the correct explanation for the case of "Bridey Murphy." But this has not been shown. Some critics alleged that the subject of the case could have acquired all the information that she showed about life in nineteenth-century Ireland from an Irish neighbor whom she was alleged to have known as a child. Ducasse (1960) carefully examined this claim and the evidence that shows it to be invalid. The subject remembered having been acquainted with the neighbor's children, but could not recall that she had ever spoken with the neighbor herself. The latter could not in any event have furnished the subject with all the recondite details about Ireland in the early nineteenth century that "Bridey Murphy" stated. Some critics of parapsychology, borrowing from each other without returning to primary sources, have cited the alleged exposure of the case without showing any knowledge of the exposure of the exposure. They should study Ducasse and also later editions of Bernstein's report of the case (Bernstein, 1965/1956).

However, although the case of Bridey Murphy is not a proven instance of cryptomnesia, it does not provide strong evidence for reincarnation, because no person corresponding to Bridey Murphy's statements has been traced.

⁹ **Responsive Xenoglossy during Hypnosis**

I have published in articles and books reports of the two cases of responsive xenoglossy during hypnosis that seem to me authentic (Stevenson, 1974c, 1976, and 1984).

¹⁰ **Historical Novels Evoked during Hypnotic Regression**

In the same way, I have conjectured that certain delusions of mentally ill persons could derive from memories of previous lives dimly remembered. Could a woman who delusionally believes herself to be the Empress Josephine have had a previous life in France during the first decade of the nineteenth century when she might have admired or strongly identified with the Empress Josephine? We once had a patient at the University of Virginia Hospital who thought she was Scarlett O'Hara, the heroine of *Gone With the Wind*. Perhaps she had some subliminal memories of a life in the antebellum South. Another of our patients, who had hallucinations of religious content, believed she was the reincarnation of St. Teresa of Avila; it is just possible that in her psychotic process vague memories of a previous life as a nun became crystallized into the delusion of having been St. Teresa.

¹¹ **Amnesia of Later Childhood**

The inability, except in rare cases, to tap memories of previous lives during hypnosis probably has the same cause as the amnesia that occurs for spontaneous memories of previous lives in later childhood. I discuss this important topic in chapter 5.

¹² **Incidence of the Experience of Déjà Vu**

I derived the figure given here (76 percent) by combining data published by Palmer (1979) based on a survey of a random sample of residents and students of a typical American city (Charlottesville, Virginia). Other samples may show different incidences. Some of the differences between surveys derive from the variety of ways the respondents have been asked about the experiences and the several ways they may interpret the question asked. Some psychologists and respondents include under déjà vu the experience of believing that an event, such as a particular conversation, has been lived through before; others restrict the term to a sense of familiarity with a place not visited before. Palmer's questionnaire included both types of experience of déjà vu: for places and for events.

The experience of déjà vu should not be regarded as a sign of mental abnormality. Many clear-headed persons have had the experience. These include, among others, the novelist Charles Dickens (1877, p. 37) and the poet A. E. Housman (Graves, 1979, p. 166).

Neppe (1983) has published a comprehensive review of the déjà vu experience.

[13] Statements by Subjects about Changes in Buildings

The cases of Parmod Sharma, Prakash Varshnay, Rabih Elawar, and Swarnlata Mishra include such statements by the subjects. (I give references to the detailed reports of their cases in the Appendix, where I have listed the subjects by the alphabetical order of their *first* names.)

[14] Déjà Vu and Previous Life Memories

If the experience of déjà vu derived often from memories of actual previous lives, I should expect that more persons having the experience would, at the same time, have an uprush of imaged memories. This happens sometimes to the children subjects of our verified cases. When they reach the village or town where they say they have lived before, they may have new memories, ones evidently stimulated by scenes that appear to be familiar to them. Occasionally, adults who have had the experience of déjà vu say that they also had then, or moments later, some unexpected knowledge about the place where the experience occurred. They will know, for example, that around the next corner one will reach a blacksmith's shop that is, from where the subject stands, still out of sight. And so it may turn out. Informants have reported a few cases of this type to me, but I have not so far obtained any corroboration from other witnesses as to whether the subject mentioned the existence of the blacksmith's shop, for example, before the subject and his companions had come to it. No doubt in some instances diffidence has kept the subject from speaking his thoughts; in others, witnesses have died or otherwise dispersed. But I think that I would have learned of corroborated cases of this kind if déjà vu often derived from paranormal cognitions, including memories of previous lives. Perhaps this note will stimulate better recording of such experiences in the future.

[15] Neurological Explanation of Déjà Vu Experience

Efron (1963) has proposed this explanation.

[16] Recurrent Nightmares and Genetic Memory

Some persons might interpret this case as an example of genetic memory, because it is almost certain that some of Mary Magruder's ancestors were involved in an Indian raid resembling that of her nightmare. I shall return to the subject of genetic memory in chapter 7.

[17] Subjects Having Both Waking Memories and Related Dreams

Prakash Varshnay, Salem Andary, and Suleyman Andary are among the subjects who had both waking memories and apparent memories of the previous life during dreams.

[18] Vividness and Paranormal Components in Dreams

A report of "vividness" occurred in 56 (45 percent) of 125 precognitive dreams that I analyzed (Stevenson, 1970c). Prince (1921, 1922) analyzed 449 "vivid" dreams in which the dreamer had dreamed of another person about whom he was not then anxious. He found that in 35 (nearly 8 percent) of these the dream had coincided with the death of the person dreamed about. Most dreamers say that vivid dreams, compared with ones that are not vivid, occur to them rarely. It appears that, although the majority of vivid dreams convey no paranormally acquired information, a dream that is vivid is more likely to include such information than one that is not.

I do not wish to exaggerate the possible importance of vividness in dreams as an indicator of paranormal processes. A dreamer who remembers a particular dream for some reason other than vividness, perhaps because it had an apparent paranormal process, may later describe it as vivid. We should therefore consider three possibilities: vivid dreams may be more readily remembered, vivid dreams may be more likely than other dreams to have a paranormally derived content, and dreams having such a content may be retrospectively characterized as vivid. The relationship between the perceptual features of dreams and their contents requires further investigation.

[19] **Hallucinogenic Drugs and Previous-Life Memories**

Grof (1975) discussed the possibility that some persons might experience memories of previous lives during intoxication with hallucinogenic drugs. Some of the experiences during intoxication with LSD that Sandison, Spencer, and Whitelaw (1954) described seem to me suggestive of memories of previous lives. They, however, preferred to interpret them as evidence of the release by LSD of repressed memories; but they did not address the question of the origin of the specific details in the allegedly repressed memories.

[20] **Memories of Previous Lives Occurring First or More Abundantly during Illness**

Examples may be found in the cases of Ma Mu Mu and Vinita Jha.

[21] **Spontaneous "Flashes" of Possible Previous-Life Memories**

Lenz (1979) published a collection of such experiences, but he accepted them at face value and made no attempt to relate them to other kinds of experiences, either psycho-pathological or paranormal.

Numerous historical novels have been published by authors who claim to have based them on real memories of previous lives. We can acknowledge the good faith of some of these writers (Grant, 1937; Hawkes, 1981) without necessarily taking their books seriously as evidence for reincarnation.

CHAPTER 4: TWELVE TYPICAL CASES OF CHILDREN WHO REMEMBER PREVIOUS LIVES

[1] **Detailed Case Reports**

As I mentioned earlier, the Appendix gives information about the publications of these reports. (The cases are listed in alphabetical order of the subjects' *first* names.) Readers should remember that the summaries of cases presented in this book are drastically condensed versions of the full reports. In case reports, brevity and thoroughness are not usually compatible.

[2] **Announcing Dreams Related to Impending Births**

This is an example of a type of dream that frequently occurs in cases of the reincarnation type. A deceased person appears to a dreamer and expresses his wish or intention to be reborn in a particular family. The dreamer is usually the woman who will become the mother of the child who will remember the life of the deceased person appearing in the dream. Sometimes a relative (as in Corliss's case) or a friend has the dream. I call these "announcing dreams," and will say more about them in later chapters. Four other examples occur in the cases of this chapter.

[3]Honorifics in Burma

Ma is an honorific given to young girls in Burma. After they grow older and achieve adult status and a recognized position in the community (whether or not they marry), they are addressed by the honorific Daw. Similar terms for young and older men are Maung and U. Honorifics are so important in Burma that they have become an almost undetachable part of the given name; accordingly, I shall use them in referring to Burmese persons mentioned in this book.

[4]Subjects' Desires to Return to the Previous Homes and Families

So many subjects of these cases exhibit a strong desire to return to the previous family that one might regard this as a recurrent feature of the cases. However, some subjects do not show this behavior. In cases with verified details I have found that the child's desire or reluctance to meet the previous family usually accords with what we can learn or infer about the concerned previous personality's relationship with its members. The case of Suleyman Andary (in this chapter) provides an example of a child who did not wish to go to the place where the previous personality had lived and where he had been unhappy.

The child's relations with his own family also affect these attitudes. I have, however, found instances in which a child has exhibited an intense longing to return to the previous family, even when, so far as I could judge, he seemed to be receiving more affection in his (present) home than the related previous personality had received in his. In these cases one or more of several other factors may influence the child. First, he may long for the previous way of life more than for the members of the previous family; a mansion with servants may seem desirable even though inhabited by an uncongenial wife. (The case of Indika Guneratne provides an example of this type.) Second, the child may have a sense of what I call "unfinished business"; examples of this would be infant children who still needed care at the time the related previous personality died. (The cases of Sukla Gupta and Lalitha Abeyawardena exemplify this group of cases.) Third, old habits carried over and the discomforts of adapting to new persons and styles of living may cause a sort of nostalgia for conditions that seem more familiar, even when, to other observers, these conditions appear to be inferior to those in which the subject is currently living. The Spanish word querencia expresses better than any English word this longing for a familiar place. (Prakash Varshnay was a subject who showed this motive—and no other—for wishing to return to the previous family of his memories.)

[5]Ma Tin Aung Myo's Antagonism toward British and American People

I learned of this detail only through direct questioning in the later phases of my study of this case. Ma Tin Aung Myo's mother had not mentioned it spontaneously during my meetings with her. The detail is therefore not included in my longer reports of this case.

[6]Subjects' Comparisons of Their Mothers with Their "Other Mothers"

The children subjects of these cases rather often compare their parents with the previous parents they claim to remember, not always to the credit of the former. Other examples of this behavior occurred in the cases of Roberta Morgan (in this chapter), Veer Singh, and Rabih Elawar.

[7]The Druse Religion

I have published elsewhere information about the Druse religion, especially with regard to the belief in reincarnation among the Druses (Stevenson, 1974b/1966,

1980). Further information about the Druse religion can be found in Makarem (1974).

[8] **Subjects' Failures to Recognize Persons and Places That Have Changed**

Twenty-five years had elapsed between the death of Abdallah Abu Hamdan and Suleyman's visits to Gharife. The people and places he was expected to have recognized had changed considerably during these years. Recognitions, as I shall explain later, provide the weakest kind of evidence in these cases; but we should make some allowances for the difficulties sometimes imposed on a subject who is asked to make recognitions to support his claim to being reborn. (The problem of changing appearances, however, does not apply to photographs.)

[9] **"Intermediate" Lives in Druse Cases**

I have provided elsewhere reports of some illustrative cases and a discussion of the evidence for "intermediate" lives (Stevenson, 1980).

[10] **Geographical Factors Connecting the Previous Personality and the Subject's Family**

In some other cases in which the two families concerned had had no prior acquaintance, a member of the subject's family has visited, not long before the subject was conceived, the area where the previous personality had lived or died. In other cases, a member of the previous personality's family has visited or moved into the area of the subject's family shortly before the subject was conceived.

In a section of chapter 11 I discuss these geographical factors further and give additional pertinent examples.

[11] **Desire to Return**

See note 4, this chapter.

[12] **Comparison of Mothers**

See note 6, this chapter.

[13] **Knowledge of Events Occurring after Death**

Michael's statement about being carried over the bridge suggests that he had memories of events after Walter Miller's death. Memories of this type are extremely rare in the cases of most cultures but frequently occur among the cases of Burma and Thailand—the case of Bongkuch Promsin providing an example.

[14] **Cases with a Triangular Relationship between Parents and the Subject**

I have investigated two cases, those of Asha Rani in India and Ma Tin Tin Myint in Burma, in which the subject said that in her previous life she had been her father's first wife.

In the case of Taru Järvi in Finland, Taru said that (in the previous life she remembered) she had been her mother's first husband. (Hers was therefore also a case of "sex change.")

CHAPTER 5: CHARACTERISTICS OF TYPICAL CASES OF THE REINCARNATION TYPE

[1] **Definition of a Case**

Some readers may already have wished to know how I define a "case," and I shall now say what I mean by this term. By a case of the reincarnation type I mean one in which a person (the subject of the case) is identified as being a particular deceased person reincarnated.

In most of the cases, the subject himself makes the identification with the deceased person by making statements that he regards as memories of the life of that person. Such subjects usually also show other common features of the cases, which this chapter will describe.

I have, however, accepted for investigation and inclusion in our collection of cases a small number in which the subject made no statements indicative of his having imaged memories of a previous life. In these cases other persons nevertheless identified the subject as the reincarnation of a specific deceased person on the basis of: a prediction by the deceased person that he would be reborn; an announcing dream (described further below); a birthmark or birth defect; some unusual behavior of the subject; or a combination of two or more of these features. (If the subject has made no statements, we require that the case have at least two of these other features before we include it in our series.)

² Measures Used in Suppressing Cases

The parents of Asia resort to a variety of measures for suppressing children's memories of previous lives. Turning the child on a wheel until he becomes dizzy (which presumably confuses the child and is thought to drive the memories out of his mind) is used commonly. Other measures include: washing out the subject's mouth with dirty water; putting partly chewed food into the child's mouth; putting a broom on the top of the child's head twice a week; slapping the child's head gently with the sole of a shoe; and applying amulets to the child. Burmese parents have much confidence in making the children eat duck eggs. Physical beating is a last resort, but happens sometimes. Among Indian subjects known to me, Jasbir Singh, Prakash Varshnay, and Ravi Shankar Gupta were beaten to suppress their talking about previous lives.

Western parents also sometimes beat such children, as we have seen in the case of Roberta Morgan.

³ Incidence of Cases

In my first book of case reports (Stevenson, 1974b/1966), I gave some crude estimates about the incidence of cases in several areas where I have found them abundantly.

⁴ Results of Searching for Cases

Thailand and Burma are neighboring countries with many features in common. Nearly all the inhabitants of each are Theravadin Buddhists who believe in rebirth. We might expect, therefore, that the real incidence of cases in the two countries would be similar; however, the numbers of reported cases differ greatly in the two countries. In Thailand, where I have been investigating cases since 1966, I have learned of only forty-five cases. In Burma, on the other hand, where I have been investigating cases only since the end of 1970, I have information about more than 500 cases, ten times as many as in Thailand.

The differences in the incidence of reported cases in Thailand and Burma may be partly due to the different states of economic development of these two countries. Thailand, although still counted as an underdeveloped country, is vastly more advanced economically than Burma. In chapter 8 I discuss the possibility that economic development has entailed significant changes in concepts about what Westerners call paranormal phenomena.

However, I attribute most of the difference between Thailand and Burma in the incidence of reported cases to the indefatigable activity of a single person: U Win Maung, my associate in Burma. He has had the time and, more important, the tireless industry to enquire about the cases through massive correspondence and numerous visits to Burmese villages. In Thailand several able and interested Thais have worked on the cases with me when I have been able to visit Thailand myself; but none has had the time or enthusiasm to look for the cases persistently in the style—perhaps inimitable—of U Win Maung.

U Win Maung's accomplishment is unique in scope, but not in kind. Other associates and subagents have also shown how readily cases can be found in Asia by those who search for them. As another example I can mention the late Ram Singh. He was a retired employee of the Maharajah of Jhalawar in Rajasthan, India, who became interested in my research and searched for cases for me in the area where he lived. From the late 1960s until his death in 1981, he identified many cases for me. He learned about some of these by reading newspapers; for others he obtained information through his own local network of informants. His endeavors led to my learning about the same number of cases from the small region where he lived as from all the other parts of Rajasthan combined. His "territory" comprised about one-twentieth of the area of Rajasthan; yet I first learned of seventeen cases from him and (up to 1984) of only sixteen more from all other informants for cases in Rajasthan.

[5] **"Fully Developed" Is Not Perfect**
The features that make a case "fully developed" tell us nothing about its evidential value. A case rich in phenomena may be poor in evidence. What constitutes good evidence I discuss in chapters 6 and 7.

[6] **Predictions of Reincarnation among the Tlingit**
The case of Corliss Chotkin, Jr. (summarized in chapter 4), illustrates both the selection of parents for the next incarnation and the prediction of birthmarks on the next body of the reincarnating person. The case of William George, Jr., provides another example of both these features.

[7] **Predictions of Reincarnation among the Tibetans**
Norbu and Turnbull (1969) provide some information about predictions of rebirth by Tibetan lamas.

The Tibetan cases known to me nearly all have as their subjects lamas who, as children, spoke about the previous lives of other lamas; I mentioned these subjects, who are known as *tulkus,* in chapter 2. They represent a small group among all Tibetans. They are said to be able, by virtue of their advanced spirituality, to control—at least to some extent—the place and circumstances of their reincarnation. The predictions made by elderly lamas before they die express their confidence in this ability. (Cases are said to occur among Tibetan laymen also, but I know of only one such case.)

In my efforts to investigate cases among Tibetan refugees in India, I have found the dispersal of potential informants (some even having remained in Tibet) handicapping; consequently, the Tibetan cases I have investigated provide weaker evidence than those of countries where informants for a case are usually accessible in one or two communities.

[8] **Announcing Dreams**
Reports of the following cases describe announcing dreams: William George,

Jr., İsmail Altınkılıç, Cevriye Bayrı, Nasır Toksöz, Corliss Chotkin, Jr., Susan East-land, Ma Tin Aung Myo, the Venerable Sayadaw U Sobhana, Maung Yin Maung, Erkan Kılıç, Ma Tin Tin Myint, Michael Wright, Samuel Helander, and Ornuma Sua Ying Yong.

I have also given some further information about announcing dreams among the Tlingit in my 1966 article on their cases.

⁹ **Birthmarks and Birth Defects**

I have so far published detailed reports of only a few cases in which the subjects had birthmarks or birth defects. Among the more important of these cases are those of Derek Pitnov, Charles Porter, Henry Elkin, William George, Jr., Corliss Chotkin, Jr., Ravi Shankar Gupta, and Wijeratne. In chapter 4 I described one of the two birthmarks on Corliss Chotkin, Jr., and two birthmarks on Jennifer Pollock. I have included some additional information about such cases in an article (Stevenson, 1977b).

¹⁰ **Age of First Speaking about a Previous Life**

For 693 cases from six cultures the combined average age of first speaking was thirty-seven months. Complete data about the subject's age at first speaking about the previous life can be found in Cook et al. (1983b) and Stevenson (1983d).

¹¹ **Subjects Commenting on Change of Body Size**

Among the children who have commented on a change in body size since the previous life are: Marta Lorenz, Michael Wright, Sukla Gupta, Parmod Sharma, Vias Rajpal, Ramoo and Rajoo Sharma, Lalitha Abeyawardena, Ruby Kusuma Silva, Bongkuch Promsin, Rabih Elawar, and Chaokhun Rajsuthajarn.

¹² **Reducing Subjects to Tears by Teasing**

This minor cruelty was practiced on Sukla Gupta and Imad Elawar. Disna Samarasinghe could be made to cry, when she was a young child, by being called "Babanona" in a teasing manner. (Babanona was the old lady whose life Disna remembered.) I witnessed one of Disna's tearful reactions to such teasing myself.

¹³ **Memories of Previous Lives during Dreams and Nightmares**

Examples may be found in the cases of Wijanama Kithsiri, Prakash Varshnay, Suleyman Andary, and Salem Andary.

¹⁴ **Forgetting of the Memories**

I have discussed at greater length elsewhere the factors that seem to me relevant for judging whether a child has forgotten or continues to remember a previous life, whatever he may say about this himself (Stevenson, 1974b/1966). Girls seem particularly apt to conceal any residual memories they may have in their teens; it is one thing for a three-year-old girl to talk about her husband and her wish to see him, quite another for a fifteen-year-old girl to do so. Sukla Gupta (in India) was a girl who "went underground" when, after puberty, it embarrassed her to talk about having a husband, something she had talked about freely with anyone who would listen when she had been a young child.

Some subjects insightfully distinguish between their original memories, which they may have largely forgotten, and memories of what others have said they said about the previous life when they were young.

¹⁵ **Reduction of Tension in the Subject after Meeting the Previous Family**

The almost sudden subsidence of tension in the child following the first meeting with the family of the previous life somewhat resembles the relief sometimes experienced by a patient with a severe neurosis, such as a phobia, when he remembers the traumatic event that caused it. When the patient brings the forgotten event into consciousness, he can associate it with other, later experiences, which process neutralizes its noxious influence. Strong emotion occurs during the breaking down of the dissociation (the isolation of different memories within the mind), but this emotion is an accompaniment of the recovery of the forgotten memory, not itself a factor in the healing process (Davis, 1958; McDougall, 1926; Marks, 1978). Smith, Hain, and Stevenson (1970) provide further references and a discussion of this important topic. The meeting of a child with the previous personality's family may contribute to the breaking down of dissociations and the integration of the memories of the previous life with the remainder of the child's personality. If the meeting stimulates additional memories, as such meetings often do, this may further accelerate the process of integration.

[16] **Factors in the Amnesia of Childhood**

Data about the different ages of forgetting in solved and unsolved cases can be found in Cook et al. (1983b).

Mere passage of time does not cause memories to fade. They become inaccessible through the interfering effect of later experiences. Readers interested in learning more about some factors concerned in the fading of memories may find helpful a discussion of this topic and references to relevant research that I have published elsewhere (Stevenson, 1975a, pp. 25–29).

[17] **Fading of Imaged Memories and the Development of Language**

Earlier authors have described two types of cognitive memories. Koestler (1969) referred to "the 'vivid fragment' or 'picture-strip' type of memory," which he distinguished from the "abstractive" type. The latter type requires language. Tulving (1972) referred to these same types of memory as "episodic" and "semantic." (Bergson [1959/1896] made the same distinction earlier.) I have subsumed both these types under what I call "imaged memories," in order to distinguish them from "behavioral memories," which I described in Chapter 1.

Richardson (1969) in his study of imagery wrote: "As we grow to adulthood in a modern industrialized society it is to be expected that verbal modes of encoding experience will take precedence over the imagery modes of early childhood" (p. 137). The same process occurs in nonindustrial societies, although perhaps more slowly.

[18] **Clustering of Memories around Death and Events Preceding It**

An occasional subject has a memory of an event that happened many years before the previous personality's death. Examination shows that memories of this kind usually derive from events that are associated with strong emotion, such as a wedding gift or a physical injury. I have given examples in the reports of the cases of Kumkum Verma and Lalitha Abeyawardena.

[19] **Proper Names in Sri Lanka**

I have discussed this topic more fully in the Introduction to my book on the cases in Sri Lanka (Stevenson, 1977a).

[20] **Experiences with Sages between Death and Presumed Reincarnation**

I have given further information about the sages whom some subjects say they encountered in the discarnate realm in my book reporting cases in Thailand and Burma (Stevenson, 1983a).

[21] **Spontaneous Recognitions**

Other examples occurred in the cases of Ratana Wongsombat, Cevriye Bayrı, Nasır Toksöz, Jasbir Singh, Imad Elawar, Mounzer Haïdar, and Rabih Elawar.

[22] **Different Responses of Subjects to Different Members of the Previous Personality's Family**

Additional examples of how the subject adopts attitudes toward members of the previous family that correspond to the attitudes the previous personality showed toward the same persons can be found in the cases of Lalitha Abeyawardena, Disna Samarasinghe, Pushpa, and Gamini Jayasena.

[23] **Acceptance of Subjects by the Families of the Previous Personalities**

Examples of families of previous personalities showing complete acceptance and support for subjects may be found in the cases of Swarnlata Mishra, Rabih Elawar, and Ram Prakash.

[24] **Rejection of the Subject by the Previous Personality's Family**

Examples may be found in the cases of Dolon Champa Mitra and Sunil Dutt Saxena. In both these cases the previous families were wealthy and probably feared that the subject's family would expect, or even demand, subsidies on his behalf.

[25] **Phobias Expressed before the Development of Speech**

Another example occurred in the case of Sujith Lakmal Jayaratne (Sri Lanka). He, too, showed a phobia of the police and also one of trucks before he had begun to speak about the previous life. The previous personality in his case had been an illegal distiller of alcohol who had had many unpleasant encounters with the police; and he had been killed by a speeding truck.

[26] **Cases with Marked Differences in the Socioeconomic Classes of the Families Concerned**

I have described other subjects who remembered a previous life in a family of higher socioeconomic class, and who showed corresponding snobbish behavior, in my reports of the cases of Jasbir Singh, Veer Singh, Indika Guneratne, and Jagdish Chandra.

Disna Samarasinghe is another example of a subject who remembered a previous life in a family of a lower socioeconomic class than that of her own.

[27] **Adult Attitude**

Suleyman Andary, Kumkum Verma, Hair Kam Kanya, and Bongkuch Promsin are among the subjects who showed such adult attitudes.

[28] **Cases of the Sex-Change Type**

Other examples of children who remember previous lives as members of the opposite sex will be found in the cases of Gnanatilleka Baddewithana, Paulo Lorenz, Ruby Kusuma Silva, and Ampan Petcherat.

[29] **Interval between Previous Personality's Death and Subject's Birth**

I have published some of these data elsewhere (Stevenson, 1983a).

[30] **Measures Taken to Suppress Cases in India**

I have derived these figures from the doctoral thesis of Dr. Satwant Pasricha (National Institute of Mental Health and Neurosciences, Bangalore, India, 1978).

[31] **Persistence of Behavior Appropriate for Opposite Sex**

American children who do not remember previous lives but who show cross-gender behavior in childhood also develop sexually in different ways as they become older. R. Green (1979) followed a group of these children, and he found that some became homosexual in youth and adulthood whereas others developed a heterosexual orientation.

[32] **Xenoglossy**

The few cases of xenoglossy that I consider authentic and important are those of Swarnlata Mishra, Jensen (Stevenson, 1974c), Gretchen (Stevenson, 1976, 1984), and Uttara Huddar.

[33] **Inability to Remember Previous Mother Tongue**

At first blush, it seems surprising that a child in India could remember that he was an Englishman named Arthur killed in World War I and not remember also how to speak the English language. (This example is from the case of Bajrang B. Saxena, not yet published.) The explanation may lie in the different images available for *spoken words* and for *events,* such as being killed violently. If I have in my mind an image of a chair, I do not necessarily at the time think the word *chair,* much less speak it out. If I should be reborn after my death and see a chair, it may seem familiar to me and in that sense I would recognize it; but this would not necessarily lead me to attach the word *chair* to the chair that I see. If I am reborn in Germany and I seem to recognize a chair there, my German parents will probably tell me that the object of my attention is a *Stuhl,* and this might tend to block any tendency that I might have retained (from my present life) to call it a *chair.*

However, nearly all the subjects remember *some* words derived from the previous life. In order for a case to be solved, the subject must (nearly always) have remembered specifying names of people and places. Some subjects remember only a few names, others remember many.

[34] **Glossophobia**

In my book reporting cases in Burma and Thailand (Stevenson, 1983a) I discuss the resistance to learning Burmese shown by some Burmese children who remembered previous lives as Japanese soldiers killed in Burma during World War II. Another example of glossophobia occurred in the case of Nawal Daw in Lebanon.

[35] **Cases with Anomalous Dates**

I have published reports of two cases of this type, those of Jasbir Singh and Chaokhun Rajsuthajarn. I hope to include reports of other such cases in a later volume of case reports.

CHAPTER 6: METHODS OF RESEARCH

[1] **Pythagoras**

My source is Iamblichus (1965).

[2] **Apollonius**

My source is Philostratus (1969/1912).

[3] **Case Investigated by Aurangzeb**

I have a photocopy of the Urdu text of a report of this case (in an eighteenth century book) and an English translation of the passage; but I have not examined the full book from which this report was copied. It is *Khulasat-ut-Tawarikh* and written by Munshi Subhan Rai.

[4] **The Case of Katsugoro**

Hearn (1897) published translations of the original Japanese documents in the case, which occurred in the 1820s. I have published a short summary of the case (Stevenson, 1960).

[5] Burmese Cases of the Late Nineteenth Century

These were published by Fielding Hall (1898).

[6] Published Reports of Cases between 1900 and 1960

Of these the most remarkable are those by Sunderlal (1924) and Sahay (1927). They each published groups of reports; Sunderlal reported four cases, and Sahay seven. Moreover, each recognized the importance of careful recording of the testimony. Sunderlal reported one case (that of Prabhu) and Sahay reported two cases (those of Jagdish Chandra and Bishen Chand Kapoor) in which a written record of what the subject said about the previous life was made before any attempt at verifying his statements.

Gupta, Sharma, and Mathur (1936) published a noteworthy report of the case of Shanti Devi. They did not record Shanti Devi's statements about the previous life she remembered before taking her to Mathura, the city of the previous life; but they constituted themselves a committee (independent of the families concerned) to investigate the case, and they published a rather detailed report of it soon after its development.

No history of the study of cases suggestive of reincarnation can omit mention of Delanne's (1924) remarkable compilation. He gave his book the modest title *Documents pour servir à l'étude de la réincarnation*. It consists largely of an anthology of reports of cases that he gathered from diverse sources; the reports are therefore of unequal value. Some snippets from magazines and newspapers are almost worthless, but Delanne also included in his book longer detailed accounts of some cases, such as those of Alexandrina Samona and Laure Raynaud. His work, moreover, is much more than a scrapbook; it includes his own perceptive comments on the cases. It has never been translated into English and has, so far as I know, influenced no English-speaking investigator other than myself; but I am much indebted to it.

[7] Forty-four Cases Analyzed in 1960

I summarized and analyzed these cases in Stevenson (1960).

[8] Incidence of Cases in India

The survey conducted by Barker and Pasricha (1979) gives some indication of the incidence of cases, at least in one region of northern India. They found an incidence of nineteen cases per thousand inhabitants.

[9] Authenticity of Cases

I remind readers of what I wrote in Chapter 1 about the important distinction between authenticity and paranormality. When we say that a case is authentic, we mean that the accounts of informants, and other evidence we obtain, have provided an adequately accurate description of events that happened. However, a case can be authentic and yet be lacking in evidence of paranormality. This is the situation with many cases in which subject and previous personality belong to the same family. The informants may be completely reliable persons, and the subject *may* have made statements about details in the life of the previous personality that he did not learn normally; but since the child was a member of the previous personality's family, he may have had opportunities to learn much about his deceased relative from other family members.

[10] **Methods of Research**

I published the most detailed account of my methods of investigation in Stevenson (1975a).

[11] **Definition of a Firsthand Informant**

A firsthand informant is one who describes what he himself heard or saw directly: he is an eyewitness. If he narrates only what someone else told him, he is a secondhand witness—in legal terms, a teller of hearsay; and he is worse than that if he spins out accounts that he never heard from anyone.

[12] **Use of Interpreters**

Although I do not think that interpreters significantly distort the testimony in the cases, I do believe that the need for one causes an important loss of information. Moreover, this loss is not only in items of communicated verbal information; it occurs also in the inability of even the most experienced interviewer to understand fully a culture other than his own—even when he can speak the language used in that culture.

[13] **The Extended Draw-a-Person Test**

I use the modification of this test published by Whitaker (1961).

[14] **Belief in Reincarnation Questionnaire (BRQ)**

L.-V. Thomas (1968) developed the prototype of this questionnaire and used it in Senegal. Following some revisions and a trial use of the questionnaire in Turkey (by Reşat Bayer and myself), Dr. Satwant Pasricha improved the questionnaire further and used it in India. It has also been used in Thailand.

CHAPTER 7: THE ANALYSIS AND INTERPRETATION
OF THE CASES

[1] **Accuracy of Written Sources**

In chapter 6 I gave some examples of the kind of written sources that I like to locate and use. These documents tend to be more accurate than oral testimony, because most written records are made and fixed (to the extent that paper and ink endure) soon after the occurrence of the event they record. However, a written record depends on the accuracy of the person furnishing the information and that of the person making the record. One should not be awestruck by written records, and they should be checked, at least sometimes, against other evidence. I once found that a gravestone had cut into it an incorrect year for the death of a previous personality.

[2] **Direct Observations by Investigators**

The child sometimes speaks directly to us about his memories. Occasionally also we can observe in the child some of the unusual behavior his parents report. And, very rarely, we have witnessed adequately controlled recognitions by the child. (I described in chapter 5 my own witnessing of recognitions that Gnanatilleka Baddewithana and Ma Choe Hnin Htet made; I also observed Imad Elawar make several recognitions, although the conditions for these were less than perfect.)

[3] **Eyewitness Testimony**

The early psychical researchers of the late nineteenth century became aware of the limitations of eyewitness testimony and began to consider its weaknesses some years before psychologists and lawyers did.

I have reviewed most of the experiments on eyewitness testimony up to 1968 (Stevenson, 1971). Marshall, a lawyer, conducted careful experiments on eyewitness testimony and published a balanced appraisal of the results (Marshall, 1969). Loftus (1979) has also conducted pertinent experiments. Rollo (1967) has analyzed the relevance of witnesses' mistakes about details to judgments concerning their reliability in general.

The subjects of typical experiments in eyewitness testimony are students, and in many of the experiments, such as those in which they see the event to be remembered on projected slides or moving pictures, they surely have little incentive to remember *anything,* let alone details. A report by Yuille and Cutshall (1986) of eyewitness testimony by bystanders who observed a real event—a shoot-out between a thief and his victim on a street—showed that memories for such events can be highly accurate, even over several months.

⁴ Unsolved Cases

My associates and I have published summary reports of seven unsolved cases, including accounts of our futile efforts in these cases to find a deceased person corresponding to the subject's statements (Cook et al., 1983a, 1983b). The cases of Ranjith Makalanda (Sri Lanka), Wijanama Kithsiri (Sri Lanka), Ornuma Sua Ying Yong (Thailand), and Ma Tin Aung Myo (Burma) are also unsolved; I have published detailed reports of these cases.

In a particularly baffling subgroup of unsolved cases the subject gives names enough—often confidently—but still we can find no one corresponding to his statements. Husam Halibi and Maung Soe Ya were such subjects.

⁵ Paranormal Information in Unsolved Cases

Sometimes subjects of an unsolved case make statements about events or other details of a place (where they say they lived) that we do not think they could have learned normally. An example occurred in the case of Thusari Wijayasinghe (of Sri Lanka) who said that "a god was burned" in Panadura, where she claimed to have lived. This statement apparently referred to the burning of a Hindu temple and its idol during a communal riot in 1958. Thusari was not born until 1969, and she lived in Colombo, 25 kilometers north of Panadura. It is most unlikely that she would have learned normally about the burning down of the Hindu temple in Panadura.

⁶ Fraudulent Cases

Two of my associates and I have investigated three cases that seem definitely fraudulent, and we will publish reports of these along with reports of other cases for which self-deception (not deception of other persons) seems the correct interpretation.

Norbu and Turnbull (1969, pp. 235–36) described a fraudulent case in Tibet.

⁷ Cryptomnesia

Critics of these cases and of other cases showing paranormal processes often claim dismissively that they *must* be instances of cryptomnesia. Such critics, working from a base of incredulity and having heard a little about cryptomnesia, apply it abstractly without demonstrating its occurrence in specific cases. Few well-investigated instances of cryptomnesia have been reported. My review of the subject refers to nearly all published instances (Stevenson, 1983b). Admittedly, more cases may occur than are reported, but those who like the explanation of cryptomnesia have some obligation to report more instances of it.

I am completely confident that we can exclude cryptomnesia in one case: that of Süleyman Zeytun. He was a congenital deaf-mute who, it was said, could not have heard a cannon fired next to him. Can anyone seriously suggest that he somehow learned normally about the man of whose life and death he showed knowledge as a young child?

[8] **Private Family Affairs Known to Subjects**

Other examples of private matters known only to family members of which subjects showed knowledge occurred in the cases of İsmail Altınkılıç, Maung Yin Maung, Imad Elawar, Rabih Elawar, and Ratana Wongsombat. (In citing these examples I have not restricted myself to long-distance cases; several of the subjects mentioned lived in the same communities as the previous personalities of their cases.)

[9] **Cases with Statements Recorded before the Two Families Had Met**

In 1975 I published a list of the few (twelve) cases of this type (Stevenson, 1975a). The list has grown slowly since then and there are now twenty cases on it.

[10] **Interval between Main Events of a Case and First Written Record of It**

The phrase *main events* here refers to the period when the two families first met. The first written record was usually made by my associates or myself, rarely by the subject's parent or another person. I published a tabulation of this interval for fourteen cases of India and Sri Lanka (Stevenson, 1975a, p. 27). The median interval in these cases was three and a half months. I believe that in later years we have shortened the average interval further, at least for cases in India and Sri Lanka; but this is only an impression, and I cannot support it with figures.

[11] **Negative Attitudes Shown by the Subject's Family toward the Case**

Examples occurred in the cases of Prakash Varshnay, Bajrang B. Saxena, Ravi Shankar Gupta, Puti Patra, and Jasbir Singh.

Members of a subject's family may adopt different attitudes toward his case; one member may want the case given publicity, while another wishes the child suppressed. For example, Gopal Gupta's father became (ultimately) enthusiastic about Gopal's case, but his wife disapproved of the disruption it caused in the family life.

[12] **Negative Attitudes Shown by the Family of the Previous Personality toward the Case**

Examples occurred in the cases of Sunil Dutt Saxena, Rabih Elawar, Dolon Champa Mitra, Puti Patra, Lalitha Abeyawardena, İsmail Altınkılıç, Cevriye Bayrı, Süleyman Zeytun (in the beginning only), and Erkan Kılıç.

[13] **Paramnesia**

Barker (Pasricha and Barker, 1981) interpreted the case of Rakesh Gaur as an instance of paramnesia, but Pasricha did not agree with him, and it is not a straightforward example of the process. For a discussion of the strengths and weaknesses of paramnesia as an explanation for this case, readers should examine the report by Pasricha and Barker and a further report about the case by Pasricha (1983).

[14] **Interval between Previous Personality's Death and Subject's Birth**

I have published elsewhere (Stevenson, 1983a) the median interval between the death of the concerned previous personality and the subject's birth for series of cases from seven different cultures. This interval ranged from six to forty-eight months.

[15] **Genetic Memory of Another Person's Death**

One of my associates has suggested that the children born before a parent's death would know the details of that death and could, from that knowledge, transmit information about it genetically to their descendants. Because, for the purposes of this discussion, we are allowing that *any* imaged memories might be transmitted genetically, we cannot exclude this possibility. The suggestion does not, however, take adequate account of the strong emotion that nearly always accompanies the subject's narrations of the previous personality's death. I doubt whether we can ever experience another person's death as we experience our own; and it is precisely the personal experience of dying oneself, not someone else's dying, that the subject seems to be communicating.

[16] **Extrasensory Perception on the Part of Subjects**

Subjects who did demonstrate a little evidence of extrasensory perception include Gnanatilleka Baddewithana, Shamlinie Prema, and Ratana Wongsombat.

[17] **The Syndrome of Behavioral Traits in a Subject**

I have here condensed arguments that I developed at greater length elsewhere (Stevenson, 1980). Hodgson (1897–98) used similar arguments in showing why he believed that the communicator G.P. through the medium Mrs. Leonore Piper could not have been built up by telepathy between Mrs. Piper and her sitters.

[18] **Possession as an Interpretation for Cases Suggestive of Reincarnation**

This interpretation for ostensible memories of a previous life dates at least from Swedenborg (1906/1758) and has had numerous advocates since.

[19] **The Flaw in Every Case**

Even a case that I considered one of the strongest ever recorded has been assailed by a not otherwise unsympathetic critic (Nicol, 1976). I refer to the case of Jagdish Chandra, whose father, K. K. N. Sahay (a lawyer), recorded the main statements Jagdish Chandra made about the previous life he remembered *before* he (K. K. N. Sahay) took steps to have these statements verified by other, independent persons. Jagdish Chandra's family lived in Bareilly, whereas the family of the previous personality lived in Benares (now Varanasi), almost at the other end of the same state. The distance between the two families concerned—about 500 kilometers—was far greater than that of most cases, and the families were additionally separated by differences of caste, still an extremely important feature of Indian life during the 1920s, when this case developed.

Jagdish Chandra's father stated in his report of the case that he had "no friends or relatives at Benares" (Sahay, 1927). Later in the same report, however, he mentioned that when he went to Benares to complete the verification of his son's statements, he stayed with a cousin. Nicol considered this discrepancy a lie, and he thought that K. K. N. Sahay might have obtained information about a family in Benares through the cousin and then coached Jagdish Chandra to make statements about a previous life based on this information. I believe this appraisal is unjust. The cousin in Benares had died by the time K. K. N. Sahay went there (with Jagdish Chandra) to verify his son's statements, and they stayed with the cousin's husband, who was still living. K. K. N. Sahay might not have considered his cousin's husband a "relative" or "friend." I regret that he did not furnish fuller information about his connection in Benares through his cousin's family, but I do not consider his failure to do this a fatal flaw in the case. Knowing members of this family as well as I have (although I never met K. K. N. Sahay, who had died before I first went to India), I think it highly unlikely that he would have staged a hoax and then included a report of it along with six other cases that he claimed to have investigated. I am aware that personal impressions about the honesty and reliability of informants count for little in the minds of some critics; but an informant's good reputation should have due weight in appraising a case.

[20] Steps toward the Detection of More Cases before the Two Families Meet

With a larger team of investigators we could deploy more persons in the field and would learn about more cases at early stages of their development and before the two families had met. I know of several long-distance cases in Sri Lanka and India in which journalists and local persons interested in the case arrived on the scene first and, without stopping to make a written record of what the subject had been saying, rushed him to the other family. They thus obtained a good newspaper story but lost a case of great potential value for this research.

We have made some effort in Sri Lanka to enlist the cooperation of journalists in educating parents (as well as other journalists) about the value of the careful recording of the details of a case. However, the parents of a subject have their own priorities. I have already mentioned that, if they do not wish to suppress the case outright, they usually yield to the demands of the child or to their own curiosity and try to find a family corresponding to the child's statements. Once when I was in a small town in India studying a case, I was just about to leave the town (and had to do so) when I learned of a case of this type (in which the two families had not yet met). I had time only to make a few notes and pledge the child's father not to take him to the other town, where the child said he had lived before, until I could return. The child's father agreed. Unfortunately, this family lived in a somewhat inaccessible part of India, and it was two years before I could get back to this town. When I finally did return, I learned that the child's father had thought I was not coming back, and he had taken the child to the other town, where they had met the previous family.

[21] Cases for Which Reincarnation Seems the Best Interpretation

I include in a list of such cases those of: Imad Elawar, Swarnlata Mishra, Jagdish Chandra, Bishen Chand Kapoor, Sukla Gupta, Prakash Varshnay, Dolon Champa Mitra, Shamlinie Prema, Gnanatilleka Baddewithana, Gamini Jayasena, Ruby Kusuma Silva, Kumkum Verma, Suleyman Andary, Rajul Shah, Parmod Sharma, Sunil Dutt Saxena, Bongkuch Promsin, and Ratana Wongsombat.

These cases are all long-distance cases. In all of them, someone made a written record of what the subject had said either before the subject's statements had been verified or within a few months thereafter. The testimony of the informants contained no major discrepancies or flaws. (See, however, note 19, above, on F. Nicol's criticism of the case of Jagdish Chandra.)

[22] "More Details"

The quotation is from Stendhal (1926, 4:169).

[23] Concurrent Testimony of Different Witnesses

The quotations from Whately (1858) are from pages 88 and 96–97.

[24] The Faggot Metaphor of the Strength of Numbers of Cases

I claim no originality for the application of Whately's principle to the study of large series of investigated cases in psychical research. Gurney, Myers, and Podmore (1886) applied it in the earliest period of scientific work in this field. Hart et al. (1956) made a particularly valuable contribution to the methodology of studying large numbers of cases—apparitions, in his work—for recurrent features.

[25] The Concept of a Type

Much progress in medicine has depended on the identification of types or syndromes. These are groupings of diverse symptoms and signs that occur together in a patient and have a common pathological cause (Hoehne, 1980).

[26] **Male/Female Ratio of Subjects and Previous Personalities**

The data for all the subjects are from an unpublished analysis, although I have published figures from smaller series, I published some data for the sex of previous personalities in Stevenson (1980).

The single exception mentioned occurred in the sexes of the subjects in Sri Lanka, where the numbers of males and females were almost equal.

[27] **Incidence of Violent Death in Cases**

These data have been published in Cook et al. (1983b) and also (for a slightly smaller series) in Stevenson (1980).

[28] **Violent Death: Artifact of Reporting or Natural Phenomenon?**

Data for the larger series of Indian cases have been published in Cook et al. (1983b); those from the smaller (survey) series have been published in Barker and Pasricha (1979).

Data for the incidence of violent death in the general population of India derive from only two states of India: Maharashtra and Rajasthan. It is unlikely, however, that accurate figures for the entire country would deviate markedly from the figure of approximately 7 percent derived from these two states.

The survey informants were asked to remember any case of which they had heard at any time. They may have tended to remember cases with violent deaths more than those with natural ones. This may have led to some bias in the reporting of these cases also. However, two factors would have reduced this bias. First, the informants were asked to search their memories for *any* case they could remember; such a "forced remembering" should have been more comprehensive in its coverage than the casual reporting of cases informants happened to remember that occurred in the larger series. Second, the survey area was restricted geographically, and the identified subject had to be living in one of the survey villages at the time his case was reported. This excluded cases of which the news had traveled from faraway places because of a sensational feature, such as a violent death.

My associates and I conducted an analysis of the reporting of apparitional cases included in *Phantasms of the Living* (Gurney, Myers, and Podmore, 1886) that bears on the point I am discussing here. We compared cases with and without violent death of the appearing person with regard to the interval of time between the occurrence of the apparition and its later reporting. We found that for cases older than five years before they were reported, those having violent death were reported more often than those with natural death; but for cases reported within five years of their occurrence, there was no difference between the groups. This result (not previously published) suggests that apparitional cases having sensational elements, such as a violent death, tend to be fixed in memory (and passed along perhaps from one informant to another) more than cases with natural death. However, investigators learning about cases within five years of their occurrence would not find this difference; nor does the difference found among cases reported more than five years after their occurrence account for all the high incidence of violent death among them.

I do not know to what extent we can extrapolate the just-mentioned analysis of apparitional cases to those of the reincarnation type. We must investigate further the reasons why violent death figures so prominently in both types of case. The evidence I have adduced in this note (and in the associated text) is indirect and inconclusive; it is, however, suggestive that violent death is a genuine feature of many cases, not a contamination from our present ways of learning about them. If so, this feature is important, and I feel justified in presenting the imperfect evidence we have instead of waiting until we have better evidence.

[29] **Data from Unsolved Cases**

The data of this section were published in Cook et al. (1983a, 1983b).

[30] **Lack of a Model to Guide Informants about Features of a Standard Case**

An exception to this occurs in the widespread belief that violent death figures prominently in the cases. Informants from many different countries hold this belief, but I do not understand how it became so widely adopted. Since, however, violent death does occur in almost two-thirds of all cases, a person given to making generalizations quickly might easily conclude, from hearing of only two or three cases, that violence played an important part in many or all of them.

CHAPTER 8: VARIATIONS IN THE CASES OF DIFFERENT CULTURES

[1] **Outcome in Schizophrenia Better in Underdeveloped Countries**

Waxler (1979) summarized pertinent data that support this statement.

[2] **Causes of Illness Other than Chance**

Although I. M. Lewis's (1971) book on ecstatic religion is not primarily about ideas concerning causes of illness, he discusses some of the personal causes I have mentioned.

[3] **Need for a Conceptual Frame to Explain Memories of a Previous Life**

In chapter 2 I suggested that the belief in reincarnation had probably arisen in different places at different times by someone's having imaged memories of another life, which he interpreted with the idea of reincarnation. Here I am suggesting that one may sometimes need the idea of reincarnation before one can make sense of any memories of a previous life that one happens to have. I do not think these suggestions are incompatible. I think a belief in reincarnation, carried over as an intuition from a previous life, would help to make more intelligible imaged memories that were also carried over. A person might, however, interpret the imaged memories as evidence of reincarnation without a prior belief in it. In a few (Western) cases the subject as a child had apparent imaged memories of a previous life that at first he could not understand. The beliefs of his family did not provide the frame of reincarnation to which the child might have attached his seeming memories. Nevertheless, and before having read anything about reincarnation, the child had concluded that he *must* have lived before. (The case of Alice Robertson, which I described in chapter 3, is an example of this development.) I am not saying that these subjects were necessarily right in the conclusion they reached, and I think some of them were almost certainly wrong; I am only trying to describe how apparent memories of previous lives may react with a person's concepts about the world and his own nature.

[4] **Relationship on the Mother's Side in Same Family Cases among the Tlingit**

I have given further information about this in my article on the Tlingit cases (Stevenson, 1966). However, the number of Tlingit cases investigated has increased considerably since the analysis included in that article.

[5] **Relationship on the Father's Side in Same-Family Cases among the Igbo**

Further information will be found in Stevenson (1985, 1986).

[6] **Forgetting of Announcing Dreams in Sri Lanka**

Failure of the dreamer to recognize the person appearing in the dream cannot be the complete explanation for the rareness of announcing dreams in Sri Lanka. The announcing dreams of all countries are usually described as vivid, and they seem to be strongly memorable even when the deceased person seeming to communicate is a stranger to the dreamer. I should expect, therefore, that we would have more reports of announcing dreams from Sri Lanka, if more occurred there than I believe do, even though the deceased persons figuring in them were usually strangers to the dreamer.

[7] **Announcing Dreams among the Druses**

I have described a few announcing dreams among the Druses (Stevenson, 1980). Two of these had a precognitive aspect. In them, a man *still living* (and considered in good health) was seen by the dreamer to be born as the son of a pregnant woman; the man then unexpectedly died, just at the time the woman gave birth to her baby. The dreams thus accorded with the Druse belief in instantaneous rebirth after death.

[8] **Interval between Previous Personality's Death and Subject's Birth**

See chapter 5, p. 117, and chapter 7, note 14.

[9] **Jain Expectation of Nine-Month Interval between Death and Birth**

A case that does fit the Jains' expectations is that of Rajul Shah. Moreover, the previous personality of this case was traced because Rajul's family confidently applied the Jain formula. Rajul stated the given name, Gita, of the previous life and the town, Junagadh, where she said she had lived. Members of her family sent a representative to Junagadh. He examined there the Municipal Registry of Deaths for the period nine months prior to Rajul's birth. For the month in question the registry listed a Gita, and from the other information available the family representative learned the name of this Gita's father and traced him. The family thus located then verified Rajul's other statements about the previous life.

In the case of Ram Prakash the previous personality was a Jain, although Ram Prakash was a Hindu of the Thakur caste. In this case also, the interval between death and presumed rebirth was said to be exactly nine months; but I am not so confident of the date of Ram Prakash's birth as I am of Rajul's.

[10] **Memories of the Previous Personality's Funeral or Burial**

Examples occurred in the cases of Disna Samarasinghe, Chaokhun Rajsuthajarn, and Erkan Kılıç.

[11] **Memories of Events Occurring Just before the Subject's Conception**

An example occurred in the case of Bongkuch Promsin.

[12] **Memories of a Discarnate Realm**

Examples occurred in the cases of Disna Samarasinghe, Sayadaw U Sobhana, Chaokhun Rajsuthajarn, and Nasır Toksöz. Disna Samarasinghe provided an exception to the usual absence of such experiences among the cases of Sri Lanka.

[13] **Rebirth of Humans as Nonhuman Animals**

The Tlingit (and some other peoples) believe that humans can sometimes be *transformed* into nonhuman animals, and perhaps back again, as in the Western legend of the prince who was turned into a frog; but this belief should not be confused with the belief in reincarnation as nonhuman animals.

The few cases known to me in which a subject has claimed to have had a previous life as a nonhuman animal have included (for obvious reasons) almost nothing that we can consider verifiable evidence of reincarnation. A girl of Burma (Ma Than Than Aye) recalled in considerable detail the life of a Buddhist nun who had died some years before the subject was born. Her memories of this life had verified details, and the subject, as a child, showed a remarkably precocious piety that accorded with the life she remembered. She also said that between the nun's death and her birth she had had an intermediate life as an ox, which had been killed by a bomb during the Japanese occupation of Burma in World War II. The life as an ox was completely unverifiable.

[14] **Sex-Change Cases among the Tlingit**

My comments about the injunction against sex change from one life to another and the absence of sex-change cases apply to the Tlingit of the southeastern (pan-handle) part of Alaska. The Tlingit farther north at Yakutat believe that sex change *is* possible, and De Laguna (1972) mentioned cases of the sex-change type among them. Other tribes still farther north (for example, the Athabaskan and the Eskimo) believe in the possibility of sex change, and they have cases of the sex-change type; but none of the coastal tribes farther south (in northwestern North America) believe in the possi-bility of sex change or have cases of the sex-change type. The line of demarcation runs at about 60 degrees north of the equator. So far as I can tell, the demarcation—with regard to the belief in the possibility of sex change—is as trenchantly separating as the line (Wallace's line) between Bali and Lombok, which divides the fauna of Aus-tralasia from that of the lands of Asia to the west of it.

De Laguna (1972) plausibly suggested that the Yakutat Tlingit, who are a coastal people, derived their belief in the possibility of sex change from the people of the interior, the Athabaskan. This would mean that the Athabaskan, who believe that one can change sex from one life to another, had infected the Yakutat Tlingit with this idea; then after a time claims of actual sex change would have appeared among the persuaded Tlingit.

[15] **Lopsided Ratio of Male-to-Female Compared with Female-to-Male Cases of the Sex-Change Type**

The exceptional culture is that of the Igbo of Nigeria.

At the present time we have in Burma, but not in any other country, a sufficient number of cases of the sex-change type to permit at least initial probing for an expla-nation of this lopsided ratio. I have published elsewhere figures and a discussion of the analysis of seventy-five cases of the sex-change type in Burma (Stevenson, 1983a).

Perhaps Burmese boys are more reluctant to tell about a previous life as a woman than girls are to describe a previous life as a man. This would make the uneven ratio of the two types of cases at least in part an artifact of our present methods of learning about cases. But other interpretations have merit also. In Burma, as in most cultures, it is thought better to be born a man than to be born a woman; and the Burmese regard rebirth as a woman (after one has been a man in a previous life) as a serious demotion. If reincarnation occurs, a man who had died and reincarnated in a girl's body might experience a shock on realizing that this had happened. The shock could stimulate additional memories of a previous life.

It is also possible that men's lives—through their greater variety and adven-turousness of experiences—may be more memorable than women's lives. I tested this conjecture on one of my female associates, and she rejected it summarily. She pointed out that women have just as many memorable experiences as men and some that men cannot have, such as giving birth to a child. It remains true, however, that there are nearly twice as many males as females among the previous personalities of the cases, of both the sex-change type and the same-sex type. I shall discuss this further in chapter 10.

¹⁶ Premortem Beliefs Become Postmortem Conditions
This is not an original idea with me. It is explicitly taught in the *Tibetan Book of the Dead* (Evans-Wentz, 1969).

CHAPTER 9: THE EXPLANATORY VALUE OF THE IDEA OF REINCARNATION

¹ Phobias of Infancy and Early Childhood
The following additional subjects had both verified memories and phobias in infancy and early childhood: Sleimann Bouhamzy, Imad Elawar, Sujith Lakmal Jayaratne (motor vehicles); Shamlinie Prema, Ruby Kusuma Silva (water); Som Pit (bladed weapons); Erkan Kılıç (airplanes); and Parmod Sharma (curd or yogurt). In all these cases except that of Imad Elawar, the phobic object figured prominently as the means in the death of the related previous personality.

² The Case of Little Hans
Wolpe and Rachman (1960) drew attention to Little Hans's traumatic experiences with horses, and they severely criticized Freud's (1950/1909) otiose symbolic interpretation of the child's phobia.

The case of Little Hans has a straightforward explanation and nothing to do with reincarnation. I mention it here, however, to illustrate how the search for symbolic meanings in phobias may distract attention from evidence of directly responsible traumas, including, perhaps, ones occurring in previous lives.

³ Other Explanations for Phobias of Infancy and Childhood
Searching inquiries should also probe for evidence that the child's mother, during her pregnancy, became frightened under circumstances that could account for her child's phobia. King James VI of Scotland (James I of England) had a phobia of swords and daggers (Calderwood, 1844; Roughead, 1926), which one might attribute to the murder of his mother's (Mary, Queen of Scots) secretary, Rizzio, who was stabbed to death in her presence while she was pregnant with James. I have not yet studied any case of the reincarnation type in which a frightening experience of a child's mother seems the best explanation for a phobia.

⁴ Expressions of Adult Vocation Shown in Childhood
Details of the examples I have cited can be found in the following sources.

George Frideric Handel	*Flower (1923)*
	Deutsch (1955)
Elizabeth Fry	*Lewis (1910)*
Florence Nightingale	*Woodham-Smith (1950)*
Heinrich Schliemann	*Schliemann (1881)*
Jean-François Champollion	*Hartleben (1906)*
Michael Ventris	*Chadwick (1967)*
St. Catherine of Siena	*Raymond of Capua (1980)*
	Gardner (1907)
	Drane (1880)

[5] **Unusual Interests Expressed in Early Childhood**

Other examples of subjects who showed during early childhood interests that were unusual in their families may be found in the cases of Gnanatilleka Baddewithana, Hair Kam Kanya (interest in religion); Daniel Jirdi, Ramesh Sukla (interest in motor vehicles); and Kumkum Verma (interest in snakes).

[6] **Expression of Previous Personality's Vocation through Play in Childhood**

Additional examples can be found in the cases of Ichtyake Alamuddin and Sukla Gupta, who played at looking after infant children; they both remembered the lives of women who had infant children they were caring for when they died. Erkan Kılıç, who remembered the life of a nightclub owner, played at running a nightclub when he was a young child; he served imaginary rakı (the Turkish distilled alcoholic beverage) and assigned a girl playmate the role of singer, giving her a stick to hold like a microphone. Ma Than Than Aye, a Burmese child who remembered the life of a Buddhist nun, played at collecting alms as a nun would do.

[7] **Names of Previous Personality's Children Used in Play**

The cases of Sukla Gupta and Sleimann Bouhamzy provide examples.

[8] **Unusual Aptitudes and Untaught Skills**

Other subjects who showed unusual aptitudes or untaught skills early in childhood are: Paulo Lorenz (ability to work a sewing machine); Bishen Chand Kapoor (ability to play tablas, a type of drum used in India); Disna Samarasinghe (ability to cook and to weave thatching for roofs); and Swarnlata Mishra (ability to perform Bengali songs and dances).

[9] **Addictions**

Subjects who showed in childhood appetites for addicting drugs and intoxicants included: Bishen Chand Kapoor, Maung Myint Tin, Ramesh Sukla, Ronald Mapatunage, Sujith Lakmal Jayaratne (alcohol); Sanjiv Sharma, Sunil Dutt Saxena (tobacco); Jagdish Chandra, Om Prakash Mathur (derivatives of cannabis).

[10] **Temperament**

Porter and Collins (1982) edited a review of research on this subject. See also Thomas and Chess (1977) and Thomas (1981).

[11] **Precocious Sexuality**

Other examples of precocious sexuality occurred in the cases of Imad Elawar and Necip Ünlütaşkıran. Another subject, Bishen Chand Kapoor, wished, in young adulthood, to resume the pleasure the previous personality of his case had had with his mistress, Padma.

The "latent period" of sexuality that Freud (1938) described coincides in the age of its beginning that he claimed for it with the usual age of the forgetting of previous lives by the children I have studied. Perhaps in the concept of the "latent period" Freud had a glimpse of some larger truth; a part is often seen before the whole.

[12] **Gender-Identity Confusion**

Examples of sex-change cases whose subjects showed some degree of gender identity confusion are those of Paulo Lorenz, Gnanatilleka Baddewithana, Ampan Petcherat, Dolon Champa Mitra, Ruby Kusuma Silva, Ma Tin Aung Myo, Erin Jackson, Rani Saxena, and Ma Khin Ma Gyi.

[13] **Biological Explanations of Gender-Identity Dysphoria**

Baker and Stoller (1968) showed that although a biological factor (such as Klinefelter's syndrome) may occur in some cases, it does not occur in others.

[14] **Lack of Evidence of Parental Influence as a Cause of Gender-Identity Dysphoria**

Zuger (1970) concluded that parental influence could not be adduced in all cases.

[15] **Exoneration of Parents by Children with Gender Dysphoria**

Examples may be found in the autobiographical accounts of transsexualism written by Martino (1977) and Morris (1974). The mother of such a child added her testimony in a magazine article (Anonymous, 1973).

[16] **Identical or One-Egg (Monozygotic) Twins**

In judging whether twins are of the one-egg (identical) or two-egg (fraternal) types, I have usually had to rely on their physical appearance, especially similarities of their facial features. Occasionally, informants have known whether there was one placenta or two at delivery; and sometimes they have reported what a doctor said about the type of twinship when the twins were born. For six pairs of twins I have arranged for determination of their status—as one-egg or two-egg twins—by examination of their blood groups.

The expression *identical twins*, which is sometimes criticized on other grounds, seems particularly inappropriate in the present context. It almost seems to imply that in one-egg twins we are concerned with only one person who happens to have two bodies instead of the usual one body per person. The term thus tends to encourage emphasis on the similarities between one-egg twins and neglect of their equally important differences.

[17] **One-Egg Twins Reared Apart**

A vast literature has developed about investigations of one-egg twins reared apart (compared with one-egg twins reared together). Farber (1981) published a review of such studies.

[18] **Criticisms of Studies of One-Egg Twins Reared Apart**

Rose, Kamin, and Lewontin (1984) and Cassou, Schiff, and Stewart (1980) have severely criticized these studies.

In the final section of this chapter I discuss this topic more fully.

[19] **Discordance for Cleft Lip between One-Egg and Two-Egg Twins**

Fraser (1970) published an extensive review of research on this subject.

[20] **Discordant Behavior in One-Egg Twins**

R. Green (1974) reported the case of (American) one-egg male twins who, at the age of eight, showed markedly different sexual orientations. The elder twin had developed normally as a boy, but the younger one showed obviously feminine behavior. This included a preference for the company of girls rather than boys, dressing like a girl, playing with dolls, and avoidance of boys' rough games. Because the twins were monozygotic, Green looked for influences in the twins' environment that could explain their different sexual behaviors, and he thought that he had found these. Green learned that the masculine twin had been named after their father; the twins' mother thought that perhaps both twins believed he had received his father's name because he was his father's favorite. On the other hand, the feminine twin developed at the age of three a serious illness (lasting two and a half years) that involved his being with his mother (on visits to the hospital) while his brother was correspondingly more with their father. Moreover, during her pregnancy with the twins, the mother had hoped to have a girl.

The different kinds of associations of the two twins with their parents and the accompanying attitudes of the parents may account for the twins' disparate sexual behavior. However, Green's report indicates important differences between the twins that were observed when they were still infants and before environmental influences could have had much effect. For example, during infancy the twin who later showed feminine behavior was easier to hold and cuddle than his brother, and he was often thought, from his physical appearance, to be a girl. I also think it doubtful that the close association of the feminine twin with his mother between the ages of three and five and a half would suffice by itself to account for such marked elements of feminine behavior as playing with dolls and cross-dressing. Many boys who are raised by single mothers do not show such feminine behavior. I regret that Green's case was not investigated with consideration of reincarnation as a contributing factor. When inquiries focus attention on two factors only—in this case genetics and postnatal environmental influences—evidence suggesting environmental factors may receive more weight than it should. In the current Western system of psychiatry, observers of troubled children and their families may exaggerate the importance of slight evidence for parental influences because they do not think of any other explanation. In countries such as India and Burma observers would appraise the case of the twins studied by Green differently, as the case of Ma Khin Ma Gyi and Ma Khin Ma Nge shows. (However, Ma Khin Ma Gyi and her twin sister were dizygotic, so their different sexual behaviors require consideration of the genetic factor as well as of postnatal environmental influences and possible previous lives).

[21] **Siamese (Conjoined) Twins**

Chang and Eng were not Siamese, although they were "discovered" when they were living in Siam (now Thailand), nor were they the first conjoined twins carefully examined. They are, however, still the most celebrated, and perhaps we know more about their personalities than about those of any other conjoined twins. Daniels (1962), Luckhardt (1941), and Newman (1940) described the differences in the personalities of Chang and Eng.

[22] **Child-Parent Relationships**

Other examples of subjects who rejected their parents and wished to find their "real parents" occurred in the cases of Prakash Varshnay, Ravi Shankar Gupta, Veer Singh, Gamini Jayasena, Warnasiri Adikari, Wijanama Kithsiri, and Rabih Elawar.

[23] **Claim by Subject to a Rank Equal or Superior to That of Parents**

The cases of Hair Kam Kanya, Chaokhun Rajsuthajarn, Thiang San Kla, and Maung Yin Maung exemplify this.

[24] **Subject Remembering Previous Life as First Spouse of a Parent**

The other two illustrative cases are those of Ma Tin Tin Myint and Asha Rani.

[25] **Animosities toward Parents Carried over from Previous Lives**

I have secondhand information about two cases in Lebanon in which a child was reported to have remembered the previous life of a man his father had murdered. In one instance, the child was said to have kept his father squirming with reproaches for his crime. The other child adopted a different strategy; he remained silent until he reached adulthood. Then he obtained a gun, a passport, and a visa. Thus equipped, he confronted his father with the father's earlier crime, shot him, and fled from Lebanon. Not surprisingly, both these cases were closed to my investigation.

[26] **Apparently Irrational Aggression**

Other subjects who showed vengefulness toward the murderer of the concerned previous personalities include Ravi Shankar Gupta and Semih Tutuşmuş.

Subjects who generalized animosities from the previous personality's killer to an entire group of persons resembling the killer in sect or occupation include Nirankar Bhatnagar (Moslems), Ravi Shankar Gupta (barbers), Salem Andary (Bedouins), and Cemil Fahrici (policemen).

[27] **"Japanese" Character Traits of Some Burmese Subjects**

I have described these traits elsewhere (Stevenson, 1983a). Ma Tin Aung Myo (chapter 4) showed some of them.

[28] **Abnormal Appetites during Pregnancy**

Other examples of this type of experience occurred in the cases of Gamini Jayasena, Sujith Lakmal Jayaratne, and Ornuma Sua Ying Yong.

[29] **Lord Nelson's Adjustment to the Loss of His Right Arm**

An edition of Southey's *Life of Nelson* that I remember from my childhood reading includes reproductions of specimens of Nelson's handwriting before and after he lost his right arm. The loss of his right arm occurred eight years before his death in 1805 (Southey, 1962/1813).

[30] **The Uniqueness of the Individual**

I have deliberately taken the title of this subsection from Medawar (1957) because I wish to challenge the idea that our uniqueness derives only from the genetic instructions for the development of our physical bodies.

[31] **Syndromes of Unusual Behavior Related to Previous Lives**

In chapter 5 I mentioned several other examples of syndromes or combinations of unusual behavior that had occurred in the cases of Ma Tin Aung Myo, Sujith Lakmal Jayaratne, Shamlinie Prema, and Erkan Kılıç.

[32] **Criticisms of Investigations of Genetic Factors in Schizophrenia**

Schulsinger (1985) provided a concise summary of results from adoption studies in a variety of disorders (including obesity and schizophrenia) and a bibliography of more detailed reports; he did not, however, address all criticisms of the method. Rose, Kamin, and Lewontin (1984) summarize these criticisms. Readers wishing to enter into more detail should consult Cassou, Schiff, and Stewart (1980), Lidz, Blatt, and Cook (1981), and Lidz and Blatt (1983). All these authors provide references to the investigations criticized.

[33] **The Myth of the Crucial Importance of Early Experiences in the Later Development of Personality**

Stone (1954) published one of the first criticisms of studies of infant isolation that were claimed to show the crucial importance of such experiences for later personality development. In the same year Clarke and Clarke (1954) published data that raised questions about the permanence of deficits in behavior observed in early childhood. In 1957 I published a paper expressing skepticism about the primacy of early (compared with later) experiences in the development of human personality (Stevenson, 1957). In that paper I did no more than show that the assumption of the special importance of the early years of life lacked support in credible observations. I did not pursue the subject further and soon afterward turned to the investigations from which this book derives.

Further reports and reviews have been published by Cass and Thomas (1979), Clarke (1968), Clarke and Clarke (1976) (an anthology of pertinent papers), and Thomas (1981).

I should emphasize that the harmful effects of severe social stress are not in question, only the idea that such social stress has a more damaging effect in the early years of life than later.

[34] Individual Differences in Newborn Infants

Korner (1969, 1971) published descriptions of some individual differences observed in neonates.

CHAPTER 10: SOME FURTHER QUESTIONS AND TOPICS RELATED TO CHILDREN WHO REMEMBER PREVIOUS LIVES

[1] The Idea of a Splitting of the Soul in Reincarnating

R. F. Spencer (1959, pp. 287–88) described this concept among the Eskimos, Norbu and Turnbull (1969) described it among the Tibetans, and De Laguna (1972) described it among the Tlingit of Yakutat. I have given an account of it among the Haida (Stevenson, 1975b).

Information about duplication or multiple reincarnations among the Igbo can be found in my paper on the belief in reincarnation among them (Stevenson, 1985).

Sometimes informants for cases, especially among the Igbo, cite particular cases in support of the idea of a splitting of a soul. They have, for example, sometimes shown me several children, all of whom are said to be the reincarnation of the same deceased person. Among the Igbo, a deceased person figuring in such a multiple case seems usually to have been someone of high status, so that descendants and collateral members of his family would wish him to reincarnate among them. This aspiration may contribute to the idea that the deceased man has reincarnated in several children. My own examination of a few such cases suggests that one child may give stronger evidence of remembering the previous life of the deceased person than the other candidates do. The Igbo seem to accept a child as being a particular person reincarnated on the basis of much slighter evidence than informants in most other cultures require before they make such a judgment. Some Igbo cases may develop from self-deception, like the alleged reincarnations of President John F. Kennedy in Turkey to which I referred in chapter 7.

The occurrence of multiple candidates to be the reincarnation of a particular deceased person leaves unanswered the question of whether souls or minds may, in fact, duplicate or split. (These are not the same concepts.)

[2] How Many People Have Lived on the Earth?

I have elsewhere (Stevenson, 1974a) given several different estimates of the number of people who have lived on earth and references to original publications of these estimates. However, in that paper I used estimates—600,000 to 1,600,000— for the number of years that have elapsed since the first hominids developed that are lower than those now accepted. More recent estimates place that origin back to between 4,000,000 and 5,000,000 years ago, or even earlier.

[3] Previous Lives as Nonhuman Animals.

The following additional subjects are among those claiming to have had intermediate lives as nonhuman animals: Warnasiri Adikari (life as a hare) and Pratomwan Inthanu (vague impression of a life as a monkey).

⁴ **Violent Death as a Fixative of Memories**

Numerous experiments by psychologists have shown a relationship between the strength of a stimulus and the size of the response it evokes. Kupalov and Gantt (1927) reviewed the abundant evidence for this statement from experiments with conditioned reflexes. Experiments with aversive stimuli have confirmed the adage that a burnt child dreads fire.

E. L. Thorndike gave a particularly clear statement of the connection: "The likelihood that any mental state or act will occur in response to any situation is in proportion to the frequency, recency, intensity and resulting satisfaction of its connection with that situation or some part of it and with the total frame of mind in which the situation is felt" (1905, p. 207).

What Thorndike wrote about "intensity and resulting satisfaction" would apply equally well if the situation evoked "intensity and *dis*satisfaction," including physical discomfort and pain.

Psychologists have also noted that an intense experience, such as being involved in a serious accident or surviving an earthquake, may lead to unusually detailed memories (hypermnesia) not only of the event itself but of events in the hours *preceding* the event, even though these, by themselves, would not have been considered unusual or particularly memorable (Colegrove, 1899; Stratton, 1919; Brown and Kulik, 1977). It is possible that the fixation of detail in memories of events that arouse strong emotion occurs, not at the time of the event, but later, and derives from reviewing the event and attributing to it a significance that it may not have been given when it occurred. One's own death might be such an event, the significance of which might seem greater later than at the moment it happened. This could be equally true of the detailed circumstances attending the death.

An ample tradition from accounts of this life suggests that a violent death may make a greater impression on the memory than a natural one. Here I am thinking of Dr. Johnson's remark about the execution of Dr. Dodd: "when a man knows he is to be hanged in a fortnight, it concentrates his mind wonderfully" (Boswell, 1931/1791, p. 725). Further testimony on this point came from a condemned criminal, who, as he was being led to execution, said: "This is going to be a great lesson to me." Dostoevsky wrote a moving account of how it felt to be about to be shot to death (Mochulsky, 1967). His own experience of expecting to be shot surely influenced the vivid description of a condemned criminal's last thoughts that he included in *The Idiot* (Dostoevsky, 1914, p. 61). In this he dwelt particularly on the heightened mental activity of the man about to die:

> How strange that criminals seldom swoon at such a moment! On the contrary, the brain is especially active, and works incessantly—probably hard, hard, hard—like an engine at full pressure. I imagine that various thoughts must beat loud and fast through his head—all unfinished ones, and strange, funny thoughts, very likely!—like this, for instance: "That man is looking at me, and he has a wart on his forehead! and the executioner has burst one of his buttons, and the lowest one is all rusty!" And meanwhile he notices and remembers everything.

The children who remember previous lives have provided apparent confirmation of Dostoevsky's insight into the intensity of perceptions during the last moments before death, especially one that is sudden or violent. Events occurring within a few hours or even minutes of death figure frequently in the children's memories.

One subject, Udho Ram (of India), recalled that just before a wall collapsed and killed the person whose life he remembered, a snake had crawled out from the building of which the wall formed part.

Ma Myint Thein, a girl of Burma, recalled a ring, a gold bracelet, and a wristwatch that the man whose life she remembered had worn when he had been killed; these articles would have come within the man's visual field as he held up his hands to ward off the sword blow that struck off his fingers. The fatal sword cut followed immediately.

Zouheir Chaar (of Lebanon) recalled a handkerchief held to her face by an aunt of the previous personality who had been in his bedroom and weeping just before he died.
⁵Suddenness of Violent Death

Improvements in medical care in the West and their widespread deployment have changed the treatment and prolonged the lives of many persons who would formerly have died suddenly from serious injuries. In the West today, therefore, a person may die from a violent cause without dying suddenly. However, in the countries of Asia where most of the cases here considered were found, modern facilities and techniques of medical care are still not available in the villages and also not in many of the towns; in these places a violent death is usually also a sudden one.
⁶Sudden Death in Other Types of Cases Having Paranormal Processes

A high incidence of death that is sudden, even though natural, has been observed in other types of cases. In an analysis of a series of apparitional cases that were first studied in the nineteenth century, my associates and I found that in 50 percent of the cases in which the death of the person seen in the apparition had been natural, it had been sudden, by the definition I have mentioned (Stevenson, 1982).

Men everywhere seem to dread a *sudden* death more than a gradual one. The Turks have a phrase: "May God take me in three days." This expresses the hope of avoiding both instantaneous death ("dropping dead") and prolonged suffering before dying. Christians have often feared a sudden death because it gives no time to prepare oneself spiritually for dying. The tombstone of a New England man (of the mid-nineteenth century) who became entangled in machinery warned passersby that "his death was sudden and awful." Indeed, an anthology of similarly monitory graveyard inscriptions has the title *Sudden and Awful* (Mann and Green, 1968). Sudden death also deprives the dying person of the opportunity of taking leave of those he loves and leaves behind. (Aldrich [1963] has described the dying patient's grief.) I think the intense wish to communicate with loved ones may account for the high incidence of sudden death among natural-death cases figuring in apparitions.
⁷Previous Personalities Dying Natural Deaths When Young

Examples occurred in the cases of Gnanatilleka Baddewithana, Jagdish Chandra, Rajul Shah, Gamini Jayasena, Veer Singh, Prakash Varshnay, and Pratomwan Inthanu.
⁸Previous Personalities Dying Natural Deaths with "Unfinished Business"

We could subsume cases with "unfinished business" under the Zeigarnik (1927) effect, named after the psychologist who first studied the tendency we have to remember the details of an uncompleted task better than we remember those of a completed one. A waiter in a German restaurant was the subject of the first informal observations of this effect. He could remember precisely what all the persons he served had eaten until they paid him, at which point he promptly forgot what they had ordered and eaten.

⁹ **Previous Personalities Dying Natural Deaths Who Left Young Children**

Examples occurred in the cases of Sukla Gupta, Lalitha Abeyawardena, Shanti Devi, and Swarnlata Mishra. The children of Biya (previous personality in the case of Swarnlata Mishra) were somewhat older than those left behind at the deaths of the previous personalities in the other cases.

¹⁰ **Previous Personalities Dying Natural Deaths with "Continuing Business"**

Examples occurred in the cases of Parmod Sharma, Suleyman Andary, Sunil Dutt Saxena, Erkan Kılıç, and Indika Guneratne. The previous personalities of all these subjects except Suleyman Andary were prosperous or even wealthy and had more than enough money for ordinary needs. For them the "continuing business" expressed a need to accumulate still more money and to keep what they had.

¹¹ **Desire to Be Reborn Quickly**

The Buddha taught that the cause of rebirth is a craving for the pleasures of a terrestrial incarnation. I am not aware of any statement in the Buddhist canon or oral traditions of Buddhism that predicts a quicker reincarnation when the craving for rebirth is strong than when it is weak; but such a belief could be a corollary of the basic belief that rebirth itself occurs because of the desire for it.

¹² **Previous Personalities Belonging to Two or More Subgroups**

Examples occurred in the cases of Puti Patra, Cevriye Bayrı (violent death with small children left behind); Gopal Gupta, Erkan Kılıç (violent death during an active business career); Ampan Petcherat, Shamlinie Prema, Susan Eastland, Gillian and Jennifer Pollock, Ruby Kusuma Silva (violent death when a child); Faruq Faris Andary, Rabih Elawar, Michael Wright, and Salem Andary (violent death when under twenty).

¹³ **Mnemonists Not Having Previous Life Memories**

Reports of mnemonists can be found in Luria (1969), Neisser (1982), and Susukita (1933–34).

¹⁴ **Previous Personalities Dying Natural Deaths Who Were Unusually Pious and Philanthropic**

Other examples occurred in the cases of Ma Than Than Aye, Kumkum Verma, Shanti Devi, Hair Kam Kanya, Chaokhun Rajsuthajarn, and the Venerable Sayadaw U Sobhana.

¹⁵ **Lopsided Ratio of "Demotion" and "Promotion" Cases in India**

The cases of Gopal Gupta, Bishen Chand Kapoor, and Sunil Dutt Saxena illustrate socioeconomic demotion; those of Swaran Lata, Kumkum Verma, Judith Krishna, and Rajul Shah, socioeconomic promotion. These are all subjects of Indian cases.

We have studied the promotion and demotion cases mainly in India. This is partly because socioeconomic differences are greater in India, where the lingering caste system accentuates them, than they are in other cultures where the cases occur frequently; and it is partly because we have a large sample of Indian cases.

Cases illustrating demotion and promotion do, however, occur in other cultures. In Sri Lanka, for example, Disna Samarasinghe and Anusha Senewardena are subjects of promotion cases; and Indika Guneratne, Wijanama Kithsiri, and Warnasiri Adikari are subjects of demotion cases.

[16] Learning from Memories of a Previous Life

Bishen Chand Kapoor said that reflecting on the life of his previous personality, a wealthy debauch who had murdered a man, had helped him to become a better person. Parmod Sharma thought the enlarged perspective provided by remembering a previous life gave him an advantage in dealing with current troubles that arose; it made him aware of the transience of fortune and misfortune.

[17] Subjects Who Have Recalled "Intermediate Lives"

Examples occurred in the cases of Pushpa, Swarnlata Mishra, Warnasiri Adikari, Gopal Gupta, Manju Tripatti, and Imad Elawar.

[18] Fading of Memories in Discarnate State

"G.P.," a mediumistic communicator with as good credentials for being a real discarnate mind as any communicator, complained of the fading of his memories with time (Hodgson, 1897–98, p. 324).

The exceptional case of Pratomwan Inthanu may not disprove the importance of the passage of time in the forgetting of memories. The two lives that she remembered were both of infants and both had occurred within a few years of Pratomwan's birth.

[19] Previous Personalities Who Remembered Previous Lives

Illustrative cases are those of Bishen Chand Kapoor, Ma Win Shwe, Maung Aung Myint, and Mounzer Haïdar.

[20] Children Who Remember Lives That Ended in Suicide

Examples occurred in the cases of Marta Lorenz, Ramez Shams, Maung Win Aung, Paulo Lorenz, and Faruq Faris Andary.

[21] The Pain of a New Idea

The quotation is from Bagehot (1873, p. 163).

[22] Familiarity a Requirement for Belief

"Pour croire complètement à un phénomène il faut y être habitué" (Richet, 1926, p. 441). My translation in the text.

[23] The Difficulty of Imaging That One Will Some Day Be Old

After King Charles II dismissed Lord Clarendon as lord chancellor in 1667, some of Clarendon's enemies (among them the king's still-young mistress, Lady Castlemaine) exulted gleefully over his fall. As he was leaving the king's palace he heard their voices through an open window, turned and said: "O Madam, is it you? Pray remember that if you live, you will grow old" (Crewe, 1893). He was right; she died in 1709 at the age of sixty-eight.

Of all the great writers of fiction who have given me pleasure, only two have attempted to portray a person throughout an entire life, from childhood into old age and death. I am thinking of Bennett's *The Old Wives' Tale* and Maupassant's *Une vie*.

Biographers have often tried to portray an entire life from birth to death, but psychologists have shown even less interest than novelists in studying a person's entire life. The longest follow-up studies of psychologists and psychiatrists rarely extend beyond a decade or two, although exceptions occur.

[24] Imaging the Process of "Younging"

The Trobrianders believe that a discarnate soul (*baloma*) undergoes a process of becoming younger before it reincarnates (Malinowski, 1916). Malinowski described the process as resembling that of a snake shedding its skin, but I am uncertain whether this somewhat inappropriate analogy is Malinowski's or was used by the Trobrianders themselves.

[25] **Children Commenting on a Change in Bodily Size**

In note 11 of chapter 5 I named twelve subjects who had commented—directly or indirectly—on their awareness of a change in body size. All these subjects, when they were small, had memories of what it was like to be fully grown. Pratomwan Inthanu had a different type of experience: as a young adult remembering the previous life of an infant, she actually felt herself being small like the infant.

[26] **Opinions about Reincarnation Type Cases among Educated Persons in Asia and Africa**

I have described stances commonly taken, but educated persons both in the West and in Asia and Africa often differ in their attitudes toward the cases and knowledge of them. The following examples may help readers to appreciate this. In Thailand, a government official (with some education in the West) worked tirelessly during many years to assist me in the study of cases; but another (former) official (also with some training in the West), although he believed that Buddhism was true beyond doubt (and he sometimes gave lectures about it that approached propaganda), considered the actual cases ridiculous and never took the trouble to study one at first hand. In Burma, one retired government official (he, too, had had considerable training in the West) assisted me for many years in the study of cases; but it was in Burma also that I met a professor of psychology with a higher degree from a Western university who, when he learned about my research, could barely remain polite to me, although the area where he lived happened to be rich in cases within a few miles of his office; he had had no idea that they were there, and he showed no interest in leaving his desk to study one.

[27] **The Brain Is the Messenger to Consciousness**

The cited sentence occurs in Hippocrates's essay "The Sacred Disease" (Hippocrates, 1952, p. 179). Later, on the same page, Hippocrates says: "the brain is the interpreter of consciousness."

[28] **Bergson on Brain and Memory**

Bergson (1913) suggested many years ago that impairments of memory related to brain disease may only indicate that we need a healthy brain in order to locate and communicate memories; they are not evidence that memories exist only in the brain.

[29] **Neuroscientists Doubtful of the Identity of Brain and Mind**

Two neuroscientists who have expressed misgivings about attempts to reduce the mind to a function of the brain are Penfield (1975) and Eccles (Popper and Eccles, 1977). A third, toward the end of his life, wrote: "That our being should consist of *two* fundamental elements offers I suppose no greater inherent improbability than that it should rest on one only." (Sherrington, 1947/1906, p. xxiv).

[30] **Brain the Instrument of Mind**

In one of the most important theoretical papers concerned with paranormal phenomena, Thouless and Wiesner (1946–49) suggested that the normal action of a person's mind on his brain and its occasional paranormal action on another person's mind, as in telepathy, might both be subsumed under the same principle.

[31] Mind the Most Direct Thing in Our Experience

The quotation is from Eddington (1930, p. 37), who is here surely referring to consciousness.

[32] The Irreducibility of Consciousness

Here I may seem to pass too quickly over the question of what we mean by consciousness, a question that has exercised philosophers for centuries. William James (1904) doubted the value of the term *consciousness*. However, he stated that he meant "only to deny that the word stands for an entity, but to insist most emphatically that it does stand for a function. . . . there is a function in experience which thoughts perform, and for the performance of which this quality of being [consciousness] is invoked. That function is *knowing*" (p. 478).

For a reader who has time for only one article about the irreducibility of conscious experience, I recommend Nagel (1979). A single article advancing the monist position could be that of Place (1956), who argued that consciousness is a brain process. Josephson and Ramachandran (1980) edited a useful introduction to the study of consciousness.

It seems to me that consciousness may never change, only the presentations in it of images and feelings. An emphasis given in publications of recent years to "states of consciousness," especially "altered" ones, may have been misguided. It has tended to link unusual mental experiences with extraneous and sometimes exotic inducers, such as hallucinogenic drugs, hypnosis, and meditation. Even persons who take hallucinogenic drugs may not undergo a change of consciousness so much as presentations of different imagery and different feelings within the same consciousness. That is certainly how I now consider my own enriching experiences with mescaline and LSD-25: not that my consciousness changed at those times, but that I had in it images and feelings vastly different from those I ordinarily have. The distinction I am trying to make may be thought a quibble, but I think it is not.

I would prefer to see wider awareness that most psychical experiences, including everyday manifestations of telepathy, apparitions, and children's memories of previous lives, occur to ordinary people in their ordinary state. At the times of their experiences, their consciousness has a new content, but their "state of consciousness" is not necessarily different from what it usually is. The people who have these experiences may differ from other persons who do not; but we have almost no knowledge about how they differ.

[33] Lack of Isomorphism between Sensory Experiences and Neuronal Patterns

Smythies (1956, 1960) and Malcolm (1977) have discussed this topic further.

[34] Inadequacy of Current Neurophysiological Explanations of Memory

Beloff (1980a, 1980b), Gauld (1982), and Malcolm (1970, 1977) have written on this subject. L. R. Baker (1981), Dreyfus (1979), and Heil (1980) have criticized the computer model of the brain and hence of the mind.

[35] Mental Space and Physical Space

In addition to Ducasse (1951) and Price (1953), Smythies (1951, 1960, 1974), Whiteman (1973), and Poynton (1983) have written about the concept of mental space. I have described my own ideas on the subject more fully elsewhere (Stevenson, 1981).

I believe Descartes (1912/1641, p. 139) made an important error in saying that minds, unlike bodies, do not have the property of extension. Despite Hume's

(1911/1739, 1:228) correction, and similar critiques by other philosophers, Descartes's mistake has continued to impede acceptance of the idea that minds as well as bodies have the property of extension.

[36] **Incompatibility of Telepathy and Materialism**

Nearly all scientists who have considered the matter hold this view. However, Godbey (1975) has argued that telepathy (and other paranormal phenomena) are *not* incompatible with materialism.

Some scientists, including a few physicists, believe that further developments in physics will provide explanations of paranormal phenomena. I am not a member of this group, and I think that the understanding of paranormal phenomena that we seek requires postulating an aspect of reality beyond that envisaged by the concepts of physics.

[37] **Telepathy a Guarantee of Survival**

I have taken this quotation from Carington (1945, p. 143).

[38] **Experiments in Paranormal Cognition**

I do not intend by this remark to devalue the contribution that many experiments have made to the evidence of telepathy and clairvoyance. That the experiments cannot be repeated *on demand* puts them on an equal footing with many of those conducted by psychologists, which are by no means free from capricious instability. And other scientists study without apology such phenomena as meteorites, volcanoes, and earthquakes, which also do not occur to order.

Persons studying paranormal phenomena make a serious mistake when they expect them to conform to the pattern of repeatability familiar in the experiments of physics and chemistry. Almost all paranormal phenomena occur under one or other of two circumstances. Some occur, as I have tried to show, during a life-threatening situation. Others derive from the special skill that only a few unusual persons can exhibit (Whiteman, 1972). Everyone does not have a little extrasensory perception any more than everyone has absolute pitch.

Experimenters fortunate enough to work with one of the rare gifted sensitives have published evidence of telepathy and clairvoyance far superior to anything that experiments with groups can generate. I am here thinking of such persons as Stefan Ossowiecki (Besterman, 1933; Borzymowski, 1965; Efrón, 1944; Geley, 1927), Olga Kahl (Osty, 1929, 1932; Toukholka, 1922), and Craig Sinclair (Sinclair, 1962/1930).

[39] **Mind-stuff a Canvas on Which Memories Are Collected**

The quotation is from Schrödinger (1955, pp. 91–92).

[40] **Conceptions of a Discarnate World**

Ducasse (1951) and Price (1953, 1972) have written on this subject. Carington (1945) also made suggestions about the nature of life after death.

The scriptural and exegetical literatures of Hinduism and Buddhism contain descriptions of a world (or rather worlds) of discarnate souls. Evans-Wentz (1969/1927) provides one of the most accessible of such accounts.

[41] **Memories of Existence as a Discarnate Person**

Examples will be found in the cases of Disna Samarasinghe, Pratima Saxena, Chaokhun Rajsuthajarn, the Venerable Sayadaw U Sobhana, and Som Pit. An example with fewer details is that of Nasır Toksöz.

[42] Lucid Dreams

Descriptions of them may be found in C. Green (1968a), van Eeden (1912–1913), and Whiteman (1961).

[43] Experiences of Persons Who Almost Die and Do Not

Examples and analyses of these experiences (now often called near-death experiences) can be found in Greyson and Stevenson (1980); Noyes and Kletti (1976, 1977); Ring (1980); Sabom (1982); and Stevenson and Greyson (1979).

[44] Information Warranting Conjectures about the Nature of Life after Death

I have not mentioned in the text the copious information furnished by many mediumistic communicators about life where they claim to be. Most of this is worthless, because it has been expressed through mediums who have not provided satisfactory evidence of having paranormal powers, for example, by furnishing detailed information about a deceased person that they could not have learned normally. In addition, much of what mediumistic communicators state about life in a discarnate realm shows obvious coloring from the medium's mind, although not necessarily her conscious mind. On the other hand, I do not discard statements about the nature of life after death made by communicators who merit our attention through their participation in a medium's demonstration of paranormal powers. Emmanuel Swedenborg, for example, provided evidence of paranormal powers sufficiently strong to satisfy Kant (1976/1766) and also described life after death (Swedenborg, 1906). Details about some other members of this small group may be found in the papers by Balfour (1935), Hodgson (1897–98), and C. D. Thomas (1945).

[45] Dominance of Images in the Discarnate World

Price (1953) suggested that the next world would be an "imagy" one.

In suggesting that the thinking of discarnate personalities would have more images than that of most living adults, I am not suggesting that it would be devoid of words. The subjects of reincarnation-type cases frequently remember proper names, and sometimes they remember words of a language used by the previous personality, but not by members of the subject's family. If these words derive from a previous life, they were presumably retained during the state between lives.

[46] Good Men Need Not Fear Death

The exposition of this belief attributed to Socrates by Plato is in the *Phaedo* (Plato, 1936).

[47] Life Review Mentioned by Children Who Claim to Remember Previous Lives

Nasır Toksöz was one of the few examples of such children.

[48] Panoramic Memory in Persons Having Near-Death Experiences

Details can be studied in Greyson and Stevenson (1980). Similar data were obtained in other series, such as those of Ring (1980) and Noyes and Kletti (1977).

[49] Telepathy the Normal Mode of Communication among Discarnate Persons

The quotation is from Driesch (1930, p. 26). (I have translated it.)

[50] Postmortem Apparitions

Examples can be found in Myers (1889, pp. 29–30); Perovsky-Petrovo-Solovovo (1930); and Gurney (1889, pp. 422–26).

[51] Death-Bed Visions

Examples can be found in Bozzano (1906); Barrett (1926); and Osis and Haraldsson (1977).

[52] **Now Equals Here**

Several persons have described having had—when near death or after death—the experience of thinking about a person or place and instantly being with the person or at the place. Chaokhun Rajsuthajarn remembered such an experience. Geddes (1937) and Radin (1926) have reported other examples.

[53] **Baudelaire and Individual Progress**

The passage I have cited occurs on page 1362 of Baudelaire (1967). (I have translated it.)

[54] **Gibbon and Chance in Birth**

The passage I have cited occurs in Gibbon (1907, p. 217).

[55] **Western Acceptance of the Idea of Chance**

Yet many Westerners, especially Americans, show ambivalence with regard to chance. The increasing profits of insurance companies and the blurring of the distinction between mistakes and malpractice when something goes wrong in medical care reveal a strong desire for a life free of risks, that is, of chance happenings. Lawsuits against obstetricians for not delivering a perfect baby are particularly germane to one topic of this book; who or what are the causes of birth defects? We tend to think that chance causes other persons' misfortunes, but should not cause any for us.

[56] **Fear of Postmortem Punishment as a Deterrent against Depravity**

A strong belief in life after death in which one would pay a penalty for one's sins did nothing to deter crime and wickedness during the Middle Ages in Europe, when such a belief certainly prevailed. However, the belief in life after death (and the possible postmortem consequences of one's actions) that was then held did influence the conduct of some persons, both blameless and peccant.

Since the Middle Ages the Christian religion has jerkily retreated doctrinally in the face of advances in science. Among educated persons in the West its representatives deserve credit for the loving lives some of them live and for the help they give to suffering others; but few people—again I speak of educated persons—believe anything these spokesmen say about life after death and what may happen therein. For most Westerners life after death has become unthinkable and—along with death itself—a tabooed subject. The idea of reincarnation—now coming forward with some supporting evidence—poses again a question most thinking Westerners would rather not think about: "What will happen to me after I die?"

CHAPTER 11: SPECULATIONS ABOUT PROCESSES POSSIBLY RELATED TO REINCARNATION

[1] **Psychophore**

I derived this word from the Greek meaning "soul bearing." (I wish to thank Professor David Kovacs of the Department of Classics, University of Virginia, for approving the word *psychophore* and for suggesting correct cognates.) The psychophore corresponds to Schrödinger's (1955, pp. 91–92) canvas on which experiences are collected.

I am familiar with a considerable literature in Hinduism and Buddhism about nonphysical bodies that are said to act as vehicles of minds between lives. However, these writings derive from religious traditions; moreover, if they have an observational basis, this must only be the subjective one of personal insights achieved by seers and transmitted to their followers. I do not devalue such evidence, but it differs from the publicly verifiable data that we find in the cases I have investigated. These cases also, I should acknowledge, provide no direct evidence for anything like a psychophore; but since they include some verifiable and apparently paranormally derived information stated by the subjects, I think we can base conjectures on them with more confidence than we can give to scriptural authority, however deserving of our respect the latter may otherwise be.

Some of the ideas of South Asian religions about such intermediate vehicles have passed—often through theosophy and its derivatives—into popular writings in the West about out-of-the-body experiences; but terms such as *astral bodies* have connotations that I think we should avoid. For these reasons, it seemed wise to devise a new word that would have no connections with religious or occultist teachings.

Since unembodied existence is difficult to conceive, philosophers and psychologists interested in the question of the survival of human personality after death have sometimes concerned themselves with the nature of an embodied postmortem existence, and this has brought them to consider the question of a postmortem vehicle or, if reincarnation occurs, an intermediate vehicle for use between incarnations (Broad, 1958; Wheatley, 1979).

[2] **Imaged Memories of Previous Lives during Infancy**

Chaokhun Rajsuthajarn claimed that during his infancy he could recall all the details of the previous life that he remembered.

Subjects of other cases have sometimes told me that they were fully aware of their surroundings in early infancy but lacked words with which to communicate their experiences to adults. Some remembered the fatuous remarks of adults who gazed down at them as they lay in their cribs and remembered also that they could only reply with helpless gurgles. None of these claims, including that of Chaokhun Rajsuthajarn, has been verified.

However, a few persons have claimed to remember some verified event that occurred during their infancy, or even before birth, when their bodies were fetal. The better examples of these cases include evidence that the persons concerned had not learned normally about the events they remembered. I have given a list of published examples elsewhere (Stevenson, 1983a, p. 140).

Physiological measurements show that newborn infants spend one-third of their day and one-half of their sleep in a state corresponding to what older children and adults report as dreaming (Roffwarg, Muzio, and Dement, 1966). The authors of the paper reporting this fact also observed that "in the REM [Rapid Eye Movement, indicating dreaming] state, newborns display facial mimicry which gives the appearance of sophisticated expressions of emotion or thought such as perplexity, disdain, skepticism, and mild amusement. We have not noted such nuances of expression, in the same newborns when awake" (p. 609). Later, in the same paper, the authors write: "There can be little question that the stage of sleep in newborns that manifests REMs . . . is related to adult REM sleep. Therefore the REM state must originate from inborn neurophysiological processes, as opposed to being engendered by experience" (p. 611). Why must it? Only on the supposition that the infant can have had no experiences before the conception of its body. However, if reincarnation occurs, then the infant, when he is in the state corresponding to adult dreaming, might have scenes of his previous life being run through his consciousness; if so, this would account for the varying expressions on the faces of the infants when they are in this state. These would reflect the different emotions that memories of past experiences were evoking.

³ **Personality and Individuality**

Ducasse (1951) used these terms in considering man's survival after death and possible reincarnation.

The question of whether what is reborn is the same or not the same as what died (or perhaps the same *and* not the same) has engaged Buddhist exegetists in discussions that the Buddha himself considered otiose. The evidence from the children who remember previous lives suggests a continuity between the two personalities concerned in a case. It also suggests similarities between them. This does not mean, however, that they are the same; everything—human minds most of all—is constantly changing.

⁴ **Learning a New Skill in Old Age**

Cato the Censor is said, on perhaps doubtful evidence, to have taken up the study of Greek in his old age (Cicero, 1923). The great mathematician Carl Friedrich Gauss began the study of Russian when he was an old man (Dunnington, 1955). If reincarnation occurs, these men did not waste their time in the efforts of their old age.

⁵ **Emotional Intensity of Shared Experiences and Psychic Links**

Any association will lead to the formation of some psychic link, and the longer the association, the stronger it will become. Intense shared experiences will also greatly strengthen such bonds. Persons sitting with each other at the same table of a cruise ship ordinarily become friendly and may continue the friendship for a time at the end of the cruise. However, the friendship lasts longer if the cruise ship sinks and the group spends a week in a lifeboat before being rescued. Similarly, the memories of sufferings that were endured and survived together sustain the societies of veterans of wars.

Intensity of experience also strengthens memory, as Thorndike (1905)—whom I quoted earlier—and, before him, Butler (1961/1877) pointed out. Butler gave another example from sea travel: "if an object . . . be very unfamiliar, as . . . an iceberg to one traveling to America for the first time, it will make a deep impression, though but little affecting our interests; but if we struck against the iceberg and were shipwrecked, or nearly so, it would produce a much deeper impression, we should think much more about icebergs, and remember much more about them, than if we had merely seen one."

⁶ **Communications in Apparitions and Telepathic Impressions between Persons Who Love Each Other**

These connections were shown for apparitions in Gurney, Myers, and Podmore (1886) and for telepathic impressions in Stevenson (1970b). The latter work provides references to similar data in other series of cases.

In addition to collective apparitions, "bystander cases" are another exception to the general rule of a close personal relationship between agent and percipient. In these rare cases a person who is with someone known to the agent sees the apparition, but the person to whom the appearing personality seems to be communicating does not. The percipient is thus a bystander, so to speak, but a person with greater sensitivity than the presumably intended percipient. I have published references to illustrative case reports (Stevenson, 1982).

[7] **Unusual Strength of Psychic Links between Family Members**

The strength of psychic links between family members may derive not only from shared emotional experiences in *one* life. In same-family cases the subject is saying, in effect, that in his previous life he shared experiences with members of his family during the life of the deceased member of it that he claims to have been. The subject of such a case would thus begin a new life already having strong ties to members of his family that would become stronger as the family unit persisted. I have suggested earlier that successive incarnations in the same group may explain not only strong family ties but also the larger circles of clan and national loyalties.

Launched on the waters of speculations like the foregoing, one might find oneself floating toward such concepts as that of a common soul or a "world soul" that unites all of us, as all continents and islands are joined beneath the oceans (Price, 1940, 1972). I do not find unattractive the idea that we are all bonded to each other, but with bonds stronger to some persons than to others. Further inquiries may one day provide an objective confirmation of what mystics have been saying for centuries. "All religions are forced to admit plurality inherent in the One" (Zaehner, 1957, p. 167).

[8] **Paucity of Telepathic and Apparitional Experiences between Strangers**

Because it is easier to verify apparently paranormal experiences with family members and close friends, the paucity of cases occurring between strangers might arise from deficiencies in investigating and reporting the latter type of case. However, Schouten (1979) in an analysis of the cases in *Phantasms of the Living* (Gurney, Myers, and Podmore, 1886) showed that the bias against "stranger cases" is almost certainly not an artifact of reporting and is therefore a feature of the process of paranormal communication.

[9] **Friendship Acting as a Psychic Link in Reincarnation Cases**

Examples occur in the cases of Maung Yin Maung, Marta Lorenz, Maung Aung Than, and Sivanthie and Sheromie Hettiaratchi.

In two of the cases of Burmese children who remembered lives as Japanese soldiers killed during World War II, the subjects' parents recalled having been friendly with a Japanese soldier (something not usual for Burmese during the Japanese occupation of Burma). Ma Tin Aung Myo is one of these subjects.

[10] **Animosity Acting as a Psychic Link in Reincarnation Cases**

Another (possible) example occurred in the case of Sampath Priyasantha.

[11] **Binding Effect of Guilt over Indebtedness**

Guilt over a debt or theft figures as an apparent motive in some apparitional cases (Myers, 1903, 2:348; Owen, 1874, pp. 226–29).

[12] **Subject's Claim to Have Known a Member of His Family in a Previous Life**

Other subjects who have made similar statements include Ratana Wongsombat and Bajrang B. Saxena.

I did not include Sukla Gupta's statement about having known members of her family in a previous life in my detailed report of her case.

In cases having twins as subjects, one or both of them has often remembered a previous life with a close association to the other twin. Examples occur in the cases of

Sivanthie and Sheromie Hettiaratchi, Ma Khin Ma Gyi and Ma Khin Ma Nge, Gillian and Jennifer Pollock, and Ramoo and Rajoo Sharma. In all of these cases both twins recalled previous lives.

[13] **Belief Concerning the Contribution of Particular Places to the Likelihood of Pregnancy**

Informants in other cases have described similar events; shortly before the subject's mother became pregnant with him, she (or sometimes her husband) had gone to see the dead body of the person whose life the subject later remembered. An example occurred in the case of Ma Hmwe Lone, another Burmese subject.

Rose (1956) described the belief among the Aranda of Australia that discarnate spirits gather around a particular stone. Women who wanted to become pregnant would go there with their husbands; those who did not, would try to pass by inconspicuously if they needed to go near the stone. Spencer and Gillen (1968/1899), also writing about the natives of central Australia, described similar places where spirits agglomerated and women were at special risk to become pregnant.

[14] **Future Parent of a Subject Visiting Area Where Previous Personality Died**

Another example occurred in the case of Puti Patra.

[15] **Analogy of Clothes and Physical Bodies for Reincarnation**

The quotation is from McTaggart (1906, p. 125). McTaggart was not the first person to think of this analogy, because the Arabic word for reincarnation—widely used by the Druses—is *taqamos*, which literally means "change one's shirt." *Qamos* is, rather obviously, cognate with such words as *camisole* and *chemise*.

[16] **Premortem Wishes to Change Sex in the Next Incarnation**

The cases of Gnanatilleka Baddewithana and Paulo Lorenz provide examples. Paulo Lorenz's case is one of the same-family type, but in Gnanatilleka's the families concerned were complete strangers before the development of the case. I should add, however, that Tillekeratne (the boy whose life Gnanatilleka remembered) expressed his desire to change sex only indirectly, yet as clearly as he could without putting the wish into explicit words.

[17] **Greater Likelihood of Male Conceptuses with Coitus Just before Ovulation**

Details will be found in Guerrero (1974) and Harlap (1979).

[18] **Date of Coitus and Sex Ratio in Natural and Artificial Insemination**

Details will be found in Guerrero (1974).

[19] **Greater Motility of Y Chromosome—Carrying Sperm**

Details will be found in Rohde, Porstmann, and Dörner (1973), Ericsson, Langevin, and Nishino (1973); and Roberts (1978).

[20] **Unsuspected Pregnancies in Healthy Women**

Whittaker, Taylor, and Lind (1983) estimated that about 8 percent of human pregnancies "are lost at such an early stage of development that the patients are unaware that conception has occurred" (p. 1126).

[21] **Marking of a Dead Body to Identify a Reincarnating Person**

Further information about the marking of bodies of children expected to reincarnate can be found in Fielding Hall (1898), Mi Mi Khaing (1962), Noon (1942), Parry (1932), Uchendu (1965), and Stevenson (1985). I have published one case of this type, that of Ampan Petcherat. Unfortunately, in her case the person who had applied the mark on the body of the boy whose life Ampan remembered forgot on which side of the body she had made the mark; however, the mark was on the upper chest, as was Ampan's birthmark.

I shall say more about this subject in my books on the cases with birthmarks and birth defects.

[22] **Manipulation of a Mother's Eggs by Two Discarnate Personalities**

When the twins' mother knew the concerned previous personalities, and especially when she had pertinent announcing dreams, she may have expected the birth of twins and induced in herself psychophysiological changes that affected her ova or a zygote; but this leaves hanging the question of why she—even unconsciously—decided to have twins in a particular pregnancy. In addition, there are cases in which the mother did not know anything about the concerned previous personalities—either when they were alive or in subsequent dreams.

In the case of Gillian and Jennifer Pollock, these twins remembered the previous lives of their own older sisters. However, their mother strongly disbelieved her husband's prediction, when she became pregnant again, that she would give birth to twins. If she brought about the twin birth, she did not do so consciously.

In considering the division of a zygote into two parts, it is unhelpful to imagine two discarnate personalities cleaving it in two as one might halve a round cheese with a kitchen knife. A better analogy would be that of two overlapping magnetic fields (in which iron filings have become aligned), which then separate and form two new magnetic fields, each taking with it a portion of the iron filings.

[23] **Sickle-Cell Anemia and Repeater Children**

Edelstein and I explored (in a preliminary way) the connections between sickle-cell disease and infant mortality in an Igbo community of Awgu, Nigeria. We found that sickle-cell anemia had contributed nothing to the high infantile mortality in the families of the children we examined (Stevenson and Edelstein, 1982). Despite this outcome, I find the possible relationship between reincarnation and sickle-cell anemia a useful one to consider, if only as a model from which we might explore the interplay between genetic and paranormal factors.

[24] **The Concept of the *Ogbanje* (Repeater Child) among the Igbo**

I have collated my account from several sources: published accounts of repeater children, informants in Nigeria whom I have interviewed on the subject, and my own investigations of cases. I have not yet investigated the case of a repeater child through a full cycle, so to speak, of birth, death, and rebirth. I have, however, seen different parts of the cycle, including children born with congenital deformities that were said to derive from mutilation of the body of a deceased repeater baby.

No studies of the efficacy of the Igbo rituals related to the *ogbanjes* have been made. A baby born with a birth defect or birthmark that is thought to derive from marking or mutilation of an *ogbanje* in a previous life is believed to have reformed and is therefore expected to live through infancy and childhood; but I learned of two such children who nevertheless had died in infancy.

Further details may be found in Edelstein (1986) and Stevenson (1985, 1986).

[25] **Demonstrations of Extraordinary Clairvoyance**

One of the best, and best-investigated, mediums of all times, Gladys Osborne Leonard, had the ability somehow to read passages in closed books, located in a house where she had never been, and to indicate the page of the passage (sometimes its position on the page) and the place of the book on its bookshelf. E. M. Sidgwick published a careful analysis of Mrs. Leonard's book tests (Sidgwick, 1921). Smith (1964) and Gauld (1982) have provided shorter summaries of the essentials of the book tests.

The clairvoyant, or possibly telepathic, feats of Olga Kahl (Osty, 1929, 1932; Toukholka, 1922) and Stefan Ossowiecki (Besterman, 1933; Borzymowski, 1965; Efrón, 1944; Geley, 1927) approach the same degree of exactitude.

Experimenting with bacteria, Nash (1984) showed a psychokinetic effect on the rate of mutation of a gene. This involves reaching and influencing a minute "target."

[26] **Voluntary Apparitions**

The records of psychical research include reports of a small number of cases in which a person has willed himself, so to speak, to appear to another distant person and has then been seen by that person as an apparition. Borzymowski (1965) and Gurney, Myers, and Podmore (1886, 1:103–10 and 2:675–76) published examples.

[27] **Biochemical Changes Accompanying Pseudocyesis**

Details will be found in the article by Schopbach, Fried, and Rakoff (1952).

[28] **Psychophysical Inhibition of Pregnancy among the Trobrianders**

I derived this information from Malinowski (1927). I have used the present tense to describe the Trobrianders' customs, but conditions among them have probably changed since Malinowski studied them.

[29] **Overripeness of the Ovum**

I based this statement on the work of Jongbloet and Zwets (1976).

[30] **Mediums Manifesting the Physical Symptoms Experienced by Dying Persons**

Examples will be found in Balfour (1935) and Osty (1923).

[31] **Doing to Ourselves What We Do to Others**

The quotation from Friar Giles occurs in Okey (1910, p. 160).

[32] **The Vale of Soul-Making**

Keats used this phrase in a letter to his brother and sister-in-law (Forman [1931], p. 362).

References

Aldrich, C. K. 1963. The dying patient's grief. *Journal of the American Medical Association* 184:329–31.

Altus, W. D. 1966. Birth order and its sequelae. *Science* 151:44–49.

Anonymous. 1973. My daughter changed sex. *Good Housekeeping,* May, p. 87.

Ayer, A. J. 1963. *The concept of a person and other essays.* London: Macmillan.

Bacon, F. 1639. *Sylva Sylvarum or, A naturall historie.* 5th ed. London: William Rawley.

———. 1915. *The advancement of learning.* London: J. M. Dent and Sons. (First published in 1605.)

Bagehot, W. 1873. *Physics and politics.* New York: D. Appleton.

Baker, H. J., and Stoller, R. J. 1968. Can a biological force contribute to gender identity? *American Journal of Psychiatry* 124:1653–58.

Baker, L. R. 1981. Why computers can't act. *American Philosophical Quarterly* 18:157–63.

Baker, R. A. 1982. The effect of suggestion on past-lives regression. *American Journal of Clinical Hypnosis* 25:71–76.

Balfour, G. W. 1935. A study of the psychological aspects of Mrs. Willett's mediumship. *Proceedings of the Society for Psychical Research* 43:43–318.

Barber, T. X. 1961. Experimental evidence for a theory of hypnotic behavior: II. Experimental controls in hypnotic age-regression. *International Journal of Clinical and Experimental Hypnosis* 9:181–93.

Barker, D. R., and Pasricha, S. 1979. Reincarnation cases in Fatehabad: A systematic survey in North India. *Journal of Asian and African Studies* 14:231–40.

Barrett, W. F. 1926. *Death-bed visions.* London: Methuen.

Baudelaire, C. 1967. *Oeuvres complètes.* Lausanne: La Guilde du Livre.

Bell, C. 1931. *The religion of Tibet.* London: Oxford University Press.

Beloff, J. 1980a. Could there be a physical explanation for psi? *Journal of the Society for Psychical Research* 50:263–72.

———. 1980b. Is normal memory a "paranormal" phenomenon? *Theoria to Theory* 14:145–62.

Berger, H. 1940. *Psyche.* Jena: Verlag von Gustav Fischer. (I have cited the translation of Berger's account of his experience from Gloor, P. 1969. Hans Berger on the electroencephalogram of man. *Electroencephalography and Clinical Neurophysiology,* supplement no. 28.)

Bergson, H. 1913. Presidential address. *Proceedings of the Society for Psychical Research* 26:462–79.

———. 1957. *L'évolution créatrice.* Paris: Presses Universitaires de France. (First published in 1907. American edition: *Creative Evolution*. Translated by Arthur Mitchel. New York: Random House, 1944.)

————. 1959. *Matière et mémoire: Essai sur la relation du corps à l'esprit*. Paris: Presses Universitaires de France. (First published in 1896.)

Bernheim, H. 1947. *Suggestive therapeutics: A treatise on the nature and uses of hypnotism*. Translated from 2d and revised French edition by Christian A. Herter. New York: London Book. (First published in 1889.)

Bernstein, M. 1965. *The search for Bridey Murphy*. New York: Lancer Books. (First published by Doubleday, 1956.)

Besterman, T. 1933. An experiment in "clairvoyance" with M. Stefan Ossowiecki. *Proceedings of the Society for Psychical Research* 41 : 345 – 51.

————. 1968. *Collected papers on the paranormal*. New York: Garrett Publications.

Birket-Smith, K. 1959. *The Eskimos*. Rev. ed. Translated by W. E. Calvert. London: Methuen. (First published in 1936.)

Björkhem, J. 1961. Hypnosis and personality change. In *Knut Lundmark and man's march into space: A memorial volume*, edited by M. Johnson. Gothenburg: Värld och Vetande.

Bloxham, A. D. 1958. *Who was Ann Ockenden?* London: Neville Spearman.

Boas, F. 1964. *The central Eskimo*. Lincoln: University of Nebraska Press. (First published by the Bureau of American Ethnology Annual Report 6, 1888.)

Borzymowski, A. 1965. Experiments with Ossowiecki. *International Journal of Parapsychology* 7 : 259 – 84.

Boswell, J. 1931. *The life of Samuel Johnson*. New York: Modern Library. (First published in 1791.)

————. 1970. An account of my last interview with David Hume, Esq. In *Boswell in extremes: 1776 – 1778*, edited by C. M. Weis and F. A. Pottle. New York: McGraw-Hill.

Bozzano, E. 1906. Des apparitions des défunts au lit de mort. *Annales des sciences psychiques* 16 : 144 – 82.

Broad, C. D. 1958. *Personal identity and survival*. London: Society for Psychical Research.

————. 1962. *Lectures on psychical research*. London: Routledge & Kegan Paul.

Brougham, H. 1871. *The life and times of Henry, Lord Brougham, written by himself*. New York: Harper and Bros.

Brown, R., and Kulik, J. 1977. Flashbulb memories. *Cognition* 5 : 73 – 99.

Brown, W. N. 1928. *The Indian and Christian miracles of walking on the water*. Chicago: Open Court Publishing.

Butler, S. 1961. *Life and habit*. London: A. C. Fifield. (First published in 1877.)

Caesar, Julius. 1917. *The Gallic war*. Translated by H. J. Edwards. London: William Heinemann.

Calderwood, D. 1844. *The history of the kirk of Scotland*. Edited by T. Thomson. Edinburgh: The Wodrow Society.

Carington, W. 1945. *Telepathy: An outline of its facts, theory, and implications*. London: Methuen.

Cass, L. K., and Thomas, C. B. 1979. *Childhood pathology and later adjustment: The question of prediction*. New York: John Wiley.

Cassou, B., Schiff, M., and Stewart, J. 1980. Génétique et schizophrénie: Réévaluation d'un consensus. *Psychiatrie de l'enfant* 23:87–201.

Chadwick, J. 1967. *The decipherment of linear B.* Cambridge: Cambridge University Press.

Cicero. 1923. *De senectute.* Translated by W. A. Falconer. London: William Heinemann.

Clarke, A. D. B. 1968. Learning and human development. *British Journal of Psychiatry* 114:1061–77.

Clarke, A. D. B., and Clarke, A. M. 1954. Cognitive changes in the feeble-minded. *British Journal of Psychology* 45:173–79.

Clarke, A. M., and Clarke, A. D. B. 1976. *Early experience: Myth and evidence.* Shepton Mallet: Open Books Publishing.

Colegrove, F. W. 1899. Individual memories. *American Journal of Psychology* 10:228–55.

Cook, E., Pasricha, S., Samararatne, G., Maung, W., and Stevenson, I. 1983a. A review and analysis of "unsolved" cases of the reincarnation type: Part I, Introduction and illustrative case reports. *Journal of the American Society for Psychical Research* 77:45–62.

———. 1983b. A review and analysis of "unsolved" cases of the reincarnation type: Part II, Comparison of features of solved and unsolved cases. *Journal of the American Society for Psychical Research* 77:115–35.

Crewe, N. 1893. *Memoirs of Nathaniel, Lord Crewe.* London: Camden Society.

Daniélou, J. 1955. *Origen.* Translated by W. Mitchell. New York: Sheed and Ward.

Daniels, W. B. 1962. The Siamese twins: Some observations on their life, last illness, and autopsy. *Transactions of the American Clinical and Climatological Association* 73:57–65.

Davidson, H. R. E. 1964. *Gods and myths of Northern Europe.* Harmondsworth, Middlesex: Penguin.

Davis, D. R. 1958. Clinical problems and experimental researches. *British Journal of Medical Psychology* 31:74–82.

De Laguna, F. 1972. *Under Mount St. Elias.* Smithsonian Contributions to Anthropology (monograph) 7:779.

Delanne, G. 1924. *Documents pour servir à l'étude de la réincarnation.* Paris: Editions de la B.P.S.

Descartes, R. 1912. *Meditations on the first philosophy.* Translated by J. Veitch. London: J. M. Dent and Sons. (First published in 1641.)

———. 1973. *Les principes de la philosophie.* In *Oeuvres philosophiques,* vol. 3. Paris: Editions Garnier Frères. (First published in 1644.)

Deschamps, H. 1970. *Les religions de l'Afrique noire.* Paris: Presses Universitaires de France.

Deutsch, O. E. 1955. *Handel: A documentary biography.* London: Adam and Charles Black.

Dickens, C. 1877. *Pictures from Italy.* New York: Harper and Bros.

Dickinson, G. L. 1911. A case of emergence of a latent memory under hypnosis. *Proceedings of the Society for Psychical Research* 25:455–67.

Dostoevsky, F. 1914. *The idiot.* Translated by E. M. Martin. London: J. M. Dent and Sons.

Drane, A. T. 1880. *The history of St. Catherine of Siena and her companions.* London: Burns and Oates.

Dreyfus, H. L. 1979. *What computers can't do.* Rev. ed. New York: Harper and Row.

Driesch, H. 1908. *The science and philosophy of the organism.* London: A. and C. Black.

————. 1914. *History and theory of vitalism.* London: Macmillan.

————. 1930. Personne et suprapersonne. In *Transactions of the Fourth International Congress for Psychical Research,* edited by T. Besterman. London: The Society for Psychical Research.

————. 1933. *Psychical research: The science of the super-normal.* Translated by T. Besterman. London: Bell and Sons. (First published in 1932 as *Parapsychologie: Die Wissenschaft von den "Okkulten" Erscheinungen.* Munich: F. Bruckmann.)

Ducasse, C. J. 1951. *Nature, mind, and death.* LaSalle, Ill.: Open Court Publishing.

————. 1960. How the case of *The search for Bridey Murphy* stands today. *Journal of the American Society for Psychical Research* 54: 3–22.

————. 1961. *A critical examination of the belief in a life after death.* Springfield, Ill.: Charles C Thomas.

Dunnington, G. W. 1955. *Carl Friedrich Gauss: Tital of science.* New York: Exposition Press.

Dywan, J., and Bowers, K. 1983. The use of hypnosis to enhance recall. *Science* 222: 184–85.

Eddington, A. S. 1930. *Science and the unseen world.* New York: Macmillan.

Edelstein, S. J. 1986. *The sickled cell.* Cambridge, Mass.: Harvard University Press.

Efrón, D. 1944. Telepathic skin-writing (the Kahl case). *Journal of Parapsychology* 8: 272–86.

Efron, R. 1963. Temporal perception, aphasia, and déjà vu. *Brain* 86: 403–24.

Ellis, H. R. 1943. *The Road to Hel.* Cambridge: Cambridge University Press.

Ericsson, R. J., Langevin, C. N., and Nishino, M. 1973. Isolation of fractions rich in human Y sperm. *Nature* 246: 421–24.

Evans-Wentz, W. Y. 1911. *The fairy-faith in Celtic countries.* New York: Oxford University Press.

————, ed. 1969. *The Tibetan book of the dead.* London: Oxford University Press. (First published in 1927.)

Farber, S. L. 1981. *Identical twins reared apart: A reanalysis.* New York: Basic Books.

Fielding Hall, H. 1898. *The soul of a people.* London: Macmillan.

Flower, N. 1923. *George Frideric Handel: His personality and his times.* London: Cassell.

Forman, M. B., ed. 1931. *The letters of John Keats.* Vol. 2. Oxford: Oxford University Press.

Fraser, F. C. 1970. The genetics of cleft lip and cleft palate. *American Journal of Human Genetics* 22: 336–52.

Freud, S. 1938. Three contributions to the theory of sex. In *The basic writings of Sigmund Freud,* edited and translated by A. A. Brill. New York: Random House.

————. 1950. Analysis of a phobia in a five-year-old boy. In *Collected papers,* vol. 3. London: Hogarth Press. (First published in 1909.)

Gallup Opinion Index. 1969. *Special report on religion.* Princeton, N.J.: American Institute of Public Opinion.

Gallup, G., Jr., with Proctor, W. 1982. *Adventures in immortality.* New York: McGraw-Hill.

Gardner, E. G. 1907. *Saint Catherine of Siena—a study in the religion, literature, and history of the fourteenth century in Italy.* London: J. M. Dent and Sons.

Gauld, A. 1982. *Mediumship and survival: A century of investigations.* London: William Heinemann.

Gauld, A., and Cornell, A. D. 1979. *Poltergeists.* London: Routledge and Kegan Paul.

Geddes, A. 1937. A voice from the grandstand. *Edinburgh Medical Journal* 44: 365–84.

Geley, G. 1927. *Clairvoyance and materialisation: A record of experiments.* Translated by S. de Brath. New York: George H. Doran. (First published in French as *L'ectoplasmie et la clairvoyance* [Paris: F. Alcan 1924].)

Gibbon, E. 1907. *Autobiography.* London: Oxford University Press.

Godbey, J. W., Jr. 1975. Central-state materialism and parapsychology. *Analysis* 36: 22–25. (Reprinted in *Philosophy and Parapsychology,* edited by J. Ludwig. Buffalo: Prometheus Books, 1978.)

Grant, J. 1937. *Winged pharaoh.* London: Arthur Barker.

Grattan-Guinness, I., ed. 1982. *Psychical research: A guide to its history, principles, and practices.* Wellingborough, England: Aquarian Press.

Graves, R. P. 1979. *A. E. Housman: The scholar-poet.* London: Routledge and Kegan Paul.

Green, C. 1960. Analysis of spontaneous cases. *Proceedings of the Society for Psychical Research* 53: 97–161.

———. 1968a. *Lucid dreams.* London: Hamish Hamilton.

———. 1968b. *Out-of-the-body experiences.* London: Hamish Hamilton.

Green, R. 1974. *Sexual identity conflict in children and adults.* New York: Basic Books.

———. 1979. Childhood cross-gender behavior and subsequent sexual preference. *American Journal of Psychiatry* 136: 106–8.

Greyson, B., and Stevenson, I. 1980. The phenomenology of near-death experiences. *American Journal of Psychiatry* 137: 1193–96.

Grof, S. 1976. *Realms of the human unconscious: Observations from LSD research.* New York: E. P. Dutton.

Gruber, E. R. 1978. Hans Driesch and the concept of spiritism. *Journal of the Society for Psychical Research* 49: 861–74.

Guerrero, R. 1974. Association of the type and time of insemination within the menstrual cycle with the human sex ratio at birth. *The New England Journal of Medicine* 291: 1056–59.

Gupta, L. D., Sharma, N. R., and Mathur, T. C. 1936. *An inquiry into the case of Shanti Devi.* Delhi: International Aryan League.

Gurney, E., (completed by Myers, F. W. H.) 1889. On apparitions occurring soon after death. *Proceedings of the Society for Psychical Research* 5: 403–85.

Gurney, E., Myers, F. W. H., and Podmore, F. 1886. *Phantasms of the living.* 2 vols. London: Trübner.

Hardy, A. 1965. *The living stream: A restatement of evolution theory and its relation to the spirit of man.* London: Collins.

————. 1966. *The divine flame: An essay towards a natural history of religion.* London: Collins.

Harlap, S. 1979. Gender of infants conceived on different days of the menstrual cycle. *The New England Journal of Medicine* 300: 1445–48.

Hart, H., and collaborators. 1956. Six theories about apparitions. *Proceedings of the Society for Psychical Research* 50: 153–239.

Hartleben, H. 1906. *Champollion, sein Leben und sein Werk.* 2 vols. Berlin: Weidmannsche Buchhandlung.

Hawkes, J. 1981. *A quest of love.* New York: George Braziller.

Hearn, L. 1897. *Gleanings in Buddha-fields.* Boston: Houghton Mifflin.

Heil, J. 1980. Cognition and representation. *Australasian Journal of Philosophy* 58: 158–68.

Heim, A. 1892. Notizen über den Tod durch Absturz ["Remarks on fatal falls."] *Jahrbuch des schweizer Alpenclub* 27: 327–37. (English translation by R. Noyes, Jr. and R. Kletti. *Omega* 3: 45–52, 1972.)

Heywood, R. 1971. *The sixth sense: An inquiry into extra-sensory perception.* London: Pan Books. (Also published as *Beyond the reach of sense.* New York: E. P. Dutton, 1974.)

Hippocrates. 1952. Vol. 2 of *Hippocrates.* Translated by W. H. S. Jones. The Loeb Classical Library. Cambridge, Mass.: Harvard University Press. (Also London: William Heinemann.)

Hodgson, R. 1897–98. A further record of observations of certain phenomena of trance. *Proceedings of the Society for Psychical Research* 13: 284–582.

Hoehne, K. A. 1980. Classification vs. typology: A difference of practical importance. *Journal of the American Medical Association* 244: 1099–1100.

Hughes, C. C., with Hughes, J. M. 1962. *An Eskimo village in the modern world.* Ithaca, N.Y.: Cornell University Press.

Hume, D. 1854. On the immortality of the soul. In *Philosophical works,* vol. 4. Boston: Little, Brown. (First published London, 1783.)

————. 1911. *A treatise of human nature.* 2 vols. London: J. M. Dent and Sons. (First published in 1739.)

Hume, R. E., trans. 1931. *The thirteen principal Upanishads.* 2d ed., rev. London: Oxford University Press.

Iamblichus. 1965. *Life of Pythagoras.* Translated by Thomas Taylor. London: John M. Watkins.

Jackson, D. D. 1966. More on Siamese twins. (Letter to the editor.) *American Journal of Psychiatry* 123: 495.

James, W. 1904. Does "consciousness" exist? *The Journal of Philosophy, Psychology, and Scientific Methods* 1: 477–91.

Jongbloet, P. H., and Zwets, J. H. J. 1976. Preovulatory overripeness of the egg in the human subject. *International Journal of Gynaecology and Obstetrics* 14: 111–16.

Josephson, B., and Ramachandran, V. S., eds. 1980. *Consciousness and the physical world.* New York: Pergamon Press.

Kampman, R. 1973. Hypnotically induced multiple personality: An experimental study. *Acta Universitatis Ouluensis*, series D, Medica no. 6. Psychiatrica no. 3, pp. 7–116.

———. 1975. The dynamic relation of the secondary personality induced by hypnosis to the present personality. *Psychiatria Fennica* (1975): 169–72.

Kampman, R., and Hirvenoja, R. 1978. Dynamic relation of the secondary personality induced by hypnosis to the present personality. In *Hypnosis at its bicentennial*, edited by F. H. Frankel and H. S. Zamansky. New York: Plenum Press.

Kant, I. 1976. *Träume eines Geistersehers, erläutert durch Träume der Metaphysik*. Stuttgart: Philipp Reclam Jun. (First published in 1766.)

Keith, A. B. 1925. The religion and philosophy of the Veda and Upanishads. 2 vols. Harvard Oriental Series, vols. 31–32. Cambridge, Mass.: Harvard University Press.

Ker, W. P. 1904. *The dark ages*. New York: Charles Scribner's Sons.

Kleinhauz, M., Horowitz, I., and Tobin, Y. 1977. The use of hypnosis in police investigation: A preliminary communication. *Journal of the Forensic Science Society* 17:77–80.

Koestler, A. 1969. Abstract and picture-strip. In *The pathology of memory*, edited by G. A. Talland and N. C. Waugh. New York: Academic Press.

Korner, A. F. 1969. Neonatal startles, smiles, erections, and reflex sucks as related to state, sex, and individuality. *Child Development* 40: 1039–53.

———. 1971. Individual differences at birth: Implications for early experience and later development. *American Journal of Orthopsychiatry* 41:608–19.

Kupalov, P. S., and Gantt, W. H. 1927. The relationship between the strength of the conditioned stimulus and the size of the resulting conditioned reflex. *Brain* 50:44–52.

Lenz, F. 1979. *Lifetimes: True accounts of reincarnation*. Indianapolis: Bobbs-Merrill.

LeRoy Ladurie, E. 1975. *Montaillou, village occitan de 1294 à 1324*. Paris: Editions Gallimard. (American edition: *Montaillou: The promised land of error*. Translated by Barbara Bray. New York: George Braziller, 1978.)

Lewis, G. K. [c. 1910.] *Elizabeth Fry*. London: Headley Bros.

Lewis, H. D. 1973. *The self and immortality*. London: Macmillan.

———. 1978. *Persons and life after death*. New York: Barnes and Noble.

Lewis, I. M. 1971. *Ecstatic religion: An anthropological study of spirit possession and shamanism*. Harmondsworth, Middlesex: Penguin.

Lidz, T., and Blatt, S. 1983. Critique of the Danish-American studies of the biological and adoptive relatives of adoptees who became schizophrenic. *American Journal of Psychiatry* 140:426–35.

Lidz, T., Blatt, S., and Cook, B. 1981. Critique of the Danish-American studies of the adopted-away offspring of schizophrenic parents. *American Journal of Psychiatry* 138: 1063–68.

Locke, J. 1947. *An essay concerning human understanding*. London: J. M. Dent and Sons. (First published in 1690.)

Loftus, E. F. 1979. *Eyewitness testimony*. Cambridge, Mass., and London: Harvard University Press.

Luckhardt, A. B. 1941. Report of the autopsy of the Siamese twins together with other interesting information concerning their life. *Surgery, Gynecology, and Obstetrics* 72 : 116–25.

Luria, A. R. 1969. *The mind of a mnemonist*. Translated by Lynn Solotaroff. London: Jonathan Cape.

McClenon, J. 1982. A survey of elite scientists: Their attitudes toward ESP and parapsychology. *Journal of Parapsychology* 46 : 127–52.

McDougall, W. 1926. *An outline of abnormal psychology*. London: Methuen.

MacKenzie, A. 1966. *The unexplained: Some strange cases in psychical research*. London: Arthur Barker.

———. 1971. *Apparitions and ghosts: A modern study*. London: Arthur Barker.

———. 1982. *Hauntings and apparitions*. London: William Heinemann.

McTaggart, J. M. E. 1906. *Some dogmas of religion*. London: Edward Arnold.

Madaule, J. 1961. *Le drame albigeois et le destin français*. Paris: Bernard Grasset.

Madell, G. 1981. *The identity of the self*. Edinburgh: Edinburgh University Press.

Makarem, S. 1974. *The Druze faith*. Delmar, N.Y.: Caravan Books.

Malcolm, N. 1970. Memory and representation. *Noûs* 4 : 59–71.

———. 1977. *Memory and mind*. Ithaca, N.Y.: Cornell University Press.

Malinowski, B. 1916. Baloma: The spirits of the dead in the Trobriand Islands. *Journal of the Royal Anthropological Institute of Great Britain and Ireland* 46 : 353–430.

———. 1927. *The father in primitive psychology*. New York: W. W. Norton.

Mann, T. C., and Greene, J. 1968. *Sudden and awful: American epitaphs and the finger of God*. Brattleboro, Vt.: Stephen Greene Press.

Marks, I. 1978. Rehearsal relief of a nightmare. *British Journal of Psychiatry* 133 : 461–65.

Marshall, J. 1969. *Law and psychology in conflict*. Garden City, N.Y.: Doubleday.

Martino, M. 1977. *Emergence: A transsexual autobiography*. New York: Crown Publishers.

Medawar, P. 1957. *The uniqueness of the individual*. New York: Basic Books.

Mi Mi Khaing. 1962. *Burmese family*. Bloomington, Ind.: Indiana University Press.

Mochulsky, K. 1967. *Dostoevsky: His life and work*. Translated by Michael A. Minihan. Princeton: Princeton University Press.

Monod, J. 1964. Le hasard et la nécessité. Paris: Editions du Seuil. (American edition: *Chance and necessity*. Translated by Austryn Wainhouse. New York: Alfred A. Knopf, 1971.)

Morris, J. 1974. *Conundrum*. London: Faber and Faber.

Munro, N. G. 1963. *Ainu: Creed and cult*. New York: Columbia University Press.

Murphy, G. 1945. Field theory and survival. *Journal of the American Society for Psychical Research* 39 : 181–209.

Murphy, G., with Dale, L. A. 1961. *Challenge of psychical research: A primer of parapsychology*. New York: Harper and Bros.

Myers, F. W. H. 1889. On recognized apparitions occurring more than a year after death. *Proceedings of the Society for Psychical Research* 6 : 13–65.

———. 1903. *Human personality and its survival of bodily death*. 2 vols. London: Longmans, Green.

Nagel, T. 1979. What is it like to be a bat? In Nagel, T. *Mortal Questions*. Cambridge:

Cambridge University Press. (Originally published in *Philosophical Review* 83:435–50, 1974.)

Nash, C. B. 1984. Test of psychokinetic control of bacterial mutation. *Journal of the American Society for Psychical Research* 78:145–52.

Neidhart, G. 1956. *Werden wir wieder geboren?* Munich: Gemeinschaft für Religiöse and Geistige Erneuerung e. V.

Neisser, U., ed. 1982. *Memory observed: Remembering in natural contexts.* San Francisco: W. H. Freeman.

Nelli, R. 1972. *Les cathares.* Paris: Grasset.

Neppe, V. M. 1983. *The psychology of déjà vu: Have I been here before?* Johannesburg: Witwatersrand University Press.

Newman, H. H. 1940. *Multiple human births.* New York: Doubleday, Doran.

Nicol, J. F. 1976. Review of *Cases of the reincarnation type:* Vol. 1, *Ten cases in India. Parapsychology Review* 7(5):12–15.

Niel, F. 1955. *Albigeois et Cathares.* Paris: Presses Universitaires de France.

Noon, J. A. 1942. A preliminary examination of death concepts of the Ibo. *American Anthropologist* 44:638–54.

Norbu, T., and Turnbull, C. 1969. *Tibet.* London: Chatto and Windus.

Noyes, R., Jr., and Kletti, R. 1976. Depersonalization in the face of life-threatening danger: A description. *Psychiatry* 39:19–27.

———. 1977. Panoramic memory: A response to the threat of death. *Omega* 8:181–94.

Obeyesekere, G. 1968. Theodicy, sin, and salvation in a sociology of Buddhism. In *Dialectic in practical religion,* edited by E. R. Leach. Cambridge: Cambridge University Press.

———. 1980. The rebirth eschatology and its transformations: A contribution to the sociology of early Buddhism. In *Karma and rebirth in classical Indian traditions,* edited by W. D. O'Flaherty. Berkeley: University of California Press.

O'Connell, D. N., Shor, R. E., and Orne, M. T. 1970. Hypnotic age regression. *Journal of Abnormal Psychology Monograph* 76:1–32.

Okey, T., ed. and trans. 1910. *The little flowers of St. Francis.* London: J. M. Dent and Sons.

Orne, M. T. 1951. The mechanisms of hypnotic age regression: An experimental study. *Journal of Abnormal and Social Psychology* 46:213–25.

Osis, K., and Haraldsson, E. 1977. *At the hour of death.* New York: Avon Books.

Osty, E. 1923. *Supernormal faculties in man: An experimental study.* Translated by Stanley de Brath. London: Methuen.

———. 1929. Ce que la médecine doit attendre de l'étude expérimentale des propriétés psychiques paranormales de l'homme. *Revue métapsychique,* no. 2, pp. 79–148.

———. 1932. Télépathie spontanée et transmission de pensée expérimentale. *Revue métapsychique,* no. 4, pp. 233–56.

Owen, R. D. 1874. *The debatable land between this world and the next.* London: Trübner.

Palmer, J. 1979. A community mail survey of psychic experiences. *Journal of the American Society for Psychical Research* 73:221–51.

Parrinder, G. 1956. Varieties of belief in reincarnation. *Hibbert Journal* 55 : 260–67.
———. 1970. *African traditional religion*. Westport, Conn.: Greenwood Press. (First published in 1954. London: Hutchinson's University Library.)

Parry, W. E. 1932. *The Lakhers*. London: Macmillan.

Pasricha, S. K. 1983. New information favoring a paranormal interpretation in the case of Rakesh Gaur. *European Journal of Parapsychology* 5 : 77–85.

Pasricha, S. K., and Barker, D. R. 1981. A case of the reincarnation type in India: The case of Rakesh Gaur. *European Journal of Parapsychology* 3 : 381–408.

Pasricha, S., and Stevenson, I. 1977. Three cases of the reincarnation type in India. *Indian Journal of Psychiatry* 19 : 36–42.

Patanjali. 1953. *How to know God: The Yoga aphorisms*. Translated by Swami Prabhavananda, and Isherwood, C. New York: Harper and Bros.

Penelhum, T. 1970. *Survival and disembodied existence*. London: Routledge and Kegan Paul.

Penfield, W. 1975. *The mystery of the mind*. Princeton: Princeton University Press.

Peris, M. 1963. Pythagoras, birth-rememberer. *University of Ceylon Review* 21: 186–212.

Perovsky-Petrovo-Solovovo, M. 1930. A phantasm of the dead conveying information unknown to the percipient. *Journal of the Society for Psychical Research* 26:95–98.

Perry, J., ed. 1975. *Personal identity*. Berkeley: University of California Press.

Philostratus. 1912. *The Life of Apollonius of Tyana*. Translated by F. C. Conybeare. London: William Heinemann.

Place, U. T. 1956. Is consciousness a brain process? *British Journal of Psychology* 47:44–50.

Plato. 1935. *The republic*. Translated by A. D. Lindsay. London: J. M. Dent and Sons.
———. 1936. *Five dialogues*. London: J. M. Dent and Sons. (This includes the *Meno* and the *Phaedo*.)

Popper, K. R., and Eccles, J. C. 1977. *The self and its brain*. New York: Springer International.

Porter, R., and Collins, G. M., eds. 1982. *Temperamental differences in infants and young children*. Ciba Foundation Symposium 89. London: Pitman.

Poynton, J. C. 1983. Correspondence section. *Journal of Parapsychology* 47 : 82–86.

Prabhavananda and Isherwood, C., trans. 1944. *The song of God: Bhagavad-Gita*. Hollywood, Calif.: Marcel Rodd.

Prasad, J., and Stevenson, I. 1968. A survey of spontaneous psychical experiences in school children of Uttar Pradesh, India. *International Journal of Parapsychology* 10:241–61.

Prat, F. 1907. *Origène, le théologien et l'exégète*. Paris: Blond.
———. 1911. Origen and Origenism. In *The Catholic Encyclopedia*. New York: Robert Appleton.

Price, H. H. 1940. Some philosophical questions about telepathy and clairvoyance. *Philosophy*. 15 : 363–85.
———. 1953. Survival and the idea of "another world." *Proceedings of the Society for Psychical Research* 50 : 1–25.
———. 1972. *Essays in the philosophy of religion*. Oxford: Oxford University Press.

Prince, W. F. 1921. Analysis of the results of an old questionnaire. *Journal of the American Society for Psychical Research* 15 : 169–84.

————. 1922. Dreams seeming, or interpreted, to indicate death. *Journal of the American Society for Psychical Research* 16 : 164–89.

————. 1928. *Noted witnesses for psychic occurrences.* Boston: Boston Society for Psychic Research.

Putnam, W. H. 1979. Hypnosis and distortions in eyewitness memory. *International Journal of Clinical and Experimental Hypnosis* 27 : 437–48.

Radhakrishnan, S. 1923. *Indian philosophy.* 2 vols. London: George Allen and Unwin.

Radin, P., ed. 1926. *Crashing thunder: The autobiography of an American Indian.* New York: D. Appleton.

Raymond of Capua. 1980. *The life of St. Catherine of Siena.* Translated by Conleth Kearns. Wilmington, Del.: Michael Glazier.

Rees, W. D. 1971. The hallucinations of widowhood. *British Medical Journal* 4 : 37–41.

Reiff, R., and Scheerer, M. 1959. *Memory and hypnotic age regression.* New York: International Universities Press.

Rhine, L. E. 1961. *Hidden channels of the mind.* New York: Sloane.

————. 1981. *The invisible picture: A study of psychic experiences.* Jefferson, N.C.: McFarland.

Richardson, A. 1969. *Mental imagery.* New York: Springer Publishing.

Richet, C. 1926. Des conditions de la certitude. *Proceedings of the Society for Psychical Research* 35 : 422–44.

Ring, K. 1980. *Life at death: A scientific investigation of the near-death experience.* New York: Coward, McCann and Geoghegan.

Roberts, A. M. 1978. The origins of fluctuations in the human secondary sex ratio. *Journal of Biosocial Science* 10 : 169–82.

Roffwarg, H. P., Muzio, J. N., and Dement, W. C. 1966. Ontogenetic development of human sleep-dream cycle. *Science* 152 : 604–19.

Rohde, W., Porstmann, T., and Dörner, G. 1973. Migration of Y-bearing human spermatozoa in cervical mucus. *Journal of Reproduction and Fertility* 33 : 167–69.

Rollo, C. 1967. Thomas Bayes and the bundle of sticks. *Proceedings of the Society for Psychical Research* 55 : 23–64.

Rorty, A. O., ed. 1976. *The identities of persons.* Berkeley: University of California Press.

Rose, R. 1956. *Living magic.* New York: Rand McNally.

Rose, S., Kamin, L. J., and Lewontin, R. C. 1984. *Not in our genes.* Harmondsworth, Middlesex: Penguin.

Roughead, W. 1926. *The rebel earl and other studies.* New York: E. P. Dutton.

Ruben, W. 1939. Schamanismus in alten Indien. *Acta orientalia* 17 : 164–205.

Runciman, S. 1947. *The medieval Manichee.* Cambridge: Cambridge University Press.

Ryall, E. W. 1974. *Second time round.* Jersey: Neville Spearman. (American edition: *Born twice: Total recall of a seventeenth-century life.* New York: Harper and Row, 1974.)

Sabom, M. 1982. *Recollections of death.* New York: Harper and Row.

Sahay, K. K. N. c. 1927. *Reincarnation: Verified cases of re-birth after death.* Bareilly: N. L. Gupta.

Saltmarsh, H. F. 1934. Report on cases of apparent precognition. *Proceedings of the Society for Psychical Research* 42:49–103.

Sandison, R. A., Spencer, A. M., and Whitelaw, J. D. A. 1954. The therapeutic value of lysergic acid diethylamide in mental illness. *Journal of Mental Science* 100:491–507.

Sannwald, G. 1959a. Statistische Untersuchungen an Spontanphänomenen. *Zeitschrift für Parapsychologie und Grenzgebiete der Psychologie* 3:59–71.

———. 1959b. Zur Psychologie paranormaler Spontanphänomene: Motivation, Thematik und Bezugspersonen "okkulter" Erlebnisse. *Zeitschrift für Parapsychologie und Grenzebiete der Psychologie* 3:149–83.

Schliemann, H. 1881. *Ilios, the city and country of the Trojans, including an autobiography of the author.* New York: Harper and Bros.

Schmeidler, G. 1961a. Evidence for two kinds of telepathy. *International Journal of Parapsychology* 3(no. 3):5–48.

———. 1961b. Are there two kinds of telepathy? *Journal of the American Society for Psychical Research* 55:87–97.

Schopbach, R. R., Fried, P. H., and Rakoff, A. E. 1952. Pseudocyesis: A psychosomatic disorder. *Psychosomatic Medicine* 14:129–34.

Schopenhauer, A. 1891. Parerga und Paralipomena. In *Arthur Schopenhauer's sämmtliche Werke.* Volume 2. Leipzig: F. U. Brockhaus.

———. 1908. *Die welt als Wille und Vorstellung.* 2 vols. Leipzig: F. U. Brockhaus.

Schouten, S. A. 1979. Analysis of spontaneous cases as reported in "Phantasms of the living." *European Journal of Parapsychology* 2:408–55.

Schrödinger, E. 1955. *What is life? The physical aspect of the living cell.* Cambridge: Cambridge University Press.

Schulsinger, F. 1985. The experience from the adoption method in genetic research. In *Medical Genetics: Past, Present, Future*, edited by K. Berg. New York: Alan R. Liss.

Sherrington, C. 1947. *The integrative action of the nervous system.* New Haven: Yale University Press. (First published in 1906.)

Shoemaker, S., and Swinburne, R. 1984. *Personal identity.* Oxford: Blackwell.

Sidgwick, [E. M.] Mrs. H. 1891–92. On the evidence for clairvoyance. *Proceedings of the Society for Psychical Research* 7:30–99.

———. 1921. An examination of book-tests obtained in sittings with Mrs. Leonard. *Proceedings of the Society for Psychical Research* 31:241–400.

Sidgwick, H., and Committee. 1894. Report on the census of hallucinations. *Proceedings of the Society for Psychical Research* 10:25–422.

Sinclair, U. 1962. *Mental radio.* Springfield, Ill.: Charles C. Thomas. (First published in 1930.)

Slobodin, R. 1970. Kutchin concepts of reincarnation. *Western Canadian Journal of Anthropology* 2:67–79.

Smart, N. 1964. *Doctrine and argument in Indian philosophy.* London: George Allen and Unwin.

Smith, B. M., Hain, J. D., and Stevenson, I. 1970. Controlled interviews with drugs. *Archives of General Psychiatry* 22:2–10.

Smith, S. 1964. *The mediumship of Mrs. Leonard.* New Hyde Park, N.Y.: University Books.

Smythies, J. R. 1951. The extension of mind: A new theoretical basis for psi phenomena. *Journal of the Society for Psychical Research* 36:477–502.

———. 1956. *Analysis of perception.* London: Routledge and Kegan Paul.

———. 1960. Three classical theories of mind. *Journal of the Society for Psychical Research* 40:385–97.

———. 1974. The mind-brain problem today: A viewpoint from the neurosciences. In *Parapsychology and the sciences,* edited by A. Angoff and B. Shapin. New York: Parapsychology Foundation.

Snellgrove, D., and Richardson, H. 1968. *A cultural history of Tibet.* New York: Frederick A. Praeger.

Southey, R. 1962. *Life of Nelson.* London: J. M. Dent and Sons. (First published in 1813.)

Spear, P. 1965. *History of India.* Vol. 2. Harmondsworth, Middlesex: Penguin.

Spencer, B., and Gillen, F. J. 1968. *The native tribes of central Australia.* New York: Dover Publications. (First published in 1899. London: Macmillan.)

Spencer, R. F. 1959. *The north Alaskan Eskimo: A study in ecology and society.* Smithsonian Institution, Bureau of American Ethnology, Bulletin 171. Washington, D.C.: United States Government Printing Office.

Stalnaker, J. M., and Riddle, E. E. 1932. The effect of hypnosis on long-delayed recall. *Journal of General Psychology* 6:429–40.

Stanley, H. M. 1909. *Autobiography.* Boston: Houghton Mifflin.

Stendhal. 1926. *Lucien Leuwen.* Paris: Librairie Ancienne Honoré Champion. (Originally published 1855.)

Stevenson, I. 1957. Is the human personality more plastic in infancy and childhood? *American Journal of Psychiatry* 114:152–61.

———. 1960. The evidence for survival from claimed memories of former incarnations. *Journal of the American Society for Psychical Research* 54:51–71, 95–117.

———. 1964. The blue orchid of Table Mountain. *Journal of the Society for Psychical Research* 42:401–9.

———. 1966. Cultural patterns in cases suggestive of reincarnation among the Tlingit Indians of southeastern Alaska. *Journal of the American Society for Psychical Research* 60:229–43.

———. 1969. The belief in reincarnation and related cases among the Eskimos of Alaska. *Proceedings of the Parapsychological Association* 6:53–55.

———. 1970a. Characteristics of cases of the reincarnation type in Turkey and their comparison with cases in two other cultures. *International Journal of Comparative Sociology* 11:1–17.

———. 1970b. Telepathic impressions. *Proceedings of the American Society for Psychical Research* 29:1–198. (Also Charlottesville: University Press of Virginia.)

———. 1970c. Precognition of disasters. *Journal of the American Society for Psychical Research* 64:187–210.

————. 1971. The substantiality of spontaneous cases. *Proceedings of the Parapsychological Association* 5:91–128.

————. 1974a. Some questions related to cases of the reincarnation type. *Journal of the American Society for Psychical Research* 68:395–416.

————. 1974b. *Twenty cases suggestive of reincarnation.* 2d rev. ed. Charlottesville: University Press of Virginia. (First published in 1966 as vol. 26 of the *Proceedings of the American Society for Psychical Research.*)

————. 1974c. *Xenoglossy: A review and report of a case.* Charlottesville: University Press of Virginia.

————. 1975a. *Cases of the reincarnation type.* Vol. 1, *Ten cases in India.* Charlottesville: University Press of Virginia.

————. 1975b. The belief and cases related to reincarnation among the Haida. *Journal of Anthropological Research* 31:364–75. (Reprinted with revisions in *Journal of the American Society for Psychical Research* 71:177–89, 1977.)

————. 1976. A preliminary report of a new case of responsive xenoglossy: The case of Gretchen. *Journal of the American Society for Psychical Research* 70:65–77.

————. 1977a. *Cases of the reincarnation type.* Vol. 2, *Ten cases in Sri Lanka.* Charlottesville: University Press of Virginia.

————. 1977b. The explanatory value of the idea of reincarnation. *Journal of Nervous and Mental Disease* 164:305–26.

————. 1977c. Research into the evidence of man's survival after death: A historical and critical survey with a summary of recent developments. *Journal of Nervous and Mental Disease* 165:152–70.

————. 1977d. The Southeast Asian interpretation of gender dysphoria: An illustrative case report. *Journal of Nervous and Mental Disease* 165:201–8.

————. 1980. *Cases of the reincarnation type.* Vol. 3, *Twelve cases in Lebanon and Turkey.* Charlottesville: University Press of Virginia.

————. 1981. Can we describe the mind? In *Research in parapsychology, 1980,* edited by W. G. Roll and J. Beloff. Metuchen, N.J.: Scarecrow Press.

————. 1982. The contribution of apparitions to the evidence for survival. *Journal of the American Society for Psychical Research* 76:341–58.

————. 1983a. *Cases of the reincarnation type.* Vol. 4, *Twelve cases in Thailand and Burma.* Charlottesville: University Press of Virginia.

————. 1983b. Cryptomnesia and parapsychology. *Journal of the Society for Psychical Research* 52:1–30.

————. 1983c. Do we need a new word to supplement "hallucination"? *American Journal of Psychiatry* 140:1609–11.

————. 1983d. American children who claim to remember previous lives. *Journal of Nervous and Mental Disease* 171:742–48.

————. 1984. *Unlearned language: New studies in xenoglossy.* Charlottesville: University Press of Virginia.

————. 1985. The belief in reincarnation among the Igbo of Nigeria. *Journal of Asian and African Studies* 20:13–30.

————. 1986. Characteristics of cases of the reincarnation type among the Igbo of Nigeria. *Journal of Asian and African Studies* 21:204–16.

Stevenson, I., and Edelstein, S. J. 1982. The belief in reincarnation among the Igbo of southeastern Nigeria with particular reference to connections between the *ogbanje* ("repeater babies") and sickle cell anemia. In *Research in Parapsychology, 1981,* edited by W. G. Roll, R. L. Morris, and R. A. White. Metuchen, N.J.: Scarecrow Press.

Stevenson, I., and Greyson, B. 1979. Near-death experiences: Relevance to the question of survival after death. *Journal of the American Medical Association* 242: 265–67.

Stevenson, I., and Pasricha, S. 1979. A case of secondary personality with xenoglossy. *American Journal of Psychiatry* 136: 1591–92.

———. 1980. A preliminary report on an unusual case of the reincarnation type with xenoglossy. *Journal of the American Society for Psychical Research* 74: 331–48.

Stone, L. J. 1954. A critique of studies on infant isolation. *Child Development* 25: 9–20.

Stratton, G. M. 1919. Retroactive hypermnesia and other emotional effects on memory. *Psychological Review* 26: 474–86.

Sunderlal, R. B. S. 1924. Cas apparents de réminiscences de vies antérieures. *Revue métapsychique* no. 4, pp. 302–7.

Susukita, T. 1933–34. Untersuchung eines ausserordentlichen Gedächtnisses in Japan, pts. I, II. *Tohoku Psychologica Folia* 1: 111–134; 2: 15–42.

Swanton, J. R. 1908. Social condition, beliefs, and linguistic relationship of the Tlingit Indians. *Twenty-sixth Annual Report of the Bureau of American Ethnology (1904–05),* pp. 391–485. Washington, D.C.: United States Government Printing Office.

Swedenborg, E. 1906. *Heaven and its wonders and Hell.* Boston: New-Church Union. (First published in Latin, 1758.)

Thakur, S. C., ed. 1976. *Philosophy and psychical research.* London: George Allen and Unwin.

Thalbourne, M. A. 1982. *A glossary of terms used in parapsychology.* London: William Heinemann.

Thomas, A. 1981. Current trends in developmental theory. *American Journal of Orthopsychiatry* 51: 580–609.

Thomas, A., and Chess, S. 1977. *Temperament and development.* New York: Brunner/Mazel.

Thomas, C. D. 1945. A discourse given through Mrs. Leonard and attributed to Sir Oliver Lodge. *Journal of the Society for Psychical Research* 33: 134–56.

Thomas, L.-V. 1968. *Cinq essais sur la mort africaine.* Dakar: Université de Dakar.

Thorndike, E. L. 1905. *The elements of psychology.* 2d ed. New York: A. G. Seiler.

Thouless, R. H. 1979. Theories about survival. *Journal of the Society for Psychical Research* 50: 1–8.

———. 1984. Do we survive bodily death? *Proceedings of the Society for Psychical Research* 57: 1–52.

Thouless, R. H., and Wiesner, B. P. 1946–49. The psi processes in normal and "paranormal" psychology. *Proceedings of the Society for Psychical Research* 48: 177–96.

Toukholka, S. 1922. Expériences de clairvoyance avec Mme. Olga Kahl. *Revue métapsychique,* no. 6, pp. 429–33.

True, R. M. 1949. Experimental control in hypnotic age regression states. *Science* 110:583–84.

Tulving, E. 1972. Episodic and semantic memory. In *Organization of memory,* edited by E. Tulving and W. Donaldson. New York: Academic Press.

Tyrrell, G. N. M. 1953. *Apparitions.* London: Duckworth.

Uchendu, V. C. 1965. *The Igbo of southeast Nigeria.* New York: Holt, Rinehart, and Winston.

Van Eeden, F. 1912–13. A study of dreams. *Proceedings of the Society for Psychical Research* 26:431–61.

Vasiliev, L. L. 1966. *Studies in mental telepathy.* Washington, D.C.: U.S. Department of Commerce, Clearinghouse for Federal Scientific and Technical Information. (Originally published in 1962 as *Vnusheniye na rasstoyanii* [Zametki fiziologa]. Moscow: Gospolitizdat Publishing House.)

Vesey, G. 1974. *Personal identity.* London: Macmillan.

Voltaire. 1960. La princesse de Babylone. In *Romans et contes.* Paris: Editions Garnier Frères.

Waxler, N. 1979. Is outcome for schizophrenia better in nonindustrial societies? The case of Sri Lanka. *Journal of Nervous and Mental Disease* 167 : 144–58.

West, D. J. 1948. A mass-observation questionnaire on hallucinations. *Journal of the Society for Psychical Research* 34 : 187–96.

Whately, R. 1858. *Elements of rhetoric: Comprising an analysis of the laws of moral evidence and of persuasion.* Rev. ed. Boston: James Munroe.

Wheatley, J. M. O. 1965. The question of survival: Some logical reflections. *Journal of the American Society for Psychical Research* 59 : 202– 10.

———. 1979. Reincarnation, "astral bodies," and "psi-components." *Journal of the American Society for Psychical Research* 73 : 109–22.

Wheatley, J. M. O., and Edge, H., eds. 1976. *Philosophical dimensions of parapsychology.* Springfield, Ill.: Charles C. Thomas.

Whitaker, L., Jr. 1961. The use of an extended draw-a-person test to identify homosexual and effeminate men. *Journal of Consulting Psychology* 25 : 482–85.

White, R. A., and Dale, L. A. 1973. *Parapsychology: Sources of information.* Metuchen, N.J.: Scarecrow Press.

Whiteman, J. H. M. 1961. *The mystical life.* London: Faber and Faber.

———. 1972. On the concept of repeatability in scientific experimentation. *Journal of the American Society for Psychical Research* 66 : 227–29.

———. 1973. Quantum theory and parapsychology. *Journal of the American Society for Psychical Research* 67 : 341–60.

Whittaker, P. G., Taylor, A., and Lind, T. 1983. Unsuspected pregnancy loss in healthy women. *The Lancet* i : 1126–27.

Wolman, B. B., ed. 1977. *Handbook of parapsychology.* New York: Van Nostrand Reinhold.

Wolpe, J., and Rachman, S. 1960. Psychoanalytic "evidence": A critique based on Freud's case of Little Hans. *Journal of Nervous and Mental Disease* 130 : 135–48.

Woodham-Smith, C. 1950. *Florence Nightingale, 1820–1910.* London: Constable.

Yuille, J. C., and Cutshall, J. L. 1986. A case study of eyewitness memory of a crime. *Journal of Applied Psychology* 71 : 291–301.

Zaehner, R. C. 1957. *Mysticism: Sacred and profane.* Oxford: The Clarendon Press.

———. 1962. *Hinduism.* London: Oxford University Press.

Zahan, D., ed. 1965. *Réincarnation et vie mystique en afrique noire.* Paris: Presses Universitaire de France.

Zeigarnik, B. 1927. Das Behalten erledigter und unerledigter Handlungen. *Psychologische Forschung* 9: 1–85.

Zelig, M., and Beidleman, W. B. 1981. The investigative use of hypnosis: A word of caution. *International Journal of Clinical and Experimental Hypnosis* 29: 401–12.

Zolik, E. S. 1958. An experimental investigation of the psychodynamic implications of the hypnotic "previous existence" fantasy. *Journal of Clinical Psychology* 14: 178–83. (Also unpublished case reports presented at the meeting of the American Psychological Association, 1958.)

———. 1962. "Reincarnation" phenomena in hypnotic states. *International Journal of Parapsychology* 4(3): 66–78.

Zuger, B. 1970. The role of familial factors in persistent effeminate behavior in boys. *American Journal of Psychiatry* 126: 1167–70.

Index

(Subjects of cases are listed in alphabetical order according to their first or given names.)